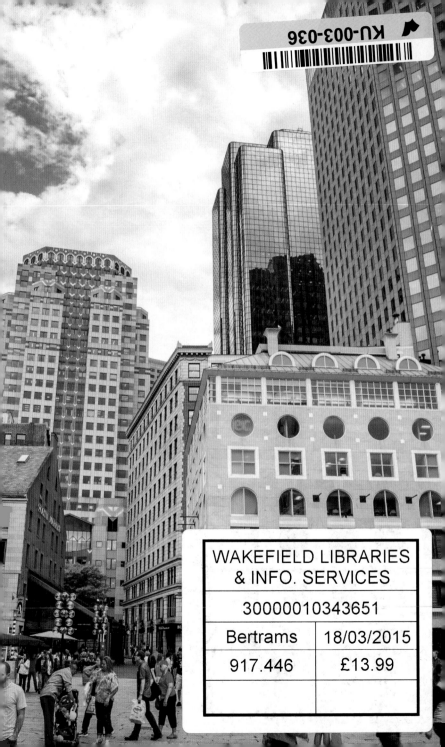

Contents

46

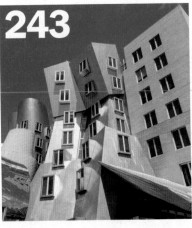

243

TimeOut **Boston**

Editorial
Editor Lisa Ritchie
Copy Editors Ros Sales, Dominic Earle
Listings Editors Caroline Hatano, Panicha Imsomboon
Proofreader John Shandy Watson

Editorial Director Sarah Guy
Group Finance Manager Margaret Wright

Design
Senior Designer Kei Ishimaru
Designer Darryl Bell
Group Commercial Senior Designer Jason Tansley

Picture Desk
Picture Editor Jael Marschner
Deputy Picture Editor Ben Rowe
Picture Researcher Lizzy Owen

Advertising
Managing Director of Advertising St John Betteridge
Vice President of Sales (North America) Jason Tosney

Marketing
Senior Publishing Brand Manager Luthfa Begum
Head of Circulation Dan Collins

Production
Production Controller Katie Mulhern-Bhudia

Time Out Group
Chairman & Founder Tony Elliott
Chief Executive Officer Tim Arthur
Publisher Alex Batho
Group IT Director Simon Chappell
Group Marketing Director Carolyn Sims

Contributors
Boston Today Robert David Sullivan. **Diary** Nolan Gawron. **Explore** Lisa Ritchie and contributors to previous editions of *Time Out Boston. SoWa So Good* Meaghan Agnew; *Baking Hot* Christina Ng; *Raising the Oyster Bar* Naomi Kooker; *Brewed in Boston* Nolan Gawron; *Perfect Formula, Second Helpings in Somerville* Naomi Kooker. **Restaurants** Naomi Kooker. **Bars** Nolan Gawron, Jessie Rogers. **Shops & Services** Meaghan Agnew, Lisa Ritchie, Jessie Rogers. **Children** Kim Foley MacKinnon. **Film** Jessie Rogers (*Essential Boston Films* Josh Rothkopf). **Gay & Lesbian** Jeremy C Fox. **Nightlife** Nolan Gawron, Jessie Rogers (*Essential Boston Albums* Jim Sullivan). **Performing Arts** Karen Campbell (*Harvard's Class Act* Jim Sullivan). **Escapes & Excursions** Lisa Ritchie and contributors to previous editions of *Time Out Boston.* **Hotels** Scott Kearnan (*Playing Away* Jim Sullivan). **History** Lisa Ritchie and contributors to previous editions of *Time Out Boston.* **Architecture** David Eisen, Lisa Ritchie.

Maps JS Graphics Ltd (john@jsgraphics.co.uk)

Cover and pull-out map photography Massimo Borchi/SIME/4Corners

Back cover photography Clockwise from top left: f11photo/Shutterstock.com; © The Sinclair; © Adrian Wilson; Jorge Salcedo/Shutterstock.com; American Spirit/Shutterstock.com

Photography Pages 2/3, 4 (bottom), 44/45, 52 (bottom), 53, 56, 57, 58, 170, 220/221, 243 (top) f11photo/Shutterstock.com; 4 (top), 26/27 (top), 44, 46, 128, 144, 150, 153 (bottom), 211, 213, 234/235, 236, 241 Marcio Jose Bastos Silva/Shutterstock.com; 7, 130 cdrin/Shutterstock.com; 10, 51, 126/127, 135, 243 (bottom), 276/277 Jorge Salcedo/Shutterstock.com; 10/11 The Isabella Stewart Gardner Museum; 11 Chuck Choi; 12 (bottom), 12/13 (top), 39 Ritu Manoj Jethani/Shutterstock.com; 13 (top) The Mary Baker Eddy Library; 13 (bottom) Danita Jo; 14 (top) Chensiyuan/Wikimedia Commons; 14 (bottom), 146 PhaseOnePhotogaphy2013; 15 (top) Tneorg/Wikimedia Commons; 15 (bottom), 18/19 The Rose Kennedy Greenway Conservancy; 17 (top) Mandy Hong; 17 (bottom) Rick Berry/Wikimedia Commons; 20 (top) ©Vanderwarker; 20 (bottom), 110, 112, 120, 204 American Spirit/Shutterstock.com; 24/25 (top) aceshot1/Shutterstock.com; 24/25 (middle), 33 (top), 106, 148/149, 171 Christopher Penler/Shutterstock.com; 24/25 (bottom) Morgan Ione Photography; 26/27 (bottom), 69 (middle), 73, 240 (bottom) Richard Cavalleri/Shutterstock.com; 28/29, 30 Mike Diskin; 30/31 (top) Jaminnbenji/Shutterstock.com; 30/31 (bottom) Liviu Toader/Shutterstock.com; 31 John Phelan/Wikimedia Commons; 33 (bottom) Michael C. Smith; 34 (top) Geoff Hargadons; 35 (top) John Kropewnicki/Shutterstock.com; 35 (bottom) Dave Green; 36, 108, 238 Stephen Orsillo/Shutterstock.com; 36/37, 74/75, 237, 240 (top) col/Shutterstock.com; 37 Peter Paradise Michaels: RavenWolfe Photography; 38/39 (top) Samuel Borges Photography/Shutterstock.com; 40 (bottom left), 71 Joel Benjamin; 40/41 (top) Jeffrey Dunn; 41, 54, 59, 70, 82, 88, 103, 115, 124, 133, 134, 141, 162, 164, 176, 180, 183, 185, 186 Michael Ascanio Peguero; 42/43 Vlad G/Shutterstock.com; 47, 239 Yevgenia Gorbulsky/Shutterstock.com; 50 Hannu J.A. Aaltonen/Shutterstock.com; 52 (top) Daniel M. Silva/Shutterstock.com; 60/61, 205 Zack Frank/Shutterstock.com; 65 Melody Mulligan/Shutterstock.com; 66 jiawangkun/Shutterstock.com; 67, 148, 153 (top right and top left), 157, 207, 208, 209 Elan Fleisher; 69 (top) JeffreyRasmussen/Shutterstock.com; 72 (top) Tupungato/Shutterstock.com; 72 (bottom) David Eby/Shutterstock.com; 76 Papa Bravo/Shutterstock.com; 77 Julien Hautcoeur/Shutterstock.com; 80 Songquan Deng/Shutterstock.com; 83 Ingfbruno/Wikimedia Commons; 85 RDSPhotography; 87 Mark Thayer, The Mary Baker Eddy Library; 89 fmua/Shutterstock.com; 94/95 © AA World Travel Library/Alamy; 96 Melissa Blackall; 104 (bottom) Andrew Takes Photos; 105 (top and bottom) © henry + mac; 105 (middle) Sara Forrest Photography; 106/107 © John Kershaw/Alamy; 111 © Bettmann/CORBIS; 114 DnDavis/Shutterstock.com; 116, 224 Wikimedia Commons; 116/117 Jon Bilous/Shutterstock.com; 122 Morganlone Yeager; 125 Nolan Gawron; 126, 137 Peter Vanderwarker; 131 Kristin Teig photography; 138 Michael Byrne/Shutterstock.com; 145 (top) Dana Tarr Photography; 154 LornaWu/Shutterstock.com; 159 diak/Shutterstock.com; 161 Eric Wolfinger; 166/167, 200 Michael J. Lutch; 168 © Les Veilleux Photography; 169 (top) Swan Boats of Boston; 169 (bottom) Marcos Carvalho / Shutterstock.com; 172 Michael Blanchard Photography; 174 Eric Scott Photography; 177 REX/c.Miramax/Everett; 178, 182 Michael von Redlich; 194 Chung Cheng; 195 Michael Meseke; 196 James Doyle; 198 Gene Schiavone; 199 Maria Baranova; 202/203 Christian Delbert/Shutterstock.com; 206 Lee Snider Photo Images/Shutterstock.com; 210 Richard Cavalleri/Shutterstock.com; 214 Douglas Mason; 215 Rolf_52/Shutterstock.com; 216 Dennis W. Donohue/Shutterstock.com; 219 CristinaMuraca/Shutterstock.com; 222/223 National Gallery of Art, Washington DC.; 226 Nathaniel Currier/Wikimedia Commons; 228 Stock Montage/Getty Images; 232 REX/Everett Collection; 242 Artifan/Shutterstock.com; 244, 250 (bottom) Michael Weschler Photography; 246, 252 Eric Roth; 248, 255 Adrian Wilson

The following images were supplied by the featured establishments: pages 5, 21, 24, 25, 26, 34 (bottom), 38/39 (bottom), 40 (bottom right), 55, 60, 69 (bottom), 74, 81, 90, 93, 94, 98, 99, 100, 104 (top), 140, 145 (bottom), 156, 158, 175, 179, 181, 190, 193, 247, 250 (top)

About the guide

GETTING AROUND

Each sightseeing chapter contains a street map of the area marked with the locations of sights and museums (❶), restaurants and cafés (❶), bars (❶) and shops (❶). There are also street maps of Boston at the back of the book, along with an overview map of the city. In addition, there is a detachable fold-out street map.

THE ESSENTIALS

For practical information, including visas, disabled access, emergency numbers, lost property, websites and local transport, see the Essential Information section. It begins on page 244.

THE LISTINGS

Addresses, phone numbers, websites, transport information, hours and prices are all included in our listings, as are selected other facilities. All were checked and correct at press time. However, business owners can alter their arrangements at any time, and fluctuating economic conditions can cause prices to change rapidly.

The very best venues in the city, the must-sees and must-dos in every category, have been marked with a red star (★). In the sightseeing chapters, we've also marked venues with free admission with a FREE symbol.

PHONE NUMBERS

The area codes for metropolitan Boston (including Cambridge, Somerville and Brookline) are 617 and 857. Even if you're dialling from within the area you're calling, you'll need to use the area code, always preceded by 1. From outside the US, dial your country's international access code (00 from the UK) or a plus symbol, followed by the number as listed in the guide; here, the initial '1' serves as the US country code. So, to reach the Museum of Fine Arts, dial +1-617 267 9300.

FEEDBACK

We welcome feedback on this guide, both on the venues we've included and on any other locations that you'd like to see featured in future editions. Please email us at guides@timeout.com.

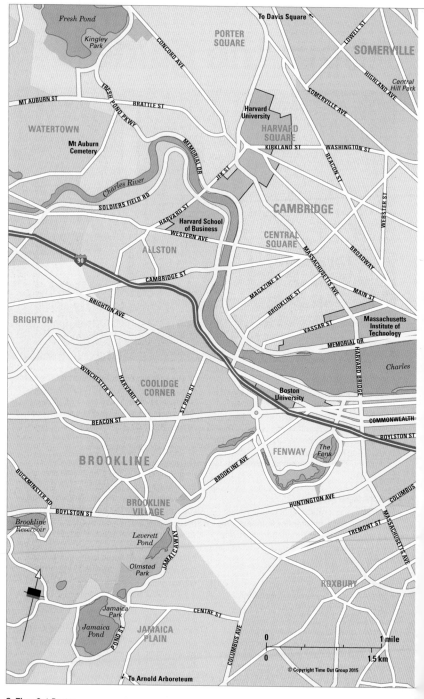

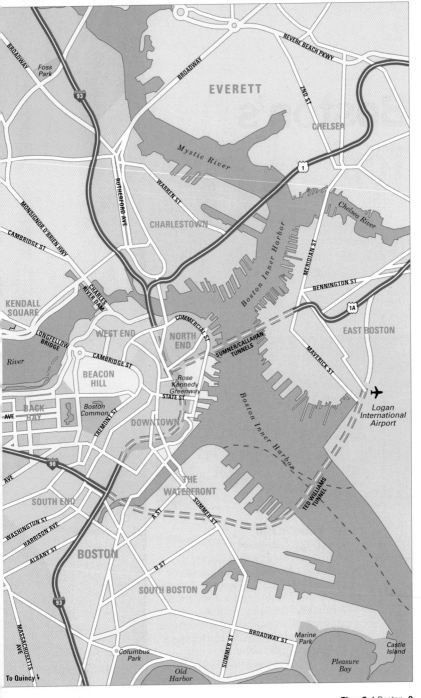

Boston's
Top
20

From fine arts to ballparks, we count down the essentials.

1 Beacon Hill
(page 62)

With its incredibly well-preserved 18th- and 19th-century townhouses, cobbled streets and gas lanterns, Beacon Hill is one of the loveliest parts of town for aimless wandering, but it also has a growing collection of standout boutiques and restaurants. From the 'black Faneuil Hall' to exquisite Louisburg Square mansions, this square-mile enclave is crammed with history.

2 Isabella Stewart Gardner Museum
(page 89)

Conceived as a complete work of art by a well-travelled Boston socialite, this delightful museum in a 1903 reproduction Venetian palace is as idiosyncratic as its founder. The exquisite courtyard is planted with seasonally changing floral displays cultivated in the on-site greenhouse. But Gardner wasn't only interested in amassing priceless relics and works by old masters such as Rembrandt and Botticelli. She was also actively involved in the art scene of her day, a friend and patron of such talents as John Singer Sargent and James McNeill Whistler. Leave time to explore the palace's many nooks and smaller objects, which include books, miniatures and correspondence. The only downside is the empty frames that once contained priceless paintings, stolen in 1990.

3 Museum of Fine Arts
(page 90)

Known for its exceptional collections of ancient Egyptian, Japanese, American and 19th-century European art, the MFA continues to improve and innovate: hot on the heels of its dramatic American Wing (designed by Foster & Partners), its Linde Family Wing for Contemporary Art has added ten new galleries. The space contains around 250 works in all media – many of them new acquisitions –

by the likes of Ellsworth Kelly, Kara Walker and Rachel Whiteread. A slew of other galleries have been renovated, including the extremely popular French Impressionism and Post-Impressionism gallery, which is home to the second-largest collection of Monets in the country.

4 SoWa
(page 99)

Over the past decade, this once-desolate warehouse district has blossomed from an emerging contemporary-art outpost comprising studios and galleries to a bona fide cultural-cum-retail destination. While the vintage market and galleries are open year-round, the place comes into its own on summer weekends with a hugely popular outdoor Sunday market, food trucks, and plenty of superb brunch options in the surrounding South End.

5 The Esplanade
(page 72)

The three-mile stretch of riverbank between the Museum of Science and the Boston University Bridge is one of the most pleasant spots in the city for strolling or picnicking, as well as being a popular jogging route. In spring, the park is frothy with cherry blossom. In summer, catch a free concert at the Hatch Memorial Shell or gaze at the flotillas of sailing boats gliding along the Charles River – an iconic Boston scene.

6 Newbury Street
(page 83)

While independent boutiques are becoming an endangered species on Newbury Street (to find those, head to the South End), Boston's premier retail strip wins hands-down for sheer volume and variety. Between Arlington Street and Massachusetts Avenue, eight blocks of bow-fronted brick townhouses are stuffed with everything from ultra-luxe designers such as Chanel and Burberry to designer chain boutiques (Scoop NYC, Intermix, Rag & Bone) and cheap fashion. With galleries, nail bars, cafés, bars and eateries in the mix, you can easily spend an entire day browsing, relaxing and posing here.

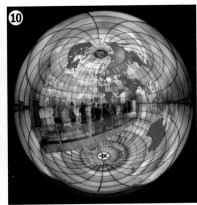

prime shopping strip, was one of the few places you could score the latest contemporary labels. Once again, it has proved itself a pioneer with a bold move to the still-evolving Seaport District. Though it feels rather out on a limb, now you can browse an exquisitely assembled mix of designer clothing and accessories for men and women, plus select beauty and home goods, against a sweeping harbour view.

7 Boston Public Garden
(page 46)

The refined adjunct of the sprawling, serviceable Boston Common, the Public Garden is the perfect park in miniature, with pathways designed for promenading, formal flower beds and a petite lagoon fringed with weeping willows. The waterfowl-shaped Swan Boats, introduced in 1877 and adored by children, are a uniquely Bostonian fixture.

8 Louis
(page 124)

Before the arrival of designer Goliaths such as Barneys New York in the Back Bay, Louis, which occupied a grand former museum building on the city's

9 Institute of Contemporary Art
(page 124)

This innovative art institution literally changed Boston's cultural landscape with its move to the city's new frontier in 2006. The starkly modern building on the waterfront, designed by NYC firm Diller Scofidio & Renfro, also pushed the boundaries of the city's traditional architectural lexicon. With a collection that spans works by some of the most important artists of our time, it's the city's hub for thought-provoking, groundbreaking shows.

10 Mapparium
(page 86)

One of Boston's stranger landmarks, the worldwide Christian Science HQ includes an eastern-influenced domed

Mother Church overlooking a 670-foot reflecting pool with echoes of the Taj Mahal. Inside the complex's library, the Mapparium is probably Boston's most oddball attraction. Stand at the middle of the world's only walk-in globe and relish the surreal acoustics and stained-glass visuals. The retro international boundaries dating from the time of its creation in 1935 make it a transporting nostalgia trip.

11 Row 34
(page 121)
It's no coincidence that Boston's oldest restaurant, the Union Oyster House, specialises in bivalves. But a new generation of oyster purveyors are carrying on the local tradition. Slurp around a dozen sustainable varieties – farm-grown in Duxbury, MA – in the industrial-chic surroundings of the waterfront sequel to Kenmore Square's acclaimed Island Creek Oyster Bar.

12 Copley Square
(page 76)
The heart of the late 19th-century 'Athens of America', Copley Square is still an uplifting spot, bracketed by the architectural marvel that is HH Richardson's Trinity Church and the august Boston Public Library. Together with the lawn and fountain, it's a surprisingly picturesque square in a major modern American metropolis.

13 Harvard Square
(page 128)
What do John F Kennedy, Leonard Bernstein, Tommy Lee Jones and Rashida Jones have in common? They all spent their days among the red-brick buildings and manicured quads of America's most revered university. Wander round the cloistered microcosm, admiring architectural gems from several eras, then browse in local literary institutions such as the Harvard Book Store and the Grolier Poetry Book Shop, and see one of the best university art collections at the just-expanded Harvard Art Museums. For lunch, your best bet is longtime student staple Mr Bartley's Gourmet Burgers.

14 Rose F Kennedy Greenway
(page 118)
For the first-time visitor, it's hard to imagine a time when a hulking elevated expressway sliced through a sizeable swathe of downtown Boston, from the North End to Chinatown, isolating neighbourhoods and cutting off access to the waterfront. Now, it's as if it never

dining spot where you can inhale cocktails as 'flavour clouds' and lick dessert off a 'tiny spoon' (don't worry, there's real food too). With a launch team that includes a Harvard professor and one of the city's top mixologists, this intriguing culinary-science experiment, appropriately set in MIT territory, is an unqualified success.

16 American Repertory Theater (ART)
(page 199)

With its highbrow name and Harvard connection, you might expect the American Repertory Theater to major exclusively in classic dramas by Tennessee Williams and Eugene O'Neill. Not a bit of it. Creative director Diane Paulus has a commendable penchant for new works, circus stunts and interactive elements, but without dumbing down the programme. Tony Award-winning Broadway hits *Pippin* and *Once* are among the productions that originated here.

17 Symphony Hall
(page 197)

A Boston landmark and one of the world's top auditoriums, Symphony Hall was designed by the illustrious architectural firm McKim, Mead & White. It opened its doors in 1900 as the home of the Boston Symphony Orchestra. Not only does it look the part as a venerable concert venue, its groundbreaking interior design, created in consultation with a Harvard physicist, ensures excellent acoustics. Extended in 1990 to include the Cohen Wing, Symphony Hall continues to update its facilities with new audio technology.

existed – and in its place is a string of parks with varied topography, fountains, a carousel and food trucks. But best of all, the Greenway provides a verdant pathway through the city, linking many key areas and making walking between them a pleasure.

15 Café ArtScience
(page 144)

What do you get when you combine a cutting-edge innovation centre with a restaurant and bar? A one-of-a-kind

BOSTON
CityPASS®

SAVE
47%
5 famous attractions

New England Aquarium

Museum of Science

Skywalk Observatory at the Prudential Center

Museum of Fine Arts, Boston

Your choice of Harvard Museum of Natural History
OR Old State House — Boston's *Revolutionary* Museum

Buy at these attractions

- **Good for 9 days**
- **Skip most ticket lines**

Connect for current pricing
citypass.com **or (888) 330-5008**

18 Toscanini's
(page 139)

Frozen treats in the middle of an arctic New England winter? It may seem perverse, but for Bostonians, ice-cream isn't just for summer. Boston has been a hotbed of ice-cream innovation since the 1970s, when Steve Herrell began mixing Oreo shards into freshly churned batches in his (now defunct) Somerville shop. These days, Cambridge is the capital of frozen nirvana, with two top scoop shops, Toscanini's and Christina's, doling out original flavours such as burnt caramel and fresh rose. Both are superb, but the more convenient location of Toscanini's gives it an advantage. On summer nights, prepare to join the queue that snakes around the premises and down the street.

19 Paul Revere House
(page 110)

Over the centuries, this incongruously squat 17th-century clapboard house on cobbled North Square has served as a flophouse and candy store, among other incarnations, and narrowly escaped destruction. The Paul Revere House would be worth a look for its architectural significance alone, but nearly 100 years after it was built, it was also home to one of the key figures in American Revolutionary lore. After your tour, sample the culinary riches of the neighbourhood, which has been Boston's 'little Italy' for decades.

20 Fenway Park
(page 89)

Seeing a game at the Red Sox's stomping ground is a quasi-religious experience for many people. The catch? As charming as the oldest ballpark in the Majors is (it dates from 1912), it's also the smallest (with about 38,000 seats), so tickets are hard to come by. Alternatively, attend a guided tour to bone up on the celebrated stadium's history. It opened just days after the *Titanic* sank; for decades, fans thought it must have been an omen as the Sox didn't win a World Series for 86 years. This was also put down to the 'Curse of the Bambino', after owner Harry Frazee sold Babe Ruth to the New York Yankees in 1919. However, the spell was famously broken in 2004, an event depicted in the US film adaptation of *Fever Pitch*. The most famous part of the stadium is its 37-foot-high left-field wall, known as the Green Monster.

Boston
Today

The 'Hub of the Universe' isn't joking.

TEXT: ROBERT DAVID SULLIVAN

Boston is growing up. The skyline is getting spikier, and the city's population has rebounded to 650,000, the highest number since the 1960s. Boston regularly shows up on 'best places to live' lists – at least, those that don't put much emphasis on the cost of living – and this most historic of American cities is driven by a quest for innovation.

In the past few years, the city has added a popular bike-hire system, joined the food truck craze, extended subway hours, and introduced smartphone apps for residents to report everything from abandoned cars to misspelled street signs. Maybe the best news for residents since the Red Sox finally won the World Series in 2004 is that the pit in the middle of downtown – abandoned for years after the iconic Filene's department store was torn down in 2007 – is being filled in. A supermarket is set to open there around the time of publication of this guide, serving the luxury apartments and condos that have blossomed in this once-neglected area.

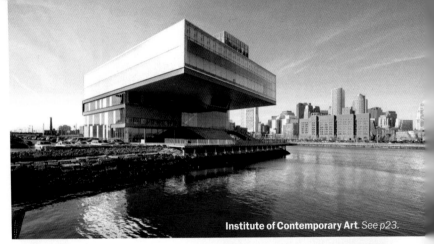

Institute of Contemporary Art. *See p23.*

WORLD-CLASS WANNABE?

The city's desire for a 'world class' label is more intense than ever. Yes, Boston knows about the snickers at its 'Hub of the Universe' nickname, but it's trying to move past its famously defensive attitude. Not everyone is comfortable with New York-like bigfooting – the city's bid to host the 2024 Summer Olympics has been greeted with horror by residents who cherish the warmer months for the decrease in noisy college students – but there's no turning back as long as the economy is strong.

The downside is that Boston has become one of the most expensive cities in America for residents, visitors and commuters. The street scene is livelier than it's been in many decades, but panhandlers are a common sight. According to a federal report, the homeless population in Massachusetts rose by 40 per cent from 2007 to 2014, faster than in any other state. The Boston area is beginning to resemble New York in its juxtapositions of extreme wealth and the down-and-out.

THE NEW BOSTONIANS

Boston's reputation for parochialism has been reinforced by gritty crime movies like *The Departed* and *Mystic River*, but the reality is that even infamous gangster Whitey Bulger's South Boston is getting cosmopolitan. Only 46 per cent of current Bostonians were born in Massachusetts, and the 2010 Census found that non-Hispanic whites made up 54 per cent of Boston's population, down from 70 per cent in 1970.

In 2014, the city reported that 27 per cent of its population was foreign-born, compared with 13 per cent for the country as a whole. While Mexicans are by far the largest immigrant group in the US, the top countries of origin for immigrants in Boston are the Dominican Republic, China, Haiti, Vietnam and El Salvador, and there are also large numbers of Brazilians and Indians in the Boston area. But the most common reported ancestry in Boston remains Irish and Italian, and you'll still find plenty of pubs and trattorias throughout the city, even if the staff no longer have Old World accents.

The immigrant population here spans all economic and educational levels, and area colleges have reported a surge in international students, evident from the array of languages you'll hear on public transit.

CENTRE-STAGE POLITICS

For nearly a century, Massachusetts has been one of the Democratic Party's strongest

These lefty tendencies are tempered by a centuries-old New England suspicion of central government, and the labour movement has been much weakened by the shift to a post-industrial economy. Massachusetts often elects moderate Republican governors to counteract its almost unanimously Democratic legislature, a habit it returned to in 2014. 'This year's race for governor unfolds beneath mostly sunny skies,' wrote the *Boston Globe* in 2014, referring to a lack of divisive issues, but the newspaper still endorsed Republican Charlie Baker to succeed Democrat Deval Patrick, who was only the second African-American to win any state's highest office.

Boston is one of the largest state capitals in the United States, and with City Hall and the State House within a few blocks of each other, the air is thick with politics. After a long history of rancorous battles divided along ethnic lines (Protestant versus Catholic in the early 20th century, white versus African-American during the fight over school integration in the 1960s and '70s), the city settled into an era of good feelings under 'urban mechanic' Tom Menino, who served as mayor from 1993 to 2014 and never had a close election. He died from cancer less than a year after leaving office.

With crime at a low point and social issues like gay marriage settled, the 2013 mayoral election revolved around development issues and the fear – prevalent here and in cities across America – that the middle class will be driven out of the city by housing costs and an uneven school system. The winner was a state legislator and former labour leader named Marty Walsh, who won both the fabled Irish stronghold of South Boston and mostly black Roxbury. Walsh has announced the goal of building 53,000 new housing units in Boston by 2030; the plan includes boosting city spending on low-income units and providing incentives for the construction of new housing away from the luxury-priced downtown. But increasing the housing stock is tough when neighbourhood groups routinely insist on lopping a few floors off planned apartment buildings.

states, and truly competitive elections are rare here. But the state still looms large in national politics. Its wealth means that even Republican candidates from other states hold fundraisers here. The Bay State has also produced more credible presidential candidates than any other state over the past 60 years, including 2004 Democratic nominee John Kerry and 2008 Republican nominee Mitt Romney, though none have reached the top since John F Kennedy in 1960. The current Bay State politician in the spotlight is Senator Elizabeth Warren, a liberal Democrat and former Harvard professor who made her name investigating predatory loans and other causes of household debt.

The state government here is known as progressive, with periodic spasms of tax-cutting fever. Massachusetts invests heavily in public education, resulting in test scores that are consistently among the highest in the US, though city districts lag behind those in the suburbs. It was the first state to legalise same-sex marriage, its universal health insurance plan was essentially copied by President Barack Obama as the Affordable Care Act and it was an early adopter of a 'cap and trade' programme designed to lower the energy emissions that cause climate change.

DOWNTOWN ON THE UP

The Hub has recovered nicely from the Great Recession, though the same can't be said of the smaller cities in New England outside the

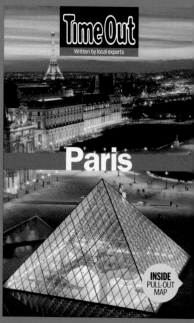

orbits of Boston and New York. Unemployment in the Boston area has consistently been below the national average, with the lowest rates in Cambridge and the suburbs to the west of the central city. 'Eds and meds' (education and health services) make up the biggest employment sector in the area, with manufacturing a shadow of its former self.

'In addition to the glitzier downtown, the city has a brand new neighbourhood on the waterfront.'

Boston's once-staid downtown is now proud – some would say alarmingly so – to show off its wealth. Before the recession, downtown was already being transformed by the Big Dig, which replaced an elevated expressway with tunnels and a 27-acre ribbon of parks called the Rose Kennedy Greenway (see p118). The most expensive road project in American history at a total cost of $24 billion, it was followed by scores of upscale hotels, luxury housing developments and trendy restaurants. Some of these replaced porn shops and holdovers from Boston's infamous red-light district, the Combat Zone; others took over what had been quirky, locally owned bars and stores.

The *Boston Business Journal* has reported that the 'fanciest penthouse' in Downtown Crossing's 60-storey Millennium Tower, due for completion in 2016, will go for $37.5 million. That may not come to pass, but multimillion-dollar residences have become so common here that the developers knew how far they'd have to go to get headlines.

In addition to a glitzier downtown, the city has a brand new neighbourhood on the waterfront. The Seaport includes a massive convention centre and the relocated Institute of Contemporary Art (see p124), as well as restaurants, offices and housing. There's also an 'Innovation District', competing with Cambridge's Kendall Square for information technology, clean technology and bio-technology start-ups – but both are trying to keep up with California's Silicon Valley.

DRINKING AND GAMBLING

The rivalry with San Francisco for hipness and innovation has the Hub trying to change its reputation for prudishness and 10pm closing times. In fact, Boston is a playground for young adults: 35 per cent of the population are between 20 and 35, the largest share of any major city in the US. But since few participate in local politics, residents who want to keep the noise down have disproportionate influence.

Mayor Marty Walsh and other civic leaders have made some progress. In 2014, the MBTA extended service by two hours at weekends, until 2.30am (half an hour after the bars close), but the agency has cut back service in the past and would no doubt do so again if passenger numbers decline. Walsh also helped to extract 75 additional liquor licences from the state, which enforces a cap on the number Boston can grant (a holdover from the days when the Yankee legislature limited the political power of the uppity Irish Catholics winning elections in Boston). The still-exorbitant price of liquor licences may not be evident downtown, but it's a problem in poorer neighbourhoods, where it's too expensive to open full-service restaurants. As for 'happy hours', they remain against the law in an effort to prevent drunk driving.

Boston has been more successful in expanding its roster of festivals, which range from Gay Pride to Italian saints' feast days in the North End. The twice-annual Boston Calling music festival, which began in 2013, has brought large crowds to City Hall Plaza, and the Greenway has hosted such events as an after-midnight food-truck festival.

But the most startling change to Boston area nightlife may be appearing in the near future. A new law allows for three casinos to be established in Massachusetts, and a state commission has approved one in Everett, which borders Boston to the north. (The proposal for a casino straddling the line between Revere and Boston lost momentum after the neighbourhood of East Boston voted against it.) For a city with a low tolerance for strip clubs and a distaste for tacky music acts and all-you-can-eat buffets, the prospect of a little Las Vegas in its backyard is disconcerting. Boston is trying very hard to get visitors to shell out a lot of money for fabulous views, fine dining, and cutting-edge music and theatre. It will be highly insulted if you take a shuttle from the airport to Everett.

Itineraries

Embark on the perfect weekend in Boston with our two-day plan.

NOON

9.30AM

7PM

Day 1

9.30AM Beat the brunch crowds at wildly popular Beacon Hill fixture **Paramount** (see p69) before strolling the neighbourhood's time-warp byways. Charles Street has a highly browsable mix of antiques shops and boutiques, most of which should be open by the time you polish off your blueberry pancakes or banana and caramel french toast – stop into the gift-friendly **Good** (see p70) and vintage-accessories trove **Twentieth Century Limited** (see p71).

11AM The Boston Brahmin bastion had a more varied demographic in its early years than you might think (see p68 **Walk**), but a stop at exclusive Louisburg Square is essential to gawk at some of the most expensive real estate in the city (and the homes of Louisa May Alcott and John Kerry).

NOON From here, it's about a 20-minute walk to the North End. There's no direct T (they don't call this 'America's walking city' for nothing), so you might want to fortify yourself with a beer at the **Sevens Ale House** (see p69)

3PM

before you set out. There are any number of great lunch options in Boston's Italian neighbourhood, from pizza napoletana at **Regina Pizzeria** (*see p115*) to fish or seafood at the **Daily Catch** (*see p112*) or **Neptune Oyster** (*see p114*). While you're here, pay your respects at the **Old North Church** (*see p114*), which played a key role in Paul Revere's 'midnight ride', and pop by his former home on picturesque North Square (*see p110*). You also may want to stop for a cappuccino at one of the numerous old-school coffee bars such as **Caffe Vittoria** (*see p112*).

3PM Head south on the **Rose F Kennedy Greenway** (*see p118*) – the strip of parks in the footprint of the elevated expressway that once cut through the city. You'll pass several landmarks, including Long Wharf on the left, and the back of Quincy Market and the Custom House clock-tower looming up on your right. Pass through several distinct spaces, including the Wharf District Parks with the dramatic circular Rings Fountain and the Urban Arboretum, where you should exit to the waterfront. Look for the incongruous shack of seafood purveyor James

Far left: **Paramount**. Top: **Old North Church**. Middle: **Rose F Kennedy Greenway & Custom House clock tower**. Bottom: **Row 34**. Right: **Sinclair**.

Hook & Co (tipped to be replaced by a skyscraper) and the 1908 Northern Swing Bridge just left of it. Cross Fort Point Channel and keep going straight on Northern Avenue until you reach the striking **Institute of Contemporary Art** (*see p124*) on Fan Pier. Before or after your culture fix, stop for a browse and a cocktail overlooking the harbour at **Louis** (*see p124*), the city's best designer boutique, which also has a good restaurant.

7PM From here, it's a short walk to the Fort Point Channel neighbourhood, which has an enticing collection of restaurants. If the waterside setting makes you crave shellfish, you can't go wrong with a dozen oysters, a lobster roll and a locally brewed beer at **Row 34** (*see p121*).

9PM Catch the T from South Station to Cambridge and end the night with a gig at Harvard Square's newest music venue, the **Sinclair** (*see p190*), or any number of great nightspots in Central Square such as **Middlesex Lounge** (*see p186*), **Phoenix Landing** (*see p186*) or veteran rock clubs **Middle East** (*see p191*) and **TT the Bear's Place** (*see p192*).

9PM

11AM

Day 2

11AM This is a Sunday-themed itinerary, so start the day with brunch in one of the chicest corners of the city, the South End. The **South End Buttery** (see p101) is a local favourite but we also recommend the Italian-inflected egg dishes at tiny, star-chef-powered *enoteca* **Coppa** (see p100).

NOON From May to October, the unmissable Sunday event is the outdoor craft and farmers' market, combined with the year-round covered vintage market, in the arty SoWa (South of Washington) enclave, which also encompasses art galleries and shops in a converted warehouse complex (see p99 **SoWa So Good**). While you're there, be sure to stop by **Bobby From Boston** (see p103), which is known for its pristine vintage menswear. If you want a snack, a fleet of food trucks parks here too.

2PM Stroll north-west through the South End's charming streets of restored brick townhouses and tidy English-style squares to Back Bay's Copley Square. Pause to take in the expansive view of **Trinity Church** (see p80) and the **Boston Public Library** (see p77) – cultural monuments of the late-19th-century 'Athens of America'. Get the subway from Copley and take your choice of Boston's two best museums: the comprehensive era- and globe-spanning **Museum of Fine Arts** (see p90) or the smaller, but unique **Isabella Stewart Gardner Museum** (see p89), in an ersatz Venetian palazzo. We're sorry, but trying to hit both in one afternoon would be over-ambitious.

5PM Now it's definitely time for a cocktail. Catch the T back to Copley and change to

NOON

2PM

BOSTON FOR FREE

WALK IS CHEAP

'America's walking city' has a wealth of marked strolls. For a free history lesson, set off on the Freedom Trail, the self-guided tour established in 1958, or one of several other themed rambles (*see p47* **Trail Blazers**). Or follow the HarborWalk along the city's waterfront. Other pleasant spots for striding out include the Esplanade, on the banks of the Charles River between Beacon Hill and the Back Bay, and Jamaica Plain's Arnold Arboretum, with its collection of more than 15,000 trees and plants (*see p154*).

HOME FREE

The city has a wealth of National Historic Sites, which are free to the public. Some of them, like Faneuil Hall and the Bunker Hill Monument, are on the Freedom Trail; others were the residences of famous figures, such as President John F Kennedy and Frederick Law Olmsted (for both, *see p157*) and Henry Wadsworth Longfellow (*see p130*). You can also pay your respects to the great and the good at their final resting places – without paying admission (*see p52* **Six Feet Under**).

STUDENT PERKS

In academic capital Cambridge, two prominent on-campus art centres offer exhibitions by high-profile artists from around the world at no charge. Harvard's Carpenter Center for the Visual Arts (*see p136*) – set in a Le Corbusier building that's worth a look in itself – and MIT's List Visual Arts Center (*see p141*) both stage boundary-pushing contemporary shows.

CASHLESS CULTURE

Most of Boston's best contemporary galleries are clustered in converted warehouses in the South End's SoWa district (*see p99* **SoWa So Good**), making an afternoon of gallery-hopping a breeze. On the first Friday of each month, you can also check out works in situ when more than 60 local artists open their studios at 450 Harrison Avenue (www.sowaartists.com) – you may even be able to snaffle free wine and snacks during the evening event.

any other Green Line train to Kenmore. You'll find expertly concocted drinks, and comfy sofas, at **Hawthorne** (*see p93*), helmed by master mixologist Jackson Cannon.

7PM If you want to stay put after a jam-packed day, nearby brasserie **Eastern Standard** (*see p92*) or **Island Creek Oyster Bar** (*see p92*) are both solid choices for dinner. But some of the city's most exciting cuisine is outside of central Boston. The beauty of its compact size is that even the further-flung areas aren't too far, so if you're up for an adventure, hop back on the subway (or call a cab) and head to a Somerville hotspot that's open until midnight on Sunday, such as **Kirkland Tap & Trotter** (*see p163*) or **Sarma** (*see p164*).

Clockwise from top left: **Coppa**; **Copley Square & Boston Public Library**; **Bobby from Boston**.

Boston Calling.
See p32.

Diary

Plan ahead with our year-round guide to the best festivals and events.

Everyone knows that Boston throws the wildest tea parties around and, given its Revolutionary pedigree, it's not surprising that the calendar features its share of historical re-enactments. But alongside such traditional events as the annual Boston Tea Party Re-enactment and the Boston Pops Fourth of July Concert are unmissable recent additions, including Boston Calling music festival, which livens up businesslike Government Center twice a year with top-calibre acts. The cultured metropolis is known for its arts events, from quirky local celebrations to the alcohol-free New Year's Eve programme, First Night, which has become a model for more than 250 cities and towns worldwide. For more festivals and events, check out the other chapters in the Arts & Entertainment section. Before you set out or plan a trip around an event, it's wise to call or check online first as dates, times and locations are subject to change.

Spring

Boston Massacre Re-enactment
Old State House, State Street, at Washington Street, Downtown (1-617 720 1713, www.bostonhistory. org). State T. **Date** early Mar.
Witness the pivotal clash that took place beneath the Old State House on an early spring night in 1770, when a group of 'cowardly' Redcoats emptied their muskets into a mob of malcontent colonists.

PAX East
Boston Convention & Exposition Center, Waterfront (www.paxsite.com). Silver Line Waterfront to World Trade Center. **Date** early-mid Mar.
Nerd out among your peers without judgement at the largest gaming convention on the East Coast – one of five PAX locations worldwide. Gamers of all types flock to town for tournaments, free play and first views of unreleased titles.

PUBLIC HOLIDAYS

New Year's Day
1 Jan

Martin Luther King, Jr Day
3rd Mon in Jan

Presidents' Day
3rd Mon in Feb

Patriots Day
3rd Mon in April

Memorial Day
Last Mon in May

Independence Day
4 July

Labor Day
1st Mon in Sept

Columbus Day
2nd Mon in Oct

Veterans Day
11 Nov

Thanksgiving Day
Last Thur in Nov

Christmas Day
25 Dec

BOSTON CALLING

The popular festival lets you 'rock at the Government Center'.

When the patron saint of Massachusetts music, Jonathan Richman, released 'Government Center' with the Modern Lovers in 1976, he probably would have never guessed that his anarchic call, 'We gotta rock at the Government Center,' was prophetic.

Unlikely though it may have seemed, in May 2013, a major music festival, **Boston Calling** (*see p32*) debuted in this business-centric patch of downtown Boston. Often decried by locals as an architectural eyesore, the vast, soulless City Hall Plaza has proven to be a surprisingly great spot for day-long outdoor performances.

Mike Snow and Brian Appel, longtime employees of the Phoenix Media Group, originally conceived of a large-scale festival that would be cross-promoted by alternative weekly the *Boston Phoenix* and affiliated radio powerhouse WBCN. But, after the presses stopped at the *Phoenix* and WBCN went off the air, they decided to continue their efforts independently with a new company, Crashline Productions. After setting the wheels in motion, the team called upon their friend Aaron Dessner, guitarist from the National, to help curate (and play) the inaugural festival. The sold-out event featuring fun., the Walkmen and the Shins, to name a few, was a huge hit and a second festival was immediately announced for that September.

It's no Bonnaroo or Coachella, but then it's not supposed to be. This festival doesn't take place in a field, but in the heart of downtown, surrounded by skyscrapers. Boston Calling continues to run twice a year and has expanded into a three-day event hosting such diverse acts as Neutral Milk Hotel, Lorde, Nas with the Roots, and the Replacements.

Clockwise: **Boston Marathon**; **Lilac Sunday**; **St Patrick's Day Parade**.

Dine Out Boston
Various locations (www.bostonusa.com/visit/dineoutboston). **Date** mid Mar & mid Aug.
While some bemoan the limited options, there's no other way you can get into so many high-end restaurants with such minimal outlay. With more than 200 establishments participating, the hungry masses can sample the cuisine and enjoy the ambience normally restricted to special occasions or the well-heeled during this two-week prix fixe event. The prices – $15-$25 for a two- or three-course lunch, $28-$38 for a three-course dinner – exclude beverages, tax and tips.

St Patrick's Day Parade
Dorchester Street & Broadway, South Boston (1-781 436 3377, www.southbostonparade.org). Broadway T. **Admission** free. **Date** mid Mar.
Boston is the undisputed capital of Irish America, and Southie is the Irish capital of Boston. Everyone and their dog wears a shamrock at the neighbourhood's St Patrick's Day parade – one of the largest in the US – complete with floats, marching bagpipers and, of course, waving politicians. Pubs along the route and throughout Boston overflow with green beer and ample merrymaking. Later on, the downtown streets are so full of soused pedestrians that hailing a taxi is tantamount to catching a fly ball at Fenway Park.

Boston Underground Film Festival
Various cinemas (www.bostonunderground.org). **Admission** varies. **Date** late Mar.
Launched in 1999, Boston's fringiest film festival gives venues and voices to local and national auteurs with little money and big dreams. Screenings at indie cinemas throughout the area culminate in an awards show where winners receive a Bacchus, the festival's coveted demonic bunny trophy. Past attendees of the BUFF include legendary Troma founder Lloyd Kaufman and zombie-film pioneer George A Romero.

Boston Marathon

Finishes at Copley Square, Back Bay (1-617 236 1652, www.bostonmarathon.org). Copley T.
Date 3rd Mon in Apr.

The 2013 race was marked by an act of terrorism, but the world's oldest annual marathon has only grown in significance since that harrowing day. Uniting and motivating the world's best athletes and onlookers, the Boston Marathon is now, more than ever, a symbol of perseverance. The race begins in Hopkinton (south-west of Boston), wraps around the campus of Boston College and finishes in Copley Square. Half a million spectators come out to cheer on the tens of thousands of contestants, soaking up the adrenaline and cheering on friends along the route; the best – and most crowded – spot is near the finish line.

Patriot's Day Re-enactments

Lexington Green, Lexington (1-781 862 1450, www.libertyride.us, www.lexingtonminutemen. com). **Date** 3rd Mon in Apr.

Massachusetts state holiday Patriot's Day commemorates the opening battle of the American Revolutionary War, which took place in suburban Lexington and Concord. Late the night before, 'Paul Revere' gallops through town, shouting his warning – 'The British are coming!' – to the colonists. On Patriot's Day itself, you can watch a full-scale re-enactment of the skirmish that produced the 'shot heard round the world'.

James Joyce Ramble

Start/finish at Endicott Estate, 656 East Street, Dedham (1-781 329 9744, www.ramble.org).
Date last Sun in Apr or 1st Sun in May.

The brainchild of a local runner and Joyce fan, who realised that struggling through *Finnegans Wake* was akin to running a particularly arduous race, this six-mile run/walk stampedes through suburban Dedham every spring. The Ramble pays tribute to its namesake by punctuating the road race with an ensemble of Joyce-reading actors dressed in period costume. Mile one features *Finnegans Wake*, mile three *A Portrait of the Artist as a Young Man* and mile six, appropriately enough, *The Dead*.

Lilac Sunday

Arnold Arboretum, 125 Arborway, at Centre Street, Jamaica Plain (1-617 524 1718, www. arboretum.harvard.edu). Forest Hills T. **Date** 2nd Sun in May.

The name says it all – float through the Arboretum in spring, when more than 400 deliciously fragrant lilac plants, of nearly 200 different varieties, are in bloom. Come for the flowers, stay for the Morris dancing – groups from all over the North-east show up to jingle and jangle their way through sword dances in honour of May Day. Refreshments are available, or bring your own picnic.

IN THE KNOW SAINTS ALIVE!

St Anthony's Feast (see p33) may be the most famous of the North End events celebrating Catholic saints, delectable dining and gondolier-style balladeers, but whether or not it is the best is up for debate. Every weekend in August, Boston's most charming neighbourhood hosts a century-old carnival-style *festa* honouring a patron saint by preparing arancini, pasta and panini. It starts with **St Agrippina's Feast**, on Hanover Street, on the first weekend of August. That's followed by the **Madonna della Cava North End Feast Celebration** (Hanover & Battery Streets) and the **Fisherman's Feast of the Madonna del Soccorso di Sciacca North End Festival** (North, Fleet & Lewis Streets) on the second and third weekends. If you can make it through to **St Lucy's Feast** (Endicott Street), following St Anthony's Feast, it's probably time to go on a diet.

Boston Calling
City Hall Plaza (www.bostoncalling.com). Haymarket, Park Street or State T. **Date** May & Sept. *See p30* **Boston Calling**. *Photo p28.*

Together Festival
Various locations in Boston (www.togetherboston. com). **Date** mid May.
Started in 2010 as a festival focused on electronica, Together now features bands, hip hop artists and discussion panels and becomes more expansive, inclusive and important every year.

Summer

The second helping of **Dine Out Boston** (*see p30*) takes place in mid August.

Boston Pride
Throughout Boston (1-617 262 9405, www.boston pride.org). **Admission** free. **Date** 1st wk in June.
Toast Gay Pride in the first state in the US to legalise same-sex marriage. Although unofficial festivities extend throughout the month of June, the main event is a week-long line-up of everything from club nights and book signings to an AIDS-awareness walk. The festival culminates with a riotous parade through Boston's own gay central, the South End, on Saturday, and further revels on Sunday.

Bunker Hill Day Celebrations
Various locations in Charlestown (1-617 242 5642, www.nps.gov/bost). Community College T. **Date** wknd in mid June.

A weekend of historical talks and re-enactments of the infamous Battle of Bunker Hill (which actually took place on neighbouring Breed's Hill) – complete with period costumes and muskets. Though British forces won the skirmish, they suffered such heavy casualties that they were forced to abandon their first major siege of Boston. The celebration finishes with a grand parade through hilly Charlestown.

River Festival
Along the Charles River, Cambridge (1-617 349 4380, www.cambridgema.gov/cac). Harvard Square T. **Date** mid June.
If crowding along the Charles on the Fourth of July isn't your bag, come early for this annual cultural celebration that dates back to 1977. Set along the riverbank between John F Kennedy Street and Western Avenue, this free Cambridge Arts Council-sponsored event features jazz, folk, roots and world music performances, dance and art demonstrations, family art-making activities, and more than 150 speciality purveyors of food, arts and crafts.

Boston Harborfest
Various locations in Boston (www.boston harborfest.com). **Date** 4th wk in June.
The annual maritime- and colonial-themed festival of fireworks, open-air concerts and (yet more) historical re-enactments in the run up to the Fourth of July now has 200-plus events taking place in more than 30 harbourside venues. The Chowderfest (a celebration of New England's traditional bivalve soup, in which top restaurants vie for the title of 'Boston's Best Clam Chowder') is the high point.

Boston Pops Fourth of July Concert
Hatch Shell, Charles River Esplanade, Back Bay (1-617 626 1250, www.july4th.org). Charles/ MGH T. **Date** 4 July.
Not surprisingly, the Fourth of July attracts hundreds of thousands of visitors to the birthplace of American independence – most of whom plant themselves along the banks of the Charles River to watch the fireworks. The Boston Pops are an American institution, and frantically territorial families show up at dawn to claim their grassy patch for the day. Technically, the event is non-alcoholic, but that doesn't stop savvy regulars from slipping drinks into plastic cups. In the early evening – after everyone is tuckered out from a sweaty day of guarding blankets (and hiding beer) – the Pops play in the Hatch Shell. The accompanying fireworks display, set off from a barge on the Charles, is not to be missed. Every year, a world-class performer or two joins the Pops for a special patriotic collaboration.

Turning of the USS Constitution
Viewing along Boston Harbor (1-617 426 1812, www.ussconstitutionmuseum.org). **Date** 4 July.

Top: **Boston Pops Fourth of July Concert**. Bottom: **Caribbean Carnival**.

Still a commissioned naval vessel, 'Old Ironsides' makes her stately annual sail around Boston Harbor to turn and re-dock in the opposite direction at the Charlestown Naval Yard. This is done not for the tourists, but to ensure that the ship weathers evenly. ▶ *You can board the ship at other times; see p151.*

Bastille Day

French Library & Cultural Center, 53 Marlborough Street, at Berkeley Street (1-617 912 0400, www. frenchculturalcenter.org). Arlington or Copley T. **Date** mid July.

This 60-year-old non-profit organisation throws a street party on an evening before or after Bastille Day, with French cuisine, Francophone musicians, children's activities and plenty of joie de vivre.

Lantern Festival

95 Forest Hills Avenue, Jamaica Plain (1-617 524 0128, www.foresthillstrust.org). Forest Hills T then 10mins walk. **Date** mid July.

A party in a graveyard? Sounds a tad morbid – but the Forest Hills Cemetery, full of lush gardens and intriguing sculpture, is one of the most gorgeous green spaces in the Boston area. Never is it more beautiful than during the annual Buddhist ritual-inspired Lantern Festival. An afternoon filled with performances from local artists (including *taiko* drummers and gospel choirs) prefaces the main event: after sunset, visitors set little lanterns adrift in Lake Hibiscus, until they form a shimmering flotilla of light.

ArtBeat

Davis Square, Somerville (1-617 625 6600, www.somervilleartscouncil.org). Davis Square T. **Date** 3rd wknd in July.

Davis Square is a breeding ground for artists, writers, musicians, performers and sundry other bohemian types, not to mention a funky place to spend an afternoon people-watching on a summer afternoon. Every year, it hosts a weekend-long celebration of all that's artsy. The revelries include concerts by local indie, blues and folk bands, theatrical performances, readings and a street art market.

Caribbean Carnival

Franklin Park, at Blue Hill Avenue, Dorchester (1-617 445 2019, www.bostoncarnivalvillage.com). Forest Hills T then 10mins walk. **Date** late Aug.

Expect ethnic food, music, dance and a colourful parade. The feathered costumes and sun-drenched festivities offer a vibrant counterpoint to Boston's buttoned-up re-enactments, and celebrate an entirely different strand of colonial history.

St Anthony's Feast

Endicott, Thacher & North Margin Streets, North End (1-617 723 8669, www.stanthonysfeast.com). Haymarket T. **Date** late Aug.

There's no better neighbourhood for a stroll than the North End, and no better time to do it than during

Clockwise from left: **What the Fluff? Festival**; **Head of the Charles Regatta**; **Beantown Jazz Festival**; **Boston Tattoo Convention**.

this annual Catholic shindig. For one weekend, the winding, cobbled streets of Boston's Italian district are lined with vendors of delectable Mediterranean fare and effigies of weeping saints. A parade and performances by Italian crooners round out the bustling weekend with carnival-type games for the kids (and playful adults).

▶ *For more saints' feasts, see p32 In the Know.*

Autumn

Boston Ahts Festival

Christopher Columbus Park, North End (1-617 635 3911, www.celebrateboston.com/boston-arts-festival.htm). Haymarket T. **Date** 1st wknd in Sept.
With a silly name that emphasises accessibility by poking fun at the Boston accent, this festival features visual art, dance, music, poetry, theatre and more in Christopher Columbus Park. A varied slate of performers, which have included the Boston Ballet and the Blue Man Group, are showcased on two stages. Art and craft activities span a wide range of media, from interactive mural-making to glass-blowing demos.

Boston Tattoo Convention

Back Bay Sheraton Hotel, 39 Dalton Street, Back Bay (1-978 744 9393, www.bostontattoo convention.com). Hynes Convention Center T. **Date** wknd in Sept.
Until 2001, Massachusetts residents had to cross the state line in order to get a tattoo. Once it was legalised, though, it didn't take long for Boston to establish itself as a hub for body art – as the Tattoo Convention proves. More than 100 tattoo artists converge at the Sheraton for the four-day event, which includes contests, vendors, galleries and performances, plus numerous ink-slingers setting up shop.

Boston Film Festival

Stuart Street Playhouse, 200 Stuart Street, Downtown (1-617 523 8388, www.bostonfilm festival.org). Chinatown T. **Date** 2nd wk in Sept.
This five-day festival of lectures, panels and screenings showcases feature-length films, shorts and independent works. There's a strong local contingent among the participants, many from nearby colleges. Past entries include the Oscar-winning *American Beauty* and Billy Ray's directorial debut, *Shattered Glass*.

Massachusetts Cannabis Reform Coalition's Freedom Rally

Boston Common, Downtown (1-781 944 2266, www.masscann.org). Park Street T. **Admission** free. **Date** mid Sept.
Every year, the city of Boston broods over issuing permits to this annual ganja-fest. Regardless, the rally always goes down, with thousands of proud stoners sneaking spliffs on to the Common. A handful of local

bands play – and not just reggae and jam bands either. In recent years, Letters to Cleo, the Dresden Dolls, Wayne Kramer and the metallic Scissorfight have all taken the stage for the cause. Now, with medical marijuana legalised in Massachusetts, the tone of the event may change.

What the Fluff? Festival

Union Square, Somerville (1-617 955 0080, www.unionsquaremain.org). Harvard Square T then bus 86, or Lechmere T then bus 87. **Date** *late Sept.*
There's more to Boston's history than the fight for independence. In 1917, for example, the entrepreneur Archibald Query invented Marshmallow Fluff – the beloved confectionary spread – right here in Somerville. Union Square celebrates its favourite local invention with a day-long festival that includes a tug-of-war over a tub of Fluff, erupting Fluff volcanoes, Fluff-based nibbles and local bands.

Beantown Jazz Festival

Various locations in Boston (www.beantownjazz.org). **Date** *Last wknd in Sept.*
Boston's lively jazz scene steals the limelight at this yearly festival, which brings hot talents to various venues. The festival includes performances at Sculler's Jazz Club, Berklee Performance Center and the Beehive. Vendors and musicians also take to the streets in the South End.
▶ *For more about Boston's jazz scene, see p192.*

Salem's Haunted Happenings

Various locations in Salem (1-978 744 3663, 1-877 725 3662, www.hauntedhappenings.org). **Date** *throughout Oct.*
As you'd expect from a place that's on the map for executing witches, spooky Salem hosts a wicked Halloween. The town is also a haven for present-day pagans. A huge costumed parade kicks off a month of jack-o'-lantern carving, haunted-house tours, candlelit vigils, modern witchcraft ceremonies, magic shows and a psychics' fair. Leave your scepticism at home – but bring your wallet and the most fabulous costume you can dream up.
▶ *For excursions to Salem, see p208.*

Lowell Celebrates Kerouac! Festival

Various locations in Lowell (1-978 970 4257, www.lowellcelebrateskerouac.org). **Date** *1st wk in Oct.*
Most famous for his seminal 1957 novel *On the Road* – an American traveller's ode to wanderlust, amphetamines and boisterous adventure – Jack Kerouac was born and buried in Lowell, a former mill town north-west of Boston. While he never claimed to have taken much from the place, the city still revels in his legacy. Every year, the town commemorates its legendary tie to the Beat Generation with a three-day festival of open mics, jazz and poetry readings.

Harvard Square Oktoberfest

Harvard Square, Cambridge (1-617 491 3434, www.harvardsquare.com). Harvard Square T. **Date** *early Oct.*
Harvard Square transforms itself into a Bavarian town for a weekend. Bands, dancers, ethnic food stalls and beer gardens line the streets, together with some 200 regional artisans and merchants displaying their wares.

Head of the Charles Regatta

Charles River, between the Boston University Bridge and the Eliot Bridge (1-617 868 6200, www.hocr.org). Central or Harvard Square T, then 10mins walk. **Date** *wknd in mid Oct.*

Thousands of rowers converge on Cambridge for this world-class regatta. The scene is spectacular – and not just because of the regatta, but also for the sight of the hundreds of thousands of spectators lining the bridges and riverbanks along the Charles.

Winter

Boston Common Tree Lighting

Boston Common, Downtown (1-617 635 4505, www.cityofboston.gov). Park Street T. **Date** late Nov or early Dec.

The story behind this annual holiday tree-lighting tradition is just as captivating as the ceremony itself. Each year, a Boston tree scout treks to Nova Scotia to select a shapely 50ft spruce. (Ever since 1917, Nova Scotia has donated its trees as a gift, out of gratitude for Boston's fast response to a devastating fire in Halifax.) A local dignitary (often the mayor) flicks the switch. The rest of the Common's trees are strung with lights as well, while an illuminated Nativity scene and menorah grace the grounds near the Park Street T station.

Christmas Revels

Sanders Theatre, Memorial Hall, 45 Quincy Street, at Cambridge Street, Cambridge (1-617 972 8300, www.revels.org). Harvard Square T. **Date** mid-late Dec.

Put on by a local non-profit performance troupe, the Revels have become a winter institution for those who like old-fashioned festive entertainment. Each year focuses on a different theme – based on culture and time period – of Christmas pageantry. Performances include dances, plays and plenty of participatory carol-singing.

Boston Tea Party Re-enactment

Old South Meeting House, 310 Washington Street, Downtown (1-617 482 6439, www.oldsouth meetinghouse.org). State T. **Date** mid Dec.

Patriots gather for a town meeting at the Old South Meeting House to condemn the crimes of nasty old King George III. Fife and drum in hand, the excitable mob then marches to Fort Point Channel, storms the brig *Beaver* and does the dirty deed. The event is in partnership with the Boston Tea Party Ships & Museum (*see p170*).

IN THE KNOW
OPEN-DOOR POLICY

From September to December – at the weekends – you can get an inside look at artists' studios in neighbourhoods across town. The **Boston Open Studios Coalition** (www.cityofboston.gov/arts) allows you a peek at the creative process (and to get deep discounts on artwork) when artists open their work spaces to the public. The **Fort Point Arts Community** (www.fortpointarts.org) hosts a particularly impressive list of artists, with doors open in mid October.

Far left:
Boston Common Tree Lighting.
Left:
Chinese New Year.

NUTCRACKER REVISITED

Variations on a theme.

Urban Nutcracker.

First Night

Various venues throughout Boston (www.firstnight. org). **Date** 31 Dec.

Boston was the first city in the country to offer this alcohol-free alternative to toasting the New Year. Launched in 1976, First Night is celebrated citywide, with more than 1,000 artists and 200 performances at indoor and outdoor venues. Events range from poetry readings to rock concerts. There are activities from noon, but the fun really starts in the early evening with the carnival-style Grand Procession in Back Bay, culminating in a midnight fireworks display at the harbour. The massive ice sculptures in Copley Square and on the Common are another signature feature.

Chinese New Year

Beach & Tyler Streets, Chinatown (1-617 350 6303, www.chinatownmainstreet.org). Boylston or Chinatown T. **Date** late Jan or early Feb.

Dragons dance and fireworks explode in a swirl of colour and sound at one of the nation's largest celebrations of the first day of the Chinese calendar. Traditionally, festivities last 15 days, and much of the action takes place in and around Chinatown.

Beanpot Hockey Tournament

TD Garden, Causeway Street, at Friend Street (1-617 624 1000, www.beanpothockey.com). North Station T. **Date** 1st & 2nd Mon in Feb.

Players from Harvard, Northeastern and Boston Universities and Boston College go head-to-head in this annual ice-hockey clash. It's a welcome reprieve from the Bruins' often disappointing performances, as an audience of rival college students assault one another with fusillades of jeers and cheers. The winning team gets a trophy shaped like a bean pot.

Visiting Boston when the cobbled streets shimmer with a fresh coat of snow and Christmas lights twinkle in the windows of Back Bay brownstones can truly be an unforgettable experience. Should you find your cup runneth over with holiday spirit, seeing a production of *The Nutcracker* is a fine way to embrace this magical time of the year. Traditionalists should go for the **Boston Ballet**'s acclaimed production of the Balanchine classic (1-617 695 6955, www. bostonballet.org), staged annually at the Opera House (see *p198*). Tickets start at around $35 and rise to more than $180.

For a more street-savvy spectacle, opt for Tony Williams Dance Center's **Urban Nutcracker** (John Hancock Hall, 180 Berkeley Street, at Stuart Street, Back Bay, 1-617 524 3066, www.urbannutcracker.com, $20-$85). The production embraces inner-city multiculturalism by weaving ballet, jazz, modern dance and various ethnic dance styles into the familiar tale, using Duke Ellington's and Billy Strayhorn's jazz version of the *Nutcracker Suite* as a springboard.

And then there is **The Slutcracker: A Burlesque** (www.theslutcracker.com, $27), an irreverent new tradition at the Somerville Theatre (see *p176*). Sit back with a glass of wine or beer to watch this loose adaptation, in which the protagonist, Clara, is dating Fritz, instead of being his older sister. And while everything seems to be perfect in their relationship, Fritz's lack of prowess between the sheets is leaving her unsatisfied. That's where Herr Drosselmeyer – traditionally Clara's mysterious gift-giving godfather and purveyor of the Nutcracker toy – steps in, and you can figure out what happens from there.

Boston's Best

Check off the essentials with our hand-picked list of highlights.

Sightseeing

VIEWS

Bunker Hill Monument p150
Climb the 294 steps to the top of this obelisk for vertiginous vistas.

Charles River Esplanade p72
Gaze out at the sailing boats on the Charles River from this idyllic strip.

Fan Pier p123
An expansive harbour panorama.

Prudential Tower p77
The Skywalk Observatory is the city's highest viewpoint.

ART

Harvard Art Museums p136
Three standout collections in one revamped space.

Isabella Stewart Gardner Museum p89
Hand-picked masterpieces and decorative art in an exquisite palace.

Institute of Contemporary Art p124
Cutting-edge exhibitions.

Museum of Fine Arts p90
Wide-ranging holdings at the city's premier art museum.

SoWa galleries p96
A cluster of contemporary art spaces.

HISTORY

Boston Athenaeum p65
A venerable cultural institution.

Granary Burying Ground p50
Pay your respects to founding fathers and historical figures.

View from the Prudential Tower.

Boston Tea Party Ships & Museum.

Faneuil Hall p56
The American Revolution was plotted here.
John F Kennedy Presidential Library & Museum p153
A dramatic monument to the assassinated leader.
Old State House p56
The site of the Boston Massacre, now a museum.
Paul Revere House p110
A colonial survivor.
Trinity Church p80
Richardson's exuberant architectural gem.

OUTDOORS
Arnold Arboretum p154
This compendium of plant life doubles as a lovely park.
Boston Public Garden p46
A genteel patch for strolling and lounging.
Rose Kennedy Greenway p78
A green path through the city.

CURIOSITIES
Harvard Museum of Natural History p170
A taxidermied menagerie and extraordinary glass flowers.
Mapparium p86
The world's only walk-in globe.
MIT Museum p144
Weird science.

CHILDREN
Boston Tea Party Ships & Museum p170
Join the tea-dumping party.

Boston Children's Museum p170
One of the best kids' museums in the country.
Swan Boats p169
Cruise the Public Garden's lagoon in a fanciful vessel.

Eating & Drinking

BLOWOUTS
L'Espalier p80
Farm-to-table haute cuisine.
O Ya p58
Deluxe Japanese tavern fare.
Troquet p59
Unflashy fine dining and wine pairing.

INSTITUTIONS
Mr Bartley's Gourmet Burgers p132
The quintessential student burger joint.
Union Oyster House p57
America's oldest restaurant.

CASUAL HOTSPOTS
Café ArtScience p144
A tasteful (and fun) experiment.
Kirkland Tap & Trotter p163
Hearty dishes served in a boisterous hangout.
Sweet Cheeks Q p92
Standout Southern specialities in a rustic setting.

Museum of Fine Arts.

SEAFOOD

Island Creek Oyster Bar p92
Boston's 'merroir' pioneer.
Neptune Oyster p114
Adventurous seafood belies
the nostalgic setting.
Row 34 p121
Slurp oysters and beer on
the harbourside.

CAFES & SANDWICH SHOPS

Caffe Vittoria p112
Octogenarian Italian café.
Cutty's p158
The sandwich redefined.
Thinking Cup p54
Superior java in three
convenient locations.
Trident Booksellers & Café p84
A worthy mid-shopping
refuelling spot.

SWEET TREATS

Toscanini's p139
Some of the coolest ice-
cream flavours around.
Maria's Pastry Shop p115
This family-run bakery sells
the North End's best *canolli*.
Union Square Donuts p104
Unusual varieties ensure they
go like hot cakes.

BARS

Brick & Mortar p139
Great cocktails and bar
snacks in nightlife central.
Delux Café p102
The ultimate neo-dive.
Doyle's p156
A gorgeous old pub beloved
by politicos.
Hawthorne p93
Local star mixologist Jackson
Cannon's home base.
Independent p165
A contemporary Irish pub.
Trillium Brewing Company p125
Queue for the innovative
tipples in this popular local
brewery's tasting room.

Clockwise from right: **Brattle Book Shop**; **Curious George Store**; **Union Square Donuts**; **Good**.

Silvertone Bar & Grill p54
Classic drinks in suitably
retro surroundings.

Shopping

GIFTS & SOUVENIRS

Black Ink p133
A jumble of giftable items.
Farm & Fable p103
Culinary collectibles for your
favourite cook.
Follain p103
Natural beauty products,
many from New England.
Good p70
A standout assemblage of
accessories and home items.
Magpie p165
Contemporary crafts.

Olives & Grace p105
Artisanal goods galore,
from jams to jewellery.

CLOTHING

Alan Bilzerian p85
Cutting-edge labels.
Ball & Buck p85
Purveyor of the modern
sportsman look.
Bodega p88
A speakeasy-style streetwear
emporium.
Louis p124
A fabulous concept store
on the waterfront.

BOOKS & MUSIC

Ars Libri p102
Rare fine-art books plus
an on-site gallery.

Brattle Book Shop p54
A well-stocked trove of antiquarian tomes.
Harvard Book Store p134
Find hefty discounts at this Harvard Square staple.
Cheapo Records p140
Vinyl lives at this septuagenarian survivor.

ANTIQUES & VINTAGE
Abodeon p133
Mid-century furnishings.
Bobby from Boston p103
Impeccable vintage menswear.
40 South Street p156
A grab bag of hip gear from the 1950s to the '90s.

FOOD & DRINK
Formaggio Kitchen p134
A cornucopia of cheeses, condiments and more.
Polcari's Coffee p115
This nostalgic gem sells much more than just java.
Wine Bottega p113
A lotta bottle squeezed into a small space.

CHILDREN
Curious George Store p133
Dedicated to the fictional monkey, this shop sells books, toys and more.

Tadpole p105
Clothes and accoutrements for urban tykes.

DEPARTMENT STORES & MALLS
Barneys New York p82
A (much smaller) outpost of the famed NYC store.
Copley Place p82
Find luxe designer labels in this upscale mall.
Neiman Marcus p83
The beauty department is a highlight of this posh store.

Nightlife

CLUBS
Middlesex Lounge p186
Popular lounge-club known for its varied weekly schedule.
Phoenix Landing p186
This hybrid Irish pub and dance spot is an unlikely hit.

MUSIC
Boston Calling p32
Diverse acts play downtown at this twice-yearly festival.
Atwood's Tavern p190
Local lights perform in a laid-back pub.
Lilypad p193
Eclectic experimental music.
Lizard Lounge p191
Get up close and personal with the musicians in this living room-size space.

Paradise Rock Club p192
Aerosmith, U2 and more have rocked this legendary house.
Sinclair p190
A slick big-ticket indie venue.
Wally's Café p193
This bare-bones joint has been jumpin' since 1947.

Arts

THEATRE
American Repertory Theater (ART) p199
Innovative new works and bound-for-Broadway shows.
Citi Performing Arts Center p199
Everything from Shakespeare to blockbusters at this three-theatre behemoth.

FILM
Brattle Theatre p174
Eclectic offerings at this Harvard Square fixture.
Coolidge Corner Theatre p176
An art deco gem.
Harvard Film Archive p176
A celluloid temple.

CLASSICAL & DANCE
Boston Ballet p197
Fine interpretations of classic and contemporary works.
Symphony Hall p197
An architectural landmark and acoustic marvel.

Explore

Downtown

In Boston's compact city centre, business people jostle with tourists admiring some of the most important historic sites of the American Revolution. Among the most visited is Faneuil Hall, site of pivotal rebel meetings, alongside the 19th-century Quincy Market. Sure, they're stuffed with shops hawking tacky gifts and chain eateries, but are an essential stop for anyone with an interest in architecture or American history.

Together, the sprawling Boston Common and more formal Public Garden form the city's central green space. To the east are the small Theatre District and the remains of a mainstream shopping district that is gradually being populated with high-rises. Weave through the side streets for the bars and restaurants of the Ladder District. Though it's being squeezed by new development, Boston's Chinatown is the third largest in the country; head here for superb cuisine in bare-bones settings.

EXPLORE

Faneuil Hall.

Don't Miss

1 Boston Public Garden
One of the city's loveliest spots for a stroll (p46).

2 Brattle Book Shop
A tucked-away trove adored by bibliophiles (p54).

3 Faneuil Hall Visit the historic hall where the rebels plotted (p56).

4 Old State House An exquisite building with a fascinating collection (p56).

5 Troquet Superb wine-centric dining near the Theatre District (p59).

Public Garden.

EXPLORE

BOSTON COMMON & THE PUBLIC GARDEN

Arlington, Boylston, Downtown Crossing or Park Street T.

America's oldest public park, the 48-acre **Boston Common** marks the beginning of the Freedom Trail (*see p47* **Trail Blazers**). It's also the sprawling anchor of the Emerald Necklace, a string of semi-connected green spaces designed by Frederick Law Olmsted that stretch seven miles across the city (*see p84* **In the Know**).

Established in 1634, the Common was originally a grazing pasture for cattle, and later became a military training ground. British redcoats also made camp here before heading north-west to Lexington and Concord in 1775. Interestingly, this leafy park had no trees at all to begin with, except one giant specimen that served as a central meeting place for the Puritans who'd settled here (until 1817, the 'Great Elm' was also used for public hangings, including that of 'witch' Ann Hibbens in 1656). The tree eventually fell victim to a series of ferocious storms that blew through the area in the mid 19th century, but by then the Common's use as a rallying point was an unshakeable tradition.

Today, watched over by the imposing gold-domed **Massachusetts State House** on Beacon Hill (*see p65*), it remains an arena for public gatherings, sunbathing in summer and ice-skating on the Frog Pond in winter. Massive protests against the Vietnam War were staged here in the 1960s; Pope John Paul II said Mass to nearly half a million people on its lawns in 1979, and more recently it's been the site of raucous marijuana legalisation rallies.

Just across Charles Street from the Boston Common is the lovely 25-acre **Public Garden**. Much younger than the Common, it was established in 1837, and was cultivated on filled-in salt marshes. As America's first public botanical garden, it was a showcase for the then-burgeoning greenhouse technology. In warmer months, its orderly English-style flowerbeds explode with colour, and numerous rare species of tree flourish.

Several monuments pay tribute to war heroes and statesmen, including a commanding bronze statue of America's first president, General George Washington, astride his horse. But the Garden's most humble statue is also the most charming. A bronze tribute to Robert McCloskey's classic children's book *Make Way for Ducklings*, which is set in the park, depicts a waddling mother duck followed by eight fluffy offspring. Also featured in the book are the famous **Swan Boats**, which have glided gracefully on the Public Garden Lagoon, powered by pedals and pulleys, since 1877. They operate from mid April to mid September; a 15-minute ride costs $3 ($1.50-$2.50 reductions).

Around the Common

At the north-east corner of Boston Common, across Park Street from the entrance to the T station, is the tall and austere **Park Street Church**. Its primary claim to fame is as the venue of abolitionist William Lloyd Garrison's first anti-slavery speech, thundered from the pulpit on 4 July 1829. Beside the church is the **Granary Burying Ground**, where lie the American patriots Paul Revere and John Hancock. Across the road, on Hamilton Place, stands the **Orpheum Theatre** (*see p190*), a refurbished music hall from 1852 that features ornate

TRAIL BLAZERS

The Freedom Trail isn't the only historical self-guided walk in town.

For the first-time visitor to Boston, the **Freedom Trail** (www.thefreedomtrail.org) provides a useful sightseeing starting point. The self-guided, two-and-a-half-mile tour is clearly marked by a red line on the sidewalk, which has wended its way past 16 of the Hub's best-known historical sites since 1958. The Trail begins at the visitor centre on Boston Common (147 Tremont Street, 1-617 426 3115), where you can pick up a map or hire an audio tour ($17), and ends at the Bunker Hill Monument (*see p150*).

More recently, historical organisations have jumped on the bandwagon with specialised rambles. The **Black Heritage Trail** traces the history of the African-American community in Boston in the late 18th and 19th centuries. Guided tours (1-617 725 0022) are offered daily from late March to late November, but a map (available at http://maah.org/trail.htm) lets you do it yourself. The tour starts at the Robert Gould Shaw and 54th Regiment Memorial, a relief sculpture on the Common in front of the State House that commemorates the valour of a young Boston Brahmin and the black regiment he commanded in the Civil War. It takes you to, among other sites, the Abiel Smith School (the country's first public school for African-American children) and the African Meeting House (1806), the oldest black church in

the US (both are part of the Museum of African American History; *see p66*).

The **Women's Heritage Trail** comprises ten separate, self-guided walking tours flung across Boston's neighbourhoods (for maps and further details, visit www.bwht.org). In the North End, for example, you can stop by the birthplace of Rose Fitzgerald Kennedy, matriarch of the American political dynasty. Downtown, there's the statue of Mary Dyer, who was hanged on Boston Common in 1660 for her Quaker beliefs. On Beacon Hill are the homes of *Little Women* author, suffragette and abolitionist Louisa May Alcott, and Rebecca Lee Crumpler, who is generally considered to have been the first African-American woman doctor.

The **Irish Heritage Trail** is a self-guided tour (maps at www.irishheritagetrail.com) that takes in museums, statues and memorials celebrating everyone from the city's first Irish-born mayor, Hugh O'Brien, to John Boyle O'Reilly, the 'poet, patriot, prisoner, sportsman and orator', who was one of the most influential Irish Americans of the 19th century. In addition to 20 stops in central Boston, it extends to landmarks in other neighbourhoods, including Dorchester's John F Kennedy Presidential Library and Museum (*see p153*) – a fitting conclusion for this tribute to 'the capital of Irish America'.

EXPLORE

Freedom Trail.

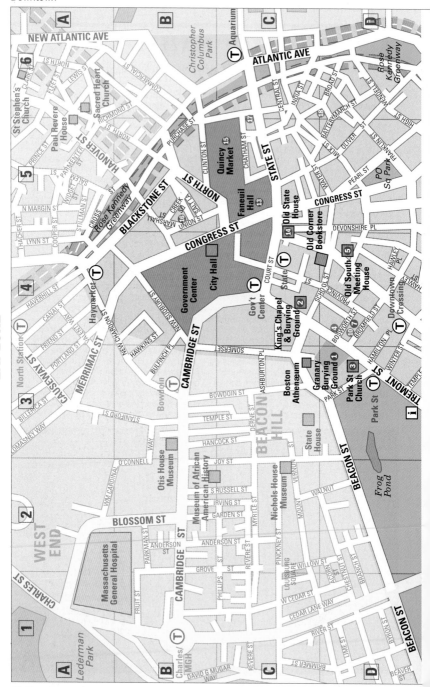

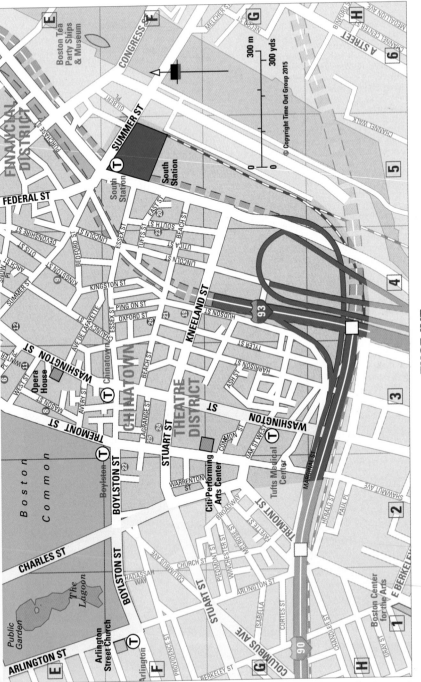

mouldings and proscenium seating. It's played host to everything from the world première of Tchaikovsky's *First Piano Concerto* (1875) to concerts by the Clash and Bob Dylan.

Heading up Tremont Street, pause to gaze up at the Gothic Revival **Tremont Temple** (no.88, between Bosworth and School Streets). Built in 1894, the Baptist church looks like a Venetian palace transported to downtown Boston; Charles Dickens and Abraham Lincoln both spoke here. On the corner of School Street is the **King's Chapel & Burying Ground**, Boston's oldest cemetery. The chapel itself, the first Anglican church in the city, was mandated by King James II, who wanted to ensure a proper foothold for the Church of England in the new colonies. School Street is so named because it was the site of the nation's first public school, **Boston Latin**, founded in 1635. Illustrious pupils included Benjamin Franklin (whose statue stands outside), John Hancock and Samuel Adams; today, the 19th-century Old City Hall stands in its place, and contains offices and a restaurant.

Sights & Museums

FREE Granary Burying Ground

At Tremont & Bromfield Streets (www.cityof boston.gov/freedomtrail/granary.asp). Park Street T. **Open** 9am-5pm daily. **Admission** free. **Map** p48 D3 ❶

So named because the adjacent Park Street Church was built on the site of a pre-Revolution storehouse for grain and supplies, the Granary Burying Ground is the third-oldest graveyard in Boston, established in 1660. In addition to Paul Revere and John Hancock, famous figures buried here include Samuel Adams, Peter Faneuil (the Huguenot merchant who built the market and Revolutionary meeting place Faneuil Hall; *see p56*), Benjamin Franklin's parents, Samuel Sewall (famous as the only Salem Witch Trial magistrate later to admit that he was wrong) and the victims of the Boston Massacre (*see p226*). Note the two gravestones for Revere – the obvious one is a more recent and elaborate pillar, but beside it is a tiny, ancient headstone that says only 'Revere's Tomb'.

FREE King's Chapel & Burying Ground

58 Tremont Street, at School Street (1-617 523 1749, www.kings-chapel.org). Government Center or Park Street T. **Open** *Chapel* 10am-4pm Mon-Sat; 1.30-4pm Sun. *Burying Ground* 9am-5pm daily. **Admission** free. **Map** p48 C4 ❷

Although the original King's Chapel – a small wooden structure – was built in the 1680s, the present one was designed by America's first architect, Peter Harrison, in 1754. The church was built on a plot of land excised from the cemetery next door after a decree from King James II (restive Bostonians were reluctant to comply with his order that land be sold at a fair price so a church could be founded to foist Anglicanism on the colonies, so the cemetery land was the only option). The burial ground is the city's oldest; eminent Bostonians who've found their final resting place here include Mary Chilton, the first woman to step off the *Mayflower*; John Winthrop, former governor of the Massachusetts Bay Colony; and Elizabeth Pain, said to be the model for the persecuted Hester Prynne in Nathaniel Hawthorne's *The Scarlet Letter*.

King's Chapel.

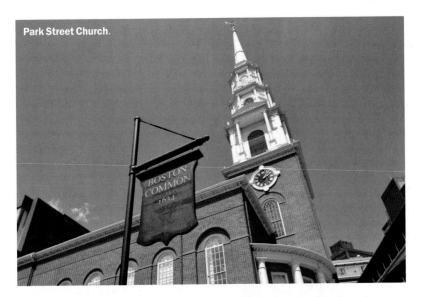

Park Street Church.

FREE Park Street Church

1 Park Street, at Tremont Street (1-617 523 3383, www.parkstreet.org). Park Street T. **Open** *Tours July, Aug 9.30am-3.30pm Tue-Sat. Services 8.30am, 11am, 4pm Sun.* **Admission** free. **Map** p48 D3 ❸

Built in 1809, the Park Street Church was known as 'Brimstone Corner' during the War of 1812 – not for its fiery sermons about hellfire and damnation, but because gunpowder was stored in a basement crypt, emitting a constant (and sometimes overwhelming) smell of sulphur. It was here that William Lloyd Garrison gave his first anti-slavery oration and, in 1818, the nation's first Sunday school class took place. Sunday services are still held here.

Bars

Highball Lounge

90 Tremont Street, at Bosworth Street (1-617 772 0202, www.highballboston.com). Park Street T. **Open** 5pm-2am Wed-Sat. **Map** p48 D4 ❹

Entering Highball Lounge is like going to a party at the posh loft of an über-rich friend who never grew up. Perched on the second floor of upscale hotel Nine Zero, the high-ceilinged space is kitted out with leather sofas, tacky artwork and stained-wood shelving stacked with vinyl. Highbrow versions of lowbrow snacks such as Korean fried chicken nuggets are offered alongside inventive cocktails such as the Dragon Lily (tequila, vermouth, serrano peppers, blackberries, cucumber and lime). View-Masters and Slinkies are nostalgic conversation starters, and old-school board games including Operation, Candyland and Chutes & Ladders can be delivered to your table for free.

LADDER DISTRICT & DOWNTOWN CROSSING

Downtown Crossing, Park Street or State T.

Walking east of the Common along Winter Street brings you to the intersection with main thoroughfare Washington Street, an area known as **Downtown Crossing**. It was once the home of now-defunct department stores Jordan Marsh and Filene's. The latter is being replaced by a mega-condo/retail tower, under construction at time of writing and tipped to include the first US flagship of Irish-owned budget-clothing giant Primark; Jordan Marsh is now a disappointing branch of **Macy's**.

The rest of Downtown Crossing is made up of various discount and chain stores, cheap jewellers and electrical-goods emporia. The area has long had a gritty, run-down feel to it – further south on Washington Street is the last remnant of the once-notorious red-light district called the Combat Zone, between Avery and Stuart Streets, which now consists of a couple of strip clubs.

But there has been some development in the area, including the **Ritz-Carlton Boston Common** (*see p246*), and the renovation of the formerly dilapidated rococo **Opera House** (*see p198*). When hip hangouts such as the retro **Silvertone Bar & Grill** started cropping up, the old appellation of the '**Ladder District**' was resurrected to reinforce the impression of an area on the up. The term, which had been in wide use for almost a century, refers

SIX FEET UNDER

Explore Boston's buried history.

With half a dozen 17th-century burial grounds in the city alone – not to mention cemeteries in the suburbs and surrounding areas – Boston is the final resting place for a mix of famous folk, from Revolutionary heroes to literary lions and former presidents.

The battered gravestones of the **Granary Burying Ground** (*see p50*) bear the famous names of Declaration of Independence signatories John Hancock and Samuel Adams. Also interred here is Paul Revere, whose 'midnight ride' alerted the militiamen in Lexington and Concord that the Redcoats were on their way in 1775. Perhaps the most intriguing plot belongs to Elizabeth Foster, who is widely thought to be the Mother Goose of nursery rhyme renown.

Further afield, at the **First Unitarian Church** on Hancock Street, in the nearby city of Quincy (*see p160*), are the crypts of two locally born US presidents – the second, John Adams, and the sixth, John Quincy Adams. And at **Holyhood Cemetery** on Heath Street, in Brookline, lie the parents of 35th president John F Kennedy: Joseph P and Rose Kennedy.

Ichabod Crane is not buried at **Sleepy Hollow Cemetery** in Concord (*see p206*); nor is his creator, Washington Irving. But several major 19th-century writers and thinkers are.

Laid to rest near their former homes are novelists Louisa May Alcott and Nathaniel Hawthorne, and essayist chums Ralph Waldo Emerson and Henry David Thoreau.

Meanwhile, more modern writers are well represented at **Forest Hills Cemetery** in Jamaica Plain (*see p155*): you can seek out the tombs of confessional poet Anne Sexton, Nobel Prize-winning playwright Eugene O'Neill and poet ee cummings.

At the **Mount Auburn Cemetery** (*see p130*) in Cambridge is the grave of Henry Wadsworth Longfellow, who is linked to two others mentioned here: not only did he immortalise Paul Revere's ride in verse, he was also Nathaniel Hawthorne's college roommate. Here, too, lie a trio of highly influential women: philanthropist Dorothea Dix, who revolutionised the care and treatment of the mentally ill; Mary Baker Eddy, founder of Christian Science; and wealthy socialite and patron of the arts Isabella Stewart Gardner, who founded a magnificent palazzo-style museum (*see p89*) to house her collections.

In spooky Salem (*see p208*), the **Burying Point** on Charter Street is home to many of the victims of the 1692 Salem Witch Trials, including Giles Corey, the 83-year-old farmer who was crushed to death by heavy stones for refusing to stand trial. There are sinister tales down in the south-western Massachusetts city of Fall River too. 'Lizzie Borden took an axe and gave her mother 40 whacks,' runs the old nursery rhyme. 'When she saw what she had done, she gave her father 41.' Lizzie was acquitted of the 1892 crime and, at **Oak Grove Cemetery** on Prospect Street, reposes with her mother and stepfather.

In **Edson Cemetery** on Gorham Street, in the mill town of Lowell, is the much-visited grave of Beat writer Jack Kerouac, who drank himself to death, at the age of 48, in 1969. Another victim of substance abuse, actor John Belushi, was a native Chicagoan, but the Massachusetts island of Martha's Vineyard (*see p218*) was his favourite vacation spot, and it's here, in historic **Abel's Hill Cemetery** in Chilmark, that his body lies.

Granary Burying Ground.

to the small side streets running between main thoroughfares Tremont and Washington Streets.

On the corner of Washington and Milk Streets, the **Old South Meeting House** was once the largest building in colonial Boston and a sparring ground for anti-British debate before the Revolution. In the small plaza across the street, the **Boston Irish Famine Memorial** was designed by Robert Shure and unveiled in 1998 to commemorate the Great Famine's 150th anniversary. Although some dismiss it as a bathetic cliché – one statue depicts a family, gaunt and kneeling, imploring the heavens for sustenance, while another shows the same family, this time well fed, striding triumphantly and purposefully into the New World – in a city as indelibly marked by Irish immigration as Boston, it's at least worth acknowledging.

Sights & Museums

Old South Meeting House

310 Washington Street, at Milk Street (1-617 482 6439, www.oldsouthmeetinghouse.org). Downtown Crossing or State T. **Open** *Apr-Oct* 9.30am-5pm daily. *Nov-Mar* 10am-4pm daily. **Admission** $6; $1-$5 reductions; free under-6s. **Map** p48 D4 ❺

Second only to Faneuil Hall as a centre of dissent during Boston's Revolutionary era, the Old South Meeting House (1729) combines the simple design of a Puritan meeting house with elements taken from Christopher Wren's then-fashionable Anglican church style, such as arched windows and a tall spire. Note the second gallery level, where those who couldn't afford a pew – including servants and slaves – were seated. Famously, the Old South was the departure point of the Boston Tea Party: after a raucous debate on British taxation on 16 December 1773, the infuriated colonists, disguised as Mohawk Indians, marched to Boston Harbor under cover of darkness and hurled 342 crates of imported tea into the Atlantic. You can see a vial of tea from that occasion among other artefacts on display in the main hall.

Restaurants & Cafés

JM Curley

21 Temple Place, at Tremont Street (1-617 338 5333, www.jmcurleyboston.com). Downtown Crossing or Park Street T. **Open** 11.30am-1am Mon-Fri; 5pm-1am Sat; 5pm-midnight Sun. **Main courses** $12-$25. **Map** p49 E3 ❻ **American**
With its locally sourced ingredients, pub-like interior and friendly staff, JM Curley (named after an early 20th-century local politico) is a let-your-hair-down release for the nearby Financial District's office crowd. The only downside is that this place is packed (and loud) during post-work hours. Arrive early or prepare to wait – Curley's addictive

caramel-popcorn-bacon snack will take the edge off your appetite. Rotating chalkboard specials include variations on the highly popular burger, a daily catch and a 'square meal', which includes protein and sides, retro style. Night owls can wait for the masses to subside and swoop in for the late-night menu, which offers a smaller, slightly cheaper version of the star burger as well as dessert 'concretes' – adult shakes, such as vanilla ice-cream whipped with pretzels, bourbon-soaked blueberries and bacon.

Marliave

10 Bosworth Street, at Province Street (1-617 422 0004, www.marliave.com). Downtown Crossing or Park Street T. **Open** 11am-1am daily. **Main courses** $21-$38. **Map** p48 D4 ❼ **French/ Italian**
Having occupied its back-alley location since 1885, this eclectic yet historic café offers a two-in-one dining escape from the bustle of Downtown. The first-floor bar with its booths and vintage tiled floor is the perfect setting for a Prohibition-era cocktail and

Downtown Crossing. See p51.

Thinking Cup.

the rarebit appetiser of melted farmhouse cheeses, bacon and lager served with toasted brioche. Upstairs, a candlelit, white-tableclothed dining room befits the menu featuring classics such as beef wellington and the popular Sunday Gravy: gnocchi with San Marzano tomatoes, beef, lamb and pork. Linger with french-pressed coffee and house-made chocolate truffles for dessert.

$ Thinking Cup
165 Tremont Street, between Avery & West Streets (1-617 482 5555, www.thinkingcup.com). Boylston or Park Street T. **Open** 7am-10pm Mon-Wed; 7am-11pm Thur-Sun. **Map** p49 E3 ❽ **Café**
As the name implies, there's an intellectual as well as a friendly vibe in this rustic, brick-walled indie café near Boston Common. Amid an unending sea of cafés serving drip coffee in paper cups, it's refreshing to sip a rich pour out of a sturdy ceramic mug. Old newspaper clippings tucked under glass tabletops and hung on the walls spark conversations between strangers sharing tables when seating is tight. Sandwiches, pastries and breakfast items are also served.
Other locations 236 Hanover Street, at Richmond Street, North End (1-857 233 5277); 85 Newbury Street, at Clarendon Street, Back Bay (1-617 247 3333).

Bars

JJ Foley's Bar & Grille
21 Kingston Street, at Summer Street (1-617 695 2529, www.jjfoleysbarandgrill.com). Downtown Crossing T. **Open** 10am-2am daily. **Map** p49 E4 ❾
This low-key, low-lit bar is an institution in Boston – a hangout for bike messengers, tattooed masses, business suits and borderline bums. Anyone who has lived in Boston for long has met someone at Foley's, or broken up with someone at Foley's, or

met and broken up with them there on the same evening – or knows someone who has.
Other location JJ Foley's Café, 117 East Berkeley Street, at Fay Street, South End (1-617 728 9101).

★ Silvertone Bar & Grill
69 Bromfield Street, at Tremont Street (1-617 338 7887, www.silvertonedowntown.com). Downtown Crossing or Park Street T. **Open** *Kitchen* 11.30am-11pm Mon-Fri; 6-11pm Sat. *Bar* 11.30am-2am Mon-Fri; 6pm-2am Sat. **Map** p48 D4 ❿
Forward-thinking in its backward-looking ways, the subterranean Silvertone Bar & Grill was a local pioneer of the trend for classic cocktails and American comfort food – and the long wagon train of regulars it immediately formed remains firmly hitched. The owners' good-natured commitment to a bygone era manifests itself in everything from the old prom pictures and liquor ads that line the walls to the confoundingly low prices charged for smart wines by the glass, served alongside such much-loved staples as macaroni and cheese, quesadillas and meatloaf.

Shops & Services

★ Brattle Book Shop
9 West Street, at Washington Street (1-617 542 0210, www.brattlebookshop.com). Downtown Crossing or Park Street T. **Open** 9am-5.30pm Mon-Sat. **Map** p49 E3 ⓫ **Books**
Established in 1825, this highly regarded antiquarian bookshop in the heart of Downtown has amassed around 250,000 books, maps, prints and other collectible items; the abundant stock spills over into a substantial outdoor space, so you can browse alfresco.

Macy's
450 Washington Street, at Summer Street (1-617 357 3000, www.macys.com). Downtown Crossing

or *Park Street T.* **Open** 10am-9pm Mon-Thur,
Sun; 10am-9.30pm Fri, Sat. **Map** p49 E4 ⑫

Department store

Macy's replaced Boston institution Jordan Marsh in
1996 (there's even a plaque outside commemorating
the dearly departed store). Macy's sells brand-name
clothing, cosmetics, homewares, furniture and lin-
gerie, but those expecting the scale or choice of the
famous New York store will likely be disappointed
by this more modest outpost.

FANEUIL HALL & AROUND

*Government Center (closed until 2016), Haymarket
or State T.*

Following either Washington Street or Tremont
Street further north brings you to **Government
Center**, which is dominated by **City Hall
Plaza** (Congress Street, at Court Street). The
result of 1960s urban 'renewal', City Hall Plaza
was the site of Scollay Square, a boisterous, if
somewhat seedy, riot of burlesque shows, jazz
joints, penny arcades, movie houses, tattoo
parlours and taverns. City planners levelled
it and in its place built the hulking City Hall.
The building is stranded in a vast paved sea
of brick that's used for public performances
and festivals. Although City Hall was among
America's most acclaimed works of architecture
when it was completed in 1968, it has drawn
vociferous local criticism for decades.

The main tourist attractions here are the
colonial **Faneuil Hall** (pronounced *fan*-yell)
and the adjacent 19th-century **Quincy
Market**. The seat of the American Revolution,
today Faneuil Hall is little more than part of
a glorified mall. Locals refer to it and Quincy
Market pretty much interchangeably, but the

whole retail/restaurant conglomeration is
called Faneuil Hall Marketplace. Although
the gift shops, food stalls and chain stores
may seem to have trivialised the importance
of the historic building, it's worth bearing
in mind that it was originally intended as a
market and gathering place for the masses.

Across the very busy Congress Street, at its
intersection with State Street, is one of the most
significant historical sites in the area: the spot
where the Boston Massacre took place. It was
under the balcony of the **Old State House**
that British troops fired on protesting rebels,
providing the spark needed to inflame the
Revolution. In typical Boston fashion, however,
even this building is not sacrosanct: its basement
serves as an entrance to the T.

From Faneuil Hall, walk north to Blackstone
Block (the block of streets off Blackstone Street,
between Hanover and North Streets). Old-school
pubs, along with one of the city's most famous
restaurants, the **Union Oyster House**), line
this cobblestoned area, making it an agreeable
place to recover from a long afternoon's

EXPLORE

Brattle Book Shop.

sightseeing with a pint of Harpoon IPA (a popular local brew) and a plate of gleamingly fresh raw shellfish.

Across the street in **Carmen Park** (at Congress and Union Streets) is the **New England Holocaust Memorial**. Six glass towers covered with six million etched numbers pay tribute to those who were killed. At night, steam rises from the transparent towers, and the dancing vapours make the monument particularly haunting.

Sights & Museums

FREE Faneuil Hall

1 Faneuil Hall Square, at Congress Street (1-617 523 1300, www.faneuilhallmarketplace.com). Government Center, Haymarket or State T. **Open** 10am-9pm Mon-Sat; 11am-7pm Sun. **Admission** free. **Map** p48 C5 ⑬

Built for the city by the wealthy merchant Peter Faneuil in 1742, the hall was later remodelled by ubiquitous Boston architect Charles Bulfinch. It had a dual function as a marketplace (on the ground floor) and a meeting hall (upstairs). In the earliest days of the American struggle for independence, the rebels frequently met here in tense, secret gatherings, under pain of execution for sedition, and fomented their plans for revolution. It became known as the 'Cradle of Liberty', as colonial heroes such as Samuel Adams regularly roused the Boston populace against the British. Later, it was here that George Washington toasted the giddy new nation on its first birthday. Through the years, the walls have heard the nation's most impassioned speakers, from the writer Oliver Wendell Holmes and early feminist Susan B Anthony, to Senator Ted Kennedy and President Bill Clinton – it still hosts the occasional political debate and symposium as a nod to its history. The building is part of Boston's National Historic Park, and rangers provide brief historical talks in the Great Hall every half hour between 9.30am and 4pm.

★ Old State House

206 Washington Street, at State Street (1-617 720 1713, www.bostonhistory.org). State T. **Open** *Late May-Aug* 9am-6pm daily. *Sept-late May* 9am-5pm daily. **Admission** $10; $8.50 reductions. **Map** p48 C4 ⑭

Incongruously but elegantly set in the midst of modern skyscrapers and congested traffic, this former legislative house is the oldest surviving public building in Boston. It was built in 1713 for the British governor (note the lion and unicorn still standing regally atop the building's façade) and the colonial legislature. Proclamations, including the 1776 Declaration of Independence, were read in this building, often from the balcony on the east side. The area below the balcony was the scene of the Boston Massacre in 1770 (commemorated by a ring of cobblestones), when British soldiers fired on an unruly crowd, killing five men.

Among them was Crispus Attucks, a black man recorded as the first casualty of the American Revolution. After Independence, the State House remained the seat of Massachusetts government until Bulfinch completed his imposing new legislative building on Beacon Hill (*see p65*). Today, it serves as the headquarters of the Bostonian Society, the historical society for the city, along with its library and museum. The collection covers the early

Old State House.

Quincy Market.

colonial period to the present, and includes artefacts such as John Hancock's red velvet coat and embroidered waistcoat, tea from the famous Tea Party and an engraving of the Massacre by Paul Revere.

FREE Quincy Market

4 South Market Building, at Congress Street (1-617 523 1300, www.faneuilhallmarketplace. com). Government Center, Haymarket or State T. **Open** 10am-9pm Mon-Sat; 11am-7pm Sun. **Admission** free. **Map** p48 C5 ⓯

Built in the mid 1820s, when Boston's population was rapidly outgrowing the smaller marketplace in Faneuil Hall, Quincy Market was originally right on the harbour (the shoreline has changed over time). Today, the neoclassical Colonnade building is lined with fast-food stands. On either side of the central hall, rows of carts loaded with souvenirs and crafts lure tourists to part with still more dollars, as do the street performers who flock to the place. Flanking the Colonnade are the North and South Markets, which are likewise filled with shops. Old-time Boston restaurant Durgin Park is touristy, but still retains an air of basic authenticity with dishes such as scrod and Indian pudding. Quincy Market also lays claim to the first stateside outpost of the popular UK-born noodle chain Wagamama, which now has a handful of Boston-area locations.

Restaurants & Cafés

Union Oyster House

41 Union Street, at Marshall Street (1-617 227 2750, www.unionoysterhouse.com). Haymarket T. **Open** *Kitchen* 11am-9.30pm Mon-Thur, Sun; 11am-10pm Fri, Sat. *Bar* 11am-midnight Mon-Sat; noon-midnight Sun. **Main courses** $23-$34. **Map** p48 B5 ⓰ **Fish & seafood**

America's oldest restaurant, established in 1826, may be targeted at tourists – as is every establishment within a block of Faneuil Hall – but, as long

as you turn a blind eye to the gift shop, the wooden booths and whitewashed walls manage to project some sense of authenticity. Stick with the historic wooden raw bar, where affable shuckers will ply you with Blue Points and cherrystones – best paired, of course, with a pint or two. Or request 'the Kennedy Booth' where JFK allegedly sat, and do no harm with a cuppa chowdah and fried seafood platter.

Bars

Black Rose

160 State Street, at India Street (1-617 742 2286, www.blackroseboston.com). Aquarium or State T. **Open** 11am-2am Mon-Fri; 9am-2am Sat, Sun. **Map** p48 C5 ⓱

One of the older Irish pubs in the city, the Black Rose plays its part well: photos of martyred patriots adorn the walls, and flags from every county hang from the ceiling. But its true selling point is the nightly programme of live Irish music (there's sometimes a cover of up to $5). If you're up for a rowdy, Guinness-fuelled singalong with friendly locals and tourists, this is the place to go.

FINANCIAL DISTRICT

Downtown Crossing or State T.

Heading south from Faneuil Hall brings you to the city's compact Financial District, roughly bordered by State, Devonshire, Purchase and Summer Streets. Amid the concrete labyrinth of one-way streets and featureless skyscrapers are some notable architectural curiosities. The **Custom House** (3 McKinley Square, at Central Street, 1-617 310 6300), now a Marriott hotel, an extraordinary marriage of the original 1847 neoclassical structure and a tower stuck on top in 1915 – which made it the city's tallest building

EXPLORE

Chinatown.

at the time. Around the corner, the flamboyant 1892 Romanesque Revival **Flour & Grain Exchange** building (177 Milk Street, at India Street), formerly the meeting hall for Boston's Chamber of Commerce, echoes the work of prominent local architect HH Richardson. Finally, **Post Office Square Park** (between Pearl and Congress Streets) provides a pleasant lunchtime oasis for office workers, overlooked by such striking art deco edifices as the **John W McCormack Post Office and Courthouse** (31 Milk Street, at Arch Street).

Bars

Mr Dooley's

77 Broad Street, at Batterymarch Street (1-617 338 5656, www.mrdooleys.com). Aquarium or State T. **Open** 11.30am-2am Mon-Fri; 9am-2am Sat, Sun. **Map** p48 D6 ⑬
Named after the fictional, opinion-rich barkeep of writer FP Dunne's syndicated newspaper columns, this Financial District mainstay has a loyal clientele of journalists and politicians, and lives up to its own billing as 'a great place for a pint and a chat'.

CHINATOWN & THEATRE DISTRICT

Boylston, Chinatown or Tufts Medical Center T.

Towards the end of the 19th century, Chinese immigrants began arriving in the city to work on the railroads and provide cheap labour in factories. By the early 20th century, there were more than 1,000 mostly Asian residents in the area originally known as South Cove, and the number expanded hugely after World War II. Today, **Chinatown** is contained within a few blocks around Kneeland, Essex, Beach and Tyler Streets. It's still one of the best parts of

the city to get a taste of authentic Asian cuisine. Next to Chinatown, on Tremont Street, is the compact **Theatre District**. You can find almost any sort of entertainment within about a block, from cabaret to serious drama. Just east of Chinatown is a small enclave of 19th-century warehouses, converted into loft apartments and businesses, called the Leather District.

Restaurants & Cafés

$ New Shanghai

21 Hudson Street, at Kneeland Street (1-617 338 6688, www.newshanghaiboston.com). Chinatown or Tufts Medical Center T. **Open** 11.30am-10.30pm Mon-Thur, Sun; 11.30am-11.30pm Fri, Sat. **Main courses** $10-$40. **Map** p49 F4 ⑲ **Chinese**
Even during its regular dinner service, the New Shanghai makes dim sum-style dining an option – and a delight. Its panoply of steamed or fried pies and buns filled with chives, soupy ground pork, bean paste and the like counts among the area's best, while an array of cold appetisers – pickled, salted and smoked – beckons the bold of palate. Other intriguing options include giant-sized lion's head meatballs (juicy pork goodness in a fine gravy) and sweet-and-spicy garlic pork, served in spongy rice-flour 'pockets'.

★ O Ya

9 East Street, between Atlantic Avenue & South Street (1-617 654 9900, www.oyarestaurantboston. com). South Station T. **Open** 5-9.30pm Tue-Thur; 5-10pm Fri, Sat. **Small plates** $8-$38. **Map** p49 F5 ⑳ **Japanese**
Bite for bite, this self-styled Japanese tavern arguably serves the most expensive food in Boston. It's also, less arguably, some of the most thrilling cuisine – daring yet meticulous, and delicate but rarely precious. Sushi isn't the half of it: chef Tim Cushman, a 2012 James Beard Award winner, transforms the

humblest fare – such as miso soup and tonkatsu – into luxuries, which sommelier Nancy Cushman pairs with sakés from her select list.

$ Peach Farm
4 Tyler Street, at Beach Street (1-617 482 3332). Chinatown T. Open 11am-3am daily. **Main courses** $9-$34. **Map** p49 F4 ㉑ **Chinese**
If the name conjures up bucolic landscapes, Peach Farm's dowdy basement digs promptly erase them. Happily, the Hong Kong-style seafood soon makes amends. Spiced dry-fried eel, enormous steamed oysters in black bean sauce, and lobster stir-fried with ginger and scallions are all superlative.

★ Troquet
140 Boylston Street, between Charles & Tremont Streets (1-617 695 9463, www.troquetboston.com). Boylston T. Open 5-10.30pm Tue-Sat. **Main courses** $29-$40. **Map** p49 F2 ㉒ **French**
Owner Chris Campbell has nailed the art of wine pairing in this sleeper hit, a block from the Theatre District; his method seems as easy as painting-by-numbers but is as satisfying as a van Gogh. The eclectic French-inspired menu suggests a selection of specific wines to go with each dish, whether it's

O Ya.

the duck confit salad with the Domaine Brunet pinot noir, or dover sole with an Italian white, and diners can choose a two- or four-ounce pour. Keep things casual at the intimate downstairs bar or sit upstairs in the comfortable dining room with white table-cloths and views of Boston Common. Those in the know dine in July and August when Campbell discounts bin ends – stray bottles of fine wine – at cost.

Les Zygomates
129 South Street, between Tufts & Beach Streets (1-617 542 5108, www.winebar.com). South Station T. Open 11.30am-2pm, 6-10.30pm Mon-Fri; 6-11.30pm Sat. **Main courses** $24-$34. **Set meal** (Fri, Sat only) $50. **Map** p49 F4 ㉓ **French**
Vintage posters and red banquettes, a zinc bar and a live jazz line-up all week define owner Ian Just's *vrai français* bistro, which has long been a bright spot in the Leather District. An eclectic, fairly priced wine list accompanies the classic bistro menu of french onion soup, precision-cooked steak frites and earthy vegetarian crêpes – for lunch and dinner.

Bars

Jacob Wirth
31-37 Stuart Street, at Washington Street (1-617 338 8586, www.jacobwirth.com). Boylston or Chinatown T. Open 11.30am-9.30pm Mon-Wed; 11.30am-10.30pm Thur; 11.30am-12.30am Fri, Sat; 11.30am-9pm Sun. **Map** p49 F3 ㉔
Walking into Jacob Wirth (established 1868) feels like stepping into old Boston: the ceilings are high, the bar ornate and staff are decked out in black and white finery. But this is an informal place. Slosh your mug of fine imported lager and tuck into a heaped plate of schnitzel or bratwurst and red cabbage.

$ Tam
222 Tremont Street, between Lagrange & Stuart Streets (1-617 482 9182). Boylston or Chinatown T. Open 8am-midnight Mon-Sat; noon-midnight Sun. **No credit cards. Map** p49 F3 ㉕
A dive bar for dive bar connoisseurs, the Tam is a Boston legend – and rightly so. Everything here is just as it should be: the beer is cheap, the whisky is plentiful, the neon is garish, the music is loud, and the toilets… er, have running water. An eccentric, eclectic crowd gathers to sample its delights.

Shops & Services

$ Ho Yuen Bakery
54 Beach Street, at Tyler Street (1-617 426 8320). Chinatown T. Open 8am-7pm daily. **No credit cards. Map** p49 F4 ㉖ **Food & drink**
Bewilderment is bliss at this wee Chinatowner. Make your way through the glassed-in proliferation of buns and tarts to a fresh, flaky snack of pastry-encased barbecued pork, lotus-seed paste or luscious, not-too-sweet egg custard.

EXPLORE

Beacon Hill & West End

Boston's most lovingly preserved neighbourhood, Beacon Hill is almost unfeasibly picturesque with its red-brick row houses and mansions, gas lanterns and steep, narrow streets – some still cobbled. That quaint period charm is largely thanks to the establishment of the Historic Beacon Hill District in 1955, which enforces strict architectural restraints. This exclusive patch contains some of the most expensive real estate in the city. For the rest of us, there are some great shops, restaurants and small museums, but it's a pleasure simply to wander.

One-time immigrant neighbourhood the West End was largely demolished to make way for high-rises in the 1950s. Though this mainly characterless area, dominated by Massachusetts General Hospital, has improved, its main attraction remains the Museum of Science & Charles Hayden Planetarium.

No.9 Park

Don't Miss

1 Boston Athenæum Channel *The Bostonians* on a tour of this refined institution (p65).

2 Louisburg Square See how the elite live in the city's poshest enclave (p62).

3 No.9 Park Barbara Lynch's timeless culinary triumph still dazzles (p69).

4 21st Amendment Hobnob with political movers and shakers (p69).

5 Good An eclectic mix of standout goods (p70).

EXPLORE

BEACON HILL

Bowdoin, Charles/MGH or Park Street T.

Beacon Hill's name derives from the beacon lit when enemy ships were sighted out at sea by a lookout posted at the summit. This has been a lofty address – both literally and figuratively – since its development in the late 18th century. Originally there were three grassy hills (the other two were subsequently levelled), and the area was known as Tremontaine, giving nearby Tremont Street its name. In Revolutionary times, it was little more than pasture land for cattle owned by politico John Hancock, who had his 'country estate' here, and the painter John Singleton Copley. But when construction began on Charles Bulfinch's new **Massachusetts State House** in 1795, well-to-do Bostonians with a nose for real estate began buying and building on the South Slope.

When the young, wealthy Charles Bulfinch left his family in Boston in 1786 for a European tour, he was expected to return home and begin life as a businessman. Bulfinch did come back, but, inspired by his travels, instead of starting in business, he thought he'd give his friends a few pointers on designing their homes first. The result of this 'help' changed the architectural landscape of Boston. And while Bulfinch's distinctive stamp can be seen throughout the city, it is most apparent in Beacon Hill, from the State House, modelled after Somerset House in London, to the Federalist brick houses with classic Boston bow fronts (so called because they bulge in the middle).

IN THE KNOW IN COD WE TRUST

Decorating the entranceway to the House of Representatives since the 18th century is what some might call a prescient symbol of the fishy politics to come at the **Massachusetts State House** (see p65). Known by the grandiose title of the **Sacred Cod**, this 4ft 11in carved pine replica of the Atlantic Ocean inhabitant hangs as a reminder of the central role of the fishing industry in the history of the Bay State. The Sacred Cod was famously stolen in 1933 for two days as part of a Harvard University prank. The Massachusetts State Police went so far as to dredge the Charles River after the cod-napping caused state-wide scandal. Feeling left out, the Massachusetts Senate also has a fish hanging from the central chandelier of its chamber, unofficially known as the Holy Mackerel.

Beacon Hill is closely associated with the 'First Families of Boston', or FFBs as they came to call themselves: the descendants of the original Puritan settlers who had become the American aristocracy. Ruthlessly exclusive, they were dubbed the 'Brahmin caste of New England' in 1861 by the writer Oliver Wendell Holmes; the sobriquet 'Boston Brahmin' stuck, and is still used today.

Some of the grandest houses are on Chestnut and Mount Vernon Streets – on the latter, look out for the splendid, Bulfinch-designed residence of prominent Bostonian Harrison Gray Otis at no.85. The poet Robert Frost lived at no.88, and Henry James's family had a house at no.131. Lodged between Mount Vernon and Pinckney Streets is **Louisburg Square**. The city's only remaining private garden square, it is one of Beacon Hill's most coveted addresses. Louisa May Alcott moved to no.10 after the financial success of *Little Women*, while novelist and influential *Atlantic Monthly* editor William Dean Howells resided at nos.4 and 16 at different points. Secretary of State John Kerry and his wife, ketchup heiress Teresa Heinz, own the former convent at no.19. Between Mount Vernon and Chestnut Streets lies the tiny, cobbled **Acorn Street** – once occupied by servants of the square's inhabitants, and now reportedly the most photographed of the Hill's many picturesque byways.

In the 19th century, Boston's free black community was concentrated in what was then part of the West End, between Pinckney and Cambridge Streets, and on the North Slope of Beacon Hill, between Joy and Charles Streets. The **Black Heritage Trail** (*see p47* **Trail Blazers**) explores this community and the abolitionist movement through the area's historical sites, although as most of the buildings featured are private residences, visitors can only enter a couple of them. Together, the **African Meeting House** and the adjacent **Abiel Smith School** form the **Museum of African American History**.

Other points of interest on Beacon Hill include the **Otis House Museum**, which, along with the neighbouring Federal-style **Old West Church** (1806), stands out on the traffic-choked thoroughfare of Cambridge Street, and the opulent **Nichols House Museum**. Visitors can also tour the **Boston Athenæum**, a beautiful private library on Beacon Street.

Charles Street, at the foot of the hill to the west, is lined with antiques shops, restaurants and boutiques. The handsome **Charles Street Meeting House**, built in 1807, now contains offices, cafés and shops.

Nearby is one of the city's most popular tourist attractions, **Cheers** (84 Beacon Street, at Brimmer Street, 1-617 227 9605, www.cheersboston.com), located in the basement of former hotel Hampshire House. Once the Bull and Finch Pub, it is credited

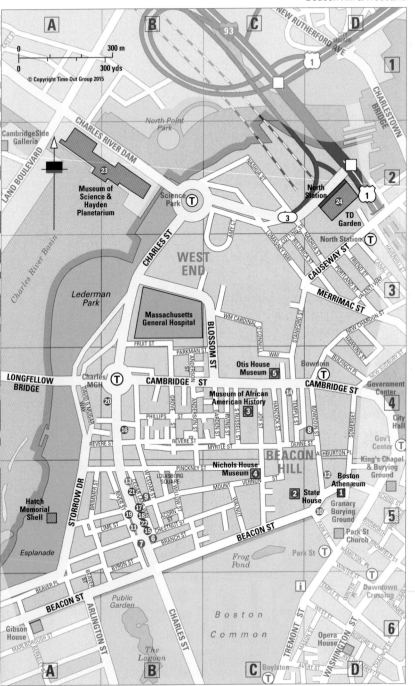

with inspiring the long-running TV sitcom. While the exterior is satisfyingly familiar – it featured in the opening shot for *Cheers* – the interior looks nothing like the show's set, and is best avoided by all but die-hard fans. A more authentic bet for sampling the Boston neighbourhood bar experience is the unpretentious **Sevens Ale House** on Charles Street.

Sights & Museums

★ FREE Boston Athenæum

10½ Beacon Street, between Bowdoin & Somerset Streets (1-617 227 0270, www.bostonathenaeum. org). Park Street T. **Open** *9am-8pm Mon-Thur; 9am-5.30pm Fri; 9am-4pm Sat; noon-4pm Sun. Tours 3pm Tue, Thur.* **Admission** *free.* **Map** p63 D5 **❶**

Founded in 1807 as a literary society, the Boston Athenæum published America's first literary magazine and acquired an extensive library of books and works of art. It moved to its current home, an imposing purpose-built structure, in 1847. The two upper floors, including the beautiful fifth-floor reading room that featured in the Merchant Ivory film adaptation of Henry James's *The Bostonians*, were added in 1913-14, followed by further expansion and renovation at the turn of the century. Among its collections are books from George Washington's library and those given to the King's Chapel by William III in the 17th century.

The Athenæum helped to establish Boston's Museum of Fine Arts (*see p90*) in the early 1870s in two of its four galleries, and much of its art collection moved with the museum. However, some notable works still remain on site, including busts of Washington, Franklin and Lafayette by Jean-Antoine Houdon, and portraits by John Singer Sargent, Mather Brown and Thomas Sully. Although much of the library is accessible only to members or scholars, the ground-floor gallery is open to the public, and free guided tours are conducted twice a week (you need to call in advance to reserve a place).

FREE Massachusetts State House

24 Beacon Street, at Park Street (1-617 727 7030, www.sec.state.ma.us/trs). Park Street T. **Open** *8.45am-5pm Mon-Fri. Tours 10am-3.30pm Mon-Fri.* **Admission** *free.* **Map** p63 C5 **❷**

Designed by Bulfinch and completed in 1798, this magnificent structure replaced the old legislative building, which had been the headquarters of the British government. The dome, originally covered in copper by Paul Revere & Sons, was later sheathed in 23-carat gold. To this day, the shining bulb is one of Boston's best-known landmarks – although it was blacked out during World War II, due to the threat of air raids. The building is the seat of state government, and the stamping ground of the Senate and House of Representatives of the Massachusetts State Legislature. When it became too small for the

IN THE KNOW HAPPY HOOKER

Statues adorning the front of the **Massachusetts State House** (*see left*) pay tribute to several historic figures, including Major General 'Fighting Joe' Hooker. A native of Hadley, Massachusetts, who distinguished himself in the Civil War, he was notorious for his bodily appetites. An accomplished boozer, the general would allow loose women to prowl his troops' tents at night. These nocturnal guests became known as 'Hooker's Ladies' – and later, simply as 'hookers'.

growing state, a somewhat incongruous yellow-brick extension was added in 1895, followed by two white marble wings in 1917.

Among the rooms covered by the guided tours (call ahead to reserve a place) are the Doric Hall, with its portraits and sculptures of historic politicians, and the House of Representatives and the Senate Chamber – in the public gallery of the House, look out for the Sacred Cod, an 18th-century carved wooden fish symbolising the importance of the country's first industry (*see p62* **In the Know**). Visitors can also follow the tour unaccompanied, as well as watch meetings from the public galleries of the legislative chambers. *Photo p66.*

▶ *For the Old State House, see p56.*

Boston Athenæum.

EXPLORE

Massachusetts State House.
See p65.

EXPLORE

**FREE Museum of African
American History**
*46 Joy Street, at Smith Court (1-617 725 0022,
ext 222, www.maah.org). Charles/MGH or
Park Street T.* **Open** 10am-4pm Mon-Sat.
Admission $5; $3 reductions; free under-12s.
Map p63 C4 ❸
The museum's premises comprise the African
Meeting House – the oldest black church in the
country – and the Abiel Smith School, which was
the nation's first public school for African-American
children. The latter was named after a 19th-century
white businessman who bequeathed $2,000 to the
city for the education of black children. A few years
after the school was built in 1834, controversy over
segregated schooling began; in 1855, following
much legal wrangling, a bill outlawing the practice
was finally passed. Children were allowed to attend
the school closest to their homes, regardless of race,
and the Abiel Smith School was closed. After extensive restoration works, it opened to the public in
2000, and now houses exhibitions.

Built by African-American artisans in 1806, the
African Meeting House played an important role
in the anti-slavery movement in the 19th century.
Abolitionist William Lloyd Garrison founded the
New England Anti-Slavery Society here in 1832 –
earning it the moniker 'the black Faneuil Hall'. At the
end of the century, when Boston's black population
shifted further south, the building became a syna-
gogue. Coinciding with the building's bicentenary,
its management embarked on the final phase of a
20-year restoration project in 2006, to return the interior to its mid 19th-century appearance.
▶ *Both buildings are stops on the Black Heritage
Trail; see p47 Trail Blazers.*

Nichols House Museum
*55 Mount Vernon Street, at Walnut Street (1-617
227 6993, www.nicholshousemuseum.org). Park
Street T.* **Open** *Apr-Oct* 11am-4pm Tue-Sat. *Nov-
Mar* 11am-4pm Thur-Sat. *Tours* every 30mins.
Admission $8; free under-12s. **Map** p63 C5 ❹
Nichols House, a Bulfinch design dating from 1804,
was occupied from 1885 to 1960 by slightly wacky
spinster, writer and landscape gardener Rose
Standish Nichols – the last of her family to live here.
In 1961, it became a museum. One of the few Beacon
Hill homes open to the public, it's furnished with
sumptuous oriental rugs, Flemish tapestries and
American, European and Asian art. The tour offers a
fascinating glimpse of upper-crust Bostonian life in
the late 19th century.

Otis House Museum
*141 Cambridge Street, at Lynde Street (1-617
994 5920, www.historicnewengland.org).
Bowdoin, Charles/MGH, Government Center
or North Station T.* **Open** 11am-5pm Wed-Sun.
Tours every 30mins. **Admission** $10; $5-$9
reductions. **Map** p63 C4 ❺
Built in 1796, this was the first of three residences
designed by Bulfinch for his friend Harrison Gray
Otis. A representative in the US Congress and, later,
mayor of Boston, Otis lived here with his young wife
for only four years (believe it or not, the impressive
Federal-style mansion was considered merely a
'starter home' for the new couple). After Harry
moved on, the house became a medical spa for ladies'
complaints, with steam baths and massage, then a
genteel boarding house. It has been painstakingly
restored to its 18th-century appearance, and contains some of the original furniture. A 45-minute

guided tour offers a vivid insight into the life of a Boston socialite. Even the fire bucket is still in place hanging behind the grand staircase (all the neighbourhood residents were obliged to rush to the scene of a fire with a bucket in hand to create a water chain).

Restaurants & Cafés

Beacon Hill Bistro

25 Charles Street, between Branch & Chestnut Streets (1-617 723 7575, www.beaconhillhotel.com). Arlington or Charles/MGH T. **Open** 7-10am, 11.30am-11pm Mon-Fri; 7.30am-11pm Sat; 7.30am-10pm Sun. **Main courses** $16-$30. **Map** p63 B5 ⑥ French

This French-style bistro and corner bar sits in the ground floor of the charming Beacon Hill Hotel. Skip the huge line at the Paramount across the street for a less mobbed brunch experience. Hotel guests and locals alike go gaga for the morning options (such as eggs with crispy chicken hash, smoked salmon omelette or vanilla pancakes), but the dry-aged duck breast and the house-ground burger are can't-lose dishes for later in the day.

Bin 26 Enoteca

26 Charles Street, between Branch & Chestnut Streets (1-617 723 5939, www.bin26.com). Arlington or Charles/MGH T. **Open** noon-10pm Mon-Thur; noon-11pm Fri; 10am-11pm Sat; 10am-10pm Sun. **Main courses** $9-$36. **Map** p63 B5 ⑦ Italian

When wine bottles serve as lamp bases and wine labels as wallpaper, you know you're in for a good glass of grape juice. The 25-page wine list at this stylish rendezvous is ever-evolving, and refreshingly

full of oenological wit and wisdom. Savour several sample glasses or linger over a carafe paired with exquisitely simple Italian plates, including assortments of cheese and charcuterie.

Grotto

37 Bowdoin Street, between Derne & Cambridge Streets (1-617 227 3434, www.grottorestaurant.com). Bowdoin or Park Street T. **Open** 11.30am-3pm, 5-10pm Mon-Fri; 5-10pm Sat, Sun. **Main courses** $23-$27. **Map** p63 D4 ⑧ Italian

Set below street level on the back slope of Beacon Hill, this Italian restaurant is as cosy as it looks. Brick walls, lace curtains and close-set tables (all of 22 seats) create an intimate setting for diners, who come for the brawny, memorable fare. The garlic soup with parmesan and truffles, and the gnocchi with short ribs and gorgonzola, are wonderfully rich. Not surprisingly, it's popular with couples of all ages.

▶ *Chef-owner Scott Herritt also owns Marliave; see p53.*

★ Lala Rokh

97 Mount Vernon Street, at West Cedar Street (1-617 720 5511, www.lalarokh.com). Arlington or Charles/MGH T. **Open** noon-3pm, 5.30-10pm Mon-Fri; 5.30-10pm Sat, Sun. **Main courses** $20-$24. **Map** p63 B5 ⑨ Persian

Armed with the recipes their mother brought with her when she emigrated from Azerbaijan in Iran, brother and sister team Azita and Babak Bina have been acting as culinary cupids for well over a decade, causing Bostonians to fall in love with intricately perfumed Persian cuisine – and each other – while on dates at this tastefully romantic hideaway.

EXPLORE

Grotto.

BOTH SIDES OF THE HILL

The historically blue-blooded enclave was surprisingly diverse.

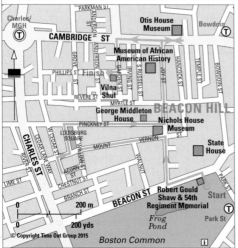

While Beacon Hill is known as Boston's Brahmin bastion, few people are aware of the immigrants who left their mark – notably the free black community before the Civil War, and late 19th-century European Jews. This walk takes in the two sides of the hill.

Begin where the two sides converge: the wealth and power of the **Massachusetts State House** (*see p65*) on Beacon Street, the work of Brahmin architect Charles Bulfinch; and, opposite, at the corner of Beacon and Park Streets, the **Robert Gould Shaw and 54th Regiment Memorial**. The bas-relief sculpture commemorates the first black regiment of the Union Army to fight in the Civil War. Colonel Shaw is depicted with drawn sword, leading his men to attack Fort Wagner; he and 62 of his soldiers would die in the battle.

Facing the State House, turn left along Beacon Street, then right on to Joy Street. Take the first left on to **Mount Vernon Street**, which Henry James hailed as the most respectable street in America. Perhaps that's because he once lived at no.131, as did Julia Ward Howe (no.32), who wrote *Battle Hymn of the Republic* and invented Mother's Day, poet Robert Frost (no.88) and the orator Daniel Webster (no.57). On the right is the **Nichols House Museum** (*see p66*), home

to suffragette and landscape gardener Rose Standish from 1885 to 1960.

Continue downhill along Mount Vernon Street until it opens into **Louisburg Square** – one of the city's wealthiest enclaves. Follow the gaze of the bust of Aristides (left) to Willow Street, then turn right into **Acorn Street**, a cobbled alley that lodged the square's staff (and is now a coveted address itself). Retrace your steps to Louisburg Square, and tarry for a moment at the doorstop of no.10, once home to Louisa May Alcott.

Walk north to Pinckney Street and turn right. It's less grand than Mount Vernon – in her earlier years, Alcott boarded at no.20. At no.15, Elizabeth Peabody founded one of the country's first kindergartens, while the **George Middleton House** (nos.5-7) is the oldest home on Beacon Hill built by African-Americans (1797), and the home of black liveryman and Revolutionary War veteran Middleton.

At the end of Pinckney Street, turn left into Joy Street and walk downhill. On your left, at no.46, is the **Abiel Smith School**, the country's first black public school and now part of the **Museum of African American History** (*see p66*). The **Black Heritage Trail** walking tour (*see p47* **Trail Blazers**) begins here. Behind the school is the **African Meeting House**, a gathering place for the community that was built by black artisans in 1806.

Further down Joy Street, at no.67, is the former home of Rebecca Lee Crumpler, the country's first black female doctor (1864). At the bottom of the hill, Joy Street dead-ends at Cambridge Street. Across the road, to the right, is the stately **Otis House Museum** (*see p66*), designed by Bulfinch in the 1790s for a prominent couple.

Walk west along Cambridge Street, turn left on to Garden Street, back up the hill, then right on to Phillips Street. The lovely **Vilna Shul** (no.18) is the only extant example of the 50 synagogues built by Boston's booming Jewish community in the early 20th century.

Acorn Street. *See p62.*

Abiel Smith School.

★ No.9 Park

9 Park Street, at Beacon Street (1-617 742 9991, www.no9park.com). Park Street T. **Open** 11.30am-2.30pm, 5.30-9pm Mon; 5.30-10pm Tue-Sat; 5.30-9pm Sun. **Main courses** $32-$45. **Map** p63 D5 ⑩ **French/Italian**

Top local chef Barbara Lynch's timeless flagship tucked inside this elegant townhouse demonstrates how 'smooth' and 'sharp' can be synonyms; the service – from the bartenders to the splendid sommelier, Cat Silirie – hits the heights of professionalism. The French/Italian cuisine, for which Lynch also earned kudos at fine-dining Menton, still attracts admirers – especially when it comes to the pastas.

Other location Menton, 354 Congress Street, at Thompson Place, Waterfront (1-617 737 0099, www.mentonboston.com).

Paramount

44 Charles Street, between Chestnut & Mount Vernon Streets (1-617 720 1152, www.paramount boston.com). Arlington or Charles/MGH T. **Open** 7am-4.30pm, 5-10pm Mon-Thur; 7am-4.30pm, 5-11pm Fri; 8am-4.30pm, 5-11pm Sat; 8am-4.30pm, 5-10pm Sun. **Main courses** $13-$23. **Map** p63 B5 ⑪ **American**

Admittedly greater than the sum of its parts, this once-classic greasy spoon (established in 1937) is now a knowingly jazzy version of its original self. Though the old stainless steel grill, Formica table-tops and cafeteria-style service at breakfast and lunch proudly advertise its blue-collar roots, the blue cheese, bacon and spinach omelettes, turkey burgers and sweet potato fries hint at a yuppie bent. The people-watching during Sunday brunch is superb.

Bars

★ 21st Amendment

150 Bowdoin Street, at Freeman Place (1-617 227 7100, www.21stboston.com). Park Street T. **Open** 11.30am-2am daily. **Map** p63 D5 ⑫

On the surface, there's nothing particularly striking about this small, low-ceilinged bar. Just across the way, however, is the State House, which leads to the spectacle of power brokers, legislators, journalists, tourists and local ne'er-do-wells sharing a drink. The 21st is the ultimate off-hour politico bar; you may well spot some in there on 'business lunches'. *Photo p70.*

Sevens Ale House

77 Charles Street, between Mount Vernon & Pinckney Streets (1-617 523 9074). Charles/MGH T. **Open** 11.30am-1am Mon-Sat; noon-1am Sun. **Map** p63 B5 ⑬

Though often prohibitively crowded, this unpretentious little pub is a good spot to seek respite from a hard day of sightseeing and antiques-hunting. The Sevens provides some welcome knuckle and grit to the relative daintiness of the area. Find a booth in the corner, settle down with a Guinness or a Bass, and you might find the Freedom Trail ends right here.

EXPLORE

Tip Tap Room

138 Cambridge Street, between Ridgeway Lane &
Temple Street (1-857 350 3344, www.thetiptap
room.com). Charles/MGH T. **Open** 11.30am-2am
Mon-Sat; 10.30am-2am Sun. **Map** p63 C4 ❷

Taking its name from the speciality steak tips (along
with lamb, turkey, chicken, swordfish and tofu versions) and taps dispensing 36 diverse beers, the Tip
Tap Room fills up early with young professionals
and MGH hospital workers still in their scrubs. An
excellent selection of artisanal bottled beers, whiskey and wine round out the menu, but it's the daily
wild game specials that set the menu apart from any
other in the city.

Shops & Services

Beauty Mark

33 Charles Street, at Chestnut Street (1-617 720
1555, www.thebeautymark.com). Charles/MGH T.
Open 11am-7pm Mon-Fri; 10am-6pm Sat; noon-
5pm Sun. **Map** p63 B5 ❶ **Health & beauty**

This sweet little white and blue shop sells a well-
edited collection of products by, among others,
Bumble and bumble (hair), Becca (make-up),
SkinCeuticals (skincare) and TokyoMilk (fragrance).
Make-up consultations are also offered.

★ Good

133 Charles Street, at Putnam Avenue (1-617 722
9200, www.shopatgood.com). Charles/MGH T.
Open 10am-7pm Mon-Fri; 10am-6pm Sat; noon-
5pm Sun. **Map** p63 B4 ❶ **Fashion/homewares**

A very fine boutique got even better with a move
down the street to more expansive digs. The new,
improved Good stocks modern-rustic furniture,
eye-catching home accessories, chunky sweaters
and dramatic necklaces. Owner Paul Niski also
uses the expanded space to host seasonal meet-and-
greets with regional furniture designers, jewellers
and ceramicists.

Holiday

53 Charles Street, between Mount Vernon &
Chestnut Streets (1-617 973 9730, www.holiday
boutique.net). Charles/MGH T. **Open** 11am-5pm
Mon; 11am-7pm Tue-Fri; 10am-6pm Sat; noon-5pm
Sun. **Map** p63 B5 ❶ **Fashion**

One-time stylist Jessika Goranson assembles contemporary European and American labels in her
small, airy boutique, including Lauren Moffatt,
Erin Fetherston, Julie Brown and Coats Factory
by Plesner; clothing is displayed in white-painted
armoires. The store also has three in-house collections, including the popular, under-$150 Pretty
Little Sister line.

Moxie

51 Charles Street, between Mount Vernon &
Chestnut Streets (1-617 557 9991, www.moxie
boston.com). Charles/MGH T. **Open** 10am-7pm
Mon-Fri; 10am-6pm Sat; 11am-6pm Sun.
Map p63 B5 ❶ **Accessories**

This stylish little boutique stocks a tempting
mix of shoes, bags, jewellery and accessories
from mid-priced designers such as Joie, Cynthia

21st Amendment. See p69.

Vincent, Tory Burch and Botkier. The general style leans towards the colourful and girly.

Persona

62 Charles Street, between Chestnut & Mount Vernon Streets (1-617 266 3003, www.persona style.com). Charles/MGH T. **Open** 10am-7pm Mon-Sat; noon-5pm Sun. **Map** p63 B5 ⑲
Accessories
Persona showcases contemporary designer jewellery collections from the likes of Kurtulan, Alexis Bittar and Yossi Harari. The stock is unusual and varied, so there should be something to suit most tastes, and prices run from down-to-earth to stratospheric. A custom design service, courtesy of co-owner and in-house designer Gary Shteyman, is also offered.

Savenor's

160 Charles Street, at Cambridge Street (1-617 723 6328, www.savenorsmarket.com). Charles/ MGH T. **Open** 11am-8pm Mon-Thur; 10am-8pm Fri, Sat; noon-7pm Sun. **Map** pp63 B3 ⑳
Food & drink
If you can't cook like Julia Child, at least you can shop like her – this butcher's most celebrated customer regularly praised its meats on her TV show. In addition to top-quality traditional cuts, Savenor's carries exotic game and a select array of gourmet groceries.
Other location 92 Kirkland Street, at Myrtle Avenue, Cambridge (1-617 576 6328).

Twentieth Century Limited

73 Charles Street, at Mount Vernon Street (1-617 742 1031, www.boston-vintagejewelry.com). Charles/MGH T. **Open** 11am-6pm Mon-Sat; noon-5pm Sun. **Map** p63 B5 ㉑ Accessories
This tiny basement shop contains a glittering cache of vintage and costume jewellery from the late 1800s to the 1980s. Also stocked are hats, handbags, and accessories for men and women, including a massive selection of vintage cufflinks. The stock draws fur-coated Beacon Hill Brahmins and retro-loving hipsters. Prices start at $35 or so for a pair of flashy, fabulous diamanté earrings from the 1950s.

Wish

49 Charles Street, between Mount Vernon & Chestnut Streets (1-617 227 4441). Charles/ MGH T. **Open** 10am-7pm Mon-Fri; 10am-6pm Sat; 11am-6pm Sun. **Map** p63 B5 ㉒ Fashion
Looking for the perfect dress? This jam-packed boutique is a good bet for finding it, stocking an almost overwhelming array of frocks in various prints and cuts by Milly, Nanette Lepore, Rebecca Taylor and Tibi, as well as separates, jeans and T-shirts from Vince, Velvet and Splendid. The house style lies between well-groomed preppy and urban sophisticate.

Good.

EXPLORE

Charles River Esplanade & Hatch Memorial Shell.

THE WEST END

Bowdoin, Haymarket, North Station or Science Park T.

The West End was once a large residential area that formed a bridge between the North End and Beacon Hill. For many years an immigrant district, its winding streets and cramped tenements housed a sizeable low-income black, Jewish, Irish, Italian and Polish population. It was also known as a destination for sailors, who patronised its shady bars and shadier brothels. Now, however, the area north of Cambridge Street barely registers on many locals' radar, and is hardly ever referred to by name.

In the 1960s, under the flag of urban renewal, city planners levelled the neighbourhood to build luxury high-rises and expand Massachusetts General Hospital. In the process, some 7,000 residents were displaced and historic architecture was demolished. On a positive note, the destruction of the West End became a cardinal example of what not to do when seeking to improve a district, and other communities whose homes were up for 'urban renewal' banded together to stop the planners.

The character of the area is improving, however. The brooding stone Charles Street Jail, overlooking the river, has been turned into the dramatic boutique-style **Liberty Hotel** (*see p249*) and the 1904 Flatiron building houses the new **Boxer Hotel** (*see p249*). Meanwhile, the restored youth playing fields, **Teddy Ebersol's Red Sox Fields** (named in memory of a young baseball fan), have revitalised the stretch of Charlesbank called Lederman Park.

Between Longfellow and Harvard Bridges, the lovely, grassy **Charles River Esplanade** is crisscrossed by walking paths and anchored by the **Hatch Memorial Shell**, a pavilion best known for the annual Fourth of July concert (*see p32*) by the Boston Pops Orchestra. On summer weekends, the Esplanade becomes crowded with sun-worshippers, frisbee players, dog walkers, cyclists and skaters, and the river is dotted with sailing boats. To the north, the **Museum of Science** perches on the Charles River Dam between Boston and Cambridge.

As you head inland towards the North End, the dismantling of the ugly raised expressway that overshadowed the streets around North Station has made the area feel more open and less seedy. Now there is a new sense of space, and style-conscious businesses such as the **Onyx Hotel** (*see p250*) have joined the sports bars and fast-food joints clustered around the monolithic **TD Garden**. The stadium, renamed yet again after a merger absorbed its former sponsor, is on the site of the late, lamented Boston Garden. Though the old venue was mildewed, rickety and weathered, it was fondly regarded as the place where the Boston Celtics basketball team won numerous NBA Championships in the 1980s, and where Boston Bruins legend Bobby Orr regularly sprayed ice with his skates. The Garden remains the only arena in town where both major sporting events and big rock concerts are staged, and also houses the Sports Museum.

Sights & Museums

Museum of Science & Charles Hayden Planetarium

Science Park, between Storrow Drive & Edwin H Land Boulevard (1-617 723 2500, www.mos.org). Science Park T. **Open** *July, Aug* 9am-7pm Mon-Thur, Sat, Sun; 9am-9pm Fri. *Sept-June* 9am-5pm Mon-Thur, Sat, Sun; 9am-9pm Fri. **Admission** *Museum of Science* $23; $20-$21 reductions. Theatres, planetarium and some special exhibitions cost extra. **Map** p63 B2 ❷

This extremely child-friendly museum is committed to providing an interactive and educational experience, making science accessible through a wealth of hands-on activities and engaging exhibits. Highlights include the Thomson Theater of Electricity, which houses a giant Van de Graaf generator, providing a safe way to experience a dramatic lightning storm at close range; the domed Mugar Omni Theater for IMAX movies, plus a 4D theatre complete with physical special effects; and the Butterfly Garden conservatory. At the multimedia Charles Hayden Planetarium, the Zeiss Star Projector reproduces a realistic night sky. There's an enormous gift shop and a decent café courtesy of celebrity chef Wolfgang Puck. The new three-storey Yawkey Gallery, focusing on the ecosystems and history of the Charles River, and offering spectacular views of the water, will debut in late 2015/early 2016. ▶ *For a child-centric review of the museum's attractions, see p170.*

Sports Museum

TD Garden, 100 Legends Way, at Causeway Street (1-617 624 1234, www.sportsmuseum.org). North Station T. **Open** 10am-4pm daily (subject to change). *Tours* (hourly) 10am-3pm daily. **Admission** $10; $5 reductions; free under-10s & active-duty military. **Map** p63 D2 ❷

Sport is a deep-rooted passion in New England. The century-old traditions in this city of champions – in a state where basketball (and arguably baseball) was invented – receive the tribute they deserve here. Located in TD Garden, which is home to the Bruins (hockey) and Celtics (basketball) teams in the colder months, the museum offers an overview of the city's sporting history via colourful displays of artefacts, antique equipment and uniforms, faded front pages and game programmes, and stunning photographs from across the decades. Whether you're interested in Bobby Orr and the Bruins, the Red Sox of Ted Williams or David Ortiz, or the century-spanning Harvard–Yale football rivalry, the Sports Museum's audio and video collections, interactive exhibits and knowledgeable staff will soon fill you in.

EXPLORE

Museum of Science & Charles Hayden Planetarium.

Back Bay & Fenway

The expansive boulevards, ostentatious belle époque mansions and venerated cultural institutions give the impression of deep-rooted permanence, but little more than 150 years ago, the entire area, from the Public Garden to the Fens, was submerged in swampland – it was, quite literally, Boston's back bay.

Home of the Boston Public Library, the Museum of Fine Arts and Symphony Hall, the elegant area evokes the city of Henry James and John Singer Sargent (both of whom hobnobbed with Isabella Stewart Gardner, founder of the unique museum that takes her name). The Back Bay is also one of the city's prime shopping and dining districts. Even formerly run-down Kenmore Square, once the domain of students, club rats and Red Sox fans heading for Fenway Park, is now buzzing with upscale brasseries and cocktail bars.

EXPLORE

Isabella Stewart Gardner Museum.

Don't Miss

1 Copley Square Trinity Church anchors this picturesque spot (p76).

2 Mapparium This offbeat attraction is delightfully surreal (p86).

3 Bodega The secret's out, but this speakeasy shop still shines (p88).

4 Isabella Stewart Gardner Museum An exquisite palace full of fascinating treasures (p89).

5 Sweet Cheeks Q Not just for carnivores (p92).

EXPLORE

Back Bay

Arlington, Back Bay, Copley, Hynes Convention Center or Prudential T.

Largely due to immigration, Boston's population soared from under 20,000 at the end of the 18th century to more than 300,000 in the mid to late 19th century. The city was bursting at its seams. To expand the narrow neck of the peninsula along the Charles River, the authorities set to work filling in mud flats along its south bank with gravel brought in by train from pits outside the city. Begun in the 1850s, the massive landfill project, undertaken in stages, took 40 years. The reclaimed land was laid out in orderly grids, with broad avenues influenced by Haussmann's new boulevards in Paris. The finished product was an immediate hit with high society, who moved into the newly built mansions and row houses, and the area became the centre for the city's most important cultural institutions.

Today's Back Bay is a mix of affluent residential streets and commercial districts. Although it contains some of the city's most important architectural sights, this is the city's main shopping destination, where you'll find everything from global mega-chains to cutting-edge designer boutiques. Prime retail strip **Newbury Street** and elegant, residential **Commonwealth Avenue**, with its median swathe of parkland, are especially pleasant for strolling. Although the neighbourhood has a conservative 'old Boston' reputation, there has been an influx of funkier businesses, not to mention the visible student presence from nearby Boston University, Berklee College of Music and Northeastern University.

The heart of Back Bay is bracketed by the Public Garden to the east, Massachusetts Avenue to the west, and Stuart Street and Huntington Avenue to the south. The area to the west known as the Fenway, home to two of the city's most important museums as well as the eponymous ballpark, is also covered in this chapter (*see p89*).

COPLEY SQUARE & BOYLSTON STREET

Despite the traffic rumbling through the intersection of Boylston and Dartmouth Streets, **Copley Square** is an expansive spot, anchored by two of the city's landmark structures: the neo-Romanesque **Trinity Church** and the imposing **Boston Public Library**. Looming behind the church, across St James Avenue, and providing a striking juxtaposition of period and style, is the 60-storey glass sheath that is the **John Hancock Tower**. The gleaming office block, designed by IM Pei, is the city's tallest building – although its observation deck closed after the 9/11 attacks. The building had a difficult beginning: during its construction in 1973, a flaw in the design caused dozens of the 500-pound windows to pop out of their frames and shatter on the sidewalk below. Miraculously, no one was hurt, but every single pane had to be replaced, and the frames that held them redesigned, at terrific expense. Walk south along Dartmouth Street for Boston's poshest mall, **Copley Place**.

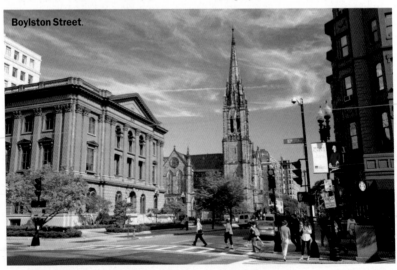

Boylston Street.

Boston Public Library.

While much of **Boylston Street** is a fairly characterless commercial thoroughfare, it has become more upmarket in recent years, with the arrival of retail development **Heritage on the Garden**, east of Copley Square, which contains such exclusive European labels as Hermès and Bottega Veneta; and, to the west, the **Mandarin Oriental Hotel** (*see p251*). Fans of ostentatious architecture should pause to gaze up at the **Berkeley** (40 Berkeley Street). Built in 1906, the office building looks like a giant wedding cake.

A block away is the rather less embellished **Arlington Street Church** (351 Boylston Street, at Arlington Street, www.ascboston.org). It was built in the mid 19th century and boasts 13 Tiffany stained-glass windows, believed to be the largest collection in any church. The **Parish Café** is a good place to refuel in the area.

A short walk south along Arlington Street brings you to the six-square-block enclave called **Bay Village**. Wedged between the Back Bay, Downtown and the South End, the tiny residential neighbourhood was created on landfill in the 1820s, decades before the South End and Back Bay. It's worth a visit for its charming architecture – similar to that of Beacon Hill, though on a smaller scale, as it was colonised by the craftspeople who built the latter's townhouses. During Prohibition, a number of the city's speakeasies were secreted in this tucked-away enclave. Today, the underground element still lives on at Boston's best-known drag venue, **Jacque's Cabaret** (*see p180*).

West of Copley Square is the **Prudential Center**, with its 50th-floor observation deck and shopping mall, which is connected to the swankier Copley Place by an enclosed, raised walkway. Nearby is the **Hynes Convention Center**, now eclipsed by the massive Boston Convention and Exhibition Center, which opened in the redeveloped waterfront area.

Sights & Museums

FREE Boston Public Library
700 Boylston Street, at Copley Square (1-617 536 5400, www.bpl.org). Copley T. **Open** 9am-9pm Mon-Thur; 9am-5pm Fri, Sat; 1-5pm Sun (except June-Sept). **Admission** free. **Map** p79 E4 ❶

The original structure, designed by Charles McKim and completed in 1895, is now the research library, while an extension opened in 1972 functions as a general library. The elegant granite exterior of the older building is generally classified as Italian Renaissance revival, although McKim cited various influences, including the Marshall Fields department store in Chicago. It's well worth visiting, and you can join an informal art and architecture tour, conducted by volunteers, most days (phone or check website for times). At the centre of the building is the cloistered courtyard, with its central fountain – a tranquil place to linger. Bates Hall (the expansive second-floor reading room named after an early benefactor) runs the entire length of the library, and features a majestic barrel-arched ceiling punctuated by half-domes at each end. Another highlight is John Singer Sargent's epic mural, *Triumph of Religion*, which dominates the third-floor gallery; there are also murals by 19th-century French painter Pierre Puvis de Chavannes, among others. The modern wing of the library – which echoes its parent's materials, lines and proportions in a modernist vocabulary – has had its critics, but has aged well.

▶ *Downstairs, the library's restaurant, Courtyard, and the Map Room Café are worthy lunch spots.*

Prudential Center & Tower
800 Boylston Street, between Dalton Street & Ring Road (1-617 236 3100, www.prudentialcenter.com). Copley, Hynes Convention Center or Prudential T. **Open** *Skywalk Observatory* Mar-Oct 10am-9.30pm daily. Nov-Feb 10am-8pm daily. *Shops* 10am-9pm Mon-Sat; 11am-6pm Sun. **Admission** *Skywalk Observatory* $16; $11-$13 reductions. **Map** p78 C4 ❷

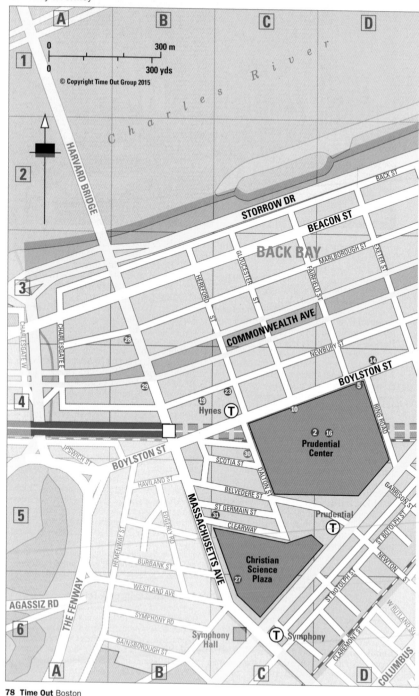

EXPLORE

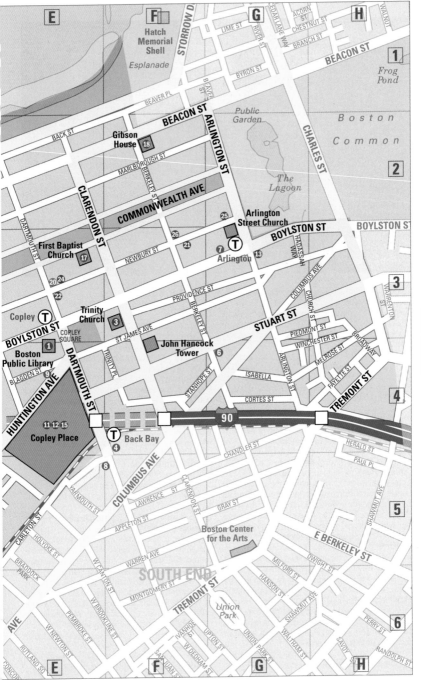

EXPLORE

Trinity Church

EXPLORE

A standard-issue shopping mall forms the base for the 52-storey office tower above. Since the closure of the John Hancock observatory deck, the Skywalk Observatory on the 50th floor is Boston's lone skyscraper view point. The glassed-in walkway offers a 360° perspective from a height of 750ft; on a clear day, you can see as far as 80 miles. Two audio tours, picking out historical sites, are available. The classic Top of the Hub Restaurant & Lounge, two floors up, is recommended more for the fabulous view than for the food.

★ Trinity Church

206 Clarendon Street, at Copley Square (1-617 536 0944, www.trinitychurchboston.org). Back Bay or Copley T. **Open** 9am-5pm Mon, Fri, Sat; 9am-6pm Tue, Thur; 11am-7pm Wed; 7am-9pm Sun. **Admission** $7; $5 reductions. **Map** p79 F3 ❸
Copley Square's visual centrepiece, the unabashedly ornate Trinity Church was restored to full splendour by a three-year renovation project in the early 2000s. The original church was on Summer Street, but was destroyed by fire in 1872. Commissioned to build a replacement, architect Henry Hobson Richardson rejected the Gothic Revival style prevalent at the time and instead took inspiration from the ancient churches of southern France. It proved to be his masterpiece, so much so that the term 'Richardsonian Romanesque' entered the architectural lexicon. The church is also known for its extensive murals – almost every inch of wall was hand-painted by a team led by American artist John La Farge. The impressive stained-glass windows include four that were designed by the English Pre-Raphaelite painter Edward Burne-Jones and made by Arts and Crafts pioneer William Morris.

Restaurants & Cafés

Douzo

131 Dartmouth Street, between Stuart Street & Columbus Avenue (1-617 859 8886, www. douzosushi.com). Back Bay or Copley T. **Open** 11.30am-11.30pm daily. **Main courses** $19-$49. **Map** p79 F4 ❹ Japanese
Scallop-kiwi maki, soft-shell crab tempura, shining baubles of monkfish pâté – Back Bay was more than ready for such heady fare, as Douzo has proven since day one. A date favourite for its multi-level nooks and mood lighting, it's no less welcoming to singles who score seats at the sushi bar, getting the inside scoop on daily specials direct from the chefs.

★ L'Espalier

774 Boylston Street, at Ring Road (1-617 262 3023, www.lespalier.com). Copley or Hynes Convention Center T. **Open** 11.30am-2.30pm, 5.30-10.30pm Mon-Fri; noon-1.45pm, 5.30-10.30pm Sat, Sun. **Set meals** $95-$205. **Map** p78 D4 ❺ French
Marriage proposals and six-figure deals are par for the course at chef-owner Frank McClelland's New French New England legend. Make that par for six courses (you can also opt for three or 11): the main menu is a seasonal *dégustation*, breathtaking in its creativity, scope, execution and price – all served by hyper-attentive yet professional servers in a setting of white tablecloths and fine crystal. From the wine cellar to the *fromage* programme, McClelland has established haute cuisine with a farm-to-table commitment (sometimes ingredients come from his own farm, Apple Street Farm in Essex). Other options – the three-course prix fixe at dinner, tea on weekends – can get you in the door without risking the mortgage.

Grill 23 & Bar

161 Berkeley Street, at Stuart Street (1-617 542 2255, www.grill23.com). Arlington T. **Open** 5.30-10.30pm Mon-Thur; 5.30-11pm Fri; 5-11pm Sat; 5.30-10pm Sun. **Main courses** $27-$69. **Map** p79 G4 ❻ **American**

Boston does not lack for steakhouses, but this original fine-dining gem in the Back Bay still stands out with its high ceilings, marble columns, white tablecloths and white-jacketed waiters, where lawyers and brokers cut deals over some of the best steaks in town. Chef Jay Murray's seasonal menu transcends steakhouse clichés with a changing array of appetisers, such as *hamachi* tartare with salsa verde and avocado, or locally made *burrata*. (There's more than red meat here.) The award-winning wine list has over 1,500 bottles and many by the glass. An excellent choice for larger groups who want to be doted on in elegant surroundings.

Parish Café

361 Boylston Street, at Arlington Street (1-617 247 4777, www.parishcafe.com). Arlington T. **Open** 11am-2am Mon-Sat; noon-2am Sun. **Main courses** $12-$15. **Map** p79 G3 ❼ **Café/bar**

What's better than cramming the city's most celebrated chefs into a single kitchen? A menu of sandwiches created by and named for those chefs, which is the main concept at this Back Bay hotspot. The culinary creativity runs the gamut from breaded veal cutlet (Chris Coombs of Dbar, Deuxave and Boston Chops) and roasted rare sirloin with caramelised onions (Michael Schlow of Tico), to slow-roasted pork butt (Michael Leviton of Lumiere) and breaded and pan-fried aubergine with black bean spread (Jamie Bissonnette of Coppa and Toro).

Local bartenders get equally creative on the cocktail list. What never changes is the kinetic energy, both inside the snug multicoloured café and out on the very popular patio.

Other location 493 Massachusetts Avenue, at Tremont Street, South End (1-617 391 0501).

Salty Pig

130 Dartmouth Street, at Columbus Avenue (1-617 536 6200, www.thesaltypig.com). Back Bay T. **Open** 11.30am-1am daily. **Main courses** $10-$19. **Map** p79 F5 ❽ **American/Italian**

With the emphasis on 'pig', this casual eatery across from the Back Bay T stop near Copley Square has a niche in own-made meats, charcuterie and cheeses, making it a prized place for small-plate grazing with a nice glass of wine or one of the rotating draught beers (cocktails are limited to cordials and liqueurs). The menu is limited but creative (there's a pork tasting option), with house-made pastas and assorted flat-breads providing an affordable way to enjoy the relaxed setting of communal wooden tables and seasonal patio.

Sorellina

1 Huntington Avenue, at Dartmouth Street (1-617 412 4600, www.sorellinaboston.com). Back Bay or Copley T. **Open** 5.30-10pm Mon-Thur, Sun; 5.30-11pm Fri, Sat. **Main courses** $17-$48. **Map** p79 E4 ❾ **Italian**

Cloaked in classic black and white stripes, this elegant dining room – Mistral's swanky sister – looks as much like a modern design showroom as the fine-dining Italian restaurant it is. The menu is equally glamorous. The ingredients are posh, sauces

Salty Pig.

Barneys New York

sparing; even the signature spaghetti (make that *maccheroncelli*) and meatballs uses wagyu beef and a splash of Barolo. You'll find plenty of the latter on the largely high-end Cal-Ital wine list as well.

▶ *For our review of Mistral, see p101.*

Towne Stove & Spirits

900 Boylston Street, at Gloucester Street (1-617 247 0400, www.towneboston.com). Prudential T. **Open** 4pm-2am Mon-Fri; 11am-2am Sat, Sun. **Main courses** $16-$48. **Map** p78 C4 ⑩ **Eclectic**
New England clam chowder may rub shoulders with house-made maki, wood-grilled pizzas, osso buco or peking duck on the frequently changing menu at this snazzy, two-storey dining destination. The food is as bold as the decor – just as partner Lydia Shire would want you to experience it (her famous lobster pizza is on the menu too). Start with drinks in the street-side lounge downstairs, where the under-lit bar dazzles with changing colours, then cosy into a banquette or take a seat at one of the white-clothed tables. With its broad menu and many-roomed options, you can go for brunch, lunch, dinner or cocktails without getting bored.

Shops & Services

Barneys New York

Copley Place, 100 Huntington Avenue, at Exeter Street (1-617 385 3300, www.barneys.com). Back Bay, Copley or Prudential T. **Open** 10am-8pm Mon-Sat; noon-6pm Sun. **Map** p79 E4 ⑪ **Department store**
This two-level branch of the super-chic New York department store within the city's premier mall has been criticised by some for bringing a less interesting selection of labels to Boston than those found in its parent store – but, given the compact size, it seems inevitable that the number of lines would be more limited. There's no doubt it's a welcome addition for style-conscious shoppers looking for contemporary

designer fashion (Isabel Marant, Alexander Wang, Phillip Lim and Martin Margiela, for example), shoes and accessories hitherto hard to find in the city, as well as less ubiquitous cosmetics.

★ Copley Place

100 Huntington Avenue, at Ring Road (1-617 262 6600, www.simon.com/mall/copley-place). Back Bay, Copley or Prudential T. **Open** 10am-8pm Mon-Sat; noon-6pm Sun. **Map** p79 E4 ⑫ **Mall**
This upmarket mall gets better and better. Copley Place has an 11-screen cinema, two hotels and 100 stores, including Barneys New York, Louis Vuitton, Jimmy Choo, Tiffany, Neiman Marcus and less rarefied names such as Banana Republic and J Crew. A glass-enclosed bridge connects it to its more pedestrian counterpart at the Prudential Center.

★ Exhale

28 Arlington Street, at Providence Street (1-617 532 7000, www.exhalespa.com). Arlington T. **Open** 6am-9pm Mon-Fri; 7.30am-8pm Sat, Sun. **Map** p79 G3 ⑬ **Health & beauty**
Located in the upscale Heritage on the Garden complex, Exhale is a wellness-oriented spa with extensive services, including an excellent fitness and yoga programme. Alongside top-notch facials, massage and the usual beautifying services, alternative therapies such as acupuncture are available.
Other location 2 Battery Wharf, at Commercial Street, Waterfront (1-617 603 3100).

First Act

745 Boylston Street, at Ring Road (1-888 551 1115, www.firstact.com). **Open** 9am-7pm Mon-Thur; 9am-5pm Fri. **Map** p78 D4 ⑭ **Books & music**
If it's good enough for Rufus Wainwright, Keane and KT Tunstall, it's good enough for you. They're just a few of the musicians who have played intimate in-store concerts at this shop, where brightly coloured guitars are mounted on the walls. Even

EXPLORE

if you're not a rock star, you can buy custom-made guitars (electric and acoustic), or at least test a few models out in the showroom.

Neiman Marcus

5 Copley Place, at Dartmouth Street (1-617 536 3660, www.neimanmarcus.com). Back Bay or Copley T. **Open** 10am-8pm Mon-Sat; noon-6pm Sun. **Map** p79 E4 ⓰ **Department store**
Situated in the posh Copley Place mall, Neiman Marcus is the place to come for big-name international designer fashion and accessories. Customer service is excellent, and the cosmetics department has a good selection of cult brands such as Chantecaille and Laura Mercier.

Saks Fifth Avenue

Prudential Center, 800 Boylston Street, at Gloucester Street (1-617 262 8500, www. saksfifthavenue.com). Copley or Prudential T. **Open** 10am-9pm Mon-Sat; noon-7pm Sun. **Map** p78 D4 ⓰ **Department store**
Entered from the Pru mall or Ring Road, this formerly staid (and much smaller) branch of the famous New York store got a slick revamp a few years ago. The ground-floor designer accessories department is arranged in mini 'boutiques', while cosmetics is similarly divided up into individually labelled stands. Saks Fifth Avenue a good place to snap up popular contemporary labels, but service can be patchy.

NEWBURY STREET & AROUND

Newbury Street has a reputation as the city's posh shopping street, and while this multi-purpose strip certainly has its share of luxe designer and contemporary fashion names (Chanel, Burberry, Marc Jacobs, Rag and Bone), it also hosts everything from a hardware store to an outlet devoted to Boston bean memorabilia. The street's personality changes palpably from one end to the other. Generally speaking, the Arlington Street end, closer to the Public Garden, is more upmarket, with a mix of designer boutiques, antiques stores and jewellers. America's oldest jeweller, **Shreve, Crump & Low**, established in 1796, now has its headquarters here.

This is also a good place to head for a spot of pampering – there are dozens of spas, salons and cheap nail bars on Newbury Street. A sceney vibe prevails on summer weekends, when locals promenade on the strip and linger at upmarket cafés. Numerous art galleries are clustered here, including the prestigious **Barbara Krakow Gallery** (10 Newbury Street, at Arlington Street (1-617 262 4490, www.barbarakrakowgallery. com), though the contemporary art buzz has shifted to the SoWa district (*see p96*). The **Society of Arts and Crafts** (no.175, between Dartmouth & Exeter Streets, 1-617 266 1810, www.societyofcrafts.org), founded in 1897, has an upstairs gallery showcasing museum-quality thematic exhibitions, while the shop below, which represents more than 300 artists from across the country, sells more affordable items.

As you head towards Massachusetts Avenue, closer to Berklee College of Music and Boston University, the mood is more casual; high-priced cafés give way to younger fashion stores, pizza joints and ice-cream shops. Indie bookshop-cum-café **Trident Booksellers & Café** is a well-loved hangout.

EXPLORE

Newbury Street.

EXPLORE

Running parallel to Newbury is the area's grandest residential street, **Commonwealth Avenue** (or Comm Ave, as it's universally known). Elegant mansions and townhouses line the thoroughfare, designed in 1865 to resemble a Parisian boulevard. The neo-Gothic **Burrage mansion** (no.314) is a particularly ostentatious example. The wide, tree-lined central promenade is a link in the Emerald Necklace series of parks designed by Frederick Law Olmsted (see above **In the Know**). Dotted with statues, memorials and benches, it draws dog-walking locals and the homeless. On the corner of Clarendon Street is the **First Baptist Church**, Richardson's prelude to his ecclesiastical masterwork, Trinity Church in Copley Square.

Crossing Commonwealth Avenue and Newbury Street and are a series of streets that run in alphabetical order (from Arlington to Hereford). Cut down one of these, heading north towards the river, and you'll come to Marlborough Street. Because of its rather odd configuration of one-way streets, Marlborough is the quietest and prettiest of Back Bay's streets. The French Academic-style residence at 273 Clarendon Street, between Marlborough and Beacon Streets, is the birthplace and former home of the Massachusetts Audubon Society, one of the country's first environmental organisations. Little more than a block away is the river, and the continuation of the **Esplanade** (*see p72*).

On Beacon Street, as you head towards Massachusetts Avenue, the stately environs are occasionally interrupted by fraternity houses – recognisable by the Greek letters hanging outside (and the riotous parties on weekends).

More sedate is the **Gibson House Museum**, which gives insight into the life of a well-to-do 19th-century family (and their staff) that lived in the neighbourhood.

Sights & Museums

FREE First Baptist Church of Boston
110 Commonwealth Avenue, at Clarendon Street (1-617 267 3148, www.firstbaptistchurchofboston. org). Copley T. **Open** 11am-2pm Tue-Fri. **Admission** free. **Map** p79 E3 ⑰
Completed in 1871, a year before HH Richardson began work on Copley Square's Trinity Church, the First Baptist Church is a similar mix of stone and wood surfaces. Richardson commissioned the bas-relief encircling the top of the belltower from Frédéric Auguste Bartholdi, the sculptor of the Statue of Liberty.

Gibson House Museum
137 Beacon Street, at Berkeley Street (1-617 267 6338, www.thegibsonhouse.org). Arlington T. **Open** *Tours* 1pm, 2pm, 3pm Wed-Sun. **Admission** $9; $3-$6 reductions. **No credit cards. Map** p79 F2 ⑱
This Italian Renaissance-style townhouse, designed by local architect Edward Clarke Cabot and completed in 1860, was one of the first to be built in Back Bay. Although the brownstone and red-brick building isn't remarkable from the outside, the interior offers a rare glimpse into how wealthy Bostonians once lived. The house was impeccably and intentionally preserved by its last occupant, the idiosyncratic Charles Gibson Jr, and converted into a museum in 1957. Visitors on the hour-long tour can see four of the home's six floors, from the ground level where the servants laboured, to the exquisite dining rooms, bedrooms and library above. Every room (except the servants' domain) is decorated with fine china, bronze sculptures and other accoutrements of 19th-century prosperity.

Restaurants & Cafés

★ Trident Booksellers & Café
338 Newbury Street, at Hereford Street (1-617 267 8688, www.tridentbookscafe.com). Hynes Convention Center T. **Open** 8am-midnight daily. **Main courses** $9.50-$12.50. **Map** p78 B4 ⑲ Café
A bohemian ambience permeates this bright, airy café within an indie bookshop. It hops all day with Berklee students and writerly types, poring over glossies from a rack of edgy, globe-spanning magazines while polishing off breakfast burritos, tuna and Swiss cheese melts, yam fries and smoothies. It's a great place to take a breather from Newbury Street shopping, catch up with friends or sit solo sipping unfurling jasmine pearl tea at the counter with the latest *Paris Review*.

Ball & Buck.

Bars

Met Back Bay

279 Dartmouth Street, at Newbury Street (1-617 267 0451, www.metbackbay.com). Copley T.
Open 8am-1am Mon-Fri; 9am-1am Sat-Sun.
Map p79 E3 ⑳
The potential stuffiness of the space (leather uphol-stery; a bar area named 'the Library') is tempered by the casual atmosphere and jean-clad servers. Show up late for a cocktail, such as the signature blood orange cosmo, and something from the ham and cheese bar. Or go for dinner and pair a burger with a fairly priced brew.

Shops & Services

Alan Bilzerian

34 Newbury Street, at Berkeley Street (1-617 536 1001, www.alanbilzerian.com). Arlington T. **Open** 10am-6pm Mon-Sat. **Map** p79 F3 ㉑
Fashion
This trailblazing boutique has been bringing cutting-edge European and Japanese fashion to the Boston area for nearly half a century. The eclectic mix for men and women includes Lanvin, Yohji Yamamoto and Ann Demeulemeester.

★ Ball & Buck

144B Newbury Street, at Dartmouth Street (1-617 818 1776, www.ballandbuck.com). Copley T. **Open** 11am-8pm daily. **Map** p79 E3 ㉒ **Fashion**
In-the-know Bostonian guys augment their ward-robes with regular trips to this urban-sportsman lair. Stock up on house-designed shirts, chunky sweat-ers, sunglasses, boat shoes and weathered wallets, as well as hipster accoutrements such as an oyster

shucker and a stars and stripes koozie (beverage sleeve). Tucked at the back of the store is a scaled-down barber's helmed by Van Capizzano, Robert De Niro's former barber.

Bauer Wine & Spirits

330 Newbury Street, at Hereford Street (1-617 262 0363, www.bauerwines.com). Hynes Convention Center T. **Open** 10am-11pm Mon-Sat; noon-8pm Sun. **Map** p78 C4 ㉓ **Food & drink**
Between its smart address and the renown of its resident expert and co-owner, Howie Rubin, this long-established liquor store could easily get away with catering exclusively to its wealthy neighbours – a fact that makes its across-the-board accessibility all the more admirable. With one of the most extensive selections in the city, this is an excellent and centrally located place to source that hard to find craft beer or Viognet.

Brodney Antiques & Jewelry

145 Newbury Street, at Dartmouth Street (1-617 536 0500, www.brodney.com). Copley T. **Open** 10am-6pm Mon-Sat; noon-5pm Sun. **Map** p79 E3 ㉔ **Antiques/accessories**
This refined treasure trove, established in 1939, sells an impressive range of antiques and curiosities. Its shelves hold an alluring mixture of pieces, from art deco jewellery, Victorian oil lamps and sterling silver punch bowls to French clocks, glassware and Asian art. While the shop is a favourite with serious connoisseurs, casual browsers are welcome. Charm bracelet lovers, take note: this place has the best collection of vintage gold charms – from tiny bejewelled typewriters to cocktail glasses and dice – we've ever seen, but be prepared to pay over $100.

Mario Russo

3rd floor, 9 Newbury Street, at Arlington Street (1-617 424 6676, www.mariorusso.com). Arlington T. **Open** 9am-7pm Mon-Fri; 8am-6pm Sat; 11am-5pm Sun. **Map** p79 G2 ㉕ **Health & beauty**

Mario Russo's hair salon, catering to fashionable, well-heeled Bostonians and visiting celebs alike, is often voted best in the city in the local press.
Other location Louis, Fan Pier, 60 Northern Avenue, Waterfront (1-857 350 3139).

Shreve, Crump & Low

39 Newbury Street, at Berkeley Street (1-617 267 9100, www.shrevecrumpandlow.com). Arlington T. **Open** 10am-6pm Mon-Wed, Sat; 10am-7pm Thur, Fri; noon-5pm Sun. **Map** p79 F3 ㉖ **Accessories/ gifts**

This traditional jewellery and luxury gift shop, established in 1796, is the oldest in North America, though it recently took up residence in these three-floor Back Bay premises. Antique pieces are sold alongside the classic diamonds, silver and gold.
► *The shop's illustrious customers have included the Kennedy family and Winston Churchill.*

MASSACHUSETTS AVENUE & AROUND

The Back Bay stretch of this major thoroughfare, commonly referred to as Mass Ave, has a gritty, urban edge that feels a world away from smart Newbury Street. That said, deluxe streetwear emporium **Bodega** (whose hidden location behind a fake convenience store façade is no longer a hipsters' secret) sits on a side street amid the run-down fast-food joints and music stores. These establishments largely cater to the students at the **Berklee College of Music**, at the corner of Mass Ave and Boylston Street, one of the country's top music schools; its **Performance Center** (*see p188*) presents shows by both students and more established musicians.

The triangle formed by the intersection with Huntington Avenue is dominated by the imposing **Christian Science Plaza**, the world headquarters of the First Church of Christ, Scientist, an organisation established by Mary Baker Eddy, based on a system of spiritual, prayer-based healing. The plaza itself, with its dramatic 670-foot reflecting pool, was designed by IM Pei's firm in the 1960s, but the key buildings are much earlier. The 'Mother Church' is actually two churches: the more intimate Romanesque original, built in 1894, and the 1906 extension – a soaring, domed structure combining Byzantine and Renaissance elements, which can accommodate 3,000 worshippers. The adjacent 1930s neoclassical Mary Baker Eddy Library contains the **Mapparium**, one of the city's more unusual sights, along with interactive

exhibitions about the faith and its founder. A 699-foot skyscraper under construction alongside the plaza will be Boston's tallest residential tower when it's completed sometime around 2017, housing a new Four Seasons hotel as well as condos.

Almost directly across Massachusetts Avenue you'll find **Symphony Hall** (*see p197*), home of the Boston Symphony Orchestra. The attractive, unfussy building, built in 1900, was partly inspired by the Gewandhaus in Leipzig, Germany. The focus on the acoustics of the design was unprecedented; during the planning stages, the architects McKim, Mead and White consulted a Harvard physicist in order to achieve the best possible sound. Tours cover the groundbreaking acoustics in detail and provide some behind-the-scenes glimpses.

Sights & Museums

★ Mapparium

Mary Baker Eddy Library, 200 Massachusetts Avenue, at Clearway Street (1-617 450 7000, www.marybakereddylibrary.org). **Open** 10am-4pm Tue-Sun. **Admission** $6; $4 reductions; free under-5s. **Map** p78 C6 ㉗
See p87 **A World of its Own**.

Restaurants & Cafés

Asta

47 Massachusetts Avenue, at Marlborough Street (1-617 585 9575, www.astaboston.com). Hynes Convention Center T. **Open** 6-10.30pm Tue-Sat. **Set meals** $45-$95. **Map** p78 B3 ㉘
Contemporary American

You'll feel like the party's in the kitchen at this intimate, somewhat noisy brick-walled spot – and it is. Guests are greeted with a free glass of sparkling wine. Those lucky enough to snag a stool (ask for a sheepskin cover) at the wooden counter overlooking the open kitchen can watch as chef-owner Alex Crabb (formerly of L'Espalier) devises intensely creative, captivating dishes from locally sourced, seasonal ingredients: creamed fresh corn with thyme; duck confit; flaky apple turnover with smoked caramel. The menus are prix fixe-only and the decor is pared-down and art-free.

Clio

Eliot Hotel, 370 Commonwealth Avenue, at Massachusetts Avenue (1-617 536 7200, www. diorestaurant.com). Hynes Convention Center T. **Open** 5.30-10pm Mon-Thur; 5.30-10.30pm Fri, Sat. **Main courses** $19-$40. **Set meals** $79-$124. **Map** p78 B4 ㉙ French

The taupe and cream colour scheme says 'refinement'; the leopard print rug says 'excitement'. The menu says both at once – and the cooking that first earned Ken Oringer his celebrity status bears

A WORLD OF ITS OWN

The Mapparium is an unmissable oddball attraction.

Here's proof that Boston really is at the centre of the universe, or at least the world. The **Mapparium** (*see p86*) – the world's largest walk-in globe – is among the city's quirkiest landmarks.

Located at the Mary Baker Eddy Library in the Christian Science Plaza, it is, essentially, a three-storey model of the globe built to scale. The perfect sphere is 30 feet in diameter, traversed by way of a glass bridge. Bouncing off the globe room's non-porous glass walls, sound is amplified tenfold. The effect is pleasantly hallucinatory – whispers across the room register directly in your ear.

The 608 stained-glass panels that comprise the Mapparium recreate the planet as it was in the mid 1930s, when the project was completed. Most of the borders are outdated; several of the countries shown have long since been swallowed up by larger, hungrier, hardier entities.

Built in 1935 for the then astronomical sum of $35,000, it was conceived as a symbol of the *Christian Science Monitor*'s global audience. Its creator, Boston-based architect Chester Lindsay Churchill, designed the rest of the library as well. Ironically, it's the map's obsolescence that gives it a new and unexpected relevance today. Over the years, as its geography has grown increasingly antiquated, the giant map has become a gentle reminder that boundaries, and the powers that dictate them, are in a state of constant flux. There's a lesson here for every Ozymandias.

A number of technological improvements have given new life to the old globe. A proper lighting system, capable of generating 16 million colour combinations, invigorates the map panels, and a multimedia presentation, 'A World of Ideas', has also been installed. You needn't be put off by its new-agey title – at seven minutes, the show is brief as well as totally doctrine-free.

The map itself, though, remains unchanged. Though it could easily have become just another kitsch relic, the enigmatic globe is still surprisingly dignified. As the Mapparium's admirers know, standing in the centre of the world is an uplifting, if somewhat surreal, experience.

EXPLORE

Bodega.

out that promise. In the tiny kitchen of the Eliot Hotel's ever buzzing special-occasion destination, Oringer and his team sculpt miniature New French masterpieces from foie gras, lobster, game and exquisite produce you've never heard of, while the deft chefs behind the counter at Uni, Clio's cosy adjoining sashimi bar, do likewise with seafood flown in weekly from Tokyo's Tsukiji market.

Bars

Bukowski Tavern

50 Dalton Street, at Scotia Street (1-617 437 9999, www.bukowskitavern.net). Hynes Convention Center T. **Open** 11.30am-2am Mon-Sat; noon-2am Sun. **No credit cards. Map** p78 C4 ③⓪
Named for the booze-loving author, the Bukowski is all attitude. The style reflects the interests of the beer-slinging crew: Sex Pistols on the jukebox and a beer menu that encompasses ales, stouts, lagers, wheat beers and such connoisseurs' quaffs as fruit beers and a Japanese ale/saké hybrid. Local brews include Harpoon on tap and Pretty Things in the bottle.
Other location 1281 Cambridge Street, at Oakland Street, Inman Square, Cambridge (1-617 497 7077).

Shops & Services

★ Bodega

6 Clearway Street, at Massachusetts Avenue (no phone, http://shop.bdgastore.com). Hynes Convention Center T. **Open** 11am-6pm Mon-Sat; noon-5pm Sun. **Map** p78 C5 ③① **Accessories**
At first glance, it looks like any other convenience store, the window lined with faded bleach bottles and paper towels. Something's odd, though – the kid behind the counter is a little too stylish, the water stains on the ceiling are too perfect, the horse race on the TV seems to be caught in a loop and none of the stock seems to have moved in months. Step in front of the faux Snapple vending machine to activate the hidden sliding door and reveal the 'secret' store

within a store. Inside is the ultra-modern interior of Boston's flyest sneaker shop – carrying rare kicks from Nike Tier Zero and Adidas Consortium, as well as deluxe streetwear and books on art and design.

Fenway & Kenmore Square

Kenmore, Museum of Fine Arts or Symphony T.

Huntington Avenue, home to Symphony Hall and the **Museum of Fine Arts** – Boston's smaller yet wide-ranging answer to New York's massive Met – was rather grandly rebranded the 'Avenue of the Arts' by former mayor Thomas Menino in 1998. While this seems somewhat hyperbolic, considering that only a handful of the city's cultural institutions reside in the vicinity – there's also the **Boston University Theatre** (*see p201*) and the **New England Conservatory**, as well as the unmissable **Isabella Stewart Gardner Museum**, around the corner from the MFA – they are certainly among the most important.

North of Huntington Avenue are the Back Bay **Fens**, a lovely patch of parkland (and a legendary gay cruising spot), bordered by the Fenway and Park Drive. Once a foul-smelling swamp, the Fens is now an important link in the Emerald Necklace (*see p84* **In the Know**). With its freshwater creek and marshland, the Fens features both wild and landscaped spaces. The section behind the MFA contains the lovely **James P Kelleher Rose Garden**, established in 1930, with its rose-trellis archways, formal flower beds and awning-shaded seats. Closer to Boylston Street, the northerly section is home to the **Fenway Victory Gardens** (www.fenwayvictorygardens.com). The seven-acre allotment site, planted during World War II, is open to the public – the main entrance is on the corner of Boylston Street and Park Drive. Further along the Riverway portion of the Emerald Necklace is **Olmsted Park**, which has a well-travelled path for cyclists and pedestrians, and straddles the Boston–Brookline border.

Near the Fens, **Kenmore Square** sits at the confluence of three major roadways: Commonwealth Avenue, Brookline Avenue and Beacon Street. The square can be easily identified by the giant, glowing 'Citgo' sign on Beacon Street. Since its arrival in 1940, the sign has become a beloved point of reference for locals; attempts to remove it in the early '80s were met with such fierce resistance that they were ultimately dropped.

Over the years, Kenmore Square's function as a transportation corridor, combined with the seasonal nature of the visitors and inhabitants of its two main tenants, Boston University and Fenway Park, engendered the area with a sense of impermanence and confusion. The abundance of students created a natural market for cheap eateries and bars, all of which contributed to the square's slightly seedy air. But the past decade has seen a shift in character. There are now some great restaurants and bars clustered around the luxury **Hotel Commonwealth** (*see p252*), including Parisian-style brasserie **Eastern Standard** and the **Hawthorne** cocktail bar.

Lurking behind Kenmore, **Lansdowne Street** has been the city's nightclub row for decades. The names have changed, but the clubs live on. In the early 20th century, retailer Eben

Jordan (founder of the *Boston Globe* and now-defunct local department store Jordan Marsh), built the structure at nos.13-15 as a stable for his horses and delivery trucks. In 1969, it became a psychedelic club called the Ark, before morphing into Boston Tea Party, a legendary rock haunt. In the 1970s, before moving to New York to open Studio 54, Steve Rubell took over and transformed the club into a glittering disco. After a series of incarnations, the building became the site of Avalon and Axis in the 1990s and is now home to the Boston chapter of the **House of Blues** (*see p188*).

Mere steps from Lansdowne Street sits historic **Fenway Park** (4 Yawkey Way, 1-877 733 7699, www.redsox.com), home of the Boston Red Sox. The celebrated baseball stadium opened on 20 April 1912, just days after the Titanic sank. For decades, fans thought it must have been an omen, as the Sox didn't win a World Series for 86 years; this was also put down to the 'Curse of the Bambino', after owner Harry Frazee sold Babe Ruth to the New York Yankees in 1919. However, the spell was famously broken in 2004, an event depicted in the US film adaptation of Nick Hornby's novel *Fever Pitch*. The most famous part of the stadium is its 37-foot high left-field wall, known affectionately as the Green Monster. Guided tours are available.

Sights & Museums

★ Isabella Stewart Gardner Museum

25 Evans Way, at the Fenway (1-617 566 1401, www.gardnermuseum.org). Museum of Fine Arts T. **Open** 11am-5pm Mon, Wed, Fri-Sun; 11am-9pm Thur. **Admission** $15; $5-$12 reductions; free under-18s. **Map** p91 D3 ㉜

As remarkable as its founder, the eccentric socialite and patron of the arts who was the inspiration for Isabel Archer in Henry James's *The Portrait of a Lady*, the Gardner museum is a lavish reconstruction

Fenway Park

EXPLORE

of a 15th-century Venetian palace, complete with a exquisite interior courtyard with a seasonally changing floral display. Initially conceived by Gardner and her husband Jack to house the growing collection of art and objects amassed during their extensive travels, the museum only came into being after Jack's death. It opened in 1903, with the widowed Gardner residing on the fourth floor until she died in 1924. She wanted the arrangement of the architecture and artworks to engage the imagination, so every item in the 2,500-piece collection, spanning European, Asian and Islamic art from classical times to the turn of the 20th century, is meticulously placed according to her personal instructions.

The result is an idiosyncratic mix of paintings, sculptures, tapestries, rare books and furniture. Among the many highlights are John Singer Sargent's *El Jaleo*, Titian's *Europa* and works by Botticelli, Rembrandt and Raphael. In 1990, 13 works, including Rembrandts, a Vermeer and Degas drawings, were stolen in America's largest art heist, and the empty spaces – which can't be filled under the terms of Gardner's will – are a poignant sight. Most of the works aren't labelled, but there are laminated guides in each room (and online). In 2012, the museum opened a glass, brick and pre-patinated-copper wing designed by architect Renzo Piano. Now the main entrance ot the museum, it houses a

guests' 'living room' (where you can browse a library of books illuminating the collection), a café and a gift shop as well as concert venue Calderwood Hall and gallery space for special exhibitions.

▶ *For more on the founder's eccentricities, see above* **In the Know**.

★ Museum of Fine Arts

465 Huntington Avenue, at Museum Road (1-617 267 9300, www.mfa.org). Museum of Fine Arts T. **Open** 10am-4.45pm Mon, Tue, Sat, Sun; 10am-9.45pm Wed-Fri. **Admission** $25; $10-$23 reductions; free under-7s; free under-18s Mon-Fri after 3pm, Sat, Sun & school holidays. Pay what you wish 4-9.45pm Wed. **Map** p91 D4 ❸
Founded in 1870, the MFA moved from Copley Square to its current home, a neoclassical granite building on Huntington Avenue – the so-called Avenue of the Arts – in 1909. The globe-spanning collection encompasses 500,000 objects. Of particular note are the collection of American art, including Paul Revere's silver Liberty Bowl and paintings by John Singleton Copley; the Egyptian collection, much of which was acquired through excavations in conjunction with Harvard University in the first half of the 20th century; the Japanese collection (the first in America, and one of the finest in the world); and the Impressionist and post-Impressionist paintings, including an impressive array by Monet – the second largest collection of his work in the US.

The Upper Rotunda in the centre of the building is adorned by John Singer Sargent's spectacular murals, which pay tribute to the museum's role as guardian of the arts through references to Greek mythology. As well as the vast permanent collection, all of which is presented in an accessible way with a contemporary eye for design and placement, the

Museum of Fine Arts.

EXPLORE

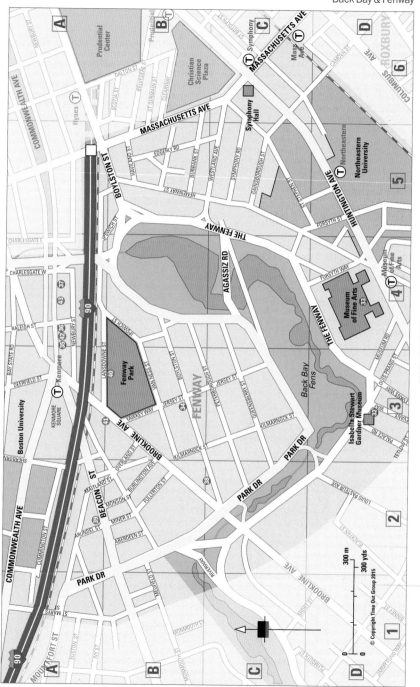

EXPLORE

MFA hosts major temporary exhibitions on such diverse themes as couture fashion, Spanish master Francisco Goya and American ceramics.

Five years and $345 million in the making, the new glass and granite Art of the Americas wing (covering North, Central and South America), designed by Foster & Partners (famous for the contemporary revamp of the British Museum's Great Court and the Gherkin in London, among other buildings) opened in 2010.

Refuelling options comprise three cafés and a more formal restaurant, Bravo. There's also a programme of arthouse films and festivals and, increasingly, new and world music, in the Remis Auditorium and outdoors in the Calderwood Courtyard.

Restaurants & Cafés

Citizen Public House & Oyster Bar

1310 Boylston Street, at Jersey Street (1-617 450 9000, www.citizenpub.com). Fenway or Kenmore T. **Open** 5pm-2am Mon-Sat; 11am-2am Sun. **Main courses** $14-$23. **Map** p91 B3 ③④ American/seafood

There's no complaining about the beer options on tap and cocktails here, but the real draw is the 100-plus whiskey varieties poured at this welcoming pub/eaterie. The oyster bar is a great option for fresh, local bivalves from Wellfleet (Cape Cod) and Island Creek (Duxbury). The star on the menu is the ground sirloin burger, but fancier diners may opt for the hanger steak frites or risotto con funghi. Pop in at the weekend to brunch on huevos rancheros or buttermilk ricotta pancakes.

Eastern Standard

Hotel Commonwealth, 500 Commonwealth Avenue, at Kenmore Square (1-617 532 9100, www.easternstandardboston.com). Kenmore T. **Open** 7am-2am daily. **Main courses** $20-$36. **Map** p91 A4 ③⑤ Brasserie

For some, it evokes the Gare du Nord; for others, New York's buzzy Grand Central without the trains; above all, this big, bustling American brasserie is a smash hit, accessible in every sense of the word. It's open early and closes late, is staffed by energetic, expert mixologists and knowledgeable servers, and is frequented by folks who know where to go for a fabulous meal, whether or not it's during baseball season (Fenway Park is around the corner). The huge bar and heated patio are big pluses. The menu is deceptively simple but appealing, sneaking in oodles of offal between the chilled shellfish and comfort classics such as steak frites and schnitzel.

Island Creek Oyster Bar

Hotel Commonwealth, 500 Commonwealth Avenue, at Kenmore Street (1-617 532 5300, www.islandcreekoysterbar.com). Kenmore T. **Open** 4-11pm Mon-Thur; 4-11.30pm Fri, Sat; 10.30am-11pm Sun. **Main courses** $16-$36. **Map** p91 A4 ③⑥ Seafood

Sustainably farmed year-round in Duxbury Bay, Island Creek bivalves are sweet, briny and delectably fresh. Expectations are high for any restaurant bearing the farm's name – and Island Creek Oyster Bar exceeds them. The space blends the rustic romance of the oyster farm with the polish of next-door neighbour Eastern Standard (chef Jeremy Sewall and bar manager Jackson Cannon have their hands in both spaces). A long bar reminiscent of Duxbury Bay's Powder Point Bridge anchors the front, while tables filled with locals, suits, trendsetters and students stretch towards the rear, where the back wall is lined with lobster cages filled with oyster shells, creating a mesmerising texture of grey ripples and crags.

Petit Robert Bistro

468 Commonwealth Avenue, near Charlesgate West (1-617 375 0699, www.petitrobertbistro. com). Kenmore T. **Open** 11am-11pm daily. **Main courses** $14-$27. **Map** p91 A4 ③⑦ French

There is no shortage of French bistros in Boston, yet this authentic stalwart, owned by *Maître Cuisinier de France* Jacky Robert, makes it all look supremely easy. Comfortable, unfussy and affordable, his townhouse kitchen reacquaints diners with the hearty joys of proper quenelles, no-nonsense soupe à l'oignon gratinée and boeuf bourguignon – topped off with a terrific, rustic tarte tatin.

Other location 480 Columbus Avenue, at Rutland Square, South End (1-617 867 0600).

★ Sweet Cheeks Q

1381 Boylston Street, at Brookline Avenue (1-617 266 1300, www.sweetcheeksq.com). Kenmore T then 15mins walk, or Fenway T. **Open** 11.30am-10pm Mon-Wed, Sun; 11.30am-11pm Thur-Sat. **Main courses** $18-$26. **Map** p91 C2 ③⑧ Barbecue

The brainchild of Tiffani Faison (of *Top Chef* fame), this barbecue haven is a rustic, kick-back find in the Fenway – and a great pre- or post-Sox game hotspot, where main dishes are served on metal trays, cocktails come in mason jars, and napkins and silverware are plucked from cans on the table. On warm nights, hit the pavement seating. Start with the bucket o' biscuits with honey butter – because one won't do. Pair the brisket or buttermilk fried chicken with Faison's famous farm salad (brussels sprouts, faro, grapes) or broccoli casserole. The giant Nutter-Butter cookie and rich and creamy butterscotch pudding is the right way to end the evening.

Bars

Audubon Boston

838 Beacon Street, at Arundel Street (1-617 421 1910, www.audubonboston.com). Kenmore T. **Open** 11.30am-1am Mon-Sat; 11am-1am Sun. **Map** p91 A2 ③⑨

Bleacher Bar.

A sleek alternative to the busy bars near Fenway Park, this great neighbourhood spot just got even better. Since being taken over by the owners of Somerville gem Trina's Starlite Lounge (*see p165*), Audubon's potential has finally been realised. The expanded beer list includes highbrow and lowbrow choices, and the creative cocktails feature house-made syrups and unlikely combinations. There's also an inventive food menu, served from lunchtime until late. If you happen here on a summer day, head out back for one of the best (and semi-secret) patios in the city.

Bleacher Bar

82A Lansdowne Street, between Brookline Avenue & Ipswich Street (1-617 262 2424, www.bleacherbarboston.com). Kenmore T. **Open** 11am-1am Mon-Wed, Sun; 11am-2am Thur-Sat. **Map** p91 B3 ④

A tour of Fenway Park isn't complete without a stop-off at Bleacher Bar. Featuring a full-on view from below the field, this annex of the oldest baseball stadium in the country has a nigh-on unbeatable cachet among the city's sports fans, despite being relatively new. Beer is the order of the day here: there's an extensive menu of bottles and draughts; the eccentric few who enjoy a cocktail with their baseball should look elsewhere.

Boston Beer Works

61 Brookline Avenue, at Lansdowne Street (1-617 536 2337, www.beerworks.net). Fenway or Kenmore T. **Open** 11am-1am daily. **Map** p91 B3 ④

Beer Works' two locations draw tons of tourists, thanks to their proximity to monster sports venues. One has a view of Fenway Park, the other is a stone's throw from TD Garden. Both brewpubs feature the same multi-tiered, gridded aluminium look with oblique angles, which will have you thinking you've stumbled into a space station that happens to serve alcohol. Once you get past the theme-park aesthetic, you'll discover some great beer. The in-house brews

have Boston-y names such as Paul Revere Rye Lager and Boston Garden Golden. The Bunker Hill Blueberry beer, which has a light, fruity taste, is really all about the optics, as the blueberries waft up and down like sea monkeys.
Other location 110 Canal Street, at Valenti Way, West End (1-617 896 2337).

Hawthorne

Hotel Commonwealth, 500 Commonwealth Avenue, at Kenmore Street (1-617 532 9150, www.thehawthornebar.com). Kenmore T. **Open** 5pm-1am daily. **Map** p91 A4 ④

Local mixology mover and shaker Jackson Cannon's swanky lounge is spread over several subterranean rooms in the Hotel Commonwealth. It can be difficult to find a free space on one of the couches, but the classic cocktails and small plates are worth the wait. The bar recently traded its hefty drinks menu for a weekly changing 'bookmark' – a slim slip of featured cocktails such as the Phil Collins (cucumber vodka, chartreuse, lime and soda) and the Dutch Oven (barrel-aged Bols Genever, bitters and absinthe).
▶ *Jackson Cannon also designed the drinks menus for Eastern Standard; see p92.*

Lower Depths Tap Room

476 Commonwealth Avenue, between Charlesgate West & Kenmore Street (1-617 266 6662, www. thelowerdepths.com). Kenmore T. **Open** 11.30am-1am daily. **No credit cards. Map** p91 A4 ④

The name comes from a dour Russian play, and the theme is life in the pits of despair – a concept trumpeted by a huge mural depicting such famous depressives as Sid Vicious and Patti Smith. Join the mug club and you get six months to drink your way through more than 150 beers, which works out at nearly a glass a day. The prize? A personalised 25oz mug. You can fill it anytime, in case you haven't lost your taste for the brown stuff. Try the rare Belgian beer, Duvel Tripel Hop, which has a champagne-like effervescence and sugary taste.

EXPLORE

South End

Sandwiched between the affluent Back Bay and the working class, predominantly African-American Roxbury, the South End was a shabby-chic 'gay ghetto' in the 1980s, where enterprising young urbanites found affordable period apartments in the heart of the city. Now as sought-after as its neighbour Back Bay, but a lot trendier, it still has a substantial gay presence, though gentrification has priced many people out of the neighbourhood. These days, the area is still decidedly chic but not at all shabby, brimming with stylish restaurants, lively bars and independent boutiques selling fashion, furnishings and gifts.

A longstanding bastion of creativity, the warehouses in the once-sketchy zone south of Washington Street (known as SoWa) that house studios and galleries have been transformed into a one-stop weekend destination for art, shopping and food.

EXPLORE

SoWa Sundays.

Don't Miss

1 Coppa Award-winning Italian cuisine in an adorable setting (p100).

2 Delux Café The ultimate neo-dive bar (p102).

3 Bobby from Boston The city's best vintage menswear (p103).

4 Farm & Fable Even non-cooks will enjoy browsing the curated kitchenware (p103).

5 SoWa Sundays This seasonal market encompasses crafts, food, art and vintage goods (p99).

Mills Gallery. *See p98.*

THE SOUTH END

Back Bay, Mass Ave or Tufts Medical Center T, or Silver Line Washington Street.

A five-minute stroll south of Copley Square brings you to the **Landmark District**, near the junction of Clarendon and Tremont Streets. This is the core of the South End, and its name derives from its status as a protected neighbourhood since 1983. It's an attractive, smartly arranged part of the city – the original street plan was laid out by celebrated Boston architect Charles Bulfinch, and the South End contains the largest collection of Victorian cast iron-girded rowhouses in the country.

In contrast to its neighbour Back Bay, the South End, with its English-style squares, was built for the mercantile class. In the 20th century, however, the area fell into disrepair as economic depression struck. By the mid 1970s, many original buildings

had been demolished; others fell victim to arson. But through the efforts of concerned citizens, who founded the South End Historical Society, the neighbourhood was restored and subsequently gained its protected status.

The South End's two parallel arteries, Tremont and Washington Streets, are at the centre of the area's thriving restaurant and bar scenes. It also has a rich cache of culture. The sprawling **Boston Center for the Arts** (*see p199*) occupies the block of Tremont Street between Berkeley and Clarendon Streets. An organ factory in the 19th century, the complex now contains four performance spaces and the large, light-filled **Mills Gallery** as well as artists' studios. The administrative headquarters and studios of the Boston Ballet are also here. The building's centrepiece is the **Cyclorama**, a circular, domed structure built in 1884 to exhibit Paul Dominique Philippoteaux' massive painting of the Civil War Battle of Gettysburg. The painting went on tour five years later, never to return – it's now on display in Gettysburg. The Cyclorama itself has served as a roller-skating arena, flower market and factory, and now hosts events and the occasional performance. The complex also contains restaurant, bar and entertainment venue the **Beehive**, which was designed in collaboration with local artists; the funky decor includes bars made from reclaimed materials, and avant-garde loos.

While there has been an artistic presence here since the 1960s, in recent years the area south of Washington Street, **SoWa**, has exploded into a bona fide contemporary art district. The

IN THE KNOW
FRIDAY NIGHT ARTS

On the first Friday of every month, many SoWa-based artists throw open their studio doors to let visitors peek behind the creative curtain. Sip wine while chatting with local painters and photographers before browsing some two dozen nearby galleries, all of which stay open late. See www.sowaboston.com for more info.

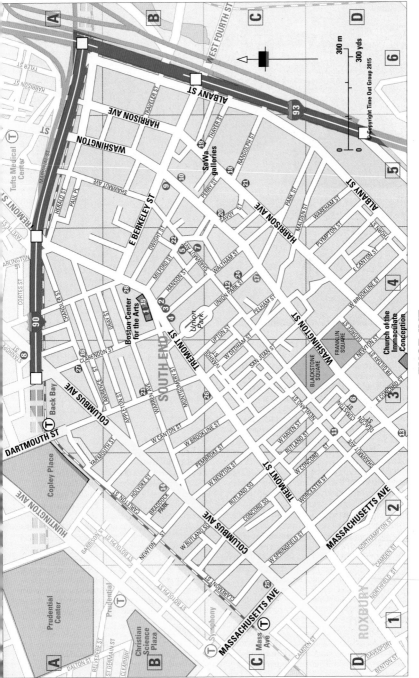

South End

EXPLORE

B&G Oysters.

converted warehouse at **450 Harrison Avenue** houses more than 70 artists' studios and 15 galleries (www.sowaartistsguild.com). The enclave now also includes shops, eateries and regular markets (*see p99* **SoWa So Good**), and upscale condos are proliferating in the vicinity.

Small shops, selling everything from kids' gear and pet accoutrements to fashion and chic home accessories, are clustered throughout the South End. As you head south-west, towards Mass Ave and Roxbury beyond, the area has a rougher edge, but gentrification has spread here too, with eateries including Ken Oringer's tapas bar **Toro** and pastry chef Joanne Chang's **Flour Bakery & Café** on this stretch of Washington Street.

Behind Columbus Avenue, the 4.7 mile **Southwest Corridor Park** cuts through the urban landscape, dotted with playgrounds and dog-exercising parks. Designed as a 'new strand' of the Emerald Necklace (*see p84* **In the Know**) at the end of the 1980s, it starts at Back Bay T station and follows the Orange Line underneath it through the South End and Roxbury to Jamaica Plain.

Sights & Museums

Mills Gallery

Boston Center for the Arts, 551 Tremont Street, at Clarendon Street, South End (1-617 426 8835, www.bcaonline.org). Back Bay T. **Open** noon-5pm Wed, Sun; noon-9pm Thur-Sat. **Map** p97 B4 ❶

One of the most experimental galleries in town, the BCA's exhibition space is best known for hosting unusual collaborative group shows in a variety of media, including performance and process-focused art. Committed to nurturing emerging talent, the gallery presents work by artists based in the organisation's studio building in an annual showcase. *Photo p96.*

Restaurants & Cafés

Addis Red Sea

544 Tremont Street, at Hanson Street (1-617 426 8727, www.addisredsea.com). Back Bay or Tufts Medical Center T, then 15mins walk. **Open** 5-11pm Mon-Fri; noon-11pm Sat, Sun. **Main courses** $8-$15. **Map** p97 B4 ❷ **Ethiopian**

If you've never scooped up a dollop of *kitfo* with a hunk of soft, spongy *injera* while seated around a multicoloured *mesob*, or if you don't even know what all that means, then this much-loved Ethiopian charmer will come as an eye-opening treat. Brightly hued woven baskets act as tables, flatbread replaces flatware and a typical meal centres on spicy, stew-like mélanges, with the soothing counterbalance of honey wine. There are plenty of options for vegetarians too.

B&G Oysters

550 Tremont Street, at Waltham Street (1-617 423 0550, www.bandgoysters.com). Back Bay or Tufts Medical Center T, then 15mins walk.

SOWA SO GOOD

The arty enclave has morphed into a culture, shopping and eating hub.

For decades, the area south of Washington Street was a derelict wasteland of vacant industrial buildings best avoided after dark. But a redevelopment boom that began in the early 2000s helped reshape it into a creative enclave, as artists were invited to rent warehouse space on Harrison Avenue and its side streets at below-market prices. That evolution attracted premier Newbury Street galleries such as **Miller Yezerski Gallery** (1-617 262 0550, www.milleryezerskigallery. com) and **Chase Young Gallery**, 1-617 859 7222, www.chaseyounggallery.com), which joined the scrappy art spaces in the up-and-coming area. Today, SoWa is a catch-all of galleries, indie boutiques, restaurants and markets – not to mention pricey real estate. Most of the action is clustered around 450 and 460 Harrison Avenue, at Thayer Street. Note that not all businesses are open every day, so check the websites or call before setting out.

MOHR MCPHERSON

The two-storey furniture and accessories store (460 Harrison Avenue, 1-617 210 7900, www.mohr-mcpherson.com) traffics in Asian imports both small and big-ticket, from grain pots and steel lanterns to table lamps and hand-carved armoires (worldwide shipping can be arranged). A recent expansion added a downstairs café; grab a latte before meandering through the store's rug gallery and discount warehouse, both located several doors down.

GALERIA CUBANA

Michelle Wojcik's glass-enclosed space (460 Harrison Avenue, 1-617 292 2822, www.lagaleriacubana.com) is among the area's most exciting galleries, and the only one in New England specialising in contemporary Cuban art. Wojcik regularly travels to the island nation to source prints, watercolours, mixed-media and sculptural pieces from more than a dozen artists.

GALVIN-IZED HEADWEAR

Self-taught milliner Marie Galvin's lower-level shop (Suite 67, 450 Harrison Avenue, 1-617 834 2910, www.galvinized-hats.com) bursts with artful, handmade Derby hats, feather headbands, wedding veils, and over-the-top fascinators. Actress Jessica Alba is just one of the designer's high-profile fans.

SIMPLEMENTE BLANCO

Most of us merely aspire to an all-white aesthetic; Fernanda Bourlot has made it her calling. The interior designer's pristine home store (Gallery 15, 460 Harrison Avenue, 1-617 734 3669, www.simplementeblanco. com) stocks alabaster linens, china, soaps, and even gardening accessories – just leave the coffee outside.

BOBBY FROM BOSTON

Bobby Garnett is the grandfather of the city's vintage shopping scene. His clubby two-room emporium (see p103) specialises in menswear, including varsity sweaters, leather bomber jackets, Borsalino hats and bow ties. The smaller women's section in back offers a curated selection of slinky cocktail dresses as well as a range of pristine handbags.

SOWA SUNDAYS

Plugged-in Bostonians know spring has arrived when SoWa Sundays (May-Oct, www.sowasundays.com) start up again. The outdoor bazaar sprawls across several blocks, and includes a farmer's market, artisanal food vendors, plus art, clothing and home accessories from regional designers. There's also an always-mobbed food truck court and a year-round indoor vintage market at 460 Harrison Avenue.

SoWa Sundays.

EXPLORE

Open 11.30am-10pm Mon; 11.30am-11pm Tue-Fri; noon-11pm Sat; noon-10pm Sun. **Main courses** $26-$33. **Map** p97 B4 ❸
Fish & seafood

'Bivalves', reads a hand-shaped sign on the gate, pointing you towards Barbara Lynch's diminutive, understated oyster bar. Decor so coolly clean that it's practically scrubbed sets the tone for an ever-changing array of oysters from both coasts, complemented by dozens of mostly white wines offered by the glass. The menu is supplemented by a small but sparkling (if rather costly) selection of seafood-centric appetisers and mains.

▶ *The Butcher Shop (see below), also owned by Barbara Lynch, is just across the road.*

Butcher Shop

552 Tremont Street, at Waltham Street (1-617 423 4800, www.thebutchershopboston.com). Back Bay or Tufts Medical Center T, then 15mins walk. **Open** noon-10pm Mon, Sun; noon-11pm Tue-Thur; noon-midnight Fri, Sat. **Main courses** $19-$22. **Map** p97 B4 ❹
French/bar

It's polished, it's chic, it's packed with designer-clad South Enders swirling wine goblets and nibbling on pâté, it's… a butcher's shop? Yes, indeed – as well as a cosy soapstone-and-slate wine bar. Owner Barbara Lynch stocks the display cases with every delicacy, from pigs' heads and whole hams to quails' eggs and truffle butter, and fills the short menu with equally delicious simple fare. House-made charcuterie and antipasti is accompanied by a selection of mostly European boutique reds.

▶ *After a bite or two, regulars often cross the street to B&G Oysters, also owned by Barbara Lynch, to complete their surf-and-turf crawl.*

★ Coppa

253 Shawmut Avenue, at Milford Street (1-617 391 0902, www.coppaboston.com). Silver Line to Washington Street at E Berkeley Street. **Open** noon-10pm Mon-Thur; noon-11pm Fri; 5-11pm Sat; 11am-10pm Sun. **Main courses** $14-$27. **Map** p97 B4 ❺ Italian

Never mind sitting elbow-to-elbow with your neighbour at this shoebox of a wood-and-brick enoteca. The famous wood-fired pizzas (especially the Parma, with mozzarella, tomato, rocket and prosciutto di parma), robust pastas and small-plate bar snacks (beef-heart pastrami *crostini* with harissa) make this cosy nook worth the tight squeeze. Owners Ken Oringer and Jamie Bissonnette (both James Beard Award-winning chefs) introduced the trend for topping everything from pastas to pizzas with a farm-fresh egg, with delicious results. But be warned: although prices appear to be more than reasonable, even on the Italian-only wines and craft beers, the half-portion pastas, small bites and four-slice pizzas are pleasing enough to tempt you into ordering more than your stomach – or wallet – can handle.

$ Flour Bakery + Cafe

1595 Washington Street, at Rutland Street (1-617 267 4300, www.flourbakery.com). Massachusetts Avenue T then 15mins walk, or Silver Line Washington Street to W Newton Street. **Open** 7am-9pm Mon-Fri; 8am-6pm Sat; 8am-5pm Sun. **Main courses** $10-$13. **Map** p97 C3 ❻ Bakery/café

In 2000, Flour put this then-desolate stretch of Washington Street on the culinary map – and X still marks Joanne Chang's sweet spot for those in search of the perfect brioche. Blue pastel hues and a chalkboard menu make this place as cute as a cupcake – or

Flour Bakery + Cafe.

any of the other goodies gracing the counter, for that matter. Chang won the Food Network's *Throwdown with Bobby Flay* for her sticky buns, but she and her staff also deliver fat chocolate-chip macaroons that could convert sworn coconut-loathers. The sandwiches are no mere afterthought – the applewood-smoked BLT and smoked turkey with cranberry chutney (recipes in her cookbooks) are big sellers. **Other locations** 131 Clarendon Street, Back Bay, (1-617 437 7700); 12 Farnsworth Street, Fort Point Channel, Waterfront (1-617 338 4333); 190 Massachusetts Avenue, Central Square, Cambridge (1-617 225 2525).

Franklin Café

278 Shawmut Avenue, at Hanson Street (1-617 350 0010, www.franklincafe.com). Back Bay or Tufts Medical Center T then 15mins walk, or Silver Line to Washington St at Union Park. **Open** 5pm-2am daily. **Main courses** $10-$20. **Map** p97 B4 **7** American

Tiny, dark and pretty much packed from cocktail hour to the wee hours, the Franklin is a favourite local haunt with a cosy bar and booths – great for quality cocktails and late-night creative-American comfort eats (rosemary roasted half chicken; *cioppino* of hake, mussels and clams in a tomato-fennel broth). The kitchen stays open until 1.30am, a rarity in town and often a draw for off-the-clock chefs. Plus, the price is right: all plates are $20 and under. The friendly buzz, funky music and laid-back vibe make it worth the wait for a table.

Mistral

223 Columbus Avenue, at Cahners Place (1-617 867 9300, www.mistralbistro.com). Back Bay T. **Open** 5.30-10pm Mon-Thur; 5.30-11pm Fri, Sat; 10.30am-2pm, 5.30-9.30pm Sun. **Main courses** $21-$44. **Map** p97 A3 **8** French/Mediterranean

With its stone floors and potted cypresses, sunnily sophisticated Mistral brings a touch of swish Saint-Tropez to the edge of the Mass Pike. This place has been on the A-listers' shortlist since it opened. For our part, we wish chef-owner Jamie Mammano would tinker a tad more often with the items on his rarely changing French-Mediterranean menu – exquisite though they may be – and with their ever-rising prices a little less. But the tête-à-têtes among the beauties and powerbrokers lining the bar are meaty enough to make eavesdropping over cocktails synonymous with feasting.

★ Myers + Chang

1145 Washington Street, at East Berkeley Street (1-617 542 5200, www.myersandchang.com). Back Bay T then 15mins walk. **Open** 11.30am-10pm Mon-Thur, Sun; 11.30am-11pm Fri-Sat. **Main courses** $14-$20. **Map** p97 B5 **9** Asian fusion

Not to be confused with chain restaurant giant PF Changs, this hip South End gem serves Asian fusion cuisine from local culinary darling Joanne Chang (Flour) and restaurateur Christopher Myers. Menu highlights include fall-off-the-bone tea-smoked spare ribs, spring rolls with a ginger dipping sauce, and exceptional dan dan noodles. The vibrant but intimate spot is great for couples – especially on Mondays and Tuesdays between 5pm and 10pm when the prix fixe meal for two is just $45. 'Cheap date night' menu options include the 'Bro Date' and 'It's Complicated'.

Oishii

1166 Washington Street, at East Berkeley Street (1-617 482 8868, www.oishiiboston.com). Tufts Medical Center T, or Silver Line Washington Street at E Berkeley Street. **Open** noon-3pm, 5.30pm-midnight Tue-Sat; 1-10pm Sun. **Main courses** $20-$120. **Map** p97 B5 **10** Japanese

Cross a Zen meditation garden with a slick postmodern lounge and what do you get? Something like the urban outpost of Oishii – which is to say, nothing like the modest 15-seat original in suburban Chestnut Hill. And that's just fine: if anyone's earned the right to show off a bit, it's the folks who brought Bostonians their first taste of Tokyo-grade sushi. Hype, you scoff? Go for the *omakase*, a multi-course meal composed of the chef's selections, before you answer that question. The spectacularly colourful combinations look as sensational as they taste. **Other location** 612 Hammond Street, Chestnut Hill (1-617 277 7888).

Orinoco: A Latin Kitchen

477 Shawmut Avenue, at West Concord Street (1-617 369 7075, www.orinocokitchen.com). Massachusetts Avenue T. **Open** noon-2.30pm, 6-9.30pm Tue-Sat; 11am-3pm, 5.30-9pm Sun. **Main courses** $13.50-$20. **Map** p97 C3 **11** Venezuelan

Amid the upscale boutiques and dog bakeries of the hyper-gentrified South End, this twinkling little tribute to the Venezuelan roadside restaurant known as a *taguarita* comes as a total surprise. So does the bold yet delicately nuanced food, served in a mask-and basket-lined dining room. The smaller plates in particular burst with flavours and textures: after a round of *antojitos* such as cheese-filled, deep-fried plantain chunks and rich, gooey bacon-wrapped dates, share a couple of the stuffed corn pockets called *arepas* – the shredded beef and mojo-laced roast pork really stand out. **Other locations** 22 Harvard Street, Brookline Village (1-617 232 9505); 56 JFK Street, Harvard Square, Cambridge (1-617 354 6900).

South End Buttery

314 Shawmut Avenue, at Union Park Street (1-617 482 1015, www.southendbuttery.com). Back Bay T then 15mins walk. **Open** 6.30am-10pm Mon-Thur, Sun; 6.30am-11pm Fri, Sat. **Main courses** $16-$23. **Map** p97 C4 **12** Eclectic

EXPLORE

Boston brunchers know that the South End is the place to be every Sunday morning, but this popular bakery-café doesn't just do brunch – by night it's a bona fide restaurant with a full liquor licence. Enter through the café and descend into the grotto-like subterranean dining room, where cosy banquettes and colourful bud vases decorate the fireplace-warmed space. The menu is short but varied, with options that range from braised beef cheeks, steak frites and eggplant parmigiana to a choice of house-made veggie burgers such as the beet and goat's cheese.

Toro

1704 Washington Street, at East Springfield Street (1-617 536 4300, www.toro-restaurant. com). Massachusetts Avenue T then 15mins walk. **Open** noon-3pm, 5.30pm-midnight Mon-Thur; noon-3pm, 5.30pm-1am Fri; 4.30pm-1am Sat; 10.30am-midnight Sun. **Main courses** $17-$38. **Map** p97 D3 ⑬ **Spanish**

Ken Oringer's smash take on a *taperia* is an atmospheric spot. With its exposed brick and wooden beams, central communal table and blackboard chalked with drinks specials, it effortlessly captures the rustic spirit of Spain – which its customers invariably catch in turn, swigging wine from juice glasses or cava from *porrónes*. The food is superb. Buttery, cider-simmered foie gras sausage, immaculate salt cod croquettes and seasonal treats showcasing glass eels or green chickpeas prove the much-touted grilled corn with aioli and crumbled *cotija* (pungent aged cheese) is no fluke.

Bars

Anchovies

433 Columbus Avenue, at Braddock Park (1-617 266 5088, www.anchoviesboston.com). Back Bay or Prudential T. **Open** 4pm-2am Mon-Sat; 3pm-2am Sun. **Map** p97 B2 ㉔

If you're all bistro'd out (always a risk in the South End), Anchovies is the perfect antidote. A cosy little hole in the wall with simple, tasty Italian vittles, a solid beer selection and a bar packed with the friendliest regulars you're likely to find in town – which means get there earlyish.

Beehive

Boston Center for the Arts, 541 Tremont Street, at Clarendon Street (1-617 423 0069, www. beehiveboston.com). Back Bay T, or Silver Line Washington Street to Union Park Street. **Open** 5pm-1am Mon-Wed; 5pm-2am Thur, Fri; 10am-2am Sat; 10am-1am Sun. **Map** p97 B4 ⑮

An annex of the Boston Center for the Arts, Beehive is a madly buzzing bohemia. Whimsical textiles, wild paintings and other odd objets offset the loft-like restaurant/bar/entertainment venue's exposed-brick grittiness, while some of the city's best-known bartenders mix the drinks. In short, Beehive is a capital-S scene. The kitchen whips up

fun, Mediterranean-tinged nibbles, salads and communal platters to fuel the revelry, plus a few main courses for square-meal sticklers.

★ Delux Café

100 Chandler Street, at Clarendon Street (1-617 338 5258). Back Bay T. **Open** 5pm-1am daily. **No credit cards. Map** p97 A3 ⑯

After briefly closing for renovations, this classic South End hole in the wall reopened in 2014 with long-time employees taking the helm. The new owners spruced up the place just enough to make it more comfortable while leaving the old spirit and kitschy eccentricities largely intact. The walls are still plastered with classic records (though different selections are showcased), the old TV still plays reruns of classic cartoons and sitcoms, and there's still a decade's worth of graffiti in the bathroom. The beers are craftier, the liquor selection more diverse, and while the food menu has expanded slightly, it still offers old favourites, such as roast chicken and quesadillas with apple salsa. Small, cosy and friendly, Delux continues to serve some of the best (and best-priced) gourmet bar food around, from one of the smallest kitchens in the city.

Gallows

1395 Washington Street, at Union Park Street (1-617 425 0200, www.thegallowsboston.com). Back Bay T. **Open** 5pm-midnight Mon-Wed; 11.30am-1am Thur-Sat; 11am-11pm Sun. **Map** p97 C4 ⑰

Situated near the spot where public hangings were performed in colonial times, the Gallows plays up its macabre location with an ominous black crow sign above the door. But inside, the bar has an unassuming vibe and an inventive cocktail list that highlights original concoctions including liquor infusions and disappearing old-timey ingredients such as mead and whey. The sangria ironically employs cheap and fruity Boone's Farm Strawberry Hill, while the dinner menu offers an extensive list of boards, burgers and poutine options for top-notch gourmet bar bites.
▶ *The gastropub is branching out with a nearby doughnut shop (see p104 Baking Hot).*

Shops & Services

Ars Libri

500 Harrison Avenue, at Randolph Street (1-617 357 5212, www.arslibri.com). Back Bay T then 15mins walk, or Silver Line Washington Street to E Berkeley Street. **Open** 10am-6pm Mon-Fri; 11am-5pm Sat. **Map** p97 C5 ⑱ **Books & music**

With tomes on everyone from Henri Matisse to David Hockney, this sprawling store is a haven for art history buffs. Set on the outskirts of the South End, Ars Libri specialises in rare and out-of-print books on fine art. Check the website for details of the latest art exhibition at the in-store satellite of the Robert Klein Gallery.

Delux Café.

▶ *Ars Libri is just a few buildings down from a cluster of contemporary galleries at 450 Harrison Avenue; see p98.*

★ Bobby from Boston
19 Thayer Street, at Harrison Avenue (1-617 423 9299). Back Bay T then 15mins walk, or Silver Line Washington Street to E Berkeley Street. **Open** noon-6pm Tue-Sat. **No credit cards. Map** p97 B5 ⓳
Fashion
Bobby Garnett's fabulous vintage emporium smack in the middle of the SoWa arts district is well known to Japanese denim aficionados, movie wardrobe professionals and local rockers. The pristine stock spans the 1930s to the '70s and, although women's clothes are sold, the focus is on menswear. Here, you'll find $30 pairs of 501s and three-figure vintage versions, American sportswear and lots of cool suits, including English labels from the 1960s.

Brix Wine Shop
1284 Washington Street, at Savoy Street (1-617 542 2749, www.brixwineshop.com). Back Bay T then 20mins walk, or Silver Line Washington Street to E Berkeley Street. **Open** 11am-9pm Mon-Sat; noon-6pm Sun. **Map** p97 C5 ⓴ **Food & drink**
Displaying an impressive sense of style and a flair for hospitality, this lovely cork-floored wine 'boutique' is known for its weekly wine tastings, which showcase the smaller producers (from both Europe and the New World) that its buyers specialise in seeking out.

December Thieves
524 Harrison Avenue, at Savoy Street (1-617 375 7879, www.decemberthieves.com). Back Bay T then 15mins walk, or Silver Line Washington Street to E Berkeley Street. **Open** 11am-6pm Tue-Thur, Sat; 11am-7pm Fri; 11am-5pm Sun. **Map** p97 C5 ㉑
Accessories
Small in size but large in ambition, this anything goes SoWa boutique stocks hand-screened scarves,

outré art, leather backpacks and sophisticated children's toys. Owner Lana Barakat discovers many of the designers during international travels and also sells pieces from Lazuli, her statement-jewellery line.

★ Farm & Fable
251 Shawmut Avenue, at Milford Street (1-617 451 1110, www.farmandfable.com). Silver Line Washington Street to E Berkeley Street. **Open** 11am-6pm Tue-Sat; 11am-5pm Sun. **Map** p97 B4 ㉒
Homewares
Owner Abigail Ruettgers has managed to marry her duelling passions for cooking and vintage finds at this charming corner store. Home chefs can browse a beautifully curated collection of antique cookbooks and kitchenware alongside new heirlooms like copper pots and hand-stitched aprons. The downstairs kitchen hosts regular local chef demos, mixology classes and other events.

★ Follain
53 Dartmouth Street, at Warren Avenue (1-844 365 5246, www.shopfollain.com). Back Bay T. **Open** 11am-7pm Mon-Sat; noon-6pm Sun. **Map** p97 B3 ㉓ **Health & beauty**
Tara Foley, a longtime natural-beauty blogger, quit her corporate job to pursue her retail dreams, with ravishing results. Her airy apothecary sources only the purest skin, hair and bath products from both local and national brands, including New England favourites like Tammy Fender, Shamanuti and Farmaesthetics. Makeup aficionados will cheer her paraben-free beauty counter.

Hudson
12 Union Park Street, between Shawmut Avenue & Washington Street (1-617 292 0900, www.hudsonboston.com). Back Bay T then 15mins walk, or Silver Line Washington Street to Union Park Street. **Open** 10am-6pm Mon-Wed, Fri, Sat; 11am-7pm Thur; 11am-5pm Sun. **Map** p97 C4 ㉔
Homewares

EXPLORE

BAKING HOT

The latest cult doughnut shops are the antithesis of a certain local chain.

Behemoth franchise Dunkin' Donuts started with a single shop in Quincy (*see p160*) in 1950; today, Boston brims with more than one store per square mile, while the worldwide tally is more than 10,000. But the city that unleashed the monster chain on America and beyond is making amends with a new era of artisanal doughnuts.

Union Square Donuts (20 Bow Street, Union Square, Somerville, 1-617 209 2257, www.unionsquaredonuts.com), which recently relocated to larger premises to satisfy the huge demand, is known for big, fluffy, made-from-scratch doughnuts in such signature flavours as brown butter hazelnut crunch and sea-salted bourbon caramel. Now the cult spot is venturing into savoury varieties such as bacon, cheddar and sage, and spinach, feta and red onion.

Saugus-based **Kane's Donuts**, a mom-and-pop business established in 1955, was, at the time of writing, preparing to open an outpost in Boston's financial district (1 International Place, at Oliver Street, www. kanesdonuts.com). The foodie favourite is known for gigantic doughnuts made from locally sourced ingredients. Popular flavours include the Bismarck and Boston cream, plus seasonal specials such as eggnog for the holidays and peach melba and pink lemonade in summer.

The local doughnut craze has elevated some pastry purveyors to rock-star status. Pop-up doughnut shop **Stacked Donuts**, run by former No9 Park sous chef and one-time *Top Chef* contestant Stephanie Cmar, reportedly sold 200 doughnuts within 20 minutes of opening. Her light, airy and offbeat creations come in flavours including bacon mocha, lemongrass, Lucky Charms and cherry cola. Cmar has since paired up with Justin Burke-Sampson's Trademark Tarts, which sells hand-made pop tarts, to form Party of Two Restaurant Group (www.partyoftwo boston.com); baked goods can be found in restaurants and shops throughout Boston and Cambridge, including **Coppa** and the **Butcher Shop** (for both, *see p100*) in the South End – but, be warned, they sell out fast. The duo hopes to open permanent digs in 2015, so check the website or social media for updates.

South End gastropub the **Gallows** (*see p102*) started featuring savoury Sriracha doughnut breakfast sandwiches on its weekend brunch menu, which proved so popular that owner Rebecca Roth Gullo decided to open a stand-alone doughnut bakery nearby. **Blackbird Doughnuts** (492 Tremont Street, www.blackbirddoughnuts. com) is slated to open by publication of this guide, so keep an eye on the website.

Stacked Donuts.

EXPLORE

Former actress and interior designer Jill Goldberg combines her native New England aesthetic with a laid-back Californian style. Among the creamy, plump armchairs and retro side tables is an array of tempting, unusual items such as an eclectic selection of patterned pillows and one-off vintage pieces.

Olives & Grace.

Laced
569 Columbus Avenue, at Massachusetts Avenue (1-617 262 5223, www.lacedboston.com). Massachusetts Avenue T. **Open** 11am-7pm Mon-Sat; noon-6pm Sun. **Map** p97 C1 ㉕ **Fashion/ skateboards**
On the South End–Roxbury border, this 'lifestyle skate boutique' has serious street cred; local sports stars such as the Red Sox's David Ortiz come here to stock up on bling-tastic limited-edition trainers by the likes of Nike SB and Air Jordan, plus T-shirts, sweatshirts, caps as well as spectacularly decorated boards.

★ Olives & Grace
623 Tremont Street, at West Canton Street, South End (1-617 236 4536, www.olivesandgrace.com). Back Bay T. **Open** 11am-7pm Tue-Fri; 10am-7pm Sat, Sun. **Map** p97 C3 ㉖ **Health & beauty/food & drink/accessories**
'A curtsy to the makers' is the tagline of this beautifully appointed, subterranean boutique. Owner Sofi Madison introduces customers to the finest artisanal finds, from organic beauty products (Fig + Yarrow) to small-batch foodstuffs (Dove & Figs jams) to locally made jewellery (Porcelain & Stone). Madison grants priority to socially conscious purveyors and lures in foot traffic with regular 'Meet the Maker' pop-up events.

Tadpole
58 Clarendon Street, at Chandler Street (1-617 778 1788, www.shoptadpole.com). Back Bay T. **Open** 10am-7pm Mon-Fri; 10am-6pm Sat; noon-5pm Sun. **Map** p97 A3 ㉗ **Children**
Aimed at the thoroughly modern child, Tadpole will outfit your little darling for life in the city with clothes and toys you'll be hard-pressed to find elsewhere. Catering to tykes from newborn to six, stock includes everything from house-designed onesies and T-shirts featuring the iconic Boston Citgo sign to environmentally friendly toy trucks.

Uniform
511 Tremont Street, at Dwight Street, South End (1-617 247 2360, www.uniformboston.com). Back Bay T. **Open** 11am-7pm Tue, Wed; 11am-8pm Thur-Sat; noon-5pm Sun. **Map** p97 B4 ㉘ **Fashion**
A one-stop shop for the fashion-conscious male, with a good selection of smart shirts, casual jackets, shoes and cheeky belt buckles. Uniform also stocks a line of Freitag messenger bags and wallets, made from recycled truck tires, and selected shaving products from the Art of Shaving and Jack Black.

EXPLORE

North End

With its network of narrow, meandering streets and huddled brick rowhouses, many of them fronted by vintage Italian cafés, pastry shops and frenetic restaurants, the North End combines an old New England setting with street scenes straight out of *GoodFellas*. First settled in the early 1630s, it's one of Boston's oldest neighbourhoods. For decades, it has been the city's Italian quarter, and it's probably better known among most Bostonians as a dining destination than for its key role on the road to American independence. As the home of silversmith Paul Revere, the North End was the starting point of his legendary midnight ride to warn rebel troops in Lexington and Concord of the arrival of British redcoats. The area also has links with Boston's most famous political dynasty – John F Kennedy's grandmother, Rose, daughter of the city's mayor, was born here. For decades the North End was quite literally cut off from the rest of the city – before being liberated by the Big Dig project.

EXPLORE

Old North Church.

Don't Miss

1 Paul Revere House Over 300 years of history at the city's sole 17th-century wooden home (p110).

2 Bricco Overwhelmed by the choice of Italian eateries? Head here (p112).

3 Caffe Vittoria The quintessential espresso stop (p112).

4 Old North Church 'One if by land…' (p114).

5 Polcari's Coffee A vintage gem stuffed with local character (p115).

From the late 1950s until 2004, a massive iron girding holding up the elevated six-lane Central Artery created a 40-foot wall separating the historic North End from the rest of downtown Boston – which may be one reason it has retained its distinctive identity. As part of the Big Dig, the traffic that once congested the Central Artery has been rerouted underground to the southbound I-93 tunnel, and the unsightly and noisy hulk of steel dismantled. Long-term residents marvel at the uninterrupted views of – and from – the area's streets. The resulting North End Parks, part of the **Rose F Kennedy Greenway**, are a lovely place for a few minutes' rest in the heart of the city.

The early township at the tip of the Shawmut Peninsula was a maze of two- and three-storey clapboard houses known as saltboxes, but a number of fires – notably the devastating blaze of 1676 – ushered in the age of brick. The area's other memorable disaster was the great molasses flood (*see right* **In the Know**).

Originally a blue-blood bastion, the neighbourhood saw an influx of European immigrants in the mid to late 19th century. First came the Irish, then German, Russian and Polish Jews, followed by a smattering of Portuguese fishermen and, finally, the Italians. By 1920, some 90 per cent of the local population was from central and southern Italy.

Today, that figure has halved and a wave of high-income professionals has moved in to occupy converted loft apartments. Nonetheless, the area retains its Italian flavour. With its tightly clustered red-brick row houses hung with wrought-iron fire escapes, traditional cafés and retro neon signs, all it needs is a Tony Bennett soundtrack to

IN THE KNOW A STICKY END

On 15 January 1919, a giant tank of molasses being stored on Commercial Street for rum-making exploded, sending 2.5 million gallons of the sticky liquid cascading through the streets. Rising to waves of up to 40 feet, the deluge crushed houses and vehicles and dragged 21 people (and 12 horses) to a sugary grave. Some claim that on a hot day you can still smell molasses on Commercial Street.

feel like a scene out of *GoodFellas*. Many locals still buy their provisions from *salumerias*, bakeries and greengrocers. Passers-by greet each other and chat in the streets, often in Italian. Elderly men cluster in modest social clubs or, when the weather is warm enough, drag their folding chairs on to the sidewalk to play backgammon and engage in heated conversations. In summer, street festivals in honour of various saints take over the area nearly every weekend (*see p32* **In the Know**).

NORTH SQUARE

Haymarket or North Station T.

Three of the sites on the Freedom Trail (*see p47* **Trail Blazers**) are in the North End. The best known is the house where silversmith Paul Revere once lived, at 19 North Square. The **Paul Revere House**, the only wooden 17th-century colonial home in central Boston, is worth visiting for its architectural and historical significance. On the other side of the courtyard stands the red-brick Georgian **Pierce/Hichborn House**. Revere's cousin and fellow revolutionary Nathaniel Hichborn lived here from 1781 until his death in 1797. Separated by little more than 30 years, the architectural contrast between the two houses is fascinating – and while Revere's may appear the more primitive of the two, it was in fact a more impressive residence in its day.

Once Walt Whitman's place of worship, the 1833 **Sacred Heart Church** (12 North Square, at North Street, 1-617 523 5638) is across picturesque, cobblestoned North Square. At no.2, a plaque marks the site of the Old North Meeting House, built in 1650, where Puritan preacher Increase Mather and his son Cotton used to preach.

While Revere's story is the area's main claim to fame, another American legend has its roots here. The oldest daughter of congressman John 'Honey Fitz' Fitzgerald (later elected mayor of Boston) was born at 4 Garden Court. Rose Fitzgerald married a fellow named Kennedy, and her sons included President John F Kennedy, Attorney General Robert F Kennedy and Senator Ted Kennedy.

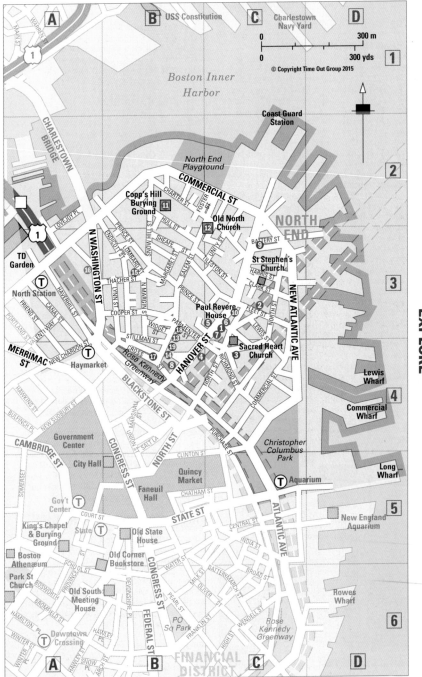

Boston Inner Harbor

Charlestown Navy Yard

USS Constitution

Coast Guard Station

North End Playground

COMMERCIAL ST

CHARTER ST

FOSTER ST

Copp's Hill Burying Ground **11**

Old North Church **12**

NORTH END

BATTERY ST **9**

St Stephen's Church

HARRIS ST

CLARK ST

2

FLEET ST

Paul Revere House **5** **10** **1** **7**

Sacred Heart Church **3**

NEW ATLANTIC AVE

LEWIS ST

COMMERCIAL ST

HANOVER ST **4**

NORTH ST

RICHMOND ST

PRINCE ST

SALEM ST

UNITY ST

HULL ST

SHEAFE ST

MARGARET ST

TILESTON ST

N ST MONS

ENDICOTT ST

LONSDALE ST

PRINCE ST

THACHER ST

LYNN ST

N MARGIN ST

COOPER ST

STILLMAN ST

WIDGET ST

CROSS ST

PARMENTER ST

16

15

N WASHINGTON ST

N Washington St

Rose Kennedy Greenway

17 **14** **8** **13** **19**

TD Garden

1

North Station **T**

HAVERHILL ST

FRIEND ST

CANAL ST

PORTLAND ST

VALENTI WAY

NEW CHARDON ST

Haymarket **T**

MERRIMAC ST

BLACKSTONE ST

NORTH ST

CAMBRIDGE ST

HAWKINS ST

BULFINCH PL

NEW SUDBURY ST

Government Center

City Hall

Gov't Center **T**

COURT ST

King's Chapel & Burying Ground

State **T**

Old State House

T

Faneuil Hall

Quincy Market

UNION ST

SALT LN

MARSHALL ST

CONGRESS ST

CLINTON ST

CHATHAM ST

STATE ST

CENTRAL ST

Christopher Columbus Park

PURCHASE ST

Aquarium **T**

ATLANTIC AVE

Lewis Wharf

Commercial Wharf

Long Wharf

New England Aquarium

Boston Athenæum

Park St Church

Old Corner Bookstore

SCHOOL ST

PROVINCE ST

DEVONSHIRE PL

Old South Meeting House

WATER ST

MILK ST

OLIVER ST

BATTERYMARCH ST

BROAD ST

INDIA ST

Rowes Wharf

Downtown Crossing **T**

FEDERAL ST

CONGRESS ST

PEARL ST

HIGH ST

WENDELL ST

FRANKLIN ST

Rose Kennedy Greenway

PO Sq Park

PEMBERTON SQ

SOMERSET ST

BOSWORTH

BROMFIELD ST

HAMILTON PL

WINTER ST

TEMPLE PL

HAWLEY PL

SNOW PL

ARCH ST

FINANCIAL DISTRICT

0   300 m
0   300 yds

© Copyright Time Out Group 2015

EXPLORE

Sights & Museums

★ Paul Revere House & Pierce/ Hichborn House

19 North Square, between Richmond & Prince Streets (1-617 523 2338, www.paulreverehouse.org). Haymarket T. **Open** *mid Apr-Oct* 9.30am-5.15pm daily. *Nov-Dec, Mar-mid Apr* 9.30am-4.15pm daily. *Jan, Feb* 9.30am-4.15pm Tue-Sun. **Admission** $3.50; $1-$3 reductions. **Map** p109 C3 **➊**

Built in 1680 – making it the oldest surviving structure in downtown Boston – the Paul Revere House was constructed on the site of the parsonage that was home to Puritan preacher Increase Mather and his family (*see p113* **In the Know**). The two-storey, wooden post-and-beam structure may seem modest, but its high ceilings and large rooms (for the period) mark it out as a home for a family of means. Revere bought the house from its first owner, wealthy merchant Robert Howard, and lived here with his wife, children (he had 16 over 30 years, but only eight resided in the house at any one time) and mother from 1770 until 1800. The third storey was removed in the 19th century, when the house fell into disrepair (at various times it served as a flophouse, candy store, cigar factory and bank).

In 1902, it was nearly demolished, but the fortuitous intercession of Revere's great-grandson saved the place from the wrecking ball; six years later, the Paul Revere House opened to the public, one of the first 'house museums' in America. One of the ground floor rooms is mainly furnished as it would have been when Howard occupied it, while the kitchen and upstairs are decorated in the style of Revere's time, with some original pieces of furniture that belonged to the family. There are rotating displays with examples of the silversmith's work.

Across the courtyard – dominated by a 900lb iron bell cast by Paul Revere & Sons – is the Pierce/ Hichborn House, one of the oldest brick buildings in Boston and a prime example of early Georgian architecture. It was built in 1711 for glazier Moses Pierce, and later purchased by Revere's cousin Nathaniel Hichborn, a shipbuilder. While the Paul Revere House is open to visitors, entry to the Pierce/ Hichborn House is by guided tour only (usually twice daily; phone to check).

Restaurants & Cafés

Prezza

24 Fleet Street, between Moon Street & North Square (1-617 227 1577, www.prezza.com). Haymarket T. **Open** 4.30-10pm Mon-Thur; 4.30-10.30pm Fri, Sat; 4-9pm Sun. **Main courses** $28-$48. **Map** p109 C3 **➋** Italian

The local boy-done-good achievement of chef-owner Anthony Caturano prevails in his white-tablecloth fine-dining haven, which combines the urbane musculature of a downtown steakhouse with the intimacy of the North End trattorias that surround it. It's why you'll glimpse as many back-slapping businessmen at the bar as you will canoodling couples in the booths. Caturano's cooking displays similar breadth: from the pumpkin ravioli with lobster and brown butter to the wood-grilled swordfish with tomato-braised baby octopus, you'll be happy to discover the 'fine' is alive and well in this dining experience. With nearly 40 wines by the glass, the bar makes a nice place to start the evening.

Shops & Services

Officina 189

189 North Street, at North Square (1-857 233 4300, www.officina189.com). Haymarket T. **Open** noon-7pm Tue-Fri; noon-8pm Sat; noon-5pm Sun. **Map** p109 C4 **➌** Accessories

Fabrizio Di Rienzo, a Milanese import himself, brings a collection of goods straight from the Boot to Boston's Italian-American neighbourhood. Finely crafted items from labels little known on these shores, including fragrances, watches, scarves, leather goods and even bicycles, are showcased in the slender, brick-walled space – most are exclusive to the store.

HANOVER STREET & AROUND

Haymarket or North Station T.

With upwards of 100 eateries packed into the small neighbourhood, the North End has been a popular dining destination with Bostonians and tourists for decades. In the vicinity of the area's two main drags, Hanover Street and Salem Street, you can find everything from humble trattorias to chic *nuovo Italiano* restaurants.

But it's not all about food. Among the Italian cafés and restaurants on Hanover Street is **St Stephen's Catholic Church** (no.401, 1-617 523 1230), the work of Boston-born architect

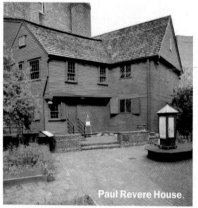

Paul Revere House.

EXPLORE

THE BRINK'S JOB

The 'crime of the century' ultimately didn't pay.

Tony Pino (centre), heading to court

On the evening of 17 January 1950, a group of armed gunmen in pea coats, chauffeur caps and rubber Halloween masks stormed the Brink's Building at 165 Prince Street in the North End. Within 20 minutes, they were gone – making off with an unheard-of $1.2 million in cash, and another $1.6 million in bonds and securities. A few months later, authorities found their getaway car – a brand-new green Ford truck, cut into pieces with an acetylene torch and wrapped in fibre bags – in a landfill in the suburban town of Stoughton.

The heist, unsolved for nearly six years, was considered 'the crime of the century', a daring and brilliant operation that was ultimately foiled not by a slip-up or canny police work, but by the robbers' own greed and bickering.

The gang – Tony Pino, Adolph 'Jazz' Maffie, James 'Specs' O'Keefe, Thomas 'Sandy' Richardson, Vincent Costa, James Faherty, Joe McGinnis, Mike Geagen, Henry Baker, Joseph Banfield and Stanley Gusciora – had meticulously cased the joint. Months before the heist, they stole the lock cylinders out of the doors one by one, had keys made by a local locksmith, and replaced them. They crept into the building dozens of times after hours to rehearse their plans. By the time the day of the job rolled around, they knew the Brink's building better than its own employees.

After making their getaway, the bandits divvied up some of the loot and made a pact not to touch it until six years had passed – the statute of limitations on robbery in Massachusetts. But six months later, O'Keefe and Gusciora were arrested in Pennsylvania on an unrelated charge and sentenced to several years in prison. O'Keefe began putting pressure on his former associates to cough up money for his defence. Relations between the gang members soured, and when O'Keefe was released from prison, several attempts were made on his life.

Mere days before the statute of limitations on the Brink's job was due to expire, O'Keefe – in prison on yet another charge, and under extreme pressure from investigators – finally summoned an FBI agent. 'All right, what do you want to know?' he asked.

Today, the spot where the Brink's building once stood is a parking garage. In the 1970s, Dino De Laurentiis produced a film about the heist, *The Brink's Job*, much of it shot on location in Boston. Local lore has it that the film crew paid a North Ender $200 to take out an air-conditioning unit for a shot, and the next morning, every window on the street had one.

After O'Keefe sang, the rest of the gang, most of whom were well known to police, were soon rounded up and convicted. Some died in prison, while others were paroled at ripe old ages. Richardson and Maffie marched in a Boston parade as guests of honour when *The Brink's Job* had its 1978 première.

As for the rat, O'Keefe? He never did time for the Brink's heist, eventually landed a job as Cary Grant's chauffeur, and died of a heart attack in 1976.

EXPLORE

Daily Catch.

Charles Bulfinch, and the only surviving example of his church designs in the city. Roughly bookended by St Stephen's and the **Old North Church** is the brick-paved **Paul Revere Mall**, also known as the Prado. Its centrepiece is a statue of Revere, designed by Cyrus E Dallin in 1865 but only cast in 1940. As well as paying tribute to the North End's favourite son, the mall (between Hanover and Unity Streets) serves as a social hub in warm weather, where locals play cards, gossip and argue over sports scores. In the square, engraved tablets on the walls list the famous residents and places in the neighbourhood. On Unity Street, to the left of the back gate of the Old North Church, is the handsome **Clough House**. Built in 1712, it was once home to Ebenezer Clough, the master mason who helped build the church.

Now occupied by a real-estate agent, the former **Joseph A Langone Funeral Home** (383 Hanover Street) found notoriety as the site of the funeral for Nicola Sacco and Bartolomeo Vanzetti. The Italian anarchists were executed in 1927, following a controversial robbery and murder trial that preyed on the xenophobia of the era. Many believed the two were innocent; what is indisputable is that their case was railroaded through the courts to appease the angry, anti-immigrant zeitgeist, and the story of their fate remains a *cause célèbre* among anti-death-penalty groups worldwide.

Heading towards the waterfront, you'll pass a handful of boutiques, including **In-jean-ius** denim shop; around the corner at 12 Fleet Street is its dressier sibling, **Twilight** (1-617 523 8008, www.twilightboutique.com).

At the opposite end of Hanover Street is the open-air produce, meat and fish market known as **Haymarket**, held on Blackstone Street between Hanover and North Streets. On Fridays and Saturdays, it's a bustling, colourful scene, open from 5am 'until we sell out', according to one of the charismatic stallholders.

Restaurants & Cafés

★ **Bricco**

241 Hanover Street, between Cross & Richmond Streets (1-617 248 6800, www.bricco.com). Haymarket T. **Open** *4-11pm daily. Late-night menu 11pm-1.45am Fri, Sat.* **Main courses** $26-$59. **Map** p109 B4 ❹ Italian

With name chefs blowing in and out of its kitchen, this dark, suave neighbourhood pioneer of *alta cucina* has hit its share of rough patches over the years. But its capacity for comebacks is astounding. Give it a try if you're feeling flush – chances are you'll score some marvellously silky pasta (the meatball-studded *timpano* is a wonder), rounded out by intriguing seasonal dishes like duck with roasted yams, and whole Mediterranean *branzino* (sea bass) baked in a wood-fired oven. Meanwhile, the allure of the obscure tints the all-Italian wine list.

★ $ **Caffe Vittoria**

290-296 Hanover Street, between Prince & Parmenter Streets (1-617 227 7606, www.vittoria caffe.com). Haymarket T. **Open** *7am-midnight Mon-Thur, Sun; 7am-12.30am Fri, Sat.* **No credit cards. Map** p109 C3 ❺ Café

Fusing the freshly scrubbed look of a small-town soda fountain with the vintage spirit of *un bar Italiano*, this is one of the North End's quintessential coffeehouses. A scattered array of antique espresso urns and French presses attest to this – and the rich, foamy cappuccino sprinkled with cocoa confirms it. The imported sodas and a selection of grappas make their case, too.

▶ *After hours, head downstairs to cigar bar Stanza dei Sigari, a Prohibition-era speakeasy that still looks the part.*

Daily Catch

323 Hanover Street, at Prince Street (1-617 523 8567, http://thedailycatch.com). Haymarket T. **Open** *11am-10pm daily.* **Main courses** $19.50-$69. **No credit cards. Map** p109 C3 ❻ Fish & seafood

When people talk about the true character of the 'old' North End, chances are they're envisioning the Daily Catch. It's essentially a kitchen nook with a blackboard menu, juice glasses in lieu of stemware and skillets that double as plates. It doesn't take credit cards, or even have a bathroom. But boy, has it got calamari – fried, stuffed, marinated and chilled, chopped and pressed into delicious meatballs. Squid ink, meanwhile, gives the linguine a kick – as does garlic galore. **Other locations** 2 Northern Avenue, Seaport District, Waterfront (1-617 772 4400); 441 Harvard Street, Brookline (1-617 734 2700).

Pomodoro
319 Hanover Street, at Prince Street (1-617 367 4348). Haymarket T. **Open** 4-11pm Mon-Fri; 11am-11pm Sat, Sun. **Main courses** $23-$28. **No credit cards. Map** p109 C3 ❼ Italian
Pomodoro still shines as a beacon of freshness and flavour in a sea of red sauce. That's why it's well worth the wait for a spot in the tiny dining room, and not just for the free tiramisu that tends to appear around dessert time. Favourite main dishes include Italian classics such as seafood *fra diavolo*, chicken carbonara and veal *scallopini* – all cooked to perfection and served with friendly flair.

Taranta
210 Hanover Street, at Cross Street (1-617 720 0052, www.tarantarist.com). Haymarket T. **Open** 5.30-10pm daily. **Main courses** $28-$39. **Map** p109 B4 ❽ Italian/Peruvian
In the hands of a lesser chef-owner, Taranta might have been a mere novelty. Under José Duarte – a visionary in the kitchen and a charmer in the dining room – this southern Italian-Peruvian joint is one of the most consistently exciting (yet warm and relaxing) eateries around. The cross-cultural fusion not only yields the piquant likes of cassava gnocchi with lamb *ragù*, and pork chops with sugar cane and *rocoto* pepper glaze, but also determines the scope of the wine list, extending from Piedmont and Puglia in Italy to Argentina and Chile.

Shops & Services

In-jean-ius
441 Hanover Street, at Salutation Street (1-617 523 5326, www.injeanius.com). Haymarket T. **Open** 11am-7pm Mon-Sat; noon-6pm Sun. **Map** p109 C3 ❾ Fashion
Find your perfect pair of jeans without the leg work – this small shop packs in up to 30 cult denim labels for women, including AG Jeans, J Brand, Mother, Joe's Jeans and Citizens of Humanity, plus the cool T-shirts and tops – by Michael Stars, Vintage Havana, Autumn Cashmere and many more – to go with them.

Wine Bottega
341 Hanover Street, between Prince & Fleet Streets (1-617 227 6607, www.thewinebottega.com).

Haymarket T. **Open** noon-8pm Mon, Sun; 11am-9pm Tue, Wed; 11am-10pm Thur; 10am-10pm Fri, Sat. **Map** p109 C3 ❿ Food & drink
Inch for inch, this is arguably Boston's best – not to mention most eclectic – wine shop. An articulate staff with a passion for the innovative and the undiscovered guarantees that the range of its inventory surpasses expectations for a shop of this size.

SALEM STREET & COPP'S HILL
Haymarket or North Station T.

Unlike the Italians, other immigrants to the area didn't leave a lasting legacy. Salem Street is so named because it was once called Shalom Street – in the mid 19th century it was the primary home of the neighbourhood's Jewish population. Today, none of the five synagogues that once stood in the North End remains, and virtually all traces of Jewish influence have vanished. Now, the southern end of the street is dominated by old-fashioned food shops, including the 1930s **Polcari's Coffee** at no.105 (*see p115*); foodies can sign up for one of the **North End Market Tours** run by resident expert Michele Topor and her team of guides (1-617 523 6032, www.bostonfoodtours.com).

More importantly, Salem Street is the site of the **Old North Church**, the city's oldest place of worship and one of its most famous Revolutionary landmarks. After paying your respects, cross Salem Street and carry on up Hull Street to reach **Copp's Hill Burying Ground**, the highest point in the North End; below it on Commercial Street is Langone Park, with its playing fields, children's playground and views of the Charlestown Navy Yard. Directly opposite the graveyard's entrance, **44 Hull Street** is Boston's narrowest house, measuring just ten feet wide. According to local lore, the sole purpose its original owners had in building it was to block their neighbours' view. Welcome to Boston, pal.

IN THE KNOW GRAVE MATTERS

Perhaps the most famous Bostonians to be interred in **Copp's Hill Burying Ground** (*see p114*) are the Puritan preachers and arch-conservative theologians Cotton Mather and his father Increase. Famed for his literary prolificacy, Cotton is believed to have written more than 400 books and pamphlets. Father and son fell out of favour in subsequent years over their handling of the Salem Witch Trials. Both were influential enough to have halted the Salem inquisition, but neither condemned the mass hysteria that the trials unleashed until it was far too late.

Nearby, 165 Prince Street, on the corner of Commercial Street, was the site of the 'Great Brink's Robbery' (*see p111* **The Brink's Job**).

Sights & Museums

`FREE` Copp's Hill Burying Ground
Hull Street, at Snowhill Street (no phone).
Haymarket or North Station T. **Open** 9am-5pm daily. **Admission** free. **Map** p109 B2 ⓫
The final resting place for around 10,000 early Bostonians – including the Mathers (*see p113* **In the Know**) – this cemetery was created on the northernmost hill of the Shawmut Peninsula in 1659. The British used the site's geographical advantage to launch cannon balls at the rebel army during the Battle of Bunker Hill; it is said that they warmed up by using some of the cemetery's gravestones for target practice. Also buried here is the slave and soldier Prince Hall, an early black leader in Boston. Hall lived in the free black community that originally settled the hill, and earned fame for his valour in the Battle of Bunker Hill.

`FREE` Old North Church
193 Salem Street, at Hull Street (1-617 523 6676,
www.oldnorth.com). Haymarket or North Station T.
Open *Jan, Feb* 10am-4pm daily. *Mar-May, Nov-Dec* 9am-5pm daily. *June-Oct* 9am-6pm daily.
Admission free. **Map** p109 C3 ⓬
Originally called Christ Church in Boston, Old North Church – indeed, the city's oldest – was built in 1723, its design inspired by Sir Christopher Wren's London churches. It played a critical role in the earliest days of the American Revolution: it was from Old North's steeple that lanterns were held aloft to warn the Minutemen of the movements of British forces. One lantern was to be displayed if the troops were seen moving by land, two if they were coming in by sea. They came by sea, and two it was, spurring Paul Revere to take his famous midnight ride – although Revere, a Puritan, never worshipped in this Anglican church.

The steeple itself wasn't part of the original church, but was added in 1740, with replacement steeples built in 1806 and 1954 after hurricanes tore the previous versions down. In the window where the two lanterns were hung sits a third lantern, lit by President Ford on 18 April 1975, symbolising hope for the nation's next century of freedom. Also look out for the bust of George Washington – the first of the country's first president. The church's plain white interior features its original chandeliers, lit for Christmas services, and wooden box pews. These were rented by local families, who were free to decorate them as they chose. The decor and positioning of each family's pew was a sign of their social status, with coveted centre pews attracting the highest rents.

Beneath the church rest the bodies of approximately 1,100 of the early colonists and British

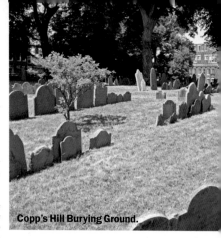
Copp's Hill Burying Ground.

subjects in 37 tombs; you can descend to the crypt as part of a guided tour (see website for details). The church's rich history attracts a steady stream of visitors, and the converted chapel next door houses a tasteful gift shop.

Restaurants & Cafés

Antico Forno
93 Salem Street, at Wiget Street (1-617 723 6733,
www.anticofornoboston.com). Haymarket T. **Open** 11.30am-10pm Mon-Thur, Sun; 11.30am-10.30pm Fri, Sat. **Main courses** $19-$24. **Map** p109 B3 ⓭
Italian
The North End is notoriously ridden with corner-cutting imitations of authentic trattorias. But Antico Forno is the genuine article, quietly eschewing red-checked clichés as it upholds Italian-American traditions. From aubergine rolls to rigatoni with sausage or thin-crust pizza, pretty much anything that emerges from the brick oven oozing ricotta and proper tomato sauce is a winner. The pasta plates also please, especially the cloud-soft gnocchi. The kitchen is open all day for impatient appetites.

★ Neptune Oyster
63 Salem Street, at Morton Street (1-617 742 3474, www.neptuneoyster.com). Haymarket T. **Open** 11.30am-9.30pm Mon-Thur, Sun; 11.30am-10pm Fri, Sat. **Main courses** $15-$34. **Map** p109 B4 ⓮ Fish & seafood
Established in 2004, Neptune Oyster is exemplary in its East Coast raw bar perfection. The simple, subway tiled interior gleams with retro charm. But if the daily oyster roster is definitive, the rest of the menu is startlingly original. The fearless eatery will try just about anything, from crispy oysters with Berkshire pig, golden raisin sauce and pistachio aïoli to Nantucket striped bass with heirloom tomato *sofrito* and roasted jalapeño. Even the classics get a seafood twist, such as the yellowfin tuna 'steak frites' and the house burger with a fried oyster. If you can grab a

EXPLORE

marble-topped table or a seat at the bar (be prepared for a wait), you're in for a treat.

Regina Pizzeria
11½ Thacher Street, at North Margin Street (1-617 227 0765, www.pizzeriaregina.com). Haymarket T. **Open** 11am-11.30pm Mon-Thur, Sun; 11am-12.30am Fri, Sat. **Main courses** $12-$23. **Map** p109 B3 ⓯ **Pizza**
With a magic oven that yields a beautifully bubbly crust on every pizza and a stalwart crew of Boston-bred tray-slingers, Regina's reputation precedes it. So, often, does the queue to get in. Though it has spawned numerous mall outposts, none can compare to the original, which opened in 1926 and has barely changed since. Squeeze yourself into a wooden booth, call for a pitcher of beer and a pizza *napoletana* or the whopping three-pound, multi-topping *giambotta*, and *mangia* like never before.

Bars

Ward 8
90 North Washington Street, at Medford Street (1-617 823 4478, www.ward8.com). Haymarket or North Station T. **Open** 4.30pm-1am Mon-Wed; 4.30pm-2am Thur, Fri; 10am-1am Sat, Sun. **Map** p109 A3 ⓰
Named after the cocktail created in Boston in the late 1890s, Ward 8 is located on the fringe of the North End and separates itself from the pack by *not* serving Italian food. The marble bar, wooden tables and tiled walls add up to a minimalist yet warm warehouse-chic vibe. The gastropub has an extensive craft-beer selection as well as a lengthy cocktail list organised by spirit. Many of the well-crafted drinks are fresh takes on old favourites, but the whisky section takes a reverent look back to classics such as a Lion's Tale, Gold Rush, and of course, the Ward 8.

Shops & Services

★ Maria's Pastry Shop
46 Cross Street, at Salem Street (1-617 523 1196, www.mariaspastry.com). Haymarket T. **Open** 7am-7pm Mon-Sat; 7am-5pm Sun. **Map** p109 B4 ⓱ **Food & drink**
This family-run old-timer fills the freshest *cannoli* in the 'hood. Actually, most of its Italian sweets deserve superlatives for adherence to tradition, from *torrone* and *marzipane* to holiday favourites such as ricotta pie.

★ Polcari's Coffee
105 Salem Street, at Parmenter Street (1-617 227 0786, www.polcariscoffee.com). Haymarket T. **Open** 10am-6.30pm Mon-Fri; 9am-6pm Sat. **Map** p109 B3 ⓲ **Food & drink**
Bobby Eustace, who took over this vintage java emporium from the son of first-generation immigrant founder Anthony Polcari, considers himself a curator, dedicated to preserving the neighbourhood fixture. In addition to an amazing variety of high-quality roasts, Polcari's stocks teas, spices, nuts and other foodstuffs and, in the summer months, tasty lemon slush that puts store-bought Luigi's to shame.

Shake the Tree
67 Salem Street, at Stillman Street (1-617 742 0484, www.shakethetreeboston.com). Haymarket T. **Open** 11am-8pm Mon-Fri; 10am-8pm Sat; noon-5pm Sun. **Map** p109 B4 ⓳ **Fashion/homewares**
This fashion and gift shop stocks a highly browsable combination of casual clothing from the likes of Ella Moss, Yumi Kim and Velvet, accessories, unusual toiletries, stationery, and decorative homewares. The jewellery collection includes pieces by Boston-area designers, such as Lena Taeger's semi-precious gemstone creations and Lori Magno's silver tag necklaces embossed with the local 617 area code.

EXPLORE

Waterfront

Although a section of Boston's waterfront was developed decades ago, when the warehouses of Commercial Wharf and Long Wharf were converted into apartments, restaurants and other businesses, vast stretches of prime land remained untapped. Finally, the city is capitalising on one of its greatest assets. Now that it has a major art museum and a destination boutique, the Seaport District is taking shape with new buildings filling in the vacant lots. Once-desolate warehouses around Fort Point Channel have been reinvigorated with artists' studios, start-ups, some of the city's hottest restaurants and a cult brewery.

Thanks to the development of the HarborWalk, visitors can access more of the waterfront than ever before, and learn about its history through interpretive signs. In the warmer months, it's the starting point for boat tours and excursions to the secluded Boston Harbor Islands.

EXPLORE

Rose F Kennedy Greenway.

Don't Miss

1 Rose F Kennedy Greenway A green path through many 'hoods (p118).

2 Row 34 Snag a table on the deck at this industrial oyster-and-beer oasis (p121).

3 Trillium Brewing Company Bold brews in a pint-sized facility (p125).

4 Institute of Contemporary Art Illuminating shows in a cool waterside setting (p124).

5 Louis A super-chic Hub institution (p124).

LONG WHARF TO ATLANTIC WHARF

Aquarium T.

On the harbourfront almost directly behind Faneuil Hall marketplace lies **Long Wharf**. Originally known as Boston Pier when it was constructed in the 17th century, it became the centre of the city's shipping trade; the brick warehouses date from the 18th century. The shoreline has changed quite a bit since then: when the **Custom House** (*see p57*) was built in 1847, it stood at the edge of the water – today, the landmark building lies several blocks inland, across the **Rose F Kennedy Greenway** (www.rosekennedygreenway.org). After the dismantling of an elevated expressway as part of the Big Dig, this verdant, mile-long ribbon of grassy parks was developed in its footprint. Snaking parallel to the waterfront from the North End to Chinatown, its varied landscape features flowerbeds, trees, fountains and public art. Food trucks congregate at various points (there's a schedule on the park's website).

Adjacent to the Greenway, at the border of Long Wharf, is **Christopher Columbus Park**. A huge wooden arbour, with vine-covered trellises and benches from which to admire the waterfront views, gives the spot a romantic air and there's a popular children's playground (*see p171*). Long Wharf is the departure point for whale-watching and sightseeing cruises or ferries to the Boston Harbor Islands, while the hulking, concrete-and-glass **New England Aquarium** sits on neighbouring Central Wharf. You can now walk uninterrupted along the **Harbor Walk** (www.bostonharborwalk.com) – a 47-mile network of waterside paths that will eventually link Charlestown to Dorchester (with a satellite walk in East Boston) – to Atlantic Wharf, where landmark industrial buildings have been converted into restaurants, including local star chef Jody Adams' **Trade**.

Sights & Museums

New England Aquarium

1 Central Wharf, at Atlantic Avenue & Milk Street (1-617 973 5200, www.neaq.org). Aquarium T. **Open** *July, Aug* 9am-6pm Mon-Thur, Sun; 9am-7pm Fri, Sat. *Sept-June* 9am-5pm Mon-Fri; 9am-6pm Sat, Sun. **Admission** $25; $18-$23 reductions; free under-3s. **Map** p119 A2 ❶

The centrepiece of this excellent aquarium is the 200,000-gallon salt-water replica of a Caribbean coral reef. The cylindrical tank, 40ft in diameter and four storeys tall, contains moray eels, stingrays, gigantic sea turtles and menacing sharks. The huge indoor penguin exhibit (constructed so almost all of the balconies overlook it) is great fun. If the lines

are too long, peek at the playful inhabitants of the outdoor seal enclosure instead.

▶ *For details of kid-centric exhibits at the Aquarium, see p169.*

Restaurants & Cafés

Meritage

Boston Harbor Hotel, 70 Rowes Wharf, at Atlantic Avenue (1-617 439 3995, www.meritagethe restaurant.com). Aquarium or South Station T. **Open** 5.30-10.30pm Tue-Sat. **Main courses** $29-$39. **Map** p119 A2 ❷ **Creative contemporary** The minimalist, second-floor dining room of the Boston Harbor Hotel creates a serene, uncluttered backdrop for chef Daniel Bruce's artful, wine-centric cuisine. Diners get the full trinity: food, wine and a stellar view of the harbour. Main courses are grouped according to the type of wine (pan-seared diver scallops for white, cabernet-braised short ribs for red), offering a foolproof yet flexible and educational rather than dogmatic approach to enjoying food and wine. (However, the portion-to-price ratio may end up teaching spendthrifts a less pleasant lesson.)

Miel

InterContinental Boston, 510 Atlantic Avenue, at Pearl Street (1-617 217 5151, www. intercontinentalboston.com). South Station T. **Open** 6.30am-2.30pm, 4-11pm daily. **Main courses** $18-$44. **Map** p119 B2 ❸ **French** Provence is the inspiration behind this hotel kitchen, where executive chef Didier Montarou executes olive oil and honey-kissed cuisine (hence the name) that some laud as healthy while others just deem delicious. For lunch, indulge in the lobster roll or niçoise salad with grilled medium-rare tuna; for dinner, honey-thyme scallops. There's Nutella-filled french toast at brunch. The regional theme may or may not explain (or excuse) the atypically frou-frou, countrified decor – but a stunning view over Boston Harbor from inside or out on the patio more than makes amends.

★ Trade

540 Atlantic Avenue, at Congress Street (1-617 451 1234, www.trade-boston.com). South Station T. **Open** 11.30am-11pm Mon-Thur; 11.30am-midnight Fri, Sat; 5.30-10pm Sun. **Small plates/main courses** $4-$27. **Map** p119 B2 ❹ **Eclectic** Chef/restaurateur Jody Adams has taken her talents to the waterfront with this airy space featuring floor-to-ceiling windows, artistic light fixtures, a cluster of high-top tables and a long marble bar – perfect for after-work crowds seeking cocktails and light fare. In fact, the focus here is on small plates – more than 15 globe-spanning choices, from scallion pancakes with chilli dipping sauce to fish tacos and spicy pork belly lettuce wraps. Sit at the bar and watch your gourmet-topped flatbread (mushroom and figs with gorgonzola, roasted squash and bacon) emerge from

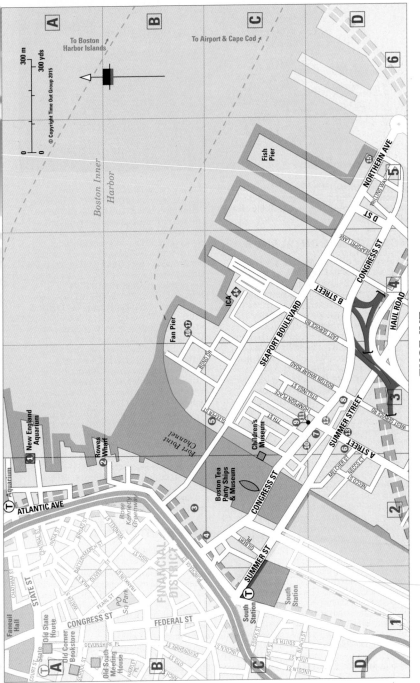

Waterfront

EXPLORE

To Boston
Harbor Islands

To Airport & Cape Cod

300 m

300 yds

© Copyright Time Out Group 2015

Boston Inner Harbor

Fish
Pier

NORTHERN AVE

FILLING WAY

D ST

CONGRESS ST

SEAPORT LANE

B STREET

HAUL ROAD

EAST SERVICE RD

SEAPORT BOULEVARD

BOSTON WHARF ROAD

WEST SERVICE RD

ICA

Fan Pier

BOND DR

STILLINGS ST

THOMPSON PLACE

7TH ST

A STREET

SUMMER STREET

NECCO ST

MELCHER ST

NECCO CT

SLEEPER ST

Fort Point Channel

New England
Aquarium

Rowes
Wharf

Aquarium

ATLANTIC AVE

Children's
Museum

Boston Tea
Party Ships
& Museum

CONGRESS ST

SUMMER ST

GILLSON ST

South Station

South
Station

FINANCIAL
DISTRICT

Faneuil Hall

Old State
House

State House

Old Corner
Bookstore

Old South
Meeting House

STATE ST

CHATHAM ST

COURT'S SQUARE

CENTRAL ST

INDIA ST

BROAD ST

BATTERYMARCH ST

MILK ST

OLIVER ST

FRANKLIN ST

KILBY ST

PEARL ST

St. Park

PO

Sq. Park

CONGRESS ST

DEVONSHIRE PL

FEDERAL ST

DEVONSHIRE ST

HAWLEY PL

ARCH ST

HIGH ST

LINCOLN ST

SOUTH ST

ESSEX ST

UTICA ST

BEACH ST

Rose
Kennedy
Greenway

Time Out Boston **119**

Georges Island.

the fiery oven. Even though desserts, such as baked alaska with mango, passion fruit and coconut sorbets are tempting to share, you'll probably want one all to yourself.

BOSTON HARBOR ISLANDS

Some of the waterfront's least-exploited assets are these 34 small islands, left by a retreating glacier about 12,000 years ago. In the 1990s, Congress designated them national parkland, and they provide a thriving wildlife habitat. Rare and endangered species of birds such as plovers and ospreys have been spotted here, and grey and harp seals live in the harbour.

Six of the islands are currently accessible by public ferry and arrangements can be made to visit a handful of the others. For more information, contact Boston Harbor Islands Partnership (1-617 223 8666, www.boston islands.com). Ferries are operated by Boston Harbor Cruises (1-617 227 4321, www.boston harborcruises.com) and depart from Long Wharf. Seasons vary by island, but the two most popular – Georges and Spectacle Islands – can be visited from May to October.

In recent years, with waterfront regeneration, the islands' fate has become a hot topic. There had once been murmurs of developments – B&Bs, amphitheatres, shops and even a water slide – on the islands. Today, some of them host festivals and family events in an attempt to bolster interest in these forgotten resources. Largely unvisited, aside from the fairly well-trafficked Fort Warren on Georges Island, they make a pleasant escape from the city on a warm afternoon.

At 28 acres, **Georges Island** is dominated by **Fort Warren**, a massive structure used during the Civil War as a Union training base and a prison for captured Confederate soldiers (including, most famously, the vice-president of the Confederacy, Alexander Hamilton Stephens). You can either take a guided tour or explore it on your own. The 105-acre **Spectacle Island** was capped off with earth displaced by the Big Dig in 2005, and now features a swimming beach, a large

marina and a visitors' centre. The views of Boston from atop its two hills are breathtaking.

Bumpkin Island, covering about 35 acres, is tucked away in Hingham Bay and doesn't see many visitors. From the early part of the 20th century to the 1940s it was used to quarantine children with polio. Today, it's one of four islands (along with Peddocks, Grape and Lovells), where camping is permitted. In all cases, reservations must be made in advance; see the Islands Partnership website for details. Also note that, inexplicably – chalk it up to prim New England culture – alcohol is not permitted on the islands.

Grape Island has never been developed; the remains of a 19th-century farmhouse are the only clue that the 50-acre island was once inhabited. It has pristine shell and gravel beaches, campsites and berries to pick.

Lovells Island covers 62 acres and has a beach, hiking trails, wooded hills and dunes. **Peddocks Island**, at 188 acres, is the largest in the archipelago. During the 1960s, a 4,100-year-old skeleton was excavated on its shores. It's the only island with residents all year round; when the Harbor Islands were first turned into a national park, the state granted the residents – most of them fishermen – life-long leases; upon their death, the land reverts back to state ownership. Peddocks, with its salt marshes and woods, is great for picnicking, camping and hiking.

FORT POINT CHANNEL

South Station T.

Fort Point, 16 December 1773: a group of 60 colonists disguised as Mohawk Indians dumps 342 chests of tea into Boston Harbor in protest at the tea tax imposed by King George III. The original ships involved are long gone (and the actual site is a subject of debate), but re-enactments take place every year, complete with period costumes and a rambunctious crowd, at the **Boston Tea Party Ships & Museum** (*see p170*).

In the late 1970s, the warehouses of this former industrial area attracted artists, who defined the neighbourhood. Although many have been forced out by developers over the last decade, several live/work buildings remain, including the looming structure at 300 Summer Street, which contains the **Fort Point Arts Community Gallery** (1-617 423 4299, www. fortpointarts.org). Check the FPAC's website for details of the annual open-studios weekend in the autumn, when more than 150 artists open their doors to the public (*see p36* **In the Know**). Almost directly across from the building, look for stairs that take you down to street level from the Summer Street overpass. At the bottom, be sure to look up if it's after dusk – the underside features an installation, *Starry Night*, which reproduces the effect of a glittering night sky. The neighbourhood is dotted with public art, both long-term and temporary; see FPAC's website for details of the latest projects. Head north on A Street and you'll reach FPAC's **Made in Fort Point** shop, which is inside a swanky condo building at no.315.

Many of the area's once-derelict warehouses are occupied by tech start-ups, as part of the waterfront 'Innovation District' (which actually sprawls over several distinct areas). It has also become one of the most happening dining areas in the city, following the arrival of three spots from star chef Barbara Lynch – fine dining restaurant **Menton**, casual eaterie **Sportello** and bar **Drink** – on the lower floors of one of the city's hip condo projects. More hotspots followed, including industrial-chic seafood destination **Row 34**. Once home to numerous industries, including manufacturing and printing, the waterfront is seeing a resurgence in Boston's brewing tradition. Stop into the small tasting room of **Trillium Brewing** (*see p125* **Brewed in Boston**) for a sample or several.

Longtime resident the **Children's Museum** underwent a 21st-century makeover, with a sleek glass extension and a new landscaped outdoor space and is one of the best places to bring kids in Boston. The oversized **Milk Bottle** (300 Congress Street) outside the museum is a Fort Point landmark that started life as a highway drive-in, and still serves ice-cream and snacks in summer.

Restaurants & Cafés

Barking Crab

88 Sleeper Street, between Northern Avenue & Seaport Boulevard (1-617 426 2722, www. barkingcrab.com). Silver Line Waterfront to Courthouse. **Open** 11.30am-11pm Mon-Wed, Sun; 11.30am-midnight Thur-Sat. **Main courses** $19-$29. **Map** p119 C3 ❺ Fish & seafood

Set right on Boston Harbor's Fort Point Channel, this red-shingled seafood shack and open-air tent is party central all summer long for local desk jockeys as well as tourists, who crowd the picnic tables beneath lamps made of Christmas light-strung lobster traps. Plastic buckets of indifferently fried clams or peel-and-eat shrimps come second to the beer-fuelled festivities. It's the live music, summertime canned-brew deals and salt air that matter most at Barking Crab.

Blue Dragon

324 A Street, nr Summer Street (1-617 338 8585, www.ming.com/blue-dragon). South Station T then 10mins walk. **Open** 11.30am-1am Mon-Fri; 3pm-1am Sat. **Main courses** $10-$14. **Map** p119 D3 ❻ Pan-Asian/eclectic

Quite a departure from his upscale Blue Ginger in suburban Wellesley, American Public Television chef Ming Tsai's funky pan-Asian gastropub is a cheap-eats find for those looking for bold bites with a global accent and a classy, laid-back vibe. The semi-open kitchen cranks out *banh mi* at lunch (black pepper shrimp with jicama salad, for example). At dinner, small plates rule: dishes might include beer-battered fish tacos, dim sum, and rice and noodle options. Larger portions include a popular buttermilk tempura whole-chicken platter. Late-night eats are more limited than the dinner menu, but both include the restaurant's one killer dessert: a warm, deep-dish chocolate chip cookie served with ice-cream and soy caramel sauce.

Pastoral

345 Congress Street, between Thomson Place & Farnsworth Street (1-617 345 0005, www. pastoralfortpoint.com). South Station T. **Open** 11.30am-1.30am daily. **Main courses** $10-$20. **Map** p119 D3 ❼ Italian/pizza

Armed with an authentic Neapolitan pizza oven, chef-owner Todd Winer has established a winner in this rustic farmhouse pizzeria. The space features plenty of reclaimed wood, antique kitchen gadgets on one wall and a collection of window frames that cleverly separate the bustling bar from the happening dining room. Bubbly, thin-crust pizzas with gourmet toppings such as house-made fennel sausage (served perched atop large, empty San Marzano tomato cans), hearty handmade pastas, salads and a tight selection of mainly local microbrews have drawn many devotees. End the night with killer warm chocolate chip cookies.

★ Row 34

383 Congress Street, at Boston Wharf Road (1-617 553 5900, www.row34.com). South Station T. **Open** 11.30am-2.30pm, 5-10pm Mon-Thur; 11.30am-2.30pm, 5-11pm Fri; 5-11pm Sat; 5-10pm Sun. **Main courses** $15-$28. **Map** p119 D3 ❽ Fish & seafood

See p122 **Raising the Oyster Bar**.

EXPLORE

RAISING THE OYSTER BAR

Catch the new wave of shellfish specialists.

Ever since **Union Oyster House** (*see p57*) opened near Faneuil Hall in 1826 (its original name was Atwood & Bacon), raw oysters have been integral to Boston's culinary scene. Today, the briny bivalves grace just about every restaurant menu and star in buck-a-shuck nights up and down the coast. Boston's new wave of boutique oyster bars prizes local farm-raised shellfish and keeps shuckers in the limelight. Early adopters include **East Coast Grill** (*see p139*), **B&G Oysters** (*see p98*) and **Neptune Oyster** (*see p114*), but a new crop continues the trend. These are the latest places to sample the freshest pearly gems from Cape Cod to Maine and beyond.

THE RAW BAR INNOVATOR: ISLAND CREEK OYSTER BAR

Island Creek's eponymous oyster farm in Duxbury supplied many of the top seafood spots (including Neptune Oyster and East Coast Grill) with plump specimens long before it opened its own outpost (*see p92*) in 2010. More than a dozen varieties – from the meaty Wellfleet (Cape Cod) to earthy freshwater East Beach Blonde (Rhode Island) – complete with notes on origin and farmer, offer fans a tour by *merroir*. (This is the marine equivalent of *terroir*, in which location shapes flavour characteristics.) While there are only ten seats at the counter to glimpse the raw-bar action, there are plenty of tables in the cavernous dining room for savouring the freshly shucked results.

THE FORT POINT PIONEER: ROW 34

In 2013, the Island Creek gang branched out with this more affordable space in Fort Point Channel (*see p121*), dubbing it the 'working man's oyster bar'. The place is named for oysters cultivated from the 34th row at the Island Creek Oyster farm. You'll find a similar, daily-changing oyster menu as at ICOB, with the same trio of cocktail sauce, horseradish and mignonette accompaniments, but in a more industrial, casual setting with concrete floors and plenty of outdoor tables. Watch the shuckers' show at the 15-seat slate and stainless steel-counter, and order from the overhead list of rotating draughts of indie beers. You can choose from more than a dozen kinds of oysters at dinner (fewer at lunch), then follow them up with a buttered lobster roll.

FOR BOOZE AND BIVALVES: CITIZEN PUBLIC HOUSE & OYSTER BAR

The 'pub' in public house is evident in this wood-panelled haven in the Fenway (*see p92*), which is famous for its 200-plus whiskey selection as well as its whole-pig roasts for large parties. The small raw bar is a cosy spot for sampling the three varieties offered daily, often locally sourced but sometimes from further afield (Virginia or Prince Edward Island), with a ringside view. You can broaden your horizons even more with the seafood platter, which includes smoked mussels, littlenecks, shrimp and lobster.

Row 34.

Sportello

348 Congress Street, at A Street (1-617 737 1234, www.sportelloboston.com). South Station T. **Open** 11.30am-11pm daily. **Main courses** $22-$31. **Map** p119 D3 ❾ **Italian**

One of the early culinary pioneers of Fort Point Channel, chef-owner Barbara Lynch launched Sportello (Italian for 'counter service') with the idea of opening a sleek, chic interpretation of an American diner serving casual Italian fare. Diners grab a stool at one of the two U-shaped white counters, and get to watch the action in the open kitchen before digging into the tagliatelle with bolognese and fried basil. At lunch, folks line up at the bakery counter for pastries, soups and sandwiches to go, and find a bench along the channel for a waterside picnic. It's an affordable alternative to Lynch's highly regarded and highly priced adjacent celebration of French-Italian cuisine, Menton (354 Congress Street, 1-617 737 0099, www.mentonboston.com), which offers four-course and seven-course tasting menus.

Tavern Road

343 Congress Street, at Farnsworth Street (1-617 790 0808, www.tavernroad.com). South Station T. **Open** 4pm-2am daily. **Main courses** $24-$27. **Map** p119 C3 ❿ **Eclectic**

Creativity runs in the family here. Chef Louis DiBicarri takes care of the house-made charcuterie, small plates, and main dishes such as espresso-rubbed venison and whole roasted snapper, while brother Michael tends to the loft-like dining room furnished with wooden tables, booths and industrial light fixtures. A massive street art-style mural on one wall pays homage to the brothers' late uncle Adio, a local sculptor whose works still grace the city. The bar is arguably the best in the neighbourhood, with creative cocktails, bottled beers (no draught) and wine. If you're short on time or want lunch to go, head next door to TR Street Foods, the restaurant's takeaway counter, which doles out inspired sandwiches and easily portable dishes such as beef tacos and turkey kebabs.

Bars

Drink

348 Congress Street, between Thompson Place & Farnsworth Street (1-617 695 1806, www.drinkfortpoint.com). South Station T. **Open** 4pm-1am daily. **Map** off p119 D3 ⓫

This below-street-level bar has been firmly planted at the top of local and national cocktail enthusiasts' must-see lists for its personal approach to mixology. Master bartenders present you not with a menu but with an ear to listen to your preferences, crafting artisanal tipples from their stock of premium spirits and mixers.

▶ *Drink is part of Barbara Lynch's mini Fort Point empire, including Menton and Sportello; see above.*

Lucky's Lounge

355 Congress Street, at A Street (1-617 357 5825, www.luckyslounge.com). South Station T. **Open** 11am-2am Mon-Fri; 10am-2am Sat, Sun. **Map** p119 D3 ⓬

Tucked away in the bowels of an old warehouse, this retro lounge was one of the first bar-eateries to colonise the now-hopping Fort Point area. A varied slate of music includes the Al Vega Trio's popular Saturday-night and Sunday-brunch tributes to Ol' Blue Eyes, plus a weekly mix of reggae, soul and R&B.

Shops & Services

Made in Fort Point

315 A Street, at Melcher Street (1-617 423 1100, www.fortpointarts.org). South Station T. **Open** 11am-6pm Mon-Fri; noon-4pm Sat. **Map** p119 D3 ⓭ **Art/accessories/fashion**

The name sums it up – this gallery-like space set within an upscale condo development sells an ever-changing mix of art, accessories, jewellery, clothing and cards, all made in the area. Artist Laura Davidson's limited-edition offset 'tunnel books' are like 3D cards with local themes; Argentinian-born Liliana Folta creates colourful and surreal sculptures and paintings; and Leslie Anne Feagley's black-and-white Boston ballpark photos reveal the unexpected beauty of Fenway Park and environs.

SEAPORT DISTRICT

Silver Line Waterfront to World Trade Center.

Also known as the South Boston Waterfront, this area is in the midst of ongoing commercial and residential development. Standing at the water's edge on Fan Pier, the **Institute of Contemporary Art** is surrounded by glossy towers and under-construction buildings. Walk west along the shore and you'll reach the city's premier designer boutique, **Louis**, which moved from Newbury Street in 2010. A few blocks inland is the flashy **Boston Convention & Exhibition Center**.

Heading east on Seaport Boulevard will take you to the 1914 **Fish Pier**, still home to wholesale seafood companies, with fishing boats berthed alongside, and the No Name Restaurant, which opened in 1917 and was once one of the city's best seafood places but is no longer recommended. Hugging the harbour past the World Trade Center is a line-up of large chain restaurants, bars and **Legal Harborside** at Liberty Wharf, capitalising on the view with floor-to-ceiling glass windows fronting the water. Also located here are the **Blue Hills Bank Pavilion** (*see p188*) and local suds-maker, **Harpoon Brewery** (306 Northern Avenue, 1-617 456 2322, www.harpoonbrewery.com), complete with a spacious beer hall.

EXPLORE

Sights & Museums

★ Institute of Contemporary Art

100 Northern Avenue (1-617 478 3100, www. icaboston.org). Silver Line Waterfront to World Trade Center. **Open** 10am-5pm Tue, Wed, Sat, Sun; 10am-9pm Thur, Fri. **Admission** $15; $10 reductions; free under-18s. Free 5-9pm Thur. **Map** p119 C4 ❷

Once crammed into a tiny building in Back Bay, the ICA moved to its spacious new home in late 2006, and is now the cultural cornerstone of the waterfront. With its 65,000sq ft floor space, the dramatic, glass-walled building houses galleries, a theatre and a café. The ICA prides itself on being a platform for challenging works – the rotating permanent collection includes pieces by Julian Opie, Paul Chan, Pipilotti Rist and Mona Hatoum, while changing exhibitions explore particular themes or materials, or focus on individual artists. The building, designed by Diller Scofidio + Renfro, has such unusual features as a downward-sloping Mediatheque that culminates in a front window framing a patch of water. After you've contemplated the art, head to the deck outside, with its expansive vista over the harbour.

Restaurants & Cafés

Legal Harborside

270 Northern Avenue, between D Street & Trilling Road (1-617 477 2900, www.legalseafoods.com). Silver Line Waterfront to World Trade Center. **Open** *Level 1* 11am-10pm Mon-Thur, Sun; 11am-11pm Fri, Sat. *Level 2* 5.30-10pm Mon-Thur; 5.30-11pm Fri, Sat; 5.30-9pm Sun. *Level 3* 4-11pm Mon-Wed; 4pm-1am Thur, Fri; noon-1am Sat; noon-11pm Sun. **Main courses** *Level 1* $13-$23. *Level 2* $26-$52. **Map** p119 D5 ❺ **Fish & seafood**

The new flagship Legal Sea Foods complex offers three floors of different dining experiences – with sweeping views of Boston Harbor. You can glimpse the oyster-shucking action in the casual first-floor dining room, which has counter seating the length of the semi-open kitchen. Here, the menu focuses on raw bar items, soups, salads, pastas, seafood such as fish and chips, and wood-grilled dishes from swordfish to steaks. The second floor is the epitome of fine dining with an elegant, carpeted room with white table-cloths, reminiscent of a ship's captain's quarters. The menu is pricey, offering caviar service, sautéed California abalone and buttered poached lobster. The third floor is reserved for private dining, but has a roof deck and bar with a retractable roof for casual, seasonal noshing on sushi and sandwiches.

Sam's at Louis

60 Northern Avenue, at Fan Pier Boulevard (1-617 295 0191, www.samsatlouis.com). Silver Line Waterfront to Courthouse. **Open** 11.30am-3pm, 5-10pm Mon-Thur; 11.30am-3pm, 5-11pm Fri, Sat; 11am-3pm, 5-9pm Sun. **Main courses** $16-$35. **Map** p119 B4 ❻ **American**

It's hard to beat this harbourside location when it comes to views, not to mention the general chicness that comes with sitting just a floor above high-end clothier Louis (*see below*). The 'Sam' is for Samantha, named after the store owner's daughter. The place comes into its own in summer – get a seat on the deck and dine on dishes that range from vegetarian options to classics such as skate wing with sage brown-butter sauce and grilled flank steak. The restaurant's proximity to the Institute of Contemporary Art makes it a great spot for post-museum cocktails.

Shops & Services

★ Louis

60 Northern Avenue, at Fan Pier Boulevard (1-617 262 6100, www.louisboston.com). Silver Line Waterfront to Courthouse. **Open** 11am-6pm Mon-Wed; 11am-7pm Thur-Sat; 11.30am-5pm Sun. **Map** p119 B4 ❼ **Fashion/accessories/ homewares**

Boston's premier concept store migrated to the still-developing Waterfront in 2010. The open-plan, warehouse-like space has sweeping harbour views, and clothing is hung on rolling racks for maximum flexibility. Louis started life as a menswear store, which is reflected in its impeccable Italian tailoring, but there are also young labels such as Greg Lauren (yes, the nephew of a certain other American designer), Belgian-born Tim Coppens and NYC duo Public School. Womenswear features such au courant names as Thomas Tait, Simone Rocha, Jonathan Saunders, Jason Wu and Suno. You'll also find carefully selected beauty products, scents and candles, home items, shoes and accessories. An outpost of celebrated snipper Mario Russo's salon is on site, as well as an excellent restaurant, Sam's (*see above*).

Sam's at Louis.

BREWED IN BOSTON

The city's pint glass runneth over.

Throughout the 19th century, Boston had more breweries per capita than anywhere in the United States, but the adoption of the 18th Amendment in 1920, ushering in the Prohibition era, ensured that most of their recipes were lost to the ages. Over the past 30 years, though, the Boston area has been a big player in the craft-beer renaissance. Opened by Jim Koch in 1985, **Samuel Adams** (30 Germania Street, Jamaica Plain, 1-617 368 5080, www.samueladams.com) is the founding father of the local brewing resurgence; **Harpoon** (*see p123*) opened just a year later. Since 2011, however, the pace has quickened, with a slew of newcomers. These include Chelsea's **Mystic** (www.mystic-brewery.com); **Idle Hands** (www.idlehands craftales.com) and **Night Shift Brewing** (www.nightshiftbrewing.com) in Everett; and Somerville's **Slumbrew** (www.slumbrew.com). Some of these spots are in out-of-the-way parts of town, but **Boston Brew Tours** (1-617 453 8687, www.bostonbrewtours.com) offers a variety of single-day, multi-brewery tours (and a designated driver). We've listed the best, most easily accessible new breweries below.

Trillium Brewing Company.

THE URBAN FARMHOUSE BREWERY

Located in the hip Fort Point neighbourhood, **Trillium Brewing Company** (369 Congress Street, at Stillings Street, 1-617 453 8745, www.trilliumbrewing.com) is one of the most exciting small-batch independent brewers in the area – and beyond. Founded by Jean-Claude Tetreault and his wife Esther in 2013, the small facility is among the few breweries within Boston's city limits. After nine years of home brewing, the Tetreaults set up shop in an industrial building on Congress Street and began producing farmhouse ales – without the farm. Queues start forming outside before the tasting room opens (4-7.30pm Tue, Wed; noon-7.30pm Thur, Fri; noon-6pm Sat), but with some patience and luck you might get the chance to try the eponymous unfiltered farmhouse ale, the Wakerobin red rye ale or Fort Point Pale. All the while, exciting, experimental beers continue to ferment.

THE FREEDOM TRAIL CIDER STOP

Just a quick stumble from the Freedom Trail, **Downeast Cider** (200 Terminal Street, 1-857 301 8881, www.downeastcider.com) is located on Charlestown's industrial waterfront under the Tobin Bridge. Tyler Mosher and Ross Brockman cut their teeth making cider during their senior year of college in Maine and opened the facility together with Ross's brother Matt. While the gigantic space is still predominantly a working brewery, it has recently opened to inquisitive drinkers for growler fills (a growler is a reusable beer bottle), by-the-glass pours from the makeshift bar (1-5pm Thur, Fri; noon-8pm Sat; 1-6pm Sun) and tours (during opening hours). In addition to the original blend and cranberry cider, which are unfiltered and made with ale yeast, Downeast offers alcoholic lemonade and honey mead.

THE SOCIAL SUDS EXPERIMENT

Somerville standout **Aeronaut Brewing Company** (14 Tyler Street, at Properzi Way, 1-617 718 0602, www.aeronautbrewing. com) is headed by Ben Holmes, Dan Rassi and Ronn Friedlander, all of whom have connections to MIT. The science-focused trio is experimenting with yeast strains developed in-house to create truly unique beers. Averaging two new prototypes a week, some of which may never make it to the tap, Aeronaut usually offers eight beers at a time, ranging from Imperial Stout and English Brown to Belgian Strong. The taproom's vibe is that of a neighbourhood block party (5pm-midnight Tue-Fri; 2pm-midnight Sat). Rotating tap lines pour out nicely priced pints and minis, while Charlie Chaplin films are projected on one wall, bands play adjacent to the distilling room and local food trucks are invited to park outside to offset the liquid diet.

Cambridge

The city just across the river from Boston is dominated by its two famous academic institutions: Harvard University and the Massachusetts Institute of Technology (MIT). The high density of students and academics has created a liberal, bohemian vibe. Over the years, the affluent areas around Harvard Square have spread, pushing lower-income immigrant communities, intellectuals and artists to the outskirts; the inflated property prices have made a mockery of its old moniker 'the People's Republic of Cambridge'.

The residential areas are characterised by colourfully painted clapboard houses – from sprawling mansions to three-family triple-deckers. Many Cambridge neighbourhoods are defined by a 'square', such as Harvard, Central and Inman, though they're not square at all; the term refers to a commercial area that has evolved at the junction of two or more thoroughfares.

EXPLORE

Harvard Art Museums.

Don't Miss

1 Harvard Art Museums A cache of varied treasures in a strikingly reimagined space (p136).

2 Toscanini's Inventively delicious ice-cream in any season (p139).

3 Cheapo Records Vinyl fetishists love this old-school store (p140).

4 Café ArtScience An utterly unique gastro experience (p144).

5 MIT Museum Weird science galore (p144).

Harvard Square.

HARVARD SQUARE & AROUND

Harvard T.

Hugging the Harvard University campus, the neighbourhood known as Harvard Square is a prime location for people-watching, as the bustle of bookish students (a few actually wearing their sweaters tied over their shoulders), bearded hipsters, camera-toting tourists, homeless panhandlers, buskers and harried business-people creates a diverse street scene.

Coming out of the Harvard Square T station, the biggest local landmark is right in front of you: **Out of Town News**, perched on an island at the confluence of Massachusetts Avenue, and Brattle and John F Kennedy Streets, stocks periodicals from all over the world, and is also the area's most popular meeting place. Next to it is a pedestrianised space known as 'the Pit' – not much to look at when no one's around, but a hangout for kids since punk rock broke in the 1970s.

There are usually street performers on every corner of the square when the weather is fine, but a favourite spot is outside the local branch of bakery-café chain **Au Bon Pain** (1100 Massachusetts Avenue, 1-617 354 4144). The café itself is unremarkable, but chess experts set up at the outdoor tables, and for a buck or two they'll let you challenge them; for a few more you can get a one-on-one lesson.

The streets of Harvard Square are lined with restaurants, cafés and shops. An influx of mega-chains, banks and high-end boutiques over the past couple of decades has pushed out characterful old establishments and undermined the neighbourhood feel, yet there are some notable survivors, including **Mr Bartley's Gourmet Burgers**, independent cinema the **Brattle Theatre**, and legendary folk venue **Club Passim**, which helped to launch the careers of Joan Baez and Suzanne Vega, among others. Retail stalwarts include **Cardullo's**, a wonderfully eccentric gourmet food shop, and **Leavitt & Peirce** (1316 Massachusetts Avenue, 1-617 547 0576, www.leavitt-peirce.com), an unchanging tobacconist established in 1883. Decorated with ancient Harvard crew oars and team photos, it has become a tourist attraction in its own right.

While it once laid claim to the most booksellers per square mile of any city in America, Cambridge is no longer the browsers' paradise it once was. Only a handful remain, protected by their passionate fan-base, including the **Grolier Poetry Book Shop** and **Harvard Book Store**.

From Harvard Square, it's a short stroll to the **Charles River**. Walk down John F Kennedy Street and you'll soon reach the embankment, along which there are walking paths in both directions. Head left for breathtaking views of Boston on the opposite bank.

IN THE KNOW FLORAL DISPLAY

The Harvard **Museum of Natural History** (*see p136*) houses an amazing collection of more than 3,000 scientifically accurate glass models of plants and flowers, created by Leopold Blaschka and his son, Rudolf. The intricate sculptures were originally made so professors could teach botany during the long New England winters.

EXPLORE

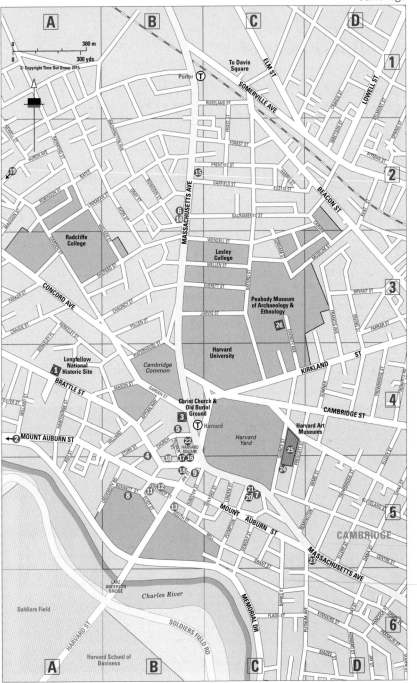

EXPLORE

In the opposite direction from Harvard Square, at Garden Street and Massachusetts Avenue, is the grassy **Cambridge Common**, where George Washington took control of the Continental Army in 1775 – a plaque marks the elm tree under which the troops were mustered. Nearby is the **Old Burial Ground**, dating from 1635, and **Christ Church** (Zero Garden Street, 1-617 876 0200, www.cccambridge.org), the site where George and Martha once worshipped. Designed in 1761 by the country's first trained architect, Peter Harrison, Christ Church was a hotbed of rebel activity during the Revolutionary War: the walls are still peppered with bullet holes.

Nearby **Brattle Street** was once called Tory Row, and several of the mansions of its former wealthy merchant residents remain. The further you venture from Harvard Square on Brattle, the older and grander the houses become. Near the end is the HQ of the Cambridge Historical Society, which, appropriately, has set up shop in the second-oldest house in Cambridge, the 1685 **Hooper-Lee-Nichols House** (159 Brattle Street, at Kennedy Road, 1-617 547 4252, www.cambridgehistory.org).

Further along Brattle or Mount Auburn Streets is the vast **Mount Auburn Cemetery**, the country's first garden cemetery. It's a lovely and peaceful place, where many of the city's most famous residents are buried. To the north is **Fresh Pond**, which was used in the 1800s as an ice source, and today is a reservoir with a two-mile perimeter and constantly changing scenery.

Carry on along Massachusetts Avenue from Cambridge Common and you will eventually reach **Porter Square**. While the square itself is unremarkable, the funky shops you'll find along the way are worth investigating – including vintage furniture store **Abodeon** and the dazzling fair-trade and folk art emporium **Nomad** (1741 Massachusetts Avenue, between Exeter Park & Prentiss Street, 1-617 497 6677, www.nomadcambridge.com). A few good bars and restaurants are also on this stretch, including standout Italian **Giulia**.

Sights & Museums

FREE Longfellow House – Washington's Headquarters National Historic Site

105 Brattle Street, at Longfellow Park (1-617 876 4491, www.nps.gov/long). Harvard T. **Open** *Tours* May-late Oct 10am-4.30pm Wed-Sun. *Grounds* dawn to dusk year-round. **Admission** free. **Map** p129 A4 **❶**

George Washington made this pretty, 28-room mansion his Continental Army headquarters from 1775 to 1776, before following the front line further south. In 1837, it became a boarding house, and a young Harvard professor, Henry Wadsworth Longfellow, moved in. When he married, his bride's father gave it to him as a wedding present, and he stayed until his death in 1882. In between entertaining such literary luminaries as Nathaniel Hawthorne, Ralph Waldo Emerson and Charles Dickens, Longfellow composed many of his best-known works here.

★ FREE Mount Auburn Cemetery

580 Mount Auburn Street, at Aberdeen Avenue (1-617 547 7105, www.mountauburn.org).

Mount Auburn Cemetery

Alden & Harlow

Harvard T then bus 71, 72, 73. **Open** 8am-5pm daily. **Admission** free. **Map** p129 A4 ➋
The final resting place for Oliver Wendell Holmes, Henry Wadsworth Longfellow and Charles Bulfinch, along with some 86,000 others. In fact, the cemetery is now so full that locals who want to spend eternity here often settle for cremation. But there's plenty of life too: there are 4,000 types of tree and 130 species of shrub alone on its 175 acres, and excellent guided tours to help you distinguish them.

FREE Old Burial Ground

Massachusetts Avenue, at Garden Street (no phone). Harvard T. **Open** dawn-dusk daily. **Admission** free. **Map** p129 B4 ➌
One of the country's first cemeteries, the Old Burial Ground contains the remains of several early Puritan settlers as well as Revolutionary War veterans and victims.

Restaurants & Cafés

Alden & Harlow

40 Brattle Street, near Church Street (1-617 864 2100, www.aldenharlow.com). Harvard T. **Open** 5pm-1am Mon-Wed; 5pm-2am Thur-Sat; 10.30am-2.30pm, 5pm-1am Sun. **Main courses** $12-$34. **Map** p129 B4 ➍ American
Duck into this subterranean hideaway – the former site of Harvard Square institution Casablanca – and discover a bustling multi-room dining and drinking destination that balances a rustic laid-back vibe with an industrial edge. The reclaimed wood and brick walls add warmth to the sprawling space, as do the honey-coloured glass lanterns that hang over the bar. There's a small atrium dining room; high-top tables in the bar area; and the main dining room, where guests can glimpse the open kitchen through metal shelving stacked with cookbooks. The American cuisine of chef-owner Michael Scelfo reflects a similar juxtaposition – chef-driven home-cooking with an edge, such as smoked lamb belly ribs with carrot and cashew tahini

and sour orange glaze. Most main courses are under $20, unless you entertain the 16-ounce Creekstone Farms New York strip.

Cambridge, 1

27 Church Street, at Palmer Street (1-617 576 1111). Harvard T. **Open** 11.30am-midnight Mon-Thur; 11.30am-1am Fri, Sat. **Main courses** $9-$30. **Map** p129 B4 ➎ Pizza
There's nothing remotely parlour-like about this Harvard Square pizza parlour. For starters, it's in a former fire station. But the cinderblock walls are warmed by large wooden booths, and the minimalist decor is carried out in the black stone table tops and streamlined menu. The place is known for its broad selection of thin-crust pizzas, which are charcoal-grilled and topped with the likes of lobster or Italian sausage, with fresh herbs and infused oils. But the salads are elegantly simple, the pastas hearty and affordable, and the only dessert is Toscanini's ice cream (a plus). You can't beat the location: it's in the heart of Harvard Square and a block away from indie film institution the Brattle Theatre. Come here, before or after. The kitchen serves until midnight.

★ Giulia

1682 Massachusetts Avenue, between Hudson & Sacramento Streets (1-617 441 2800, http:// giuliarestaurant.com). Harvard T then 15min walk, or bus 77, 96. **Open** 5.30-10pm Mon-Thur; 5.30-11pm Fri, Sat. **Main courses** $17-$38. **Map** p129 B2 ➏ Italian
Chef-owner Michael Pagliarini and his wife Pamela Ralston (she'll greet you at the door) pamper their guests with a warm welcome, friendly, professional service and killer pastas that are hand made by day on a custom-made table used to accommodate large groups at night. Brick walls and candlelight keep the vibe romantic and rustic. The all-Italian wines pair well with the dishes, which are often inspired by the chef's travels to Italy. Patrons who gawk at others' plates quickly get recommendations – try

EXPLORE

the popular pappardelle with wild boar or spaghetti alle vongole – both are al dente, flavourful and prove Pagliarini's mettle. As good as the pastas and *secondi* are, though, you won't want to forgo dessert – in particular, the chocolate terrine.

★ $ Mr Bartley's Gourmet Burgers

1246 Massachusetts Avenue, near Plympton Street (1-617 354 6559, www.mrbartley.com). Harvard T. **Open** 11am-9pm Mon-Sat. **Main courses** $6-$18. **No credit cards.** **Map** p129 C5 ❼ American

There's barely room to move amid the memorabilia that clutters this Harvard Square institution (est. 1960), never mind the crush of diners scoffing thick, juicy burgers and even thicker frappes (New England-speak for milkshakes). But don't let that stop you; the tight squeeze is all part of the fun at a joint that features 30 different burgers named after local and national celebs (Stephen Colbert, Kevin Love), all accompanied by kitschy comments (The Kim Kardashian/please make her go away).

Rialto

Charles Hotel, 1 Bennett Street, near Eliot Street (1-617 661 5050, www.rialto-restaurant.com). Harvard T. **Open** 5.30-11pm Mon-Sat; 5.30-10pm Sun. **Main courses** $26-$45. **Map** p129 B5 ❽ Italian

Jody Adams (James Beard Award winner, *Top Chef Masters* contestant) provides one of the city's most memorable dining experiences, proving she's earned all the accolades. The dining room is breezy and elegant, with sheer curtains and splashes of orange. The menu, or should we say menus, are just as sensual and revealing as Adams' passion for – and frequent travels to – Italy. Guests can choose from à la carte dining, four-course fixed-price menus that focus on an Italian region each month ($75), or the bargain-buyer's three-course teatro menu, which is offered in the bar/lounge area only for $40 (or in the dining room upon request). It'll get you in for a song, and that's all that counts.

Russell House Tavern

14 John F Kennedy Street, at Brattle Street (1-617 500 3055, www.russellhousecambridge. com). Harvard T. **Open** 11am-1am Mon-Wed; 11am-2am Thur, Fri; 10am-2am Sat; 10am-1am Sun. **Main courses** $13-$35. **Map** p129 B5 ❾ American

This upscale tavern offers various seating options and above-average comfort food with a twist, making it a good choice in the Square. In the summer, sip a cocktail from the list of classics and enjoy prime people-watching from the patio or the breezy open windows of the upper level. Downstairs, the tavern vibe kicks in with a large horseshoe bar, black banquette and high-top seating in a brick and dark wood dining room. The creative American menu spans the gamut, from pan-seared arctic char, to slow-cooked

chicken or a grass-fed burger. Anyone looking for classier late-night fare will love the $1 oysters, available every night of the week after 11pm, as well as lobster sliders and lamb-belly meatballs. Eggs Benedict and stuffed brioche french toast make the grade at brunch.

Bars

★ Beat Hôtel

13 Brattle Street, near Palmer Street (1-617 499 0001, www.beathotel.com). Harvard T. **Open** 4pm-midnight Mon, Tue; 4pm-1am Wed; 4pm-2am Thur, Fri; 10am-2am Sat; 10am-midnight Sun. **Map** p129 B5 ❿

Beat Hôtel isn't a hotel at all – the younger sibling of the Beehive (*see p102*) is an American brasserie with a nod to the intellectual and artistic movements of '60s bohemian culture. With illuminated peace signs and whimsically painted walls, the decor might try too hard, but the free, nightly jazz bands in the cavernous room secure its place as the hippest watering hole in Harvard Square. Exciting American wines are available, while the cocktail menu dusts off drinks you may have forgotten, such as the rusty nail, harvey wallbanger, tequila sunrise and the stinger.

Charlie's Kitchen

10 Eliot Street, at Winthrop Street (1-617 492 9646, http://charlieskitchen.com). Harvard T. **Open** 11am-1am Mon-Wed, Sun; 11am-2am Thur-Sat. **Map** p129 B5 ⓫

Despite the rampant fancifying of everything within a five-mile radius of Harvard, the stalwart Charlie's Kitchen has hardly changed a bit. This place may be known as the double cheeseburger king, but the loud, ready-to-drink crowd of punks, students, professors and local rock luminaries piles into the upstairs bar for the massive glasses of Hoegaarden, cheap eats, snippy waitresses and the best jukebox in Cambridge.

Grendel's Den

89 Winthrop Street, nr John F Kennedy Street (1-617 491 1160, www.grendelsden.com). Harvard T. **Open** 11.30am-1am daily. **Map** p129 B5 ⓬

This unpretentious little basement bar continues to attract throngs of thirsty Harvard students. From 5pm until 7.30pm (plus 9pm until 11.30pm Sunday to Thursday), everything on the food menu is half price after you've bought a $3 drink. You'd be surprised how much tomorrow's leaders could use a bargain now and again.

Shays Pub & Wine Bar

58 John F Kennedy Street, between Eliot & Winthrop Streets (1-617 864 9161). Harvard T. **Open** 11am-1am Mon-Sat; noon-1am Sun. **Map** p129 B5 ⓭

Owned and operated by English expats, Shays is one of the nicer bars in the area. Sunk a few feet

EXPLORE

below the sidewalk and sporting a handy outdoor patio, the bar itself is rather poky. It attracts a lively mix of academics, artists and die-hard regulars. Though many patrons quaff from the bar's extensive beer menu, this is primarily a wine bar – and there are no spirits.

West Side Lounge

1680 Massachusetts Avenue, at Sacramento Street (1-617 441 5566, www.westsidelounge.com). Porter T. **Open** 5pm-1am Mon-Sat; 10.30am-1am Sun. **Map** p129 B2

With its candlelit tables, high-backed booths and reserved seats for walk-ins, West Side Lounge is an ideal place to get your night started. Be warned – once you start in on the fairly priced cocktails and small plate-focused menu, you might choose to skip your next destination entirely.

Shops & Services

Abodeon

1731 Massachusetts Avenue, at Prentiss Street (1-617 497 0137, www.abodeon.com). Porter T. **Open** 10am-6pm Mon-Sat; noon-5pm Sun. **Map** p129 B2 **Homewares**

Mid 20th-century modern style is the speciality of this fabulous vintage home store; as well as furniture, there's classic tableware, kitchen appliances and quirky knick-knacks.

★ Black Ink

5 Brattle Street, at Harvard Square (1-866 497 1221, www.blackinkboston.com). Harvard T. **Open** 10am-8pm Mon-Sat; 11am-7pm Sun. **Map** p129 B5 **Homewares/gifts**

It's wall-to-wall fun at the Cambridge outpost of a Beacon Hill original, where the eclectic stock – everything from Tintin T-shirts and Japanese toys to colourful melamine tableware, hip stationery and strikingly packaged toiletries – is arrayed on floor-to-ceiling shelves for easy browsing.

Other location 101 Charles Street, at Pinckney Street, Beacon Hill (1-617 723 3883).

Cardullo's Gourmet Shoppe

6 Brattle Street, at Harvard Square (1-617 491 8888, www.cardullos.com). Harvard T. **Open** 9am-9pm Mon-Sat; 10am-7pm Sun. **Map** p129 B5 **Food & drink**

Call it a novelty shop for foodies. Negotiating Cardullo's riotous aisles, you'll encounter chai truffles and white chocolate ants; cans of spotted dick and jars of cassoulet; pecan vinegar and piña colada jam; wines from Cape Cod and caviar from the Mississippi River. You can score some fine sandwiches from the deli counter too. Brits abroad will find store-cupboard standbys such as McVitie's biscuits and Marmite – at a price.

Curious George Store

1 John F Kennedy Street, at Brattle Street (1-617 547 4500, www.thecuriousgeorgestore.com). Harvard T. **Open** 10am-8pm Mon-Sat; 10am-6pm Sun. **Map** p129 B5 **Children**

Parent shop WordsWorth has closed, but the children's branch (named after the fictional monkey whose creator, Margret Rey, used to frequent the old bookstore) lives on. The jungle-themed upstairs room offers parenting and baby books, board books, picture books, early readers and non-fiction tomes; older readers will find chapter books, Tintin, Asterix

Curious George Store.

Mint Julep

and anime works downstairs. But beware: your kids may not even notice the books among the profusion of toys, games and art supplies.

★ Formaggio Kitchen

244 Huron Avenue, at Appleton Street, Huron Village (1-617 354 4750, www.formaggiokitchen. com). Harvard T then bus 72. **Open** 9am-7pm Mon-Fri; 9am-6pm Sat; 10am-4pm Sun. **Map** p129 A2 ⑲ **Food & drink**

Ihsan Gurdal's store is among the nation's top gourmet shops and continues to dazzle connoisseurs with a vast collection of artisanal cheeses from all over the world. Specially constructed cheese caves in the basement keep them at the ideal temperature and humidity. There's a cornucopia of accoutrements too. Here, you'll find condiments, charcuterie, confectionery and speciality ingredients, ranging from flowering teas and heirloom cattle beans to Hawaiian red sea salt and Piedmontese chickpea flour.

Other location 268 Shawmut Avenue, between Milford & Hanson Streets, South End (1-617 350 6996, www.southendformaggio.com).

Grolier Poetry Book Shop

6 Plympton Street, at Massachusetts Avenue (1-617 547 4648, www.grolierpoetrybookshop.com). Harvard T. **Open** 11am-7pm Tue, Wed; 11am-6pm Thur-Sat. **Map** p129 C5 ⑳ **Books & music**

Down a side street from the Harvard Book Store, the tiny Grolier has been catering to the voracious appetites of Cambridge poetry lovers for more than 80 years. Every available surface is piled with new books of verse, ranging from anthologies for casual readers to collections by obscure poets in translation. The Grolier further encourages the appreciation of poetry through its annual prizes and well-attended readings.

★ Harvard Book Store

1256 Massachusetts Avenue, at Plympton Street (1-617 661 1515, www.harvard.com). Harvard T. **Open** 9am-11pm Mon-Sat; 10am-10pm Sun. **Map** p129 C5 ㉑ **Books & music**

This independent bookseller works hard to rival the larger chain stores with its varied selection of general-interest books and helpful staff, always ready to recommend a title or two. Students crowd the substantial philosophy and cultural theory sections. Meanwhile, local bibliophiles make a beeline for the basement, where the used and remainder bookshelves are packed with everything from dog-eared cookbooks to gorgeous art books, all at a hefty discount.

Mint Julep

6 Church Street, at Massachusetts Avenue (1-617 576 6468, www.shopmintjulep.com). Harvard T. **Open** 10am-7pm Mon-Wed; 10am-8pm Thur-Sat; 11am-6pm Sun. **Map** p129 B4 ㉒ **Fashion**

The first branch of this women's boutique was launched by two Harvard graduates in Brookline in 2004, swiftly followed by this larger Harvard Square shop. Mint Julep offers an appealing melange of labels (both European and American), styles, prints and prices – the only unifying factor is an underlying postmodern country-club aura. You'll find lots of retro-influenced dresses, cool T-shirts and colourful accessories by the likes of Tibi, Milly, Orla Kiely and Kensie, as well as less expensive brands.

Other location 1302 Beacon Street, at Pleasant Street, Coolidge Corner, Brookline (1-617 232 3600).

Pyara Spa & Salon

1050 Massachusetts Avenue, at Mount Auburn Street (1-617 497 9300, www.pyaraaveda.com). Harvard T. **Open** 8am-10pm Mon-Fri; 8am-8pm Sat; 10am-6pm Sun. **Map** p129 D5 ㉓ **Health & beauty**

This chic Harvard Square establishment uses Aveda's excellent natural, eco-conscious products. For the cleanest, softest skin ever, the Pyara Caribbean Therapy Body Treatment is a relaxing ritual that exfoliates, then detoxifies and nourishes with a warm seaweed mask and body wrap, before a Vichy shower water massage and restorative face, scalp and body massage leaves you floating on a cloud.

HARVARD UNIVERSITY

Harvard Square T.

Harvard has more than 400 buildings scattered around Cambridge and Boston, but for the campus you've seen in the movies, head to **Harvard Yard** (for tours, call 1-617 495 1573), a grassy, tree-lined quadrangle surrounded by red-brick buildings. First-year students still live in dormitories in the Yard, and you'll find them studying and reading (or flirting or sleeping) on the grassy sections of the quad.

As you enter the Yard from Massachusetts Avenue through Johnston Gate (a half-block from the Harvard Square T), look for **Massachusetts Hall** on the right. Built in 1720, the Hall sheltered the soldiers of the fledgling Continental Army during the Revolutionary War. Massachusetts Hall just edges out the **Wadsworth House** (built in 1726) as the oldest building in the Yard, though the latter's yellow clapboard structure is more picturesque. This building served as temporary headquarters for George Washington when he was leading the nation's army in 1775.

University Hall, designed by Charles Bulfinch in 1815, sits directly in front of the Yard's most popular sight: the **statue of John Harvard**. Cast in 1884 by Daniel Chester French (who also sculpted the Lincoln Memorial in Washington, DC), it's known as the 'statue of three lies'. Its inscription reads 'John Harvard, Founder, 1638', which is three times untrue since John Harvard was a donor, not a founder; the college was set up in 1636; and nobody knows what he really looked like – French used a Harvard student as a model. Touching John Harvard's shoe is rumored to bring good luck, but students know better: peeing on the foot is an undergraduate rite of passage.

So are liaisons among the stacks of **Widener Library**, which sits on the quiet square directly behind University Hall. The imposing, classically styled building houses the headquarters of the oldest university library in the country and the largest academic library system in the world; it holds 3.2 million volumes.

Though most visitors don't venture beyond the main quad, it's worth exploring further in order to see the neo-Gothic **Memorial Hall** (45 Quincy Street), which houses the Sanders Theatre (*see p197*), and the **Carpenter Center for the Visual Arts**, designed in 1963 by the French modernist architect Le Corbusier – his only North American building. Other notable buildings on campus include the **Science Center**, just north of the central quad – which is said to look like a Polaroid camera, and is one of several buildings at Harvard designed by Josep Lluís Sert. (For an architectural tour of the campus, *see p240* **Walk**.)

John Harvard statue.

Outside Harvard Yard

The 12 houses that serve as Harvard's undergraduate dorms are clustered near Harvard Square: walk down Plympton Street, past the gold cupola of **Adams House**, and turn right on to Mount Auburn Street and past the enormous blue bell tower of **Lowell House**. Lying between Harvard Yard and Memorial Drive is the **Harvard Lampoon Castle** (44 Bow Street), offices of the satirical publication the *Harvard Lampoon*, which has spawned countless writers and comedians, including John Updike and Conan O'Brien. You can't go inside, but it's still worth seeing the exterior. It's wedged on to a tiny sliver of land between Mount Auburn and Bow Streets, but architects Wheelwright & Haven made the most of the site in 1909, creating a cartoonish, miniature castle that reflects its mischievous inhabitants.

Harvard has an impressive array of museums that range from the authoritative to the bizarre. The **Peabody Museum of Archaeology & Ethnology** is a repository of rare fossils and ancient artefacts; its connected to the Harvard **Museum of Natural History**, which has several halls filled with casualties of the 'shoot it and stuff it' school of science, a collection of intricate, minutely detailed flowers modelled out of glass, and Vladimir Nabokov's meticulous catalogue of butterfly genitalia. The spoils of 100 years of excavations in the Near East are free for anyone to view at the Harvard **Semitic Museum** (6 Divinity Avenue, 1-617 495 4631, www.semiticmuseum.fas.harvard.edu). Thanks to the lofty aspirations and generous donations of generations of Harvard alumni, the collections on display in the recently expanded and consolidated **Harvard Art Museums** are impressive.

Sights & Museums

FREE Carpenter Center for the Visual Arts

24 Quincy Street, at Harvard Yard (1-617 495 3251, www.ccva.fas.harvard.edu). Harvard T. **Open** noon-7pm Wed-Sun. **Admission** free. **Map** p129 C5 ㉔
The Le Corbusier-designed Carpenter Center for the Visual Arts hosts exhibitions by prominent artists in its ground- and third-floor galleries. The focus is on contemporary work, with a particular emphasis on photography. The Center also houses the Harvard Film Archive (*see p175*).

★ Harvard Art Museums

32 Quincy Street, at Broadway (1-617 495 9400, www.harvardartmuseums.org). Harvard Square T. **Open** 10am-5pm daily. **Admission** $15; $10-$13 reductions; free under-18s. **Map** p129 C4 ㉕
See p137 **Three Into One Will Go.**

Peabody Museum of Archaeology & Ethnology/Harvard Museum of Natural History

11 Divinity Avenue, at Kirkland Street (1-617 496 1027, www.peabody.harvard.edu). Harvard T. **Open** 9am-5pm daily. **Admission** $12; $8-$10 reductions; free under-3s. **Map** p129 C3 ㉖
The Peabody features fossils and anthropological artefacts from as far back as the Palaeolithic period, with exhibitions on North American Indians and Central America. Connected to the Peabody is Harvard's Museum of Natural History (*see p170*), which exhibits dinosaur fossils, mineral and rock collections and a menagerie of stuffed animals that includes pheasants once owned by George Washington. A highlight of the museum is the world's only mounted kronosaurus, a 42ft-long prehistoric marine reptile.
▶ *For other highlights, see p128 In the Know.*

CENTRAL SQUARE & INMAN SQUARE

Central T.

Once a predominantly working-class neighbourhood, Central Square has become a desirable residential area for young professionals – high-priced condos and the ubiquitous chains have followed. Yet it has somehow managed to hang on to some of its distinct, slightly gritty, identity.

With a high concentration of restaurants, bars and nightspots, Central Square is a popular evening destination. Fabled rock clubs the **Middle East** and **TT the Bear's Place** share the same block. There's also a sprinkling of indie shops that have survived for decades, including the venerable vintage emporium **Great Eastern Trading Co** and second-hand vinyl fixture **Cheapo Records**.

About a 15-minute walk up Prospect Street from Central, at the intersection of Hampshire and Cambridge Streets, is **Inman Square**, an intersection with a high concentration of good restaurants – including many Brazilian eateries, quirky shops and wonderful ice-cream at **Christina's Homemade Ice-cream**.

Restaurants & Cafés

Baraka Café

80½ Pearl Street, between Auburn & William Streets, Central Square (1-617 868 3951, www.barakacafe.com). Central T. **Open** 11.30am-3pm, 5.30-10pm Tue-Sat; 5.30-10pm Sun. **Main courses** $11-$21. **No credit cards.** **Map** p142 B4 ㉗
North African
It's small wonder this vivid, richly colourful North African café remains unknown even to many Central Square locals – with only 25 seats, this is one little

THREE INTO ONE WILL GO

The unified Harvard Art Museums finally has the space it deserves.

Given Harvard's history and status, it stands to reason it has one of the country's best university art collections, spanning some 250,000 pieces from Neolithic sculpture to 21st-century conceptual installations. For decades, however, many of these riches were hidden away in storage, and what was on display was divided into three separate spaces – the Fogg Museum, known for its European and American collections; the Busch-Reisinger Museum, with its focus on works from German-speaking countries, including an impressive cache of expressionist and Bauhaus works; and the Arthur M Sackler Museum, which housed one of the most important Asian art collections in the West.

In 2008, all but the Sackler closed for a massive expansion project to bring them under one roof, newly constructed glass roof. Six years later, the unified **Harvard Art Museums** (*see p136*) opened in late 2014. Harvard engaged Renzo Piano, the man behind extensions to the Isabella Stewart Gardner Museum (*see p89*) and NYC's Morgan Library, as well as numerous high-profile buildings. The architect retained the Georgian Revival façade of the 1927 Fogg and that museum's serene courtyard with its travertine archways reminiscent of a Romanesque cloister, but opened up the interior of the upper levels with glass-walled arcades. Casual visitors can enter the light-suffused Calderwood Courtyard via the museum's Prescott Street entrance without paying admission, linger over coffee

at its café tables and get a free peek at contemporary installations on the lower level.

At the back, a modern, cedar-clad extension has increased gallery space by 40 per cent. Conservation is an important aspect of the institution (you can glimpse the prestigious Straus Center for Conservation and Technical Studies through a glass wall on the fifth floor). While the museum was closed, every object was painstakingly examined and restored, including works from the bequest of Maurice Wertheim (class of 1906), who stipulated that his collection – containing masterpieces by Renoir, Degas, Matisse and Picasso, among others – be on continuous view in a single gallery.

While the museum is still loosely delineated by its original collections, the experience is more fluid. On the second floor, for example, you can move seamlessly from a display of 17th-century Japanese screens through Islamic ceramics to Italian Renaissance paintings, while the third floor presents an interesting juxtaposition of a second-century marble Cupid with a 1986 Louise Bourgeois sculpture. A new third-floor gallery hosts special exhibitions. Since this is a study museum, anyone – not just students and academics – can request to see works that are not on display. Select from the collection database on the website and schedule your very own private viewing (at least two weeks in advance) in the fourth floor's Art Study Center.

EXPLORE

Harvard Art Museums.

secret devotees tend to keep to themselves. And once you've tasted the complex yet zesty spicing of meze such as merguez (lamb and beef sausage) and *karentika* (harissa-laced chickpea custard), with stellar *cherbat* (lemonade infused with rose petals), you'll be hard put to blame them. Well-organised types can call 36 hours before their visit to order the remarkable *bastilla*, a fragrant squab pie.

Bondir

279A Broadway, between Elm & Columbia Streets, near Central Square (1-617 661 0009, www.bondircambridge.com). Central T then 10min walk. **Open** 5-10pm Mon, Wed-Sun. **Main courses** $18-$30. **Map** p142 C2
American

You'd never guess that beyond the nondescript brick façade are an enchanting farmhouse dining room, a roaring fireplace and a daily edited menu that takes full advantage of the ebb and flow of seasonal and local ingredients. Chef-owner Jason Bond spent 20 years in New England restaurant kitchens before showcasing his talents via local produce, seafood and meats. It shows in the small yet careful selection of four courses – Maine halibut with baby brussels sprouts and shellfish emulsion, pistachio steam cake with poached figs, for example – and house-made breads. Presentations are elegant, not stuffy. Guests sip an aperitif in front of the fire before heading to their table where old church pews (with pillows) serve as seats.

★ $ Christina's Homemade Ice Cream

1255 Cambridge Street, at Prospect Street, Inman Square (1-617 492 7021, www.christinas icecream.com). Central T then 15mins walk, or bus 83, 91. **Open** 11.30am-10.30pm daily. **Ice-cream** $3-$5. **No credit cards**. **Map** p142 C1 Ice-cream

Whether or not they advertise the fact, many local restaurants scream for ice cream from this Inman Square shop to supplement their dessert menus. Among the beautifully realised seasonal flavours such as pumpkin and eggnog, keep your eyes peeled – and your mouth primed – for fresh rose, burnt sugar and ginger molasses. Not to mention the creative (and delicious) use of spices and the dependable, crave-worthy sundaes made with warm chocolate fudge and freshly whipped cream.

★ Craigie on Main

853 Main Street, at Bishop Allen Drive, Central Square (1-617 497 5511, www.craigieonmain. com). Central T. **Open** 5.30-11pm Tue-Sun. **Main courses** $38-$43. **Map** p142 C4
Creative contemporary

The buzz surrounding this upscale culinary hot-spot is centred on respected chef/proprietor Tony Maws, whose Franco-American creations use the best local and organic ingredients. He's a local pioneer of the 'snout to tail' movement. Craigie on Main's knowledgeable and friendly staff (including a handful of smiling cocktail mavens) will guide you through the seasonal menus. While there are plenty of à la carte choices, the eight-course tasting menu ($118) is a favourite, and might include crispy-fried Florida frogs' legs, hiramasa sashimi salad or rhubarb-hibiscus mousse. But the Chef's Whim, a six- or four-course tasting menu ($57 and $45, respectively) offered Sunday evenings after 9pm, is an affordable way to sample the experience without breaking the piggybank.

Inman Square. See p136.

EXPLORE

East by Northeast

1128 Cambridge Street, at Norfolk Street, Inman Square (1-617 876 0286, www.exnecambridge. com). Central T then 15mins walk. **Open** 5-10pm Tue-Sat; 5-9.30pm Sun. **Small plates** $5-$12. **Map** p142 C1 ③ **Chinese**

Chef-owner Phillip Tang offers a nuanced take on his family's oldest recipes at this intimate Chinese bistro. Small plates of noodles, dumplings and pickled vegetables make up the bulk of the menu, which features à la carte as well as fixed-price options. Daily specials ensure there is always something new to try. Bring an adventurous friend or two who like to share, and don't forget to check out the cocktail list – it's as inventive as the cuisine.

East Coast Grill

1271 Cambridge Street, between Prospect & Oakland Streets, Inman Square (1-617 491 6568, www.eastcoastgrill.net). Central T, then 15mins walk or bus 83, 91. **Open** 5.30-10pm Mon-Thur; 5.30-10.30pm Fri; 11am-2.30pm, 5.30-10.30pm Sat; 11am-2.30pm, 5.30-10pm Sun. **Main courses** $21-$32. **Map** p142 C1 ② **Seafood/BBQ**

On paper, the concept must have looked pretty fuzzy back in 1985: how could the then-unknown Chris Schlesinger possibly pull off a tropically tinged seafood shack/barbecue pit complete with raw bar and tiki lounge? But the disparate elements proved wildly harmonic – and successful. Schlesinger, author of many grilling cookbooks, sold the joint to reliable staff members who are carrying on the tradition more than a quarter of a century later with the same bold tropical-spicy flavours (grilled mahi mahi with pineapple salsa) and BBQ heat.

★ Oleana

134 Hampshire Street, between Elm & Norfolk Streets, Inman Square (1-617 661 0505, www. oleanarestaurant.com). Central T, then 15mins walk or bus 83, 91. **Open** 5.30-10pm Mon-Thur, Sun; 5.30-11pm Fri, Sat. **Main courses** $23-$27. **Map** p142 C2 ③ **Mediterranean**

Two tiny, coolly pretty dining rooms and an enormously popular garden patio provide a showcase for chef-owner Ana Sortun's passion for – and mastery of – the aromatic cuisines of Turkey, Greece, Armenia, Morocco, Egypt and Sicily. Most of the small plates are memorable, while many of the desserts are downright extraordinary.

Puritan & Company

1166 Cambridge Street, between Tremont & Norfolk Streets, Inman Square (1-617 615 6195, www.puritancambridge.com). **Open** 5.30-10pm Mon-Thur; 5.30-11pm Fri, Sat; 10.30am-2pm, 5.30-10pm Sun. **Main courses** $20-$31. **Map** p142 C1 ③ **Contemporary American**

There's a shabby-chic vibe at this Inman Square find, where kitchen towels serve as napkins and the dining room is dotted with vintage furniture. (The host stand is a vintage Glenwood oven.) But the star is chef-owner Will Gilson's cuisine – locally sourced (when possible) New England fare with a pinch of ethnic oomph and flavour-driving details. Take the house-made Parker House rolls, for example, served with butter whipped with yogurt and sea salt. Then there's the swordfish pastrami, Moxie-glazed lamb belly, roasted pork T-bone, and desserts including sweet potato pudding with rum raisins.

★ $ Toscanini's

899 Main Street, at Massachusetts Avenue, Central T. **Open** 8am-11pm Mon-Fri; 9am-11pm Sat, Sun. **Ice-cream** $3-$6. **Map** p142 C4 ③ **Ice-cream**

The *New York Times* called it the best ice-cream in the world. *People* magazine said it had the best vanilla ice-cream in the United States. Not bad, but the folks at Toscanini's aren't ones to rest on their laurels – and that's what makes them one of our favourites. The staff are constantly coming up with such new and intriguing flavours as B3 (brownies, brown sugar, brown butter) and the amazing burnt caramel, which was actually created by accident.

Bars

★ Brick & Mortar

567 Massachusetts Avenue, at Pearl Street, Central Square (1-617 491 0016, www.brickmortarltd. com). Central T. **Open** 5pm-1am Mon-Wed, Sun; 5pm-2am Thur-Sat. **Map** p142 B3 ③

It's still just as hard to find as its predecessor, the Enormous Room, but once you head through the nondescript door and up the stairs, the similarities end. A giant horseshoe-shaped bar and ample bar-stool seating have replaced the low, rug-strewn platforms and hybrid drink/bathroom line. The cocktails shine and the bar snacks (which include bacon-wrapped dates and deep-fried house-made pickles) are done just right.

Green Street Grill

280 Green Street, between Magazine & Pearl Streets, Central Square (1-617 876 1655, www.greenstreetgrill.com). Central T. **Open** 5.30pm-1am daily. **Map** p142 B3 ③

You'd never know it from the unassuming exterior, but Green Street mixes some of the city's best drinks. The long, narrow bar area fills up at peak hours – show up for last call or on weeknights to avoid the crush. Coast-spanning craft beers include selections from local brewery Pretty Things and the cocktail list offers plenty of choice, but if don't see something you like, ask the bartender for the 'special' cocktail binder for hundreds of more options.

Miracle of Science Bar + Grill

321 Massachusetts Avenue, at State Street, Central Square (1-617 868 2866, www.miradeofscience.us). Central T. **Open** 11am-1am daily. **Map** p142 C4 ③

Cheapo Records.

The Miracle of Science combines ultra-modern design, a well-selected variety of beers and a comfortable, sun-bathed interior, thanks to its huge windows looking out over Mass Ave. In honour of the many MIT students who frequent the place, the menu is laid out like the periodic table.

Plough & Stars
912 Massachusetts Avenue, at Hancock Street, Central Square (1-617 576 0032, www.plough andstars.com). Central T. **Open** 11am-1am Mon; 11.30am-1am Tue, Wed; 11.30am-2am Thur, Fri; 10am-2am Sat; 10am-1am Sun. **Map** p142 A2 ⑳
The spiritual forefather of Greater Boston's thriving Irish pub scene, the Plough opened in 1969. In the daytime, it offers good pub grub. At night, the tiny bar is transformed into a hotbed of clashing elbows and live music.

Shops & Services

Central Bottle Wine & Provisions
196 Massachusetts Avenue, at Smart Street, Central Square (1-617 225 0040, www.centralbottle.com). Central T or bus 1. **Open** 11am-8pm Mon-Wed, Sat; 11am-9pm Thur, Fri; noon-6pm Sun. **Map** p142 C4 ⑳ **Food & drink**
This glass-fronted *enoteca* is the brainchild of four friends who were so enamored with those of Venice that they opened their own similarly intimate gathering place when they returned to the States. Much more than just a wine store, the Bottle offers weekly tastings and stocks a variety of cheeses, *salumi*, craft beers and condiments.

★ Cheapo Records
538 Massachusetts Avenue, at Norfolk Street, Central Square (1-617 354 4455, www.cheaporecords.com). Central T. **Open** 11am-7pm Mon-Wed, Sat; 11am-9pm Thur, Fri; 11am-5pm Sun. **Map** p142 B3 ⑳ **Books & Music**

When Skippy White's – the fabled store for serious connoisseurs of old-school R&B, jazz, gospel and hip hop – closed back in 2006, the equally legendary Cheapo Records moved into the space. It still stocks some of the best vinyl in the area, with good prices and solid sections for pop/rock, folk, oldies, jazz and country, along with CDs and hard-to-find box sets.

Great Eastern Trading Co
49 River Street, at Auburn Street, Central Square (1-617 354 5279). Central T. **Open** noon-7pm Mon-Sat; noon-5pm Sun. **Map** p142 A3 ⑳ **Fashion**
This fun, friendly vintage shop on River Street was one of the first in the city, and it still maintains a high standard of second-hand clothing and accessories – expect an enticing melange of western shirts, belly-dancing outfits, DJs and glittery platform boots.

Keezer's
140 River Street, at Kinnaird Street, Central Square (1-617 547 2455, www.keezers.com). Central T. **Open** 10am-6pm Mon-Sat. **Map** p142 A4 ⑳ **Fashion**
Established in 1895, Keezer's is the oldest second-hand clothing store in the country and a cherished local resource. Max Keezer started the company by going into Harvard dorms in order to buy barely worn fine clothing from allowance-starved heirs. As well as renting out formalwear (they outfit the Boston Symphony Orchestra), the shop sells second-hand and end-of-the-line men's suits, sports coats, overcoats and casualwear, all in good or mint condition, and with at least 75% off. Since stock comes from Neiman's, Louis and Saks, you may find Armani and Zegna among the labels.

Stellabella Toys
1360 Cambridge Street, at Hampshire Street, Inman Square (1-617 491 6290, www.stellabella toys.com). Central T then bus 83, 91. **Open** 10am-6pm Mon-Sat; 10am-5pm Sun. **Map** p142 C1 ⑳ **Children**

This Cambridge favourite, selling a wide array of traditional and educational toys, now has a second branch between Davis and Porter Squares that visitors may find more convenient to reach by subway than its original tucked-away Inman Square location. However, only the original offers the popular programme of activities such as singalongs and playgroups.
Other location 196 Elm Street, at Tenny Street, Porter Square, Cambridge (1-617 864 6290).

Weirdo Records

844 Massachusetts Avenue, at Clinton Street, Central Square (1-857 413 0154, www.weirdo records.com). Central T. **Open** 11am-9pm daily. **Map** p142 A3 🕑 **Books & Music**
If stepping into this Central Square spot feels a bit like revisiting your first post-college apartment, you may not be surprised to learn that owner Angela Sawyer ran the business out of her tiny Somerville flat until 2009. No Beatles LPs here – Weirdo specialises in experimental and foreign music, from free jazz to Indonesian psychedelia. The store sports a colourful aesthetic, with bobble-head dolls lining the shelves and sky-printed fabrics adorning the walls.

KENDALL SQUARE & AROUND

Kendall/MIT T.

Aside from Harvard, some incredibly bright folks attend that other top Cambridge college, the **Massachusetts Institute of Technology** in Kendall Square, a short walk from Central Square along Massachusetts Avenue. MIT was founded in 1861 and rose to prominence during World War II, when radar was invented in its labs. The architecture of its various buildings is wildly diverse, ranging from the neoclassical walls of Building 10 to some striking modern structures by Eero Saarinen, Alvar Aalto, IM Pei and, latterly, the Frank Gehry-designed **Ray and Maria Stata Center**. (For more on MIT's architecture, *see p242*.)

At the heart of it all, cutting through the centre of campus and coming out from under the university's imposing dome, is the so-called 'Infinite Corridor', a long passage – punctuated by unexpected art installations – that connects many of the institute's departments.

MIT's cutting-edge **List Visual Arts Center** and multimedia **MIT Museum** are both worth visiting. Sculptures by the likes of Alexander Calder and Henry Moore also dot the grounds. In Building 10, the **Compton Gallery** (1-617 253 4444) features alternating shows that draw on the institute's historical collections of art and scientific objects. Hidden away in the back of the fourth floor of Building 4 is the Edgerton Center's **Strobe Alley**. The narrow passage displays the work of Harold ('Doc') Edgerton, the pioneer of high-speed photography, who shot the famous

images of a bullet explosively tunnelling through an apple and of a crown-shaped splash of milk. The centre carries on his research in high-speed and scientific imaging.

Dominated by modern buildings, Kendall Square doesn't have the same picturesque charm as Harvard Square, but in the past few years it's become a destination in its own right, with an explosion of new bars and restaurants, including new-concept hybrid hotspot **Café ArtScience**. It also has a popular arthouse cinema (*see p175*).

Sights & Museums

List Visual Arts Center

20 Ames Street, at Amherst Street (1-617 253 4680, http://listart.mit.edu). Kendall/MIT T. **Open** noon-6pm Tue, Wed, Fri-Sun; noon-8pm Thur. **Admission** free **Map** p143 E4 🕑
Located on the Wiesner Building's first floor, the List Visual Arts Center holds between five and eight shows a year, featuring American and international artists, working in wide variety of media. From conceptual installations to digital displays and video projects, the exhibitions typically push the boundaries of contemporary art.

Keezer's.

Cambridge

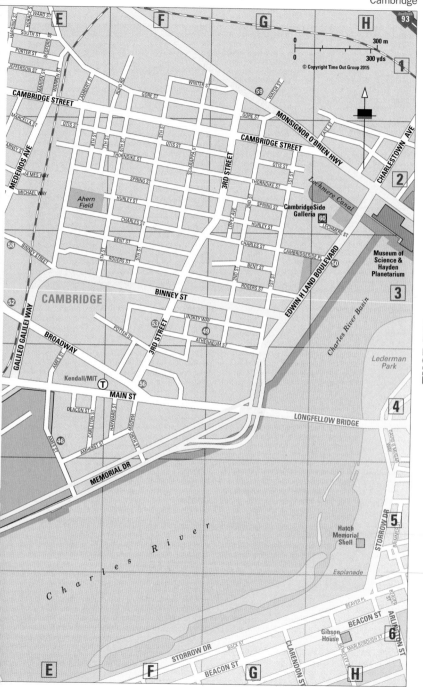

Massachusetts Institute of Technology. See p141.

★ MIT Museum

265 Massachusetts Avenue, at Front Street (1-617 253 5927, www.web.mit.edu/museum). Central or Kendall/MIT T, then 15mins walk. **Open** 10am-5pm daily. **Admission** $10; $8 reductions; free under-3s. Free to all last Sun of each mth from Sept to June. **No credit cards.** **Map** p142 C4 ❹
Five blocks from MIT's campus, this fascinating museum serves as a historical record of the institute and a showcase for its amazing inventions and related art. Collections span science and technology, architecture and design, and holography – you can see everything from exploding chairs and robotic hands to historic lasers developed for NASA.

Alexander Graham Bell carried out research on the MIT campus, so there's a retrospective of early telephonic devices too. Also on display are the kinetic sculptures of Arthur Ganson – ingenious, often hilarious machines that seem to have minds of their own – and the world's largest collection of holographic art, featuring, among other images, a woman transmogrifying into a tiger.

▶ *When you're blinded by science, swing by nearby Toscanini's (see p139) to sample some experimental ice-cream flavours.*

Restaurants & Cafés

Blue Room

1 Kendall Square, between Binney & Hampshire Streets (1-617 494 9034, www.theblueroom.net). Kendall/MIT T. **Open** 5-10pm Mon-Thur; 5-11pm Fri, Sat; 11am-2.30pm, 5-9pm Sun. **Main courses** $19-$28. **Map** p142 D3 ❹ **Creative contemporary**

Following an indie flick at arthouse Kendall Square Cinema, culture vultures refuel at this eclectic, welcoming hideaway. Best known for its interesting, fairly priced wine list and funky Sunday brunch buffet, it cultivates the spirit of adventure at dinner time, too, incorporating far-flung influences and interesting ingredients such as game (duck confit and pappardelle) and offal into its regularly changing menu.

★ Café ArtScience

650 East Kendall Street, between Athenaeum Street & Linskey Way (1-857 999 2193, www.cafeartscience.com). Kendall/MIT T. **Open** 7am-midnight Mon-Fri; 5pm-midnight Sat (food served until 11pm). **Small plates/main courses** $12-$28. **Map** p143 F3 ❹ **Eclectic** *See p146* **Perfect Formula**.

Dante

Royal Sonesta Boston, 40 Edwin H Land Boulevard, at Cambridgeside Place (1-617 497 4200, www.restaurantdante.com). Lechmere or Science Park T. **Open** 5.30-10pm Mon-Thur; 5.30-11pm Fri, Sat; 5-9pm Sun. **Main courses** $21-$34. **Map** p143 H3 ❺ **Italian**
Named after its talented chef-owner, Dante de Magistris, this cool Italian eatery has got the goods to generate a major cocktail-hour buzz: a spacious lounge, a seasonal patio overlooking the Charles River and, of course, sharp drinks and fancy snacks such as burrata with candied pistachios and arancini with truffle honey. But it usually delivers at mealtimes, too, via dishes that pack as much flair, such as the gnocchi with short-rib ragù and slow-roasted monkfish with braised endive.

Hungry Mother

*233 Cardinal Medeiros Avenue, at Bristol Street
(1-617 499 0090, www.hungrymothercambridge.
com). Kendall/MIT T.* **Open** 5-10.30pm Tue-Sun.
Main courses $18-$24. **Map** p142 D3 ⑤
American regional

This adorable spot manages to combine a commitment to sourcing ingredients locally with inspiration
from further afield – specifically from the base of the
Mississippi River Delta. The concise menu bursts
with Southern flavours and a soupçon of French
influence, from shrimp *escabeche* to cornmeal catfish
with dirty rice. The place is conveniently located
across from the Kendall Square Cinema, and if you
arrive to dine before 6pm you can score discounted
movie tickets – Hungry Mother will even pick them
up for you.

▶ *For information about the Kendall Square
Cinema, see p175.*

West Bridge

*1 Kendall Square, at Hampshire Street (1-617 945
0221, www.westbridgerestaurant.com). Kendall/MIT
T.* **Open** 11.30am-midnight Mon-Fri; 3pm-midnight
Sat, Sun. **Small plates** $12-$17. **Main courses** $16-
$45. **Map** p143 E3 ⑤ American

When West Bridge slipped into Kendall Square in
2012, the restaurant scene here was just heating up.
Chef-owner Matthew Gaudet ushers in inventive and
expertly created dishes using New England bounty in
various portions: small plates, sides, main courses to
share and larger 'table' dishes that can be turned into

Hungry Mother.

an affordable feast for parties of three or more. A cult
favourite is his 'Egg in a Jar' – a duck egg baked in a
mason jar with hen-of-the-woods mushrooms and
potato purée. Skate and shrimp with grits are to share,
and chicken with jus provides for the table. An abundance of natural light, reclaimed wood tables and custom lamps warm the sparse, industrial space, which
is marked by high ceilings and floor-to-ceiling windows. Night owls know it's where to go for dinner (the
kitchen is open until midnight) and drinks (the bar is
open until 1am). And if you're in a muddle about what
to drink, let one of the friendly plaid-shirted bartenders recommend a cocktail, or check out the rotating
tap, which sometimes pours prosecco.

Bars

Abigail's Restaurant

*291 Third Street, at Athenaeum Street (1-617 945
9086, www.abigailskendall.com). Kendall/MIT T.*
Open 11.30am-10pm Mon-Fri; 5-10pm Sat;
10am-3pm, 5-10pm Sun. **Map** p143 F3 ⑤
While many of the area's bars fill up on weekend
nights, there's seemingly always a place for you at
Abigail's long bar. This cocktail spot has something
for everyone – ranging from 'Lite N' Easy' offerings
such as the Pimm's Cup to the party-starting (or,
depending on your tolerance, night-ending) Hadron
Collider – a half-pint of stout, a shot of Jameson and
a glass of champagne. The bartenders are friendly
and knowledgeable, and there's even patio seating in
the warmer months.

West Bridge.

EXPLORE

PERFECT FORMULA

Art + science + food + drink = a unique experience.

EXPLORE

It's not a laboratory in the traditional sense of beakers and lab-coat technicians, though servers wear white shirts and bartenders extract 'alcohol paints' with a fractional distiller. And the molecular structure of skin – shaped like honeycomb, apparently, when viewed through a microscope – finds its way into the interior design. **Café ArtScience** (see p144) is a one-of-a-kind restaurant – half familiar dining experience, half sensory trip.

The brainchild of Harvard University professor David Edwards, it's the food and beverage arm of his adjacent art/design/scientific innovation hub, **Le Laboratoire** (www.lelaboratoirecambridge.com). Originally established in Paris but transplanted to Cambridge, the centre presents cutting-edge sensory exhibitions, dynamic public programming, and immersive food and drink experiences – enter Café Artscience.

During the day, the restaurant is awash in natural light from floor-to-ceiling windows; at night, it glows like a beacon. The cosy couch seating, along with marble tables and chairs, encourages chemistry between people.

Executive chef Patrick Campbell (No.9 Park) gives classic cuisine a contemporary touch with his inventive small plates, such as cauliflower velouté with sea urchin, lobster oil and curry salt; and saffron *cavatelli* with Prince Edward Island mussels and Calabrian chilli. Desserts are equally inviting, such as the huckleberry and lime Creamsicle or a 'tiny spoon' (literally a spoonful) of PB&J or other flavours.

Renowned mixologist Todd Maul (Clio) commands the WikiBar – a long, curved 24-seat bar with white leather seats. Like an open kitchen, theatre unfolds behind it: bartenders use a blowtorch to burnish the orange and cherry for the Burnt Cherry Wood Old-Fashioned. Maul creates cocktails for customers on the spot. The 'alcohol paint' is distilled flavours that 'collapse into the drink as you make it,' adding colour and flavour, says Maul. The -40°F ice cubes (literally cube-shaped) melt slowly like mini opaque glaciers, barely diluting the beverage.

While linen napkins and warm focaccia bread are reassuring signs of a restaurant as we know it, Edwards is breaking barriers on sensory experiences and experimentation. You can smell your way through dinner with Le Whaf, savour his cutting-edge WikiFoods and take home Le Whif.

WikiFood is Edwards' version of food inside an edible casing. WikiPearls of foie gras – foie gras spheres flash-frozen in liquid nitrogen – are encased in an apple 'skin' and dusted with fennel pollen. Le Whaf are 'flavour clouds' – elements turned into vapours that are inhaled, not eaten, such as the Whaf Tiki cocktail. Cachaça rum is turned into a vapour, served over flavoured ice (almond, and pineapple-mango) in a snifter. An angostura-rose tuile sits on top of the drink, which you inhale, not sip. Le Whif is a portable line of 'breathable food' that comes in flavours such as chocolate-raspberry – giving you the essence of the food without the calories.

Café ArtScience.

Belly Wine Bar
1 Kendall Square, at Hampshire Street (1-617 494 0968, www.bellywinebar.com). Kendall T. **Open** 5-11pm Mon-Wed, Sun; 5pm-midnight Thur-Sat. **Map** p142 D3 ⑤
Belly's owners also run the well-stocked wine-and-cheese store Central Bottle in nearby Central Square (and the Blue Room next door). This cosy, low-key spot offers a menu of snacks to fuel the sipping and an underrated cocktail selection.

Cambridge Brewing Company
Building 100, 1 Kendall Square, at Hampshire Street (1-617 494 1994, www.cambridge brewingcompany.com). Kendall T. **Open** 11.30am-10pm Mon-Thur; 11.30am-11pm Fri; 11am-11pm Sat; 11am-10pm Sun. **Map** p142 D3 ⑤
CBC is a veteran of the Boston beer scene. It certainly has the merchandising down: hats, T-shirts and pint glasses are all for sale. Founded in 1989, it's the oldest brewery-restaurant in the city, and the first commercial brewery in the country to produce a Belgian beer: the Tripel Threat. The room itself is spacious and comfortable, with lots of long, shiny pine surfaces. The brewing tanks are visible from every seat in the house, but the best tables are to be found on the front patio.

Firebrand Saints
1 Broadway, at Third Street (1-617 401 3399, www.firebrandsaints.com). Kendall/MIT T. **Open** 11.30am-1am Mon-Wed; 11.30am-2am Thur-Sun. **Map** p143 F4 ⑤
During the colder months, sip a well-crafted cocktail at the bar and watch the kitchen at work or the five TVs above, which loop and mash up whatever happens to be on. During the summer, snag a picnic table on the patio and order draught beer by the pint or pitcher until it's time to go home.

Lord Hobo
92 Hampshire Street, at Windsor Street (1-617 250 8454, www.lordhobo.com). Central T then 15mins walk, or bus 83, 91. **Open** 4.30pm-1am Mon-Wed; 4.30pm-2am Thur, Fri; 11am-2am Sat; 11am-1am Sun. **Map** p142 D2 ⑤
Enter through dark curtains and your attention is immediately drawn to the bar, with its 40 taps raised up in the centre like an altar to the god of hops. Here, the bartenders are more than happy to introduce you to the delicious and obscure – such as a pale ale lovingly brewed by a Belgian father and son in their spare time away from their day job at a big brewery.

State Park
Building 300, 1 Kendall Square, at Hampshire Street (1-617 848 4355, www.statepark.is). Kendall/MIT T. **Open** 5pm-1am Mon, Sun; 11.30am-1am Tue, Wed; 11.30am-2am Thur, Fri; 5pm-2am Sat. **Map** p143 E3 ⑤

Conceived by the owners of nearby Hungry Mother, State Park combines a dive bar feel with the selection and expertise of an upscale cocktail bar. A collection of old neon signs casts a glow on the repurposed furniture acquired from defunct local bars, while wood and carpeted walls line the perimeter of this spacious, yet still often packed destination. Bartenders can mix up classics and bespoke creations to your taste. Antique pinball machines, a pool table, shuffleboard and an era-spanning jukebox seal the deal. With the James Beard-nominated chef-owner Barry Maiden of Hungry Mother in charge of the menu, Southern-style specialities are updated with a New England twist, using super-fresh, sustainable ingredients.

Shops & Services

Cambridge Antique Market
201 Monsignor O'Brien Highway, at Third Street (1-617 868 9655, www.marketantique.com). Lechmere T. **Open** 11am-6pm Tue-Sun. **Map** p143 G1 ⑤ **Antiques**
Akin to wandering through someone's attic, this five-storey warehouse features more than 150 dealers, peddling everything from antique furniture, homewares and dolls to clothing, lighting fixtures, books and vintage bikes. Word to the wise: the highest prices are on the more accessible floors; it's worth your while to wander up and down the slightly tilted staircase to seek out deals.

CambridgeSide Galleria
100 CambridgeSide Place, off Edwin H Land Boulevard (1-617 621 8666, www.cambridge sidegalleria.com). Kendall/MIT T then 15mins walk, or Lechmere T. **Open** 10am-9pm Mon-Sat; noon-7pm Sun. **Map** p143 H2 ⑤ **Mall**
The only major retail centre within striking distance of curiously shop-free Kendall Square, the Galleria is good for stocking up on inexpensive basics from the likes of J Crew, Old Navy and Abercrombie & Fitch. It also has one of the Boston area's Apple Stores – a bonus for students from MIT.

Garment District & By the Pound
200 Broadway, at Davis Street (1-617 876 5230, www.garment-district.com). Kendall/MIT T. **Open** 11am-8pm Mon-Fri, Sun; 9am-8pm Sat. **Map** p142 D3 ⑤ **Fashion/fancy dress**
A source of second-hand and vintage threads for cash-strapped students and rockers since the 1980s, Garment District shares its crumbling warehouse premises with a costume shop – the perfect combination if you're off to a fancy-dress party. On the ground floor is the fabled By the Pound – literally a pile of clothes, shoes, belts, bags and assorted junk dumped in a pile on the floor that's sold at $1.50 a pound. Head upstairs for a vast array of second-hand jeans, branded clothing and vintage attire.

Other Neighbourhoods

While the centre of town is compact and walkable, Greater Boston sprawls out in all directions into numerous distinct areas; we've focused on those that are of most interest to visitors. While some, like Allston and Jamaica Plain, are simply further-flung neighbourhoods, others, such as Cambridge (*see pp126-147*), Somerville and Brookline, are separately administered cities, though they feel like parts of Boston. Not only will you find worthwhile sights, restaurants and other venues, exploring these residential areas can give you a more complete picture of life in the city.

Ironically, given Boston's reputation for liberalism and its association with the 19th-century Abolitionist movement, the city's working-class neighbourhoods were largely segregated by race in the 20th century, although widespread immigration and gentrification have since created a more diverse ethnic mix across the board.

Arnold Arboretum.

Don't Miss

1 **John F Kennedy Presidential Library & Museum** Get the story on the doomed, Boston-bred leader (p153).

2 **Arnold Arboretum** Tree-huggers' heaven (p154).

3 **Doyle's** The city's most elegant pub (p156).

4 **Kirkland Tap & Trotter** The casual successor to Craigie on Main is another culinary knockout (p163).

5 **Magpie** Cool crafts from across the US (p165).

EXPLORE

EXPLORE

CHARLESTOWN

*Community College T, or Haymarket T then bus 92
or 93, or North Station T then 10-15mins walk.*

A short walk across Charlestown Bridge from
the North End, this neighbourhood was, for
many years, known as the tough, working-class
area on the edge of the Boston skyline – insular,
with mob ties and a predominantly Irish-Catholic
population. But its reputation, like that of many
of the city's neighbourhoods, is changing fast.
Over the last couple of decades, it has been
infiltrated by young professionals, lured by its
elegant waterfront properties and proximity
to downtown Boston. Even so, it maintains a
small-town feel, with its tight, winding streets,
clapboard 'triple-decker' three-family houses
and corner pubs.

Settled in 1628, two years before Boston, it
became part of its larger neighbour in the late
19th century. Its prosperity reflected the ebb
and flow of business in the Navy Yard, which
was founded in 1800 when the new republic,
desperate to respond to attacks on merchant
ships by Barbary pirates off the coast of North
Africa, decided to beef up its navy. From that
point onwards, it became one of the most critical
and, during wartime, busiest shipbuilding and
repair yards in the country: at the start of World
War II, it employed 47,000 workers. Due to lack of
demand, it closed in 1974, and some tough years
followed. Today, the **Charlestown Navy Yard**
(entrance at Gate 1, Constitution Road, 1-617
242 5601, www.nps.gov) serves as a museum of
American naval history. The most famous ship
in the yard (if not in the country) is the **USS
Constitution**, built in 1797 and now a museum.

From the yard, you can see the obelisk of the
Bunker Hill Monument shining in the near
distance. Dominating picturesque Monument
Square, it commemorates one of the most famous
battles of the Revolutionary War, and its summit
commands spectacular views. Just across the
street, an airy museum recounts its bloody
history. Although the antique charm of the
nearby **Warren Tavern** (2 Pleasant Street,

Bunker Hill Monument.

at Main Street, 1-617 241 8142) is somewhat
marred by a blaring TV and modern bar fittings,
it retains some of its period atmosphere.

Sights & Museums

FREE **Bunker Hill Monument**
*Monument Square, Breed's Hill (1-617 242 5642,
www.nps.gov). Community College T.* **Open** *Apr-
Oct* 9am-4.45pm daily. *Nov-Mar* 9am-5pm daily.
Admission free.
This 221ft granite obelisk, completed in 1842, commemorates the first major battle of the American
Revolution. Technically speaking, it didn't go well
for America: after a bloody conflict, the rebels had to
retreat and the British declared victory. But England
sustained severe casualties – almost half of its 2,200
troops were killed, compared to 440 American soldiers – and the fight emboldened the colonists. The
legendary battle's name is actually a misnomer, as
much of the fighting took place on Breed's Hill, the
site of the monument – Bunker Hill is nearby, visible from the top of Breed's Hill. This isn't the first
structure to commemorate the event; an 18ft wooden
pillar with a gilt urn was erected in 1794.

Visitors can listen to free talks from park rangers, or climb the monument's 294 steps (a brisk
ascent takes five minutes) for a breathtaking view
of Boston. In front of the tower is a statue of Colonel
William Prescott, an American officer whose instruc-
tion to troops in the Battle of Bunker Hill – 'Don't fire
until you see the whites of their eyes!' – has become
part of American military lore. Across the street, the

IN THE KNOW TAVERN LORE

Named after Dr Joseph Warren, a popular
revolutionary who died in the final clash in
the Battle of Bunker Hill, **Warren Tavern**
(*see above*) was built just after most of
Charlestown burned down in the late 18th
century, making it one of the oldest structures
in the area. Paul Revere presided over
Masonic meetings as a grand master here,
and George Washington visited as president.

Bunker Hill Museum, features several displays of weaponry, a 360° painting of the battle and an enormous diorama of fighting soldiers.

USS Constitution Museum

Building 22, Charlestown Navy Yard, off Constitution Road (1-617 242 5670, www.uss constitutionmuseum.org). North Station T then 15mins walk, or Haymarket T then bus 93. **Open** *Apr-Oct* 9am-6pm daily. *Nov-Mar* 10am-5pm daily. **Admission** *Suggested donation* $5-10; $3-$5 reductions. **No credit cards. Map** p273 M1.

Built in 1797, this legendary old frigate became one of the most celebrated warships of its era, taking part in more than 30 battles and engagements. Ottoman polacres, French brigs and British privateers all felt the force of her guns. 'Old Ironsides' earned its nickname during the War of 1812, when a sailor watched as shots fired by a British cannon bounced off its hull. The sailor is said to have shouted, 'Her sides are made of iron!' Although 'Ironsides' is actually made of oak, the nickname stuck. Today, it is the oldest commissioned warship in America. In March 2015, the ship is being moved from its regular spot at Pier 1 to dry dock, where it is being restored over the next three years, but visitors will still be able to tour the vessel during that time (see www.history.navy.mil/ussconstitution for updates). Located in a converted pumphouse in the Yard, the museum has exhibitions that relate both to the *Constitution* itself and to more general naval history. Interactive displays offer a simulated hands-on seafaring experience: the thrill of battle on deck and handling the ship's massive sails.

ALLSTON

Harvard Avenue, Griggs Street, Packards Corner or Pleasant Street T.

Head west on Commonwealth Avenue from Boston University and you'll hit Allston. Though the neighbourhood has a reputation as a 'student ghetto', where undergrads rent their first apartment, it has a diverse demographic, including Korean, Vietnamese, Brazilian and Colombian immigrants, which is reflected in a wide array of cheap ethnic restaurants.

Some of the city's best music clubs, including the **Paradise Rock Club** (*see p192*) and **Great Scott** (*see p191*), are in 'Allston Rock City' and it seems as if everyone you meet is in a band, or they used to be, or their roommate is.

Restaurants & Cafés

Lone Star Taco Bar

479 Cambridge Street, at Brighton Avenue (1-617 782 8226, www.lonestar-boston.com). Harvard Avenue T or bus 57, 66. **Open** 11am-2am Mon-Fri; 10am-2am Sat, Sun. **Main courses** $3-$9. Mexican

There's a lot of value in this Mexican street-food find, where you can enjoy a local draught, or a chilli-spiked margarita and a *carnitas* taco for under $20 (including a side of rice and beans), proving that exceptional, artisanal food can be had for college student prices. From the wooden stools at the bar to the line of tables and benches, there's an understated simplicity and camaraderie that pervades the narrow dining room. And you gotta love a place that serves brunch daily until 4pm, with a breakfast taco and *huevos rancheros* on the regular menu. The owners also operate Deep Ellum (*see below*) next door.

Soul Fire

182 Harvard Avenue, at Glenville Avenue (1-617 787 3003, www.soulfirebbq.com). Harvard Avenue T. **Open** 11.30am-11pm daily. **Main courses** $12-$26. Barbecue

The folks at Soul Fire are mighty serious about their barbecue. They respect the process as both a science and an art – and their dedication shows in the results. Quality meats are coated in an assortment of dry rubs and slathered with different sauces to suit every taste; accompany your meal with a $2.50 draught PBR. Great sides include mac and cheese and baked beans.

Bars

★ Deep Ellum

477 Cambridge Street, at North Beacon Street (1-617 787 2337, www.deepellum-boston.com). Harvard Avenue T or bus 57, 66. **Open** 11am-2am Mon-Fri; 10am-2am Sat, Sun.

Former bartenders from Bukowski Tavern decided that they could beat their alma mater at its own game. The result is a cosy bar with exposed brick, dim lighting, a summer porch and very knowledgeable staff. Deep Ellum stocks a stylish collection of everything from Abbey-style craft beers for the adventurous and well-heeled, to PBR for the bike messengers, students and other low-budget hipsters who flock here.

Model Cafe

7 North Beacon Street, at Cambridge Street (1-617 254 9365). Harvard Avenue T or bus 57, 66. **Open** 7pm-2am Mon-Fri, Sun; 2pm-2am Sat. **No credit cards.**

The Model started off as an unpretentious little neighbourhood dive and then one day, through no fault of its own, suddenly became the bar of choice for the hipster/arty contingent (who inexplicably started calling it the 'Mow-dell'). Nowadays, the trendy crowd and the original local crowd share the place. The jukebox is among the best around.

Sunset Grill & Tap

130 Brighton Avenue, at Harvard Avenue (1-617 254 1331, www.allstonsfinest.com). Harvard Avenue T or bus 57, 66. **Open** 11.30am-1am Mon-Sat; 11am-1am Sun. **Map** p276 A5.

EXPLORE

Sunset is the granddaddy of all the draught beer purveyors in town. You won't get sublime atmosphere or an exhaustive selection of obscure brews, but this place has by far the most taps running at once: more than 100. It has all the ambience of an amusement park, with beer signage and memorabilia crowding the walls, and BU students and sundry Allstonians crowding the tables and bars. It's a good spot when you're feeling rowdy.

Shops & Services

At the Buzzer

81 Harvard Avenue, at Gardner Street (1-617 783 2899, www.atbboston.com). Harvard Avenue T. **Open** noon-8pm Mon-Sat; noon-6pm Sun. **Shoes** This shoe consignment shop caters to sneakerheads and collectors looking for something beyond general releases. It carries a wide selection of vintage Air Jordans, Nike SBs and Reeboks, among others. Be warned: you can expect to drop a lot of cash for these rarities.

In Your Ear

957 Commonwealth Avenue, near Harry Agganis Way (1-617 787 9755, www.iye.com). Pleasant Street T. **Open** varies (usually 11am-8pm Mon-Fri; noon-7pm Sun). **Books & music** When stacks of records overflow outside a store's front door, you know you're in for a deliciously disorganised display. In Your Ear doesn't disappoint. The main location stocks 100,000 LPs and CDs; there are crates in the aisles and a massive odds-and-ends bin featuring three-for-a-buck bargains. The eight-track selection is uncommonly large, the magazine section has random back issues of *Relix* and *Rolling Stone* and the corner of the store is plastered with kitschy Mexican movie posters such as *El Regreso de King Kong*. It's a glorious mess.

ROXBURY & DORCHESTER

Roxbury: Jackson Square, Mass Avenue, Roxbury Crossing or Ruggles T, or Silver Line Washington Street. Dorchester: Ashmont, Fields Corner, JFK/UMass, Savin Hill or Shawmut T.

Roxbury is considered the heart of Boston's African-American community, but it hasn't been on most tourists' itineraries. The inner-city neighbourhood is emerging from hard times: in the 1980s and early '90s, it was known for its high crime rate and low employment, with the warehouses and factories that once generated a booming manufacturing trade long abandoned. In recent years, however, the area has been receiving more constructive attention. Community events, grassroots activism and a boost in state funding have helped revitalise the neighbourhood. Parts of it can still feel quite threatening to visitors, but **Discover Roxbury** (183 Roxbury Street, 1-617 427 1006, www.discoverroxbury.org) is gaining recognition for its historical and cultural tours.

Founded in 1630 by British colonists, Roxbury flourished first as a farming community, and later as a bustling industrial centre. During the 1950s, it became famous for its swinging jazz scene. It was during this period that Roxbury's most illustrious resident moved to town. For several years, Malcolm Little, aka Malcolm X, lived here with his half-sister Ella.

One sight worth visiting is the beautiful **First Church in Roxbury** (10 Putnam Street, at Dudley Street, 1-617 318 6010, www.uuum.org) near John Eliot Square. Built in 1803, this is the oldest wooden church in Boston, with a bell that was cast by patriot and silversmith Paul Revere. Also in the area is the **Shirley-Eustis House** – one of the few remaining examples of pre-Revolutionary architecture.

The **Eliot Burying Ground** (Eustis Street, at Washington Street), which was established in 1630, is another surviving early site. Several colonial governors, as well as Reverend John Eliot (who was known as the 'Apostle to the Indians', for translating the Bible into Algonquin), are buried here.

Although Roxbury is home to many immigrant groups, its recent history as a predominantly black neighbourhood is reflected in the **Museum of the National Center of Afro-American Artists**, on Walnut Avenue.

Nearby Dorchester, known locally as Dot, is, geographically, Boston's largest neighbourhood. It has also seen its fair share of crime and poverty, but began to be gentrified in the 1980s. The restored mansions in the affluent Ashmont Hill area, lining Ocean Street and Welles Avenue, for example, are as impressive as any you'd find in Cambridge, and expensive condos are replacing old triple-decker apartment buildings. Attracted by the low rents, artists have set up studios and experimental galleries such as **HallSpace** (950 Dorchester Avenue, between Crescent Avenue & Harbor View Street, www.hallspace.org), but the area's prime draw for visitors is the **John F Kennedy Presidential Library & Museum**, which shares Columbia Point with the University of Massachusetts (UMass) Boston campus.

Sights & Museums

★ John F Kennedy Presidential Library & Museum

Columbia Point, off Morrissey Boulevard, Dorchester (1-617 514 1600, www.jfklibrary.org). JFK/UMass T then free shuttle bus. **Open** 9am-5pm daily. **Admission** $14; $10-$12 reductions; free under-12s.

A looming concrete-and-glass monolith designed by IM Pei (completed in 1979), this shrine to the life and work of the 35th US president overlooks the outer harbour from the top of the Columbia Point peninsula. On the ground floor, the stunning 115ft-high atrium commands panoramic views of the sea and the city. Downstairs, the museum contains an extensive display of memorabilia, as well as temporary shows. Presented as a series of multimedia retro room sets and visitor-friendly displays, the permanent exhibition comprises a timeline of Kennedy's rise to power (including excerpts from his famous televised debate with Nixon, and documentary footage on the Cuban Missile Crisis), achievements (promoting the space race), his family life and reproductions of the Oval Office and the office of JFK's brother, Attorney General Robert F Kennedy.

The historical archives, which can only be viewed by appointment, include an extensive collection of Ernest Hemingway's letters and papers, donated by his wife Mary – Kennedy allowed her to re-enter Fidel Castro's Cuba in order to remove the writer's effects from the couple's abandoned home in Havana.

▶ *For JFK's birthplace, see p157.*

Museum of the National Center of Afro-American Artists

300 Walnut Avenue, at Dennison Street, Roxbury (1-617 442 8614, www.ncaaa.org). Ruggles T then bus 22, 29. **Open** 1-5pm Tue-Sun. **Admission** $5; $4 reductions. **No credit cards.**

The NCAAA's museum, affiliated with the Museum of Fine Arts (*see p90*) in Back Bay, is the only place in New England committed exclusively to African, Caribbean and Afro-American visual arts. Its Victorian mansion in Roxbury houses diverse exhibitions, including a permanent display recreating a Nubian king's burial chamber.

John F Kennedy Presidential Library & Museum.

EXPLORE

Arnold Arboretum.

Shirley-Eustis House

33 Shirley Street, at Clifton Street, Roxbury (1-617 442 2275, www.shirleyeustishouse.org). Ruggles T then bus 15. **Open** *June-mid Oct 1-4pm Thur-Sun. Oct-May by appt.* **Admission** $8; $5 reductions. **No credit cards.**

This Georgian mansion, the only remaining house in America that was built by a royal colonial governor, is a National Historic Landmark. It went up between 1747 and 1751, and was built by William Shirley, who was appointed to his post by King George II. After that, the building, which was used as barracks for Revolutionary forces during the war, and was later home to federal governor William Eustis, played host to a Who's Who of historical figures; illustrious visitors included George Washington and Benjamin Franklin. Today, guided tours show off the restored marble floors and lovely period furniture of this perfectly preserved slice of pre-Revolutionary Roxbury.

JAMAICA PLAIN

Forest Hills, Green Street or Stony Brook T.

Jamaica Plain – or JP, as it's known – has been slowly evolving for decades. It's one of Boston's densest Latino neighbourhoods, and its impressive Victorian properties, coupled with low rents, also attracts young, arty types, creating a bohemian buzz. Trendy restaurants and bars such as the **Centre Street Café** and **Ten Tables** sit alongside Latino bakeries and barber shops. Once a quirky bowling alley, restaurant and nightspot, the **Bella Luna Restaurant & Milky Way Lounge** has since reopened – without the bowling alley – in a new, higher-rent location in the Brewery Complex. Art studios abound in the area – once a year, many are opened

to the public for the Jamaica Plain Open Studios weekend (www.jpopenstudios.com). The main drag, Centre Street, is especially vibrant, with mural-splashed buildings. Landmark Irish pub **Doyle's** has been drawing politicos for decades.

Blessed with acres of parkland, JP is easily one of the most verdant parts of the city. In the spring, the **Arnold Arboretum**, a sprawling botanical park, explodes with colourful blossoms, attracting eager walkers, joggers and cyclists. **Franklin Park**, a somewhat careworn 527-acre spread, features a woodland reserve, golf course and zoo *(see p168)*. The largest link in Boston's Emerald Necklace *(see p84* **In the Know***)*, designed by Frederick Law Olmsted, it is undergoing restoration with the help of local volunteers. Across the way, **Forest Hills Cemetery** contains the graves of several literary notables and colonial heroes.

Sights & Museums

★ FREE Arnold Arboretum
125 Arborway, at Centre Street (1-617 524 1718, www.arboretum.harvard.edu). Forest Hills T. **Open** *Grounds* dawn-dusk daily. *Visitor centre Apr-Oct* 10am-5pm Mon, Tue, Thur-Sun. *Nov-Mar* noon-4pm Mon, Tue, Thur-Sun. **Admission** free.

The arboretum, one of the world's leading centres for plant study, was established in 1872. In a beautiful, 265-acre park setting, this living museum is administered by Harvard University. It provides the opportunity to see more than 15,000 specimens of trees and plants from around the world. Free guided tours are available on designated days throughout the year – phone for details.

▶ *In May, Lilac Sunday is a day-long celebration of the fragrant, flowering shrub; see p31.*

FREE Forest Hills Cemetery

95 Forest Hills Avenue, at Route 203 (1-617 524 0128, www.foresthillscemetery.com). Forest Hills T. **Open** 7am-dusk daily. **Admission** free.

Literary giants ee cummings, Eugene O'Neill and Anne Sexton are all buried here, as is the prominent abolitionist William Lloyd Garrison. The mile-long Contemporary Sculpture Path, established in 2001, gives the cemetery the feel of an open-air museum.

Loring-Greenough House

12 South Street, at Centre Street (1-617 524 3158, www.loring-greenough.org). Green Street T then 15mins walk, or Forest Hills T then bus 39. **Open** *Apr-Dec* 1am-3pm Sun. *Jan-Mar* by appointment. **Admission** *Suggested donation* $5. **No credit cards.**

Built in 1760 for a wealthy British naval officer, this house was used as a hospital during the Revolutionary War, then housed five generations of another prosperous family before becoming a museum in 1924. Its decor spans a variety of periods, and includes collections of Victorian card cases and late 19th-century clothing. Visitors can freely roam its two acres of landscaped lawns and gardens, but may only enter the house with a guided tour.

Samuel Adams Brewery

30 Germania Street, at Brookside Avenue (1-617 368 5080, www.samueladams.com). Stony Brook T. **Tours** 10am-3pm Mon-Thur, Sat; 10am-5.30pm Fri. **Admission** *Suggested donation* $2. **No credit cards.**

Samuel Adams lager, named after the brewer turned Revolutionary leader, is on tap around the city and beyond. Brewery tours allow you to follow the beer-making process, from the selection of ingredients to the finished product – which you get to sample.

▶ *For more on Samuel Adams, see p228.*

Restaurants & Cafés

Centre Street Café

669A Centre Street, at Seaverns Avenue (1-617 524 9217, www.centrestreetcafejp.com). Green Street T then 10mins walk. **Open** 11.30am-2.30pm, 5.30-10pm Mon-Thur; 11.30am-2.30pm, 5.30-11pm Fri; 5.30-11pm Sat; 5.30-10pm Sun. **Main courses** $12-$29. **Italian/Mediterranean**

Once a bohemian haunt, the Centre Street Café has been refashioned by new owners (the folks behind nearby Tres Gatos; *see right*) into a sophisticated version of a neighbourhood café with a well-edited Italian-inflected menu. Colourful patterned wallpaper brightens the dark-wood and cream dining room. The semi-open kitchen sends out creative pastas (*fusilli con funghi* with brussels sprouts, asago, crème fraiche and lemon thyme) and delectable main dishes including stuffed short-rib *braciole*. Lunch is a casual affair, and the café is set to resume its popular weekend brunch (call for details of the extended hours).

$ JP Licks

659 Centre Street, at Starr Lane (1-617 524 6740, www.jplicks.com). Green Street T or bus 39. **Open** 6am-midnight daily. **Ice-cream** $4.50-$7. **Ice-cream**

This is the flagship location of the Jamaica Plain-born ice-cream institution (other shops have popped up on Newbury Street and in Harvard Square, among other areas). The local chain is known for its funky cow motif, lively atmosphere, hip scoopers and exciting flavours, so expect to wait in line on hot days. But don't worry, it just gives you more time to decide between the wild Maine blueberry or the brownie batter. The place also roasts its own coffee. **Other locations** throughout the city.

★ Ten Tables

597 Centre Street, at Pond Street (1-617 524 8810, www.tentables.net). Green Street T then 10mins walk, or bus 39. **Open** 5.30-10pm Mon-Sat; 5-9pm Sun. **Main courses** $22-$30. **Creative contemporary**

By virtue of its size (ten tables), the lucky few who manage to get reservations at this diminutive bistro have front-row seats for the show in the open kitchen. Then they get to enjoy the results, distinguished by owner Krista Kranyak's commitment to locally grown organic produce, artisan products and creativity; witness the charcuterie, pastas and main courses, such as the pan-seared bluefish with juniper. The four-course tasting menu for $48 is a good deal.

Tres Gatos

470 Centre Street, at Roseway Street (1-617 477 4851, www.tresgatosjp.com) Stony Brook T then 10mins walk or bus 39. **Open** 5.30-10pm Mon-Wed; 5.30-11pm Thur, Fri; 10am-11pm Sat; 10am-10pm Sun. **Small plates** $6-$15. **Spanish**

You've got to love the concept: serve creative tapas in a renovated home that doubles as an indie book and music store. Take advantage of the business's split personality with a stop at the sleek bar for a glass of cava followed by a browse in the back, where stock is a mix of new and secondhand books, CDs and vinyl. The dining room is broken into small rooms, all in deep blues, soft greys and smoky oranges, and aglow with candlelight. The menu is a feast of Spanish cuisine, with vegetarian options, and portions are mostly generous for the price. The chilled tortilla Española with *pimentón* aïoli is perfection, and the grass-fed beef empanadas, wrapped in a beautifully cooked pastry, have a floral appeal. In the summer, grab a seat out on the sunny patio or in front of the big bay window, where you can gaze out on to Centre Street. *Photo p156.*

$ Ula Café

284 Amory Street, at the Brewery Complex (1-617 524 7890, www.ulacafe.com). Stony Brook T. **Open** 7am-7pm Mon-Fri; 8am-7pm Sat, Sun. **Main courses** $8-$9. **Café/vegetarian**

EXPLORE

Truly a JP gem, Ula was founded with the intention of creating a friendly neighbourhood space for locals and visitors to interact – and dine on satisfying and healthy food. Veggie-friendly sandwiches, such as sweet potato and avocado, add to the impressive range of baked goods. It's the perfect place to refuel with a hearty soup or salad, or strike up a conversation with a kindred spirit on the patio when weather allows.

Bars

Bella Luna Restaurant & Milky Way Lounge

284 Amory Street, at the Brewery Complex (1-617 524 6060, www.milkywayjp.com). Stony Brook T. **Open** 5-11pm Mon, Tue, Sun; 5pm-midnight Wed; 5pm-1am Thur, Fri; noon-1am Sat.

When JP's beloved bowling alley, dance club and restaurant combo relocated to the Brewery Complex, the lanes were conspicuously absent. Still, the new space features the same familiarly kooky decor, a pool table and a patio on which you can enjoy craft beers and slices of gourmet pizza.

Brendan Behan Pub

378 Centre Street, at Sheridan Street (1-617 522 5386, www.brendanbehanpub.com). Jackson Square T then 15mins walk, or bus 39. **Open** noon-1am daily. **No credit cards**.

This is one of the jewels of Boston's Irish pub scene. Named after the Irish playwright, it once hosted standing-room-only *seisiúns*, attended by the likes of Patrick McCabe and JP Donleavy. Behan's is not a fancy place – it's small and dimly lit, with no food on offer – but that's part of its charm. Locals love it because they are encouraged to bring their own food

– usually from the various take-out joints that dot Centre Street – to nibble on between pints from the incredible beer selection.

★ Doyle's

3484 Washington Street, at Williams Street (1-617 524 2345, www.doylescafeboston.com). Green Street T. **Open** 9am-midnight daily.

In business for more than a century, this old Irish charmer has long been popular with politicos. The ceilings are lofty, the rooms capacious, and the murals high on the walls (scenes of colonial Massachusetts) are gorgeous. The generous portions of comfort food and wide selection of ales and scotches are its other strengths.

▶ *If you're lucky, you may get to taste a brand new brew from the Samuel Adams Brewery (see p155), which makes beer just down the road and sometimes tests out recipes at Doyle's.*

Shops & Services

For **Boomerangs**, another great Jamaica Plain thrift shop, *see p184*.

40 South Street

40 South Street, at Sedgwick Street (1-617 522 5066, www.fortysouthst.com). Green Street T. **Open** 1-7pm Thur, Fri; 11am-6pm Sat; noon-5pm Sun. **Fashion**

The most varied and laid-back of Boston's local thrift stores is 40 South Street (née Gumshoe). Run by local rock legend Hilken Mancini, it walks the line between vintage and thrift so adeptly, you'd be hard pressed to know there was ever a line there to begin with. You can find clothing dating from the 1950s to the '90s, and all of it is high quality, clean, and moderately priced. If you're looking for a plaid shirt or a

Tres Gatos. *See p155.*

pair of jeans, you have definitely come to the right place – the selection is almost overwhelming, but in the best way possible.

Caramelo Clothing Company

606 Centre Street, at Pond Street (1-617 942 8127, www.carameloclothing.com). Green Street T. **Open** 11am-6pm Tue, Wed; 11am-7pm Thur, Fri; 10am-6pm Sat; noon-5pm Sun. **Fashion**

This neighbourhood retail haven stocks all manner of US- and European-made menswear, from button-down shirts and cardigans to ties and sunglasses. Local designers represented include Osmium (shirts and vests), Polkadile (cuff-links), and Beanfield (Boston-related graphic tees); whiskered types will appreciate the expansive collection of grooming products and accessories.

★ Fat Ram's Pumpkin Tattoo

380 Centre Street, at Sheridan Street (1-617 522 6444, www.pumpkintattoo.com). Jackson Square T. **Open** 10am-10pm Mon-Sat; noon-8pm Sun. **Tattoos**

About as far away from 'Mom' as you can get, the artworks created by the five tattooists here run from baby portraits to colourful abstracts. Staff are friendly, knowledgeable and certain to turn your dream ink into a reality.

BROOKLINE

Brookline Village, Cleveland Circle, Coolidge Corner or Longwood T.

Located four miles west of downtown Boston, Brookline is one of its prettiest and most affluent suburban communities. Cinephiles should check out the restored art deco **Coolidge Corner Theatre** (*see p175*), Greater Boston's only not-for-profit cinema; across the street, **Brookline Booksmith** is great for new and used titles.

The birthplace and boyhood home of the town's most famous son, John F Kennedy, is a short walk away. The small house was carefully restored after the assassination under the supervision of his mother, Rose.

If cars are your thing, check out America's oldest collection of automobiles, at the **Larz Anderson Auto Museum**, in the vast, verdant Larz Anderson Park. The **Frederick Law Olmsted National Historic Site**, former home and office of the renowned landscape architect, has reopened after restoration.

Sights & Museums

Frederick Law Olmsted National Historic Site

99 Warren Street, at Dudley Street (www.nps.gov/ frla). Brookline Hills T then 15mins walk or bus 60.

Larz Anderson Auto Museum.

Open *House* varies by season; usually noon-4pm Wed, Thur; 9.30am-4pm Fri, Sat (see website or call for summer and winter hours). *Grounds* dawn-dusk daily. **Admission** free.

The pioneering landscape architect behind New York's Central Park and Boston's Emerald Necklace, Olmsted moved to this 1810 house, Fairsted, in 1883, establishing his family firm on the premises. In addition to a massive archive of plans, drawings, photographs and other documents, displays in several rooms – including Olmsted's original design studio – chart his legacy and family history. The grounds reflect hallmarks of his artfully 'wild' style in miniature, including a lawn, rock garden and a short, winding path through mountain laurels.

John F Kennedy National Historic Site

83 Beals Street, at Gibbs Street (1-617 566 7937, www.nps.gov/jofi). Coolidge Corner T then 10mins walk. **Open** *Late May-Oct* 9.30am-5pm Wed-Sun; *Nov-late May* by appt. **Admission** free.

The modest former home of the country's 35th president has been restored to its appearance at the time of his birth in 1917. It includes the earliest of presidential artefacts: the bed in which JFK was born, and the piano he learned to play on. Tours are available of the house and surrounding neighbourhood.

Larz Anderson Auto Museum

Larz Anderson Park, 15 Newton Street (1-617 522 6547, www.larzanderson.org). Cleveland Circle or Reservoir T, then bus 51. **Open** 10am-4pm Tue-Sun. **Admission** $10; $5 reductions; free under-6s.

In the early 20th century, the 64-acre Larz Anderson Park was the private estate of distinguished couple Larz and Isabel Anderson; it was bequeathed to the town of Brookline after the widow's death in 1948.

The car-mad pair's collection of vintage vehicles is contained in their former carriage house. The non-profit museum also has rotating exhibitions, and hosts weekend car shows in the summer, when models are displayed on the lawn.

Restaurants & Cafés

★ Cutty's

284 Washington Street, at Davis Avenue (1-617 505 1844, www.cuttysfoods.com). Brookline Village T. **Open** 8am-3pm Mon-Sat. **Sandwiches** $5-$10. Sandwiches

This tiny shop has redefined the sandwich with its gourmet combos on chewy bread, alongside addictive house-made potato crispy chips and baked goods such as brownies and cookies. These are quick, affordable and easy eats – Cutty's is a good place for families, if you can squeeze around a table (or opt for takeaway). There are breakfast sandwiches (served only in the morning), the popular 'spuckie' – layers of fennel salami, hot capicola, mortadella and mozzarella with an olive-carrot salad on ciabatta – and the slow-roasted pork and pickled fennel (Saturdays only). Cutty's fans mark their calendars by the monthly Super Cluckin' Sundays, when the buttermilk fried chicken sandwich is the only thing on the menu until they run out.

Dok Bua

411 Harvard Street, at Fuller Street (1-617 232 2955, www.dokbua-thai.com). Coolidge Corner T then 10mins walk or bus 66. **Open** 11am-11pm daily. **Main courses** $8-$19. Thai

The kitsch will tickle you; the kitchen will floor you. This gaudy former grocery serves some of Boston's freshest, most fiery Thai fare. The sprawling menu grants diners numerous opportunities to nosh on something new, be it ground pork mixed with steamed egg, sour curry with root vegetables or black sesame dumplings. The familiar favourites are all there too, from tom yum soup to red curry.

★ La Morra

48 Boylston Street, at High Street (1-617 739 0007, www.lamorra.com). Brookline Village T. **Open** 5.30-10pm Mon-Thur; 5.30-10.30pm Fri; 5-10.30pm Sat; 5-9pm Sun. **Main courses** $19-$24. Italian

From the outside, it's a nondescript building on a major thoroughfare. Inside, Josh and Jennifer Ziskin's two-storey eaterie evokes a cosy Tuscan farmhouse, serving cuisine to match. Ziskin relishes blurring the lines between humble and elegant, hearty and delicate, be it chicken livers glazed with *vin santo*, marrow risotto or wood-grilled chops with herbed polenta. Looking for something slightly lighter? Settle in at the ground-floor bar for a sampling of what Venetians call *cicchetti* – an anchovy between fried sage leaves here, a *crostino* slathered with salt cod there.

Magic Beans.

Taberna de Haro

999 Beacon Street, at St Marys Street (1-617 277 8272, www.tabernaboston.com). St Marys Street T. **Open** 5.30-10pm Mon-Wed; 5pm-midnight Thur-Sat. **Tapas** $5-$25. Spanish

Low-key Taberna de Haro, whose owners used to run an eaterie in Madrid, enjoys something of a cult following. Recent renovations upped the ante with a larger bar area dubbed Straight Loft, the simply but cheerfully decorated dining room dominated by an open kitchen, and a bustling pavement café in the summer. The plethora of rustic tapas – house-made *butifarra* (veal sausage) with lemony aïoli, garlicky frogs' legs, exemplary *papas arrugadas*, blue cheese whipped with brandy – is complemented by the catalogue of little-known regional wines and sherries.

Bars

Matt Murphy's

14 Harvard Street, at Webster Place (1-617 232 0188, www.mattmurphyspub.com). Brookline Village T. **Open** 11am-11pm daily. No credit cards.

One of the better Irish pubs in a city that has no shortage of them, Matt Murphy's is well worth a journey into the Brookline outlands. The Guinness poured here is sublime, but what makes the pub such a hit among locals is its food. The fish and chips (served wrapped in newspaper, naturally) is deservedly famous and the shepherd's pie superb. The kitchen even makes its own ketchup. If it's not as youth-oriented as some Irish bars, Murphy's still gets its customers moving once the music starts – if they're capable of moving after dinner, that is.

★ Publick House

1648 Beacon Street, at Washington Street (1-617 277 2880, www.thepublickhousebeerbar.com). Washington Square T. **Open** 5pm-2am Mon-Fri; noon-2am Sat, Sun.

This is the place where bartenders from all of the other bars in town will send you if they don't have a

EXPLORE

particular Belgian Trappist ale or abbey beer. Here, authenticity is key – and the collection of beers is astounding. The highlights: Belgian (strong, dark to white), Hefeweizen, Schwarzbier, Scottish Ale, Imperial Stouts, Sweet Stout. Publick also uses beer in its dishes, which are equally varied and delicious.

Shops & Services

Brookline Booksmith
279 Harvard Street, at Green Street (1-617 566 6660, www.brooklinebooksmith.com). Coolidge Corner T. **Open** 8.30am-11pm Mon-Fri; 9am-11pm Sat; 9am-9pm Sun. **Books & music**
It's easy to find what you're looking for at this cheery Coolidge Corner bookstore, with its friendly staff and fine selection of new books. There's a charming children's reading area in the back, near a gift section stocked with greeting cards, toys and novelties. In the used-book cellar, shelves are pushed aside for readings with local and emerging writers.

Magic Beans
312 Harvard Street, at Babcock Street (1-617 383 8250, www.mbeans.com). Coolidge Corner T. **Open** 10am-7pm Mon-Thur; 10am-8pm Fri, Sat; 10am-6pm Sun. **Children**
Hands-down the best toy store in town, Magic Beans also carries books for kids and parents, and has a large range of baby and nursing gear. Plunk your offspring in the fenced play area in the back and shop for board games, Lego, Playmobil, Thomas the Tank Engine trains, Groovy Girls and art supplies.
▶ *Teens can stroll over to New England Comics next door at No.316, or to Eureka Puzzles & Games*

around the corner at 1349 Beacon Street (1-617 738 7352, www.eurekapuzzles.com).

SOUTH BOSTON
Broadway or Andrew T.

Known as Southie, this area feels removed from central Boston. That's partly been due to the wasteland of disused piers and warehouses that lay between the two, but with the redevelopment of the waterfront, the area is becoming more integrated. Perhaps because of its physical isolation, the blue collar, Irish-Catholic community remained virtually unchanged for almost a century. Dominated by organised crime in the 20th century, it gained a reputation as one of Boston's toughest areas. But like nearly every corner of the city, it's now been colonised by young professionals looking for affordable rents. The mood on Southie's two main thoroughfares is changing accordingly.

Smart eateries and shops have been popping up on East and West Broadway, including designer boutique **Habit** (703 East Broadway, at K Street, 1-617 269 1998, www.habitshop.com) and high-end resale shop **Covet** (395 West Broadway, between E & F Streets, 1-617 268 1100, www.covetboston.com). **Woody's L Street Tavern** (195 L Street, between East 8th Street & Marine Road, 1-617 268 4335), has been given a facelift, but is still recognisable as the dive where Matt Damon and Ben Affleck hung out in *Good Will Hunting*. Be warned, it's a long walk (or a ride on the no.11 bus) from the T.

EXPLORE

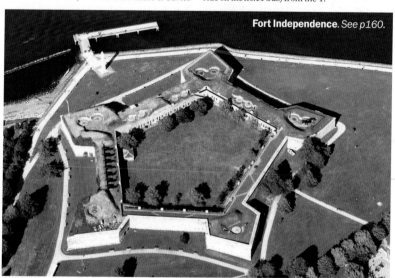

Fort Independence. *See p160.*

The area's signature 'triple-decker' homes reflect its past as a purpose-built immigrant district, dating from the early 19th century, but there's not much in the way of tourist sights, apart from the **Dorchester Heights Monument** (Thomas Park, south of Broadway and G Street). Built in 1898, it marks the site of a former military encampment used by the troops of General George Washington when he was pushing the British out of Boston. It's said that when Washington brought his forces up to Dorchester Heights on 17 March 1776, he ordered his troops to use the password 'St Patrick', which explains why St Patrick's Day (a huge celebration) is also called Evacuation Day here.

On the coast, **Castle Island** used to live up to its name, but was connected to the mainland in the 1930s when streetcars served the beach at Pleasure Bay. On the peninsula sits the National Historic Landmark, **Fort Independence**.

Sights & Museums

FREE Castle Island Park & Fort Independence
East end of William J Day Boulevard, at Shore Road (1-617 727 5290, www.bostonfort independence.com). Broadway T then bus 9, 11. **Open** *Park* dusk-dawn. *Fort* Late May-mid Oct 12.30-3pm Sat, Sun. **Admission** free.
South Boston lays claim to one of the city's most appealing shoreline parks: 22-acre Castle Island. It's also among the oldest fortified military sites in North America, centred on Fort Independence, a pentagonal granite structure that was finished in the 1850s. Prior to its construction, seven other forts had been built and destroyed in the area, occupied by American and British troops in turn. Today, the island's wide-open green spaces make for a pleasant outing. *Photo p159.*

QUINCY

Quincy Center T.

Although most of this neighbouring city – about seven miles south-east down the coast from downtown Boston – looks like an average suburb, with strip malls and pizza parlours, it's earned the right to declare itself 'the Birthplace of the American Dream'. Founding fathers (and cousins) John and Samuel Adams and John Hancock were born here, and another of its native sons, John Quincy Adams, was the country's sixth president (1825-29). The Romanesque **Thomas Crane Public Library** in the town centre (40 Washington Street, 1-617 376 1300, www. thomascranelibrary.org), built in 1881 by Trinity Church architect HH Richardson, is also worth a look. Quincy (locals pronounce it 'Quinzy') was also an important centre for shipbuilding, which reached its peak during World War II.

Sights & Museums

Adams National Historical Park
1250 Hancock Street, at Saville Avenue (1-617 770 1175, www.nps.gov/adam). Quincy Center T. **Open** *Grounds & visitor centre* Late Apr-early Nov 9am-5pm daily. Early Nov-late Apr 10am-4pm Tue-Fri. *Tours* Late Apr-early Nov 9am-3pm. **Admission** $5; free under-16s.
Trolleys depart from the visitor centre (which contains a medley of historical displays) to take you to the park for a guided tour with a ranger (around two hours in total). The park contains three important houses: the saltbox-style home where John Adams, the second American president, was born; the larger colonial home where his son (and America's sixth president) John Quincy Adams was born; and the Old House, a mansion built in 1731 that both used during their presidencies as the summer White House. Nearby is the Stone Library, built in 1873, which contains more than 14,000 books owned by the family. The grounds include an 18th-century-style formal garden and a lovely orchard.

SOMERVILLE

Assembly, Davis or Sullivan T.

Once snubbed by many Bostonians as 'Slummerville', the city just north of Cambridge is having the last laugh. Some of the most exciting bars and restaurants in the Boston area have opened in the vicinity of Union Square, which is also a hotbed of breweries and artisanal food producers such as Mexican-inspired chocolate company Taza (www.tazachocolate.com). The high concentration of watering holes here, from speakeasy cocktail den **Backbar** to laid-back Irish pub the **Independent**, make it a prime bar-hopping patch.

While Somerville suffered for years from limited public transport options, recent extensions to the Red and Orange MBTA lines are making it an even more popular place to live and go out. More accessible than Union, Davis Square, just two stops from Harvard on the Red Line, has worthwhile performance venues including **Johnny D's Uptown Restaurant & Music Club** (*see p192*), a great place to catch folk and blues, and the 1914 **Somerville Theatre** (*see p176*), a vaudeville house turned cinema which also hosts sporadic gigs. Down the street the vintage boxcar **Rosebud** diner has been renamed and rebooted with a new menu. Reflecting the DIY spirit of Somerville's hipster-heavy demographic, contemporary craft shop **Magpie** assembles crafts and handmade gifts from around the country. In contrast, the city is the site of the Boston area's new outlet mall, **Assembly Row**, the first in close proximity to the metropolis.

SECOND HELPINGS IN SOMERVILLE

Well-known chefs are crossing the Cambridge border for casual sequels.

Bronwyn.

About two miles north-west of Boston is a vibrant mash-up city of hipsters, innovators, professionals and immigrants, well on its way to gentrification. Somerville's urban yet homey feel and its proximity to Boston give it an edge. Recently, chef-proprietors with established, big-ticket restaurants in Boston and Cambridge have been opening more affordable, casual offshoots here.

James Beard Award-winning chef Tony Maws followed up his refined **Craigie on Main** (*see p138*) in Cambridge with the boisterous **Kirkland Tap & Trotter** (*see p163*), on the Cambridge-Somerville border. 'At Craigie on Main, we say you roll up your sleeves one or two times,' he says. 'At Kirkland, you roll them up past the elbows.'

Exposed industrial piping and brickwork, mismatched chairs and a wood floor keep it casual, as do self-pour bottles of water on the table and the $28-and-under fare. Maws' talented team (and Maws himself, who's often seen behind the line), crank out craft cocktails and home-style eats from an open kitchen. Dishes include grilled half salmon head ('People flip out,' says Maws), pastas, fire-roasted half chicken, and, yes, a juicy burger (different but just as delicious as Craigie's), plus house-made hot dogs. There's also a house-made kielbasa platter with 'kraut and fries, a hearty vegetable and barley stew, and braised skate wing with Wellfleet clams.

Cassie Pluma worked closely with chef Ana Sortun – also a James Beard Award winner

– at **Oleana** (*see p139*), Sortun's upscale Middle Eastern restaurant in Cambridge. Now Pluma has taken the reins as chef of **Sarma** (*see p164*), which she co-owns with Sortun. Sarma is a colourful *meyhane* – a traditional Turkish café serving meze and drinks.

'We wanted to open a restaurant off the beaten path in a real neighbourhood, and this location fitted the bill,' says Pluma. Deep-hued walls in blue and green add a touch of exoticism. The creative small plates reflect Pluma's personal twist on Middle Eastern fare: harissa-barbecued duck with carrot and orange blossom; sesame fried chicken with tahini remoulade; and lamb kofte sliders with tomato, yoghurt and pickles are just a few of Pluma's signature bites, each under $16.

Across town in Union Square, husband and wife team Tim and Bronwyn Wiechmann (of TW Food in Cambridge) offer a wide selection of German-style and imported beers (16 taps) and eastern and central European cuisine in a medieval-pub setting at **Bronwyn** (*see p162*). Burlap coffee sacks serve as barstool seats; and an iron chandelier and handmade gothic chairs set the tone for the plates of wurst, pretzels and a blackboard-special-only hotdog in a poppy seed potato roll for $10. Tim Wiechmann also taps his German heritage to provide the contemporary spins on comfort food such as schnitzel with lemon-ginger hollandaise, and squid goulash, all under $22. There's a *Biergarten* that's popular in the warmer months.

EXPLORE

Restaurants & Cafés

Bergamot

*118 Beacon Street, at Washington Street
(1-617 576 7700, www.bergamotrestaurant.
com). Harvard T then 15mins walk.* **Open** 5.30pm-
midnight daily. **Main courses** $25-$30. **American**
With an inviting, low-lit white-tablecloth dining
room and impeccable service, Bergamot serves 'progressive American' cuisine – food inspired by the
seasons and with global influences. Co-owner and
chef Keith Pooler offers à la carte, prix-fixe and tasting menu options, and the small bar mixes up creative cocktails. Appetisers include roasted beets with
goat's cheese and blueberry *gastrique*; pan-roasted
monkfish basks in a caramelised onion fenugreek
sauce. Creative desserts include chocolate cream
puff with Earl Grey cream. All good to know, since
you'll want to watch yourself with the bread basket
(the focaccia that shows up on your table is incredibly hard to resist).

★ Bronwyn

*255 Washington Street, at Sanborn Court, Union
Square (1-617 776 9900, www.bronwynrestaurant.
com). Harvard T then bus 86.* **Open** 5-11pm Tue,
Wed; 5pm-midnight Thur-Sat; 11am-11pm Sun.
Main courses $17-$22. **German**
See p161 **Second Helpings in Somerville**.

Casa B

*253 Washington Street, at Sanborn Court, Union
Square (1-617 764 2180, www.casabrestaurant.
com). Harvard T then bus 86.* **Open** 5-10pm Tue-
Thur, Sun; 5-11pm Fri, Sat. **Small plate**s $8-$16.
Spanish/Caribbean

Run by a husband and wife team of former caterers,
this stylish and romantic gem serves shareable
small plates that mix his Puerto Rican roots with her
Colombian background. The result is a fusion of Latin
and Caribbean flavours manifested in *tablas* (wooden
boards of dips, cheeses, ceviches or other bites),
pinchos (a different take Basque-style bar food such
as cod salad with guacamole and sautéed chorizo) and
an impressive array of tapas. On warmer nights, get
a table in the airy upstairs dining room with a view
on to the square, or descend below ground level for
the larger dining area with banquette seating and
entertaining open-kitchen views.

Dalí

*415 Washington Street, at Beacon Street (1-617
661 3254, www.dalirestaurant.com). Harvard
or Sullivan Square T, then bus 86.* **Open** 5.30-
11.30pm Mon-Thur, Sun; 5.30pm-12.30am Fri,
Sat. **Main courses** $26-$32. **Tapas** $4.50-$17.
Spanish
Somerville's elaborately decorated Spanish stronghold glitters and glows, shimmers and shines. From
the tiled bar where the owners' wooden pig statue
(there since the place opened more than 25 years
ago) keeps watch on the patrons to the lace curtains,
this is a sexy place for traditional, solid if not
swoon-generating tapas. *Gambas al ajillo* (sizzling
shrimp and garlic) and *pulpo a'feira* (grilled octopus) are among the many popular plates backed up
by an exceptional list of wines and sherries, and
great sangria.

Foundry on Elm

*255 Elm Street, at Chester Street, Davis Square
(1-617 628 9999, www.foundryonelm.com).*

Foundry on Elm.

Davis T. **Open** 11.30am-1am Mon-Thur; 11.30am-2am Fri; 11am-2am Sat; 10.30am-1am Sun. **Main courses** $13-$24. American

Foundry on Elm is one of the classier joints in the student-saturated Davis Square area. The spacious dining room is modelled after an old-school Parisian brasserie with black-and-white mosaic tiles, a 43ft Italian marble bar and brass wall sconces. The wide-ranging menu also riffs on the brasserie theme but with an American slant. An ever-present raw bar and a rotating charcuterie board top the menu, with dishes such as Cobb salad, *steak frites* and pan-seared salmon with roasted cauliflower rounding out the dinner options. The cocktail menu features classics and the strong beer programme highlights local and regional craft brews.

Highland Kitchen

150 Highland Avenue, at Central Street (1-617 625 1131, www.highlandkitchen.com). Central T then bus 83. **Open** 5pm-1am Mon-Sat; 11am-2.30pm, 5pm-1am Sun. **Main courses** $17-$24. American

Winter Hill's comfort-food eaterie is worth the trek (literally uphill from pretty much anywhere) for the shrimp and grits, but if you've got a long afternoon to burn through we'd recommend trying a bit of everything – from buffalo-fried brussels sprouts to the pulled pork sandwich to the spicy coconut curried goat stew. The cocktail list is dominated by bourbon and gin, and ranges from old-school classics to local favourites and invented concoctions. There's a respectable wine list plus a wide variety of local and imported beers – all the more digestible when you cue up an oldie on the jukebox.

Journeyman

9 Sanborn Court, at Washington Street, Union Square (1-617 718 2333, www.journeyman restaurant.com). Harvard T then bus 86. **Open** 5.30-10.30pm Wed-Sun. **Tasting menu** $65-$95. New American

Journeyman is a dining experience unlike anything else you'll find in the Boston area. Serious foodies seek out the industrially outfitted space for the daily-changing, inventive nine-course tasting menu, built on local produce and the whims of chefs Diana Kudayarova and Tse Wei Lim. You don't

get to pick the dishes; you just buy a ticket via the website, specify any allergies or if you're vegetarian, then show up for your reservation. Portions are small, but gourmands will appreciate the care that goes into each bite of artfully plated pork rillettes, shaved frozen foie gras or celeriac brûlée. Those in the know take their chances on Wednesday, Thursday and Sunday after 8.30pm, when 'walk-ins only' get a four-course tasting menu for $40 – that's if there's space.

★ Kirkland Tap & Trotter

425 Washington Street, at Beacon Street (1-857 259 6585, www.kirklandtapandtrotter.com). Harvard T then 15mins walk. **Open** 5.30pm-midnight Mon-Thur; 5.30pm-1am Fri, Sat; 10am-2pm, 5.30pm-midnight Sun. **Main courses** $16-$28. American

See p161 **Second Helpings in Somerville**.

Petsi Pies

285 Beacon Street, at Eustis Street, Porter Square (1-617 661 7437, www.petsipies.com). Porter T then 10mins walk, or bus 83. **Open** 7am-7pm Mon-Fri; 8am-4pm Sat, Sun. Bakery-café

Whimsically decorated pastries such as mini smiley-faced pumpkin pies line the window of this otherwise plain little bakery and coffee shop. Cookies, tarts and more beckon from the display cases inside, all bearing testament to owner Renee McLeod's wonderful way with sugar, butter and flour. Her savoury pies include a traditional pot pie, and a butternut squash with caramelised onions, gorgonzola and walnuts. Resistance is not merely futile but simply foolish; the scones, in particular, are sublime.

Other locations 31 Putnam Avenue, at Green Street, Cambridge (1-617 499 0801); 441 Cambridge Street, at 5th Street, Cambridge (1-617 945 5278).

Posto

187 Elm Street, at Windom Street, Davis Square (1-617 625 0600, www.postoboston.com). Davis T. **Open** 5.30-10pm Mon-Thur; 5-11pm Fri, Sat; 4.30-10pm Sun. **Main courses** $16-$27. Italian

Posto is serious about pizza. Mozzarella is handmade in house and each wood-fired pie is made according to guidelines laid out by the Associazione Verace Pizza Napoletana. But Posto is more than just a pizza joint. It's a modern Italian restaurant with an inviting wood-and-brick dining room; the menu offers Italian classics from antipasti to pastas, including gnocchi with braised beef short ribs. There's even a whole roast pig dinner that feeds ten to 12 (and must be ordered in advance).

Redbones

55 Chester Street, at Elm Street, Davis Square (1-617 628 2200, www.redbones.com). Davis T. **Open** 11.30am-12.30am Mon-Sat; noon-12.30am Sun. **Main courses** $9-$24. Barbecue

EXPLORE

Expect sensory overload at this popular barbecue joint where the walls have fluorescent colours, the ribs are slathered in sauce – and the crammed-in patrons are pleasantly steeped in beer. Actually, the global selection of brews are superior to the 'cue, though the fried catfish and corn fritters are mouth-watering. Redbones is just a block away from the Somerville Theatre (see p176), known for showing indie flicks and hosting concerts.

Rosebud American Kitchen & Bar

381 Summer Street, at Cutter Avenue, Davis Square (1-617 629 9500, www.rosebudkitchen. com). Davis T. **Open** 5pm-1am Mon-Thur; 4pm-1am Fri; 10am-3pm, 4pm-1am Sat; 10am-3pm, 5pm-1am Sun. **Main courses** $11-$24. **American** Listed on the National Register of Historic Places, this vintage Worcester diner (yep, they count) has had a makeover and was resurrected sans counter, but with that bottomless cup of coffee – perfect to go with the pie of the month. The menu, heavy on the bacon and barbecue, represents different regions of the States and the world: fried green tomatoes, and chicken-fried catfish on the one hand, and a falafel sub and a wilted kale salad with dashi broth and pork crackling on the other. Pancakes and biscuits and gravy do justice to brunch. Oh, and the pies? If the display case at the host stand doesn't do it for you, we can't help.

★ Sarma

249 Pearl Street, at Marshall Street (1-617 764 4464, www.sarmarestaurant.com). Davis T then bus 88, 90. **Open** 5pm-midnight Mon-Thur, Sun; 5pm-1am Fri, Sat. **Meze** $7-$16. **Mediterranean** *See p161* **Second Helpings in Somerville**.

Bars

Backbar

7 Sanborn Court, at Washington Street, Union Square (1-617 718 0249, www.backbarunion.com). Harvard T then bus 86. **Open** 4pm-midnight daily. This hidden sister bar to Journeyman (see p163) is best found by looking for the disoriented would-be patrons wandering the parking lot between neighbours Bronwyn and the Independent. Once inside, you'll be treated to outstanding service and meticulously crafted cocktails while seated at low-key wooden tables. Show up early or book – staff make people wait rather than letting them crowd the space.

Burren

247 Elm Street, at Chester Street, Davis Square (1-617 776 6896, www.burren.com). Davis T. **Open** 11am-1am Mon-Thur; 11am-2am Fri; 10am-2am Sat; 10am-1am Sun. A Davis Square mainstay, the Burren is one of the most popular (and largest) Irish pubs on the north side of the river. During the afternoon, the front room – with its wooden floors and gentle light pouring through the windows – is full of folks tucking into bowls of beef stew, sipping pints of Guinness (or any number of local brews) and listening to informal Irish *seisiúns*. At night, the Burren is packed, largely with students from nearby Tufts University, who crowd the large back room to hear live (and loud) roots rock.

Daddy Jones

525 Medford Street, at Broadway, Magoun Square (1-617 690 9095, www.daddyjonesbar.com). Davis T then bus 80, 89. **Open** 5pm-midnight Mon-Sat; 10am-midnight Sun.

Backbar.

EXPLORE

The brainchild of Boston industry veteran Dimitra Tsourianis, Daddy Jones serves Greek food, craft cocktails and local brews. While more and more local bars offer Prohibition-inspired cocktails, the list here focuses on reimagined cocktails, the list here focuses on reimagined favourites from the 1980s.

★ Independent

75 Union Square, at Washington Street (1-617 440 6022, www.theindo.com). Harvard T then bus 86. **Open** 3pm-1am Mon-Thur; 3pm-2am Fri; 11am-2am Sat; 11am-1am Sun.

Marked by the comfort of a neighbourhood haunt and a low-key sort of elegance, 'the Indo' is a Somerville favourite. The kitchen produces quality pub grub and snacks – oysters, fish and chips, burgers, fried almonds – until 11pm. And the adjoining bar is Irish without being too much so, with a fine wine list and one of the better pints of Guinness in town. DJs spin every night.

Olde Magoun's Saloon

518 Medford Street, at Lowell Street, Magoun Square (1-617 776 2600, www.magounssaloon. com). Davis T then bus 88. **Open** 11.30am-1am Mon-Thur; 11.30am-2am Fri; 10am-2am Sat; 10am-1am Sun.

Though a casual neighbourhood place at first glance, Olde Magoun's Saloon has more than 25 beers on tap and an impressive array of small-batch bourbons. Making matters even better are the eight variations of mac and cheese, each served in a cast-iron skillet.

Saloon

255 Elm Street, at Chester Street, Davis Square (1-617 628 4444, www.saloondavis.com). Davis T. **Open** 5pm-1am Mon-Thur, Sun; 5pm-2am Fri, Sat.

This unmarked speakeasy relies on word of mouth: look for the Davis Square Theater entrance and take a left at the bottom of the steps. Aged mirrors and padded leather banquettes enhance the Prohibition-era vibe. While the drinks menu includes some crafty new concoctions, Saloon maintains a heavy focus on the classics. Old-fashioneds, manhattans and sazeracs are all well crafted and remain the bar's most popular cocktails. Beer, wine and other spirits are well represented, but the menu is primarily whisky-focused and features an extensive list of brown spirits divided by style (bourbon, Tennessee, rare, blended, single barrel, Irish, Asian).

Spoke Wine Bar

89 Holland Street, at Simpson Avenue, Teele Square (1-617 718 9463, www.spokewinebar. com). Davis T. **Open** 5.30pm-midnight Mon-Thur; 5.30pm-1am Fri, Sat.

Spoke's well-curated wine list is matched by a menu that's focused on cheese, cured ham and oysters – perfect for pairing with the vino. However, this unpretentious offshoot of revered Dave's Fresh Pasta, on the outskirts of Davis Square, also offers skilfully executed cocktails and a varied list of draught beers.

★ Trina's Starlite Lounge

3 Beacon Street, at Dickinson Street, Inman Square (1-617 576-0006, http://trinastarlitelounge.com). Central T then bus 83, 91. **Open** 5pm-1am Mon; 5pm-1am Tue-Thur; 5pm-2am Fri, Sat. **Map** p276 C2.

Rising from the ashes of the classic-but-grimy Abbey Lounge, this Inman Square space has remained a meeting spot for savvy locals. Trina's low lighting and dark-wood panelling are brightened up by retro images just about everywhere you look (the bathrooms are wallpapered in mid-century magazine pages), but it's the menu full of diner-style comfort food that really keeps the clientele smiling into their expertly executed cocktails. Head here for brunch on Mondays to recover from the weekend's excesses.

Shops & Services

Assembly Row

100 Foley Street, at Assembly Square (1-617 440 5565, www.assemblyrow.com). Assembly T. **Open** 10am-9pm Mon-Sat; 11am-6pm Sun. **Mall**

An industrial no-man's land has morphed into Somerville's one-stop shopping destination, with discount outlets (Lucky Brand, Saks off 5th, Pendleton, Adidas, Nike), beauty salons and eateries, including the waterside Legal on the Mystic, the newest outpost of the Legal Seafoods chain, and a beer garden in the works. The Legoland Discovery Center and the movie theatre are the principal family draws, while extras such as regular music performances and outdoor fitness classes encourage warm-weather socialising.

★ Magpie

416 Highland Avenue, at Grove Street, Davis Square (1-617 623 3330, www.magpie-store. com). Davis T. **Open** 11am-7pm Mon-Fri; 11am-6pm Sat; 11am-5pm Sun. **Gifts/Fashion/ Homewares**

Crafts are cool again, as Magpie amply proves. Owned by four young creatives, it showcases handmade gifts, art, homewares and clothes by independent designers (some of whom live in hip Somerville), at reasonable prices. The displays are as unique as the wares: arty magnets are stuck to an old, wall-mounted fridge door, and notebooks and cards lean on a vintage typewriter. Adorable hand-painted animal-themed mugs and bowls by Cambridge ceramicist Abby Berkson, toast-shaped fleece heating pads by Somerville-based Jasminedoodles and Supermaggie screen-printed T-shirts are just a few examples of the stock.

EXPLORE

Arts & Entertainment

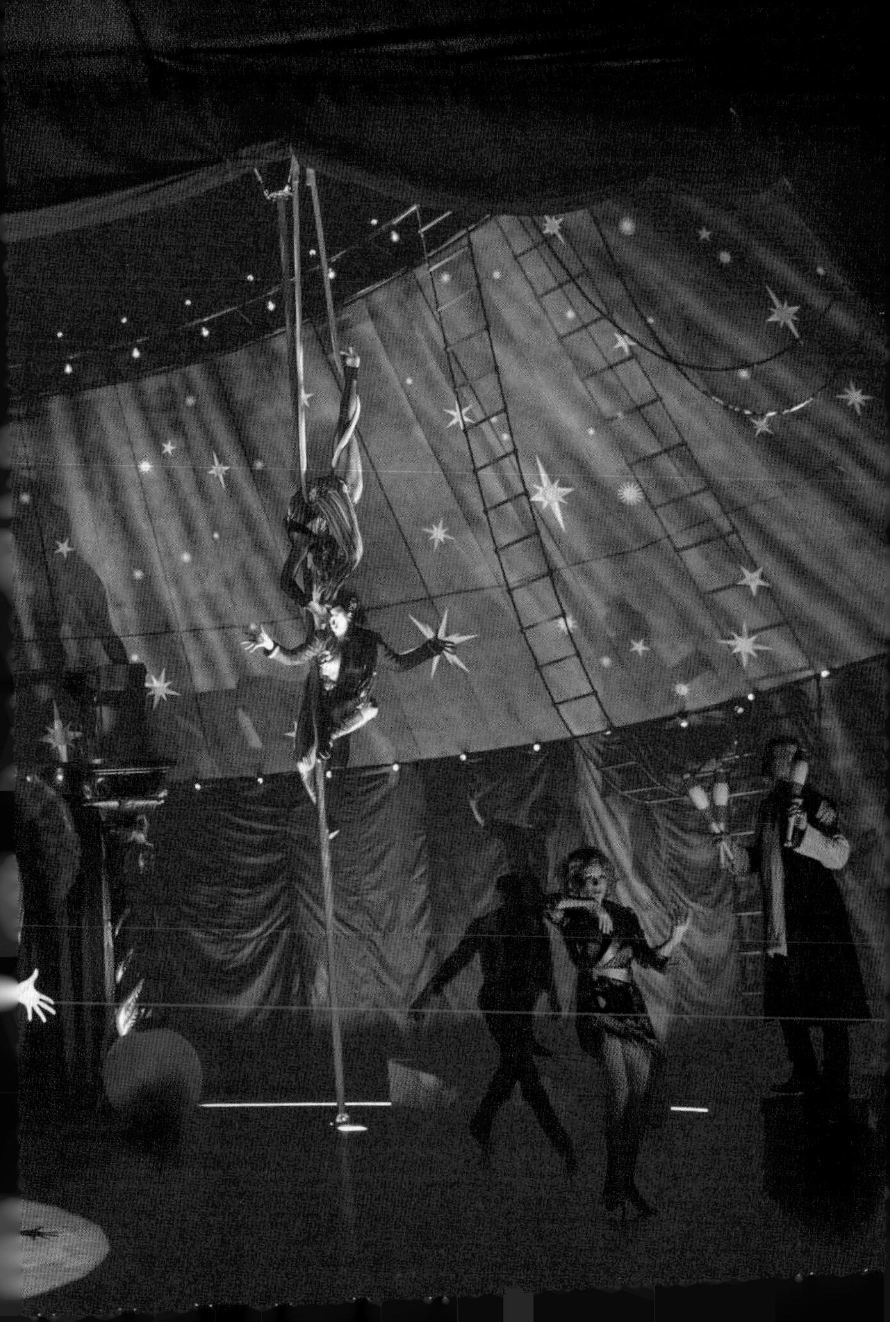

Children

Boston is rich in history, but children only have so much patience for standing in old buildings and listening to a guide, even one dressed in a funny-looking costume. But one of the newest local attractions for young visitors takes that one step further: at the rebuilt Boston Tea Party Ships & Museum, the past springs to vivid life through technology-driven exhibits, and kids can pretend to be colonists and toss tea chests into the harbour.

Ample green spaces and waterfront areas are perfect for family exploration. The USS Constitution Museum rarely fails to fire young imaginations, and Georges Island has a 19th-century fort where kids can run around. Rainy days can be more of a challenge, but there are some outstanding child-friendly museums in addition to the excellent Boston Children's Museum. Nature-loving tykes will have a blast at the New England Aquarium and the highly interactive Museum of Science.

SIGHTSEEING & ACTIVITIES

If you're here during the February or April school holidays or summer vacation, you'll find daily kids' activities at every museum and library in town. For more ideas, try local newspaper the *Boston Globe*, which highlights events in the area. Or check out the *Boston Parents Paper* magazine, available at newsstands, street boxes or, more reliably, online at http://bostonparentspaper.com. Boston's web-savvy parents also rely on www.bostoncentral.com and www.mommypoppins.com.

Animals & Nature

The **New England Aquarium** enthralls kids with its noisy penguins, a four-storey tank filled with sea turtles and sharks, and hands-on touch tanks. To spot bigger marine creatures, book a place on one of the Aquarium's summer **Whale Watch** trips. A catamaran takes you out to Stellwagen Bank, accompanied by trained naturalists who can tell you the names of all the humpbacks you see.

Paddling around Boston's waterways can offer a fresh perspective on the city. **Charles River Canoe & Kayak** (1-617 965 5110, www.ski-paddle.com) rents boats by the hour or day in Boston, Cambridge and Newton during the summer months.

Franklin Park Zoo

1 Franklin Park Road, Dorchester (1-617 541 5466, www.zoonewengland.org). Forest Hills T then bus 16. **Open** *Apr-Sept* 10am-5pm Mon-Fri; 10am-6pm Sat, Sun. *Oct-Mar* 10am-4pm daily. **Admission** $18; $12-$15 reductions; free under-2s.

Kids can walk right up to the glass enclosures at Franklin Park Zoo and make faces at young gorillas or watch stalking lions; and they can pet the sheep and goats at the Franklin Farm Contact Corral. Brilliantly coloured birds dart through the Tropical Forest over the heads of pygmy hippos and capybaras (and visitors), while butterflies will flutter on to outstretched hands at the Butterfly Landing (June-Sept). Some children will happily ignore the animals altogether, and tackle the zoo-themed playground equipment instead. A new interactive children's zoo called Nature's Neighborhood is slated to open in spring 2016.

Swan Boats.

New England Aquarium

For listings, *see p118*.

The breathtaking centrepiece of this excellent aquarium is the colossal 200,000-gallon salt-water replica of a Caribbean coral reef. The cylindrical tank, 40ft in diameter and four stories tall, is alive with moray eels, stingrays, gigantic sea turtles and menacing sharks. On a smaller scale, a touch tank exhibit lets children plunge their hands into the cold water and stroke harmless cownose and Atlantic rays and epaulette sharks as they swim by in a shallow tank. The huge indoor penguin exhibit (constructed so almost all of the balconies overlook it) is a hoot. If the lines are too long, peek at the playful inhabitants of the outdoor seal enclosure instead. The IMAX theatre offers state-of-the-art 3D glasses to put viewers in the middle of the action. Quieter tykes will enjoy the Curious George Discovery Corner, which explores the ocean and its inhabitants through toys and videos.

▶ *From April to October, the Aquarium runs a naturalist-narrated Whale Watch boat trip, which visits one of the largest whale feeding grounds in the world; see www.neaq.org for details.*

New England Aquarium.

★ Swan Boats

Public Garden, entrance on Arlington Street, Back Bay (1-617 522 1966, http://swanboats.com). Arlington T. **Open** *Mid June-Aug* 10am-5pm daily. *Apr-mid June* 10am-4pm daily. *Sept* noon-4pm Mon-Fri; 10am-4pm Sat, Sun. **Admission** $3; $1.50-$2.50 reductions; free under-2s. **No credit cards. Map** p280 H5.

What child could resist sitting in a swan? These quirky watercraft were created by designer Robert Paget in 1877, when the swan-drawn boat in the opera *Lohengrin* was a tad more familiar. Contemporary kids are more likely to know about Robert McCloskey's classic book *Make Way for Ducklings*, in which the Mallard family decides to move to Boston Pond, lured by the peanuts tossed by swan boat riders. (After your ride, look for the iconic sculptures of the ducks nearby.) You'll spend 15 minutes cruising around the small lagoon, amid the ducks and willow trees, as your children play at being swashbuckling pirates.

▶ *The Mallards also feature in an annual Duckling Day parade in mid May; for details, see http:// friendsofthepublicgarden.org.*

Museums & Attractions

Most of the city's grown-up institutions run excellent children's programmes at weekends and holidays. The **Museum of Fine Arts** (*see p90*) hosts Family Art Cart events (on weekends between September and June, and some Wednesdays in July and August), which send children out into the galleries with activities that encourage them to take a closer look at art. You can always pick up a variety of family-friendly self-guided activity sheets at the visitors' centre or download them online. The **Institute of Contemporary Art** (*see p124*) hosts a 'Play Date' on the last Saturday of the month, featuring hands-on art activities and free admission for two adults and children aged 12 and under. It also has a great outside deck overlooking the harbour – perfect for running after seagulls. If you take a shopping expedition to the Boston area's new

Boston Children's Museum

outlet mall in Somerville, **Assembly Row** (see p165), be sure to visit the **Lego Discovery Center**, which features mini local landmarks.

★ Boston Children's Museum

308 Congress Street, at Children's Wharf, Fort Point Channel, Waterfront (1-617 426 6500, www. bostonchildrensmuseum.org). South Station T. **Open** 10am-5pm Mon-Thur, Sat, Sun; 10am-9pm Fri. **Admission** $14; $8 reductions; $1 for all 5-9pm Fri. **Map** p281 M5.

More than a century after it opened, in 1913, some 400,000 visitors a year come to play at the Boston Children's Museum, overlooking Boston Harbor's Fort Point Channel. A $47 million restoration project, finished in 2007, transformed the building into a series of light, spacious, open areas, with plenty of room for energetic kids. It also turned it into Boston's first LEED-certified museum.

The centrepiece is the New Balance Climb, a twisty, turning three-storey climbing structure made of serpentine wires and platforms. On the ground floor, the Kid Power exhibit explores health and fitness, complete with climbing wall, bikes and an interactive light-up dancefloor to stomp on.

Other exhibits cover local or global themes; the Boston Black exhibit examines the city's ethnic diversity – kids can play steel drums for an Afro-Caribbean parade or go shopping in a Dominican grocery store. Next to it is a 100-year-old Japanese house from Kyoto, which they can explore as long as they first respectfully remove their shoes. For under-3s, there's the toddler-friendly PlaySpace, which has amusements such as toy trains and an aquarium. A number of performances take place throughout the day at the Kidstage.

★ Boston Tea Party Ships & Museum

306 Congress Street, Fort Point Channel, Waterfront (1-617 338 1773, www.boston teapartyship.com). South Station T. **Open** 10am-5pm daily. **Admission** $25; $13.50-$22.50 reductions; free under-3s. **Map** p281 M5. See p172 **Join the Tea Party**.

▶ *For more nautical adventures, visit the USS Constitution Museum; see p151.*

Harvard Museum of Natural History

26 Oxford Street, at Harvard Square, Cambridge (1-617 495 3045, www.hmnh.harvard.edu). Harvard Square T. **Open** 9am-5pm daily. **Admission** $12; $8-$10 reductions; free under-3s. **Map** p284 B2.

This historic museum has a vast and slightly creepy collection of stuffed, mounted and glass-encased creatures from around the globe, from beady-eyed llamas to coelacanths and butterflies. Fossil-mad children can gawk at dinosaur skeletons and admire the 42ft kronosaurus, a prehistoric marine reptile, while rock fans head straight for the meteorites and gemstones. The New England Forests exhibit in the Zofnass Family Gallery is a multimedia experience with motion detectors and soundtracks concealed around the space. Families can pick up the free 'Look Listen Touch' guide to the exhibit, then prick up their ears for meadowlarks singing, frogs croaking and other animals found in the area's forests.

▶ *Entry includes admission to the Peabody Museum of Archaeology & Ethnology; see p136.*

Museum of Science & Charles Hayden Planetarium

For listings, *see p73*.

Although not exclusively a children's domain, the Museum of Science – visited by more than 250,000 students in school groups each year – is largely geared towards youngsters. Its 700-plus hands-on displays and straightforward explanations aim to make science fun. All areas are covered, from the natural world to the latest high-tech inventions. Disciplines such as physics are explored in terms of everyday life, such as the Science in the Park exhibit with fully functional swings and seesaws. There is much to excite, from dinosaurs and the Butterfly Garden conservatory to space capsules and steam engines. In the Discovery Center, babies and toddlers can crawl safely while their older siblings put together animal skeletons or perform simple experiments. The domed Mugar Omni Theater shows a changing programme of IMAX movies, and the multimedia Charles Hayden Planetarium is a treat for small star-gazers. Adrenaline fans love the full-motion simulator, which offers a five-minute immersive experience to launch the Hubble Space Telescope, visit the Bermuda Triangle, dive in a submarine or take flight in a biplane (an additional fee applies).

Playgrounds

Christopher Columbus Park

Atlantic Avenue, adjacent to Commercial Wharf, Waterfront (www.bostonharborwalk.com). Aquarium T. **Open** dawn-dusk daily. **Map** p281 M3.
Ahoy, land-lubbers! Kids can wave at the ferries cruising to the Harbor Islands from this nautical-themed park, a short walk away from Faneuil Hall and the North End. There's a big blue-and-white climbing structure and a beach-sized sandpit, plus spray showers to play in on hot days. The flat ground means easy access for strollers.

Clarendon Street Playground

Corner of Clarendon Street & Commonwealth Avenue, Back Bay (1-617 247 3961, www. nabbonline.com/commitees/darendon_street_ playground). Copley T. **Open** dawn-dusk daily. **Map** p283 H5.
Set amid Back Bay's Victorian townhouses, Clarendon Street Playground provides a shaded urban oasis. It's sunk slightly below street level, muffling street noise – but you'll hear plenty of happy shrieks from the swings, slides, climbing

---

IN THE KNOW PARK THE KIDS

When little ones tire of sightseeing, the **Rose Kennedy Greenway** *(see p118)*, a short walk from Faneuil Hall and the North End, offers a Massachusetts-centric carousel (cod, grasshopper, seal and the like, instead of horses), water-spray features, food trucks and more. While the kids run around, you might get a chance to enjoy the free Wi-Fi.

---

frames and large open area for plain old romping. Local folks leave riding toys out for anyone to use.

Tadpole Playground

Boston Common, Downtown (www.tadpole playground.org). Park Street T. **Open** dawn-dusk daily. **Map** p280 K4.
Bronze frogs, fish and lily pads adorn this gated playground by Boston Common's Frog Pond ice-skating rink/sprinkler wading pool. The park has climbing frames and slides to occupy the kids, and plenty of benches where weary parents can rest.
▶ *For more about Boston Common, see p46.*

Theatre

In addition to the kid-centric theatres below, every Saturday morning the **Coolidge Corner Theatre** *(see p175)* in Brookline presents a family-friendly show, from variety acts with jugglers, magicians, comedians and the like, to movies such as the *Parent Trap* and *The Muppet Movie*. Games, prizes and bubbles are also part of the fun.

Boston Children's Theatre

1-617 424 6634, www.bostonchildrenstheatre.org.
One of the country's oldest theatre organisations, the BCT puts on a variety of plays and musicals, including adaptations of classic books and new

ARTS & ENTERTAINMENT

Carousel on the Rose Kennedy Greenway.

Children

JOIN THE TEA PARTY

Acting up is all part of the experience at this fun historical museum.

On the night of 16 December 1773, a group of American colonists, fed up with 'taxation without representation', boarded three ships harboured at Griffin's Wharf and dumped 342 crates of British-owned tea into the sea. It's a story every American schoolchild knows.

For more than a decade, Boston had no museum commemorating the historic event. After a fire in 2001, the old Tea Party Museum was demolished. It took 11 years for a new one to open, but most people who visit the **Boston Party Tea Ships & Museum** (*see p170*) will agree that it was worth the wait.

Located on the site where the colonists performed their revolutionary act, the floating museum, attached to the Congress Street bridge, sits astride wooden pylons. Historically accurate replicas of two of the three tall ships that were present that fateful night – the *Beaver* and the *Eleanor* – are docked adjacent, with the *Dartmouth* slated to be added in late 2015.

Tell the kids to check their preconceptions of dusty old history museums at the door. Instead, get ready for an interactive journey through time as actors in period costumes greet you at the entrance, assign you the persona of a colonist, encourage comments at a rally, then urge you to throw chests of tea into the harbour. (The tea chest props are attached by a rope, to be pulled up later.) Visitors can board the ships to explore the decks, crew's quarters and cargo holds.

Inside the museum building, portraits seemingly come to life and start talking in front of you (motion sensors trigger pre-recorded videos of actors). King Richard III and Samuel Adams get into a lively debate, then return to their poses, while 3D holograms of colonists chat on a Boston street in another amazing display. Other highlights include the Robinson Tea Chest, one of the only two original tea chests known to have survived; and the award-winning short film *Let It Begin Here*, which is screened in a state-of-the-art panoramic theatre that makes you feel as if you're on a battlefield during the American Revolution.

Make time to visit Abigail's Tea Room & Terrace on the way out. Try the signature blend, reminiscent of the tea tossed overboard, which was crafted for the museum by one of American's top tea experts, Bruce Richardson.

works, in venues around the city. Productions – by kids, for kids – coincide with the school holidays. Check the website for details of shows and prices.

Puppet Showplace Theater

32 Station Street, at Washington Street, Brookline (1-617 731 6400, www.puppetshowplace.org). Brookline Village T. **Box office** 10am-4pm Tue, Sat, Sun; 9.30am-4pm Wed-Fri. **Tickets** $12.
Traditional fairy tales, from *Cinderella* to *Jack and the Beanstalk*, are brought to life by the theatre's puppeteers, along with more contemporary stories. On Wednesday and Thursday mornings, the theatre hosts a special 'Puppet Playtime' for kids aged three and under.

Wheelock Family Theatre

200 The Riverway, at Short Street, Fenway (1-617 879 2300, www.wheelockfamilytheatre.org). Fenway T. **Box office** 10am-6pm Tue-Fri. **Tickets** $20-$35.
This professional theatre company has been staging children's shows at Wheelock College since 1982. Productions range from the classic *Pinocchio*, to *Shrek the Musical*, based on the popular movie.

Tours

For the child-friendly **Boston Old Town Trolley Tours** and the amphibious **Boston Duck Tours**, *see p260*.

Boston by Little Feet

Meet at the Samuel Adams statue on Congress Street, Downtown (1-617 367 2345, www.boston byfoot.org). State Street T. **Open** *tours* call or see website for schedule. **Tickets** $10; free under-6s.
This hour-long tour for children aged six to 12 (accompanied by a grown-up) is organised by the acclaimed Boston by Foot tour group. It provides a child's-eye view of sites along the Freedom Trail.

RESTAURANTS & CAFÉS

The city is strong on eateries that are familiar enough to keep children happy, yet with enough interest to satisfy adults. Pizzerias such as **Antico Forno** (*see p114*) and **Pizzeria Regina** (*see p115*) always appeal, as do the marvellous flavours at **Christina's Homemade Ice Cream** (*see p138*).

Fire + Ice

50 Church Street, at Brattle Street, Cambridge (1-617 547 9007, www.fire-ice.com). Harvard T. **Open** 11.30am-10pm Mon-Thur, Sun; 11.30am-11pm Fri, Sat. **Main courses** $19. **Map** p284 A2.
Don't let the sleek, trendy interior fool you – this is a child-friendly place. Picky eaters can choose their own ingredients, then watch their meal being cooked on the grill before their eyes. It's an all-you-can-eat establishment, with reduced rates for younger kids.
Other locations 205 Berkeley Street, at St James Avenue, Back Bay (1-617 482 3473).

Full Moon

344 Huron Avenue, between Gurney & Fayerweather Streets, Huron Village, Cambridge (1-617 354 6699, http://fullmoonrestaurant.com). Harvard T then bus 72. **Open** 11.30am-2.30pm, 5-9pm Mon-Fri; 9am-2.30pm, 5-9pm Sat, Sun. **Main courses** $17-$20.
Full Moon is stocked with baskets of toys, books, a chalkboard and a dolls' house to keep the children sweet. While the kids play, you can sample such adult-friendly fare as grilled rosemary chicken skewers with polenta and mushroom ragu, or fettuccine with duck meatballs, accompanied by a glass of Chianti. The children's menu spans hot dogs and fries to cheesy quesadillas. Best to book ahead, as it's popular with families.

Hard Rock Cafe

22-24 Clinton Street, at Faneuil Hall, Downtown (1-617 424 7625, www.hardrock.com). Haymarket T. **Open** 11am-midnight Mon-Thur, Sun; 11am-2am Fri, Sat. **Main courses** $15-$25. **Map** p281 L3.
Noisy, boisterous and filled with memorabilia from the golden age of rock, this ever-popular burger joint may be cheesy, but kids can be as raucous as they want and nobody will get angry.

★ Jasper White's Summer Shack

50 Dalton Street, at Scotia Street, Back Bay (1-617 867 9955, www.summershackrestaurant.com). Hynes Convention Center T. **Open** 11.30am-4pm, 5-10pm Mon-Thur; 11.30am-4pm, 5-11pm Fri; 11.30am-11pm Sat; 11.30am-10pm Sun. **Main courses** $14-$28. **Map** p282 F7.
If you don't have time for a clam bake on the beach, head here. Its cheery, colourful decor and friendly vibe make it great for families. Kids can try corn dogs, clam chowder or chicken wings, while older diners savour wood-grilled lobster or oysters from the raw bar.
Other locations 149 Alewife Brook Parkway, Cambridge (1-617 520 9500).

BABYSITTING

Care

1-855 781 1303, www.care.com. **Open** 8am-5pm Mon-Fri. **Rates** placement fee varies; sitter salary $15-$35/hr.

Nanny Poppins

1-617 697 0052, www.nannypoppins.com. **Open** 9am-6.30pm daily. **Rates** placement fee varies; sitter salary $15-$25/hr.

Film

As a result of tax breaks, more and more movies – from *Ted 2* to *Black Mass* – are being filmed in-state. Although film shoots aren't as prolific on the streets of Boston as in celluloid capitals such as NYC or LA, Denzel Washington, Johnny Depp and local boys Mark Wahlberg, Ben Affleck and Matt Damon have all worked here. If you're more interested in seeing stars on the big screen than on location, Boston offers cinemagoers a range of options, from multiplexes to contemporary arthouses. Vintage gems, including the former vaudeville venue Somerville Theatre and the art deco Coolidge Corner Theatre, turn a night at the pictures into an event, with screening series, one-offs, second-runs and visiting performers all a part of the regular programming.

For local movie listings, critics' picks and reviews of the latest releases, visit timeout.com/boston.

CINEMAS

The city's screening venues range from glitzy stadium theatres showing the latest Hollywood blockbusters, such as the giant **Regal Fenway**, to funky Cambridge repertory houses such as the **Kendall Square Cinema** and the single-screen **Brattle Theatre**. To see a flick in a non-traditional venue, check out the Ruth and Carl J Shapiro Film Program at the **Museum of Fine Arts** (*see p90*) for new narrative and documentary films and international fare, as well as work from local filmmakers and director retrospectives. The **Institute of Contemporary Art** (*see p124*) offers contemporary film and video art in addition to special screenings and festival events.

Arthouse & Revival

★ Brattle Theatre
40 Brattle Street, at Harvard Square, Cambridge (1-617 876 6837, www.brattlefilm.org). Harvard T. Tickets $10; $7-$8 reductions. **Map** p284 A2.
Built as a theatre in 1890 by the Cambridge Social Union, the slightly ragged Brattle became a movie house in the 1950s, when it offered Humphrey Bogart marathons as a stress reliever for students during exam weeks. In the half century since then, it has kept Bogart in the annual line-up – including a Valentine's Day screening of *Casablanca*. A non-profit that's dangled close to the edge of bankruptcy several times, the historic single-screen carries on, marching to the beat of its own eclectic programming. With classic films, cartoon marathons, new documentaries, rare Japanese horror, best-of-the-year recaps and staff picks all on the roster, it's a good bet for open minds and omnivorous tastes. More easy-going than the nearby Harvard Film

---

IN THE KNOW
A BEER WITH MATT AND BEN

Low-key watering hole **Woody's L Street Tavern** (195 L Street, between East 8th Street & Marine Road, South Boston, 1-617 268 4335) doesn't have the trappings of a tourist magnet, but fans of *Good Will Hunting* venture deep into the residential neighbourhood for a drink at Matt Damon and Ben Affleck's dive-bar hangout in the 1997 film.

Archive, the Brattle serves beer and also hosts book events and live music on occasion. Showtimes can be a little erratic, so it's best to check the website.

★ Coolidge Corner Theatre

290 Harvard Street, at Green Street, Brookline (1-617 734 2500, www.coolidge.org). Coolidge Corner T. **Tickets** $11; $4-$9 reductions.

Once the Beacon Universalists Church, the Coolidge was transformed into a movie palace in 1933, and given a much-needed renovation in 2006 that restored its art deco fixtures and brought comfortable new seats. Today, the much-loved non-profit works all the angles by juggling tons of series with its regular independent and foreign programming – 'Science on Screen' pairs a movie with a related science talk and 'After Midnite' does cult films and horror, for example. The annual Coolidge Award has honoured the likes of Meryl Streep and Jonathan Demme, and attracted many a big name into town. Like the Somerville Theatre, the Coolidge has added more screens to compete with multiplexes – in addition to the main 1930s theatre, there are three smaller screens. But be warned: one is very small.

★ Harvard Film Archive

Carpenter Center for the Visual Arts, 24 Quincy Street, at Harvard University, Cambridge (1-617 495 4700, http://hcl.harvard.edu/hfa). Harvard T. **Tickets** $9-$12; $7 reductions. **No credit cards.** **Map** p284 B2.

Home to the largest collection of 35mm films in New England, Harvard's film temple and screening space provides access to a diverse catalogue of often hard-to-find films. The selection in a given month might include anything from Hong Kong cinema

to historically important Hollywood gems to pure experimental stuff. The HFA also hosts retrospectives, with filmmakers frequently brought in for Q&As. The poured cement exterior of the Carpenter Center might not be much to look at, but it's the only Le Corbusier building in North America.

Kendall Square Cinema

1 Kendall Square Building, at Cardinal Medeiros Avenue, Cambridge (1-617 621 1202, www.landmarktheatres.com). Kendall/MIT T. **Tickets** $11; $9 reductions.

This MIT-area staple is a good place to see first-run independent films, but purists wouldn't call it an independent movie house; the indies run alongside big blockbusters and the whole place is owned by Landmark Theatres, who wrangle more than 50 cinemas nationwide. *Photo p176.*

▶ *For restaurants, cafés and bars around Kendall Square, see p141.*

Paramount Center

559 Washington Street, at Avenue de Lafayette, Downtown (1-617 824 8400, http://artsemerson.org). Chinatown T. **Tickets** usually $10. **Map** p280 K5.

Emerson College's Paramount Center is an old classic that rose from the ashes in 2010, thanks to extensive renovations. The restored art deco building is dominated by an iconic flashing marquee, and still has the Paramount Pictures logo carved into the façade. The complex now houses two theatres for performing arts and the Bright Family Screening Room, with 170 seats and both film and digital projection capabilities. Cinematic offerings include unusual foreign films, animation, shorts, children's

Coolidge Corner Theatre.

programming and new avant-garde fare. It's a far cry from the seedy collection of sex clubs and adult theatres that used to define this stretch of Washington Street as Boston's 'Combat Zone'.

Somerville Theatre

55 Davis Square, at Elm Street, Somerville (1-617 625 5700, http://feitheatres.com/somerville-theatre). Davis T. **Tickets** $7-$10; $7 reductions.
Mere steps from the Davis T station, the Somerville Theatre opened in 1914 as a vaudeville and movie venue, transitioning into the picture business full-time during the Great Depression. The Somerville's tradition of attracting audiences by giving away prizes like turkeys and domestic appliances ended in the 1970s, but a crowd-pleasing, multi-purpose spirit is still intact. As well as showing new, one-off and second-run movies, the theatre is a venue for the Independent Film Festival Boston every spring, and also hosts occasional concerts by major acts. Four smaller screens were added in 1996, but the original colourful, gold-and-plaster main theatre remains in good shape. Beer and wine are sold for all shows.

Mainstream & First-run

AMC Loews Boston Common

175 Tremont Street, at Avery Street, Downtown (1-617 423 5801, www.amctheatres.com). Boylston or Chinatown T. **Tickets** $13-$18.50; $7 reductions. **Map** p280 K5.
The mothership of Boston multiplexes, the AMC Loews is a winner for its convenient location and 19 screens. Summer blockbusters, Oscar favourites, pre-screeners, opening events, AMC independents, IMAX and RealD 3D – you'll find it all here.

Regal Fenway Stadium

201 Brookline Avenue, at Fullerton Street, Fenway (1-617 424 6111, www.regmovies.com). Fenway T. **Tickets** $12.50-$16.50; $7-$10 reductions.
Tucked just behind Fenway Park, the Regal is a hangout for both college students and local families, though it still tends to be much less crowded than its multiplex competitor on the Common.

FILM FESTIVALS

Although it's a long way from becoming the home of the next Sundance, Boston has a fine array of film festivals in its cultural calendar. The week-long **Boston Film Festival** (*see p34*) in September shows a substantial roster of feature films and shorts. The **Boston Underground Film Festival** (*see p30*) screens bizarre and provocative cinematic fare, while spring's **Independent Film Festival Boston** (www.iffboston.org) has premières of indie films heading for general release. The Museum of Fine Arts (*see p90*) hosts various annual fests, including the **Palestine Film Festival** and the **Jewish Film Festival**.

A couple of highly regarded out-of-town summer festivals allow you to combine sun, sand and screenings. Down on the Cape, the **Provincetown International Film Festival** (1-508 487 3456, www.ptownfilmfest.org) blends indie and queer themes in a packed June weekend, while the **Nantucket Film Festival** (1-508 325 6275, www.nantucketfilmfestival.org), also held in June, is a favourite excursion for Boston film-lovers, who take in feature films, shorts and documentaries by emerging talents and celebrated screenwriters.

Kendall Square Cinema. *See p175.*

ESSENTIAL BOSTON FILMS

Six movies that capture the spirit of the city.

Good Will Hunting.

THE DEPARTED
MARTIN SCORSESE (2006)

When it comes to Scorsese, we expect the mean streets of New York City. But there's no denying the director knocked it out of the park for his Boston-set crime classic. This Oscar-winning picture is cast with authentically rooted actors (such as Dorchester's own scrappy Mark Wahlberg), was shot on location and infused with the dark legend of Whitey Bulger, via an unhinged Jack Nicholson.

GOOD WILL HUNTING
GUS VAN SANT (1997)

Returning to this compassionate drama is bound to bring a tear to your eye, especially when therapist Robin Williams insists to a young, troubled Matt Damon: 'It's not your fault.' (Wow, this room must be really dusty.) The years have been kind to this thoroughly Boston story, which features a now-immortal bench in the Public Garden, several Cambridge pubs and a respectable job with the accents.

THE VERDICT
SIDNEY LUMET (1982)

Take time to savour the nuances of this superb David Mamet-scripted legal thriller, starring an inspired Paul Newman as a lawyer with a drinking problem grasping for redemption. His comeback case, a medical-malpractice suit, involves the Archdiocese of Boston as a defendant; fittingly, the film evokes a fleeting state of grace, even as Newman rummages around grungy courthouses and Quincy Market.

LOVE STORY
ARTHUR HILLER (1970)

This schmaltzfest starring Ryan O'Neal and Ali MacGraw launched a catchphrase – 'Love means never having to say you're sorry' – one we don't recommend trying at home. Still, it makes our shortlist for being among the handful of films granted extensive permission to shoot on Harvard's campus, a privilege that paid handsome dividends. Doomed romance gets a cosy Ivy League shell, emphasising youthful promise cut short.

THE FRIENDS OF
EDDIE COYLE
PETER YATES (1973)

Never heard of it? No other movie gets so much punch out of Boston's early '70s charm as this gangster film, featuring Robert Mitchum as a criminal turned informant. Dark taverns and working-class neighbourhoods are shown off magnificently, but top honours go to a sequence shot at a Bruins hockey game, complete with a drunken monologue saluting Bobby Orr: 'Jeez, what a future he's got, huh?'

MYSTIC RIVER
CLINT EASTWOOD (2003)

Massively acclaimed upon its release and a masterful portrait of buried psychological trauma, this boys-to-men mystery drama has the ultimate local pedigree: it's based on a novel by Dennis Lehane, as close to Boston's Elmore Leonard as it gets. The movie sprung a seismic performance out of Sean Penn, playing ex-con James 'Jimmy' Markum, whose malfeasance comes back to haunt him in a terrible way.

Gay & Lesbian

Though button-down Boston's gay scene is less flamboyant than that of some US cities, it offers opportunities for gay, lesbian, bisexual and transgender visitors of many interests to comfortably experience nightlife, take in some culture and shopping, and explore a rich history.

Boston's Puritan roots still show in its reserved attitude towards outsiders, and you may have to take the initiative if you want to make a new friend. But the city was key to the early gay rights movement and legally recognised same-sex marriage, and it remains a place where all kinds of couples can walk hand-in-hand down most streets without raising eyebrows. The dozens of colleges and universities in Greater Boston, and its large banking and technology sectors, draw students, faculty and professionals from around the world, ensuring a diverse and educated LGBT community that belies the city's insular, Irish-Catholic stereotypes.

THE SCENE

Unlike some cities, Boston doesn't have a single gay centre but instead several pockets with distinct populations. Dispersed from the old South End 'gaybourhood' in the 2000s by gentrification and by the movement of some lesbians and gay men to the suburbs to raise families, the LGBT community remains visible there while staking outposts around the city.

Jamaica Plain, long a draw for lesbians, and a centre of casual, low-key nightlife, is increasingly populated by gay men and people across the gender spectrum, including a visible female-to-male transgender community. Somerville's Davis Square continues to be a haven for younger lesbians and hipsters of all persuasions, while many gay men make their homes in sections of Dorchester, particularly the increasingly trendy Savin Hill area, as the city has become more welcoming to the LGBT community in all but its most insular ethnic enclaves.

While many LGBT residents have been priced out, the South End area around and south of Columbus Avenue still contains Boston's largest concentration of conspicuously queer-owned or queer-friendly bars, restaurants, businesses and non-profit organisations. The funkier, more affordable and community-oriented mix of local businesses in Davis Square and on Jamaica Plain's Centre Street also provide a mix of shopping, dining, drinking and dancing venues for a sometimes surprising mix of LGBT residents and old-school townie types.

INFORMATION & MEDIA

Bay Windows (www.baywindows.com) is the city's main paper for the gay and lesbian community, though ongoing financial struggles have cut its coverage to the bare bones. The weekly is distributed on Thursdays in bookstores, cafés and gay bars throughout Boston, Cambridge and Somerville, and is also available online. The *Rainbow Times* (www. therainbowtimesmass.com) is a similarly slender publication, but covers LGBT events and issues across New England, while *Edge Boston* (www. edgeboston.com) is an online-only portal to coverage of LGBT news, entertainment and nightlife. *DigBoston* (*see p263*), a free alternative weekly newspaper, also features articles related to gay and lesbian issues. The glossy LGBT magazine *Boston Spirit* (www.bostonspirit magazine.com) is published every other month and offers free subscriptions through its website.

BARS & CLUBS

Gay and lesbian nightlife options in Boston and neighbouring Cambridge have long been limited, but in recent years the list has grown even shorter, due in part to increasingly high rents, the difficulty and expense of getting a liquor licence, neighbourhood opposition to late-night noise, and perhaps the widespread use of dating and hook-up apps that make cruising bars unnecessary. It may also be that many LGBT residents, especially those in long-term relationships, simply don't see a need for specifically gay spaces when their favourite neighbourhood bar is welcoming and within walking distance.

Boston's nightlife options – gay, straight or otherwise – are also limited by the mandated 2am closing time, though the city's new mayor has begun an effort to allow later hours, and the MBTA has extended weekend hours so that the last subway trains leave at 2.30am, allowing safe travel home after a few drinks. There are also limited after-hours options, such as the members-only club **Rise** (1-617 423 7473, www. riseclub.us), which runs a gay night on the second

Saturday of each month and is conveniently located near several South End gay bars.

Alley

14 Pi Alley, at Court Square, Downtown (1-617 263 1449, www.thealleybar.com). Government Center or State T. **Open** 2pm-2am Mon-Fri; noon-2am Sat, Sun. **No credit cards. Map** p280 K4.

If you identify as a bear, cub, otter, wolf, panda or other furry fauna, this is the place for you. Located off Boston's historic Pi Alley near Downtown Crossing, this dimly lit dive bar is relaxed, unpretentious and welcoming even to those with barely any chest hair, including the occasional woman. It's old-school in its style and atmosphere, with a single pool table, TVs showing the sport of the season, a digital jukebox and cheap, strong drinks.

Cathedral Station

1222 Washington Street, at Perry Street, South End (1-617 338 6060, www.cathedralstation.com). Tufts Medical Center T. **Open** 2pm-2am Mon-Fri; 10am-2am Sat; 11am-2am Sun. **Map** p283 J7.

ARTS & ENTERTAINMENT

Cathedral Station.

Eagle.

The first new Boston gay bar to open in years, Cathedral Station is the successor to Fritz, the nearby sports bar replaced in 2014 by Trophy Room (*see p182*). Formerly home to the Red Fez, its new space is more than twice the size of Fritz and includes dining and drinks – both available on the patio in warm weather – with an elaborate list of kitschy cocktails, but it maintains Fritz's mix of younger and older men, a few women and an overall down-to-earth, sporty vibe.

★ Club Café

209 Columbus Avenue, at Berkeley Street, South End (1-617 536 0966, www.clubcafe.com). Back Bay T. **Open** 11am-2am daily. **Map** p283 H6.
Boston's biggest and most varied gay bar, and one of its oldest, Club Café remains a mainstay because it offers something for almost everyone – it's the bar where young people just out of the closet bring their mothers for their first experience of gay nightlife. Its attractions include drinks and dining in the restaurant; the back-room Moonshine Dance Club; and cabaret performances in the Napoleon Room, which pays homage to the long-shut Napoleon Club in nearby Bay Village. The crowd is mixed by gender, age and ethnicity, though preppy men in their twenties are rarely outnumbered.
▶ *For the restaurant at Club Café, see p183.*

Dbar

1236 Dorchester Avenue, at Hancock Street, Dorchester (1-617 265 4490, www.dbarboston. com). Savin Hill T. **Open** 5pm-midnight Mon-Wed, Sun; 5pm-2am Thur-Sat.

The dinner hour brings a large and mixed gay and straight crowd to this former Irish pub in Savin Hill to enjoy upscale cocktails and dishes. The crowd gets gayer and more focused on the bar as the night goes on. The food is well prepared and the atmosphere comfortable and stylish, but the gay crowd is rarely large or diverse, consisting almost entirely of young, white, professional men.

Eagle

520 Tremont Street, at Berkeley Street, South End (1-617 542 4494, www.clubcafe.com). Back Bay T. **Open** 4pm-2am Mon-Fri; 1pm-2am Sat; noon-2am Sun. **No credit cards.** **Map** p283 J7.
If the Eagle bars in other cities have led you to expect leather, think again. Boston's Eagle is the dive of last resort for those without a date as the city's 2am closing time approaches. Between opening and 12.30am or so, only the most dedicated barflies enter, but after that it's a free-for-all where every man is eyed as fresh meat and every woman scorned as a pointless distraction. Do not take female friends.

★ Jacque's Cabaret

79 Broadway, between Piedmont & Winchester Streets, Back Bay (1-617 426 8902, www.jacques-cabaret.com). Arlington or Tufts Medical Center T. **Open** 11am-midnight Mon-Sat; noon-midnight Sun. **Admission** $7-$10. **No credit cards.** **Map** p283 J6.
A decade ago, this longtime drag bar was the most fun you could have in Boston for a $7 cover,

ARTS & ENTERTAINMENT

MAKE A NIGHT OF IT

Despite limited LGBT venues, there's a party for every night of the week.

Boston isn't known for nightlife, but that's partly because some of the best options are off the radar of visitors, and even some residents. As devoted gay bars disappear, the action has shifted to LGBT nights hosted by DJs and promoters, often at venues that are straight every other night. Some are weekly but others happen only once a month, so check websites and social media.

Mondays are for drag queens, with performances at **Jacque's Cabaret** (*see p180*), **Machine**'s **All Star Mondays** (*see p182*), and **Club Café**'s **Drag Bingo** (*see p180*). On Tuesdays, the artsy crowd goes to **Zuesday** at ZuZu (www.zuzubar.com) at the **Middle East** (*see p191*), and the middle of the week brings **Latino Wednesdays** (not just for Latinos) at downtown's **Cure Lounge** (www.curelounge. com). On Thursdays, lesbians croon at the **Midway Café**'s **Queeraoke** night (*see p182*) and twinks gyrate at **Estate**'s **Glamlife** night (*see p186*), one of four nights hosted by Chris Harris (www.chrisharrispresents.com).

Harris's **Queer Fridays** at **Guilt** (www. guiltboston.com), also downtown, attract more youngsters, while the very young head to **Machine**'s 18-plus night. On the first Friday of the month, the Welcoming Committee (www.thewelcomingcommittee.com) hosts **Guerilla Queer Bar**, drawing a large and

diverse crowd to a straight bar announced one day ahead. First Fridays also bring the woman-centric **La Boum** to the **Milky Way Lounge** (*see p156*), home to femme-focused **Fourth Fridays** hosted by Dyke Night (www. dykenight.com). Bears head to the **Alley** (*see p179*) on second Fridays for **Fur and Gold** (www.furgold.com), whose hosts DJ Brent Covington and VJ Sean Johnson present **Boyfriends** at the **Milky Way** on third Fridays.

On Saturday, Chris Harris offers **Epic Saturdays** at the **House of Blues** (*see p188*), and legendary DJ Chris Ewen plays new wave at the 18-plus night **Heroes** at **TT the Bear's Place** (*see p192*). Each fourth Saturday, DJ Colby Drasher hosts gay/straight/artsy/wild **Don't Ask Don't Tell** (www.pleasedontask donttell.blogspot.com) at **Great Scott** (*see p191*). For the women, Dyke Night hosts **Second Saturdays** at **Machine**, and the Welcoming Committee stages its **Flannel Takeover** – a female-focused Guerrilla Queer Bar – each third Saturday.

To close the weekend, downtown's **Candibar** (www.candibarboston.com) has Chris Harris's **Hot Mess Sundays** and Ladder District lounge **Mojitos** offers **Unzipped Sundays** (www.latingaynights.com). Some weeks, the **Midway Café** offers **Plastique**, with DJ's Brian Halligan and James Derek Dwyer.

Guerilla Queer Bar

ARTS & ENTERTAINMENT

Gold Dust Orphans.

but beware – hen parties got wind of the queens' bawdy antics and now fill back-to-back shows on weekends. If you don't want to be the only audience member not wearing a pink tiara, come on a Sunday or a weeknight, and watch out for transgressive, performance-art queens such as Katya Zamolodchikova and Violencia Exclamation Point. Or head downstairs to Jacque's Underground for local indie-rock performances and dance nights.

Machine

1256 Boylston Street, at Ipswich Street, Fenway (1-617 536 1950, www.machineboston.club). Kenmore T. **Open** noon-2am daily. **Admission** $5-$10. **No credit cards. Map** p282 D7.

In recent years, this previously subterranean dance club has expanded into the former Ramrod leather bar upstairs, and broadened its offerings to serve a more diverse crowd. Its biggest night is Friday, when it opens its doors to boys 18 and up and the twinks descend. It's also the home to periodic performances of clever parody-plays by drag impresario Ryan Landry and his Gold Dust Orphans (*see p183* **In the Know**), so check the schedule.

Midway Café

3496 Washington Street, at Williams Street, Jamaica Plain (1-617 524 9038, www.midway cafe.com). Green Street T. **Open** 4pm-2am daily. **Admission** free-$10. **No credit cards**.

A true neighbourhood dive bar, between its indie-rock performances the Midway becomes the unofficial centre of Jamaica Plain's young lesbian nightlife. Even after expanding a few years back, it's still a tight and often steamy place, packed with hipsterish young women and the occasional man, especially for Thursday night Queeraoke, where you can see for yourself who can and who can't carry a Tegan and Sara tune.

Paradise

180 Massachusetts Avenue, at Albany Street, Kendall Square, Cambridge (1-617 868 3000, www.paradisecambridge.com). Central Square T then 10mins walk, or bus 1. **Open** 9pm-1am Mon-Wed, Sun; 9pm-2am Thur; 7pm-2am Fri, Sat. **Admission** free-$5. **No credit cards. Map** p284 C4.

If cheap drinks and a seedy atmosphere are your thing, you'll find them just across the Charles River from Boston at the bar known affectionately to locals as 'the Parasite'. The crowd ranges from twinks to gentlemen of a certain age, who stare raptly at go-go boys dancing up to the edge of Massachusetts' public-nudity laws. Filmed bodies thrash in gay porn on upstairs TVs, while live bodies gyrate to Top 40 divas below in the dimly lit basement.

★ Trophy Room

Chandler Inn, 26 Chandler Street, at Berkeley Street, South End (1-617 482 4428,

Paradise.

www.trophyroomboston.com). Back Bay T. **Open**
4pm-2am Mon-Fri; noon-2am Sat; 10am-2am Sun.
Map p283 H7.

The successor to what was the Fritz retains some of
the sports bar's clientele as well as its dedication to
showing local teams on its several screens, but the
setting has gone upscale, with high ceilings and
stark white subway tiles to brighten and open up the
formerly dark space. With an expanded kitchen, an
array of draught beers, and fancy cocktails on the
menu, no one would mistake Trophy Room for its
predecessor, but the friendly crowd – mixed, but still
more gay men than not – doesn't seem to mind.

RESTAURANTS & CAFÉS

Any eateries in the South End are, by virtue of
their location, gay-friendly. The ones listed here
are particularly popular with queer patrons.

★ Back Bay Harry's

*142 Berkeley Street, at Stanhope Street, South
End (1-617 424 6711, www.backbayharrys.com).
Back Bay T.* **Open** 11.30am-midnight Mon-Wed;
11.30am-1am Thur; 11.30am-2am Fri; 5pm-2am
Sat; 11am-midnight Sun. **Main courses** $12-$29.
Map p283 H7.

Located next door to Club Café in a space formerly
occupied by the Laurel and Geoffrey's Café, Back Bay
Harry's maintains its tradition of a gay-friendly space
that attracts diners of all kinds. With a more elegant
atmosphere than the kitschy Geoffrey's and finer
food than the hit-and-miss Laurel, it's a good spot for
casual drinks or a satisfying meal of reinvented comfort food, before (or instead of) hitting the club.

City Girl Café

*204 Hampshire Street, at Inman Street, Inman
Square, Cambridge (1-617 864 2809, www.citygirl
cafe.com). Central T then 15mins walk.* **Open**
5-10pm Tue-Fri; 10am-3pm, 5-10pm Sat; 10am-3pm
Sun. **Main courses** $11.50-$18.50. **Map** p284 C2.

This tiny, friendly, funky lesbian-owned café in the
heart of Inman Square offers a variety of vegetarian
options but can satisfy meat-eaters too. The brunch
may be its most popular offering, but you can also
find freshly made pizza, pasta, sandwiches and
salads, as well as a decent cup of coffee. The place
also serves wine and beer.

★ Club Café

For listings, *see p180* **Club Café**.

The restaurant at Club Café, formerly known as
209, had long been a cruisey standby on the lounge

scene, with a contemporary American menu that was mostly incidental to the action at the bar. A new chef and an updated menu have shifted the focus from staples such as nachos (still available and tasty) to main dishes ($15-$26.50) including grilled salmon and aubergine parmesan. It's also one of the few places in Boston where you'll see gay men and lesbians congregating in comparable numbers on a regular basis.

▶ For our review of the Club Café bar, see p180.

★ Diesel Cafe
257 Elm Street, at Chester Street, Davis Square, Somerville (1-617 629 8717, www.diesel-cafe.com). Davis T. **Open** 6am-11pm Mon-Fri; 7am-11pm Sat, Sun.
This longtime hipster hangout is popular among Davis Square's young lesbian contingent, but also with anyone who enjoys a quality bagel, a good cup of coffee, and/or spending time ogling its cute, androgynous baristas. Locals stop in to fuel up on espresso, giggle in the instant-photo booth or line up shots at one of the café's pool tables. Wi-Fi is available.

SHOPS & SERVICES

Blade Barbershop
603 Tremont Street, at Dartmouth Street, South End (1-617 267 2200, www.bladebarbershop.com). Back Bay T. **Open** 10am-7.30pm Mon, Tue; 11am-6.30pm Wed, Thur; 9am-7.30pm Fri; 9am-4.30pm Sat. **Map** p283 H7.
It might seem a bit on the pricey side for a quaint, old-school barbershop with chequerboard floors (a haircut costs $25) – but the guys at Blade Barbershop pay special attention to detail, and the gossip you'll overhear is worth the price alone. Everyone likes a clean-cut boy, so call ahead and book an appointment.

★ Boomerangs
716 Centre Street, at Harris Avenue, Jamaica Plain (1-617 524 5120, www.shopboomerangs. com). Green Street T then 10mins walk, or bus 39. **Open** 10am-7pm Mon-Wed, Fri, Sat; 10am-8pm Thur; 11am-6pm Sun.
Now expanded to four locations across Boston and Cambridge, this chain of second-hand stores run by the AIDS Action Committee offers a wide variety of used clothes, books, records, furniture and household items. The quality is usually a cut above the thrift-store norm, and prices also tend to be higher, but it's worth paying a little more for the great blend of rare vintage items and the pure kitsch.
Other locations 1870 Centre Street, West Roxbury (1-617 323 0262); 563 Massachusetts Avenue, Central Square, Cambridge (1-617 758 6128); 1407 Washington Street, South End (1-617 456 0996).

★ Calamus Bookstore
92B South Street, at East Street, Downtown (1-617 338 1931, www.calamusbooks.com). South Station T. **Open** 11am-7pm Mon-Sat; noon-6pm Sun. **Map** p281 L5.
In 2013, it looked as if the future of Boston's last brick-and-mortar LGBT bookstore was in jeopardy due to the death of proprietor John Mitzel. However, the store has survived under new ownership, and hosts readings by important authors such as Eileen Myles and Felice Picano.

Good Vibrations
308A Harvard Street, at Babcock Street, Coolidge Corner, Brookline (1-617 264 4400, www.goodvibes.com). Coolidge Corner T. **Open** 10am-9pm Mon-Thur, Sun; 10am-10pm Fri, Sat.
This friendly Brookline sex shop isn't as much fun or as independent-minded as its predecessor (Grand Opening), but it's still a nice, brightly lit, female-centred place to pick up a few toys. As a bonus, there's a museum of antique – and alarming – vibrators in the back.

Marquis Leathers
92 South Street, at East Street, Downtown (1-617 426 2120). South Station T. **Open** 10am-11pm Mon-Sat; 10am-8pm Sun. **Map** p281 L5.
Marquis Leathers' store is, aptly, found in downtown's Leather District, above Calamus Bookstore. Inside the cavernous space, shoppers can rent or buy gay male DVDs to suit varied tastes, as well as jockstraps, sex toys, leather extras and lube.

Mike's Fitness Jamaica Plain
284 Amory Street, at New Minton Street, Jamaica Plain (1-617 524 6357, www.mikesfitnessjp.com). Stony Brook T. **Open** 5.30am-10pm Mon-Fri; 7am-8pm Sat; 8am-8pm Sun.
Though less gay and cruisey than in the heyday of its old South End location, Mike's Fitness still draws plenty of neighbourhood LGBT residents to its open, high-ceilinged former industrial space in Jamaica Plain's Samuel Adams Brewery Complex. It lacks some amenities offered by fancier gyms, but has a variety of weights, cardio machines, personal training and group classes.

Teddy Shoes
548 Massachusetts Avenue, at Pearl Street, Central Square, Cambridge (1-617 547 0443, www.teddyshoes.com). Central T. **Open** 10am-7pm Mon-Thur; 10am-8pm Fri; 10am-6pm Sat; noon-5pm Sun. **Map** p284 C3.
At Teddy's Shoes, drag-worthy PVC thigh-highs go toe to toe with ballet slippers and serious ballroom-dancing gear. Behind the unprepossessing shopfront lies a massive collection of fetish shoes, platforms and stilettos, in sizes up to a manly 16.

Nightlife

Maybe it's the 2am closing time, or maybe it's because live music has always been more popular here, but Boston is not especially known for nightclubs. But what it lacks in dancefloor square footage, it makes up for with sheer variety (and you'll also find dancefloors in some unlikely places, such as Irish pubs). Hip hop is the most prominent genre, but a house and techno scene is emerging. And you can find DJs spinning eclectic mixes of Italo disco, soul, Latin sounds and whatever else ends up in the crate on a given night. Similarly, the compact comedy circuit showcases some outsize talent. While the city has its share of megastar-magnet major venues, the lifeblood of the music scene is in smaller stages and clubs, many of which have thrived for decades, particularly in Cambridge and Allston. Local music-lovers recently got even more choice with the opening of the 525-capacity Sinclair, with acts booked by big-league promoters Bowery Presents.

Clubs

While **Lansdowne Street** was once the hub of Boston's nightlife scene, the **Theatre District** has stepped up its game of late. Tucked between Chinatown and Back Bay, it's the headquarters for the Prada-clad international set. Here you'll find a high concentration of seemingly perfect-looking people with money to burn. If that's your scene, this is your place.

Nearby, **Boylston Place** (known as 'the Alley') is lined with bars, restaurants and clubs, and drunken twentysomethings wobble from one spot to the next most weekend nights. The sole after-hours club in town is **Rise** (306 Stuart Street, 1-617 423 7473, www.riseclub.us), which stays open until the sun comes up. The place is officially a private club for members and their guests, but you can register on the website for one-night admission.

Club nights change at a rapid rate in this town, so call ahead to check that that low-key spot still plays sleek downtempo instead of the latest tracks from the Black Eyed Peas.

While most clubs accept credit cards at the bar, admission at the door is generally cash only.

DANCE CLUBS & DJ BARS

Bijou
51 Stuart Street, at Tremont Street, Downtown (1-617 357 4565, www.bijouboston.com). Chinatown T. **Open** varies (usually 10pm-2am Wed-Sat). **Admission** $15-$20. **Map** p283 J6.
For some reason, Bijou nightclub notes that its name is derived from the first American playhouse to be

---

IN THE KNOW GETTING IN

To avoid student shenanigans, the majority of nightclubs in town maintain a '21 and over' entry policy – though the occasional '18 and over' night springs up now and then. Dress codes are looser than they used to be, but as a general rule, avoid caps, trainers and athletic wear – anything that might identify you as a potential meathead.

Good Life.

lit by electricity back in Boston in 1882. But besides the name, there is no correlation to the Bijou of old, not even metaphorical. Catering to an upscale, international crowd, Bijou draws a combination of local, national and international DJs – NYC's Danny Tenaglia and the UK's Steve Lawler, for example. Arrive early (around 10pm or 11pm) if you don't want to wait in line – or worse, not get in at all. The space is small and intimate, but often loud and crowded. If you're feeling flush, reserve a VIP table ahead of time to live it up among the posh set.

Estate

1 Boylston Place, at Boylston Street, Downtown (1-617 351 7000, www.theestateboston.com). Boylston T. **Open** *10pm-2am Thur-Sat.* **Admission** *varies.* **Map** *p283 J5.*
The cul-de-sac of clubbery that is Boylston Place is a reliable hotspot on weekends, and the Estate remains the classiest and largest on the strip, with lots of leather, fireplaces and balconies. Thursdays cater to the LGBT community with an emphasis on hip hop and Top 40, while Fridays and Saturdays host guest DJs playing EDM and the best in vocal house music.

Good Life

28 Kingston Street, at Summer Street, Downtown (1-617 451 2622, www.goodlifebar.com). Downtown Crossing or South Station T. **Open** *11.30am-2am Mon-Fri; 5pm-2am Sat.* **Admission** *free-$10.* **Map** *p280 K5.*
One of several spots that have helped to drag downtown Boston out of late-night wasteland, Good Life caters to many different scenes, and remains the coolest and most casual club option in the area. The DJs may be spinning underground hip hop, reggae, cutting-edge electro music, mash-ups and party jams, and there's even the occasional live show. Don't like the scene upstairs? Then head down to the more intimate, but grimier subterranean lounge area.

★ Middlesex Lounge

315 Massachusetts Avenue, between State & Windsor Streets, Central Square, Cambridge (1-617 868 6739, www.middlesexlounge.us). Central T. **Open** *5pm-1am Mon-Wed; 5pm-2am Thur-Sat; varies Sun.* **Admission** *free-$10.* **Map** *p284 C4.*
Middlesex transforms from a bar/lounge to an all-out dance party when the DJ takes to the turntables at 10pm. During the day, the padded roll-away benches can be artfully arranged to accommodate even the most disorganised of parties, enabling the space to transform into a laid-back hipster hangout or an MIT tech-nerd after-work party space. Around nightfall, these benches are taken away and the small, dark, casual space hosts some of the best DJs in the city. Renowned local spinner DJ Kon has been the Saturday night resident (when he's not on tour) since the place opened. At the time of writing there were plans to cut hours, so check the website or call in advance.

Naga

450 Massachusetts Avenue, at Brookline Street, Central Square, Cambridge (1-617 955 4900, www. nagacambridge.com). Central T. **Open** *10pm-1am Mon-Wed, Sun; 10pm-2am Thur-Sat.* **Admission** *varies.* **Map** *p284 C3.*
With modern, state-of-the-art sound and lighting, hip hop and Top 40 tunes, not to mention bottle service, Naga offers Cambridge the upscale alternative that always seemed more at home in Boston. Stop by the front-room restaurant, Moksa, beforehand for critically acclaimed creative Asian tapas and cocktails.

★ Phoenix Landing

512 Massachusetts Avenue, at Brookline Street, Central Square, Cambridge (1-617 576 6260, www.phoenixlandingbar.com). Central T. **Open** *11am-1am Mon-Wed; 11am-2am Thur-Sat; 10am-1am Sun.* **Admission** *free-$10.* **Map** *p284 C3.*

Deep house and Guinness may not seem like the most natural match, but Phoenix Landing pulls off the hybrid Irish pub /club marvellously. The decor is unremarkable, but the no-frills atmosphere fits well with the gritty underground sounds that find their way through the speakers. The floor is tiny, but the variety is huge: hip hop, reggae, house, techno and the area's longest-running drum 'n' bass night all have a home here.

Royale

279 Tremont Street, at Stuart Street, Downtown (1-617 338 7699, www.royaleboston.com). Boylston or Tufts Medical Center T. **Open** *Club nights* 10pm-2am Fri, Sat. *Live music varies.* **Admission** $15-$20. **Map** p283 J6.

When the Roxy's shabby sort of elegance became just plain shabbiness, new owners took over and revamped the entire interior, renaming the space Royale. The massive room has a grand stage, an elegant marble foyer, cushy seating nooks, a fantastic sound system, a festive light show and more bustier-wearing bartenders than you can shake a glowstick at. There are VIP balconies if you feel like getting away from it all, but Boston clubs rarely reach the size of this place, so why not take the opportunity to get lost in the crowd? The DJ spins house/dance, mainly on weekend nights, while hipper-than-thou promoters Bowery Boston (yes, the city's own chapter of the much-loved Bowery group in NYC) bring in a diverse range of indie and mainstream rock, pop and hip hop acts.

▶ *For upcoming concerts promoted by the Bowery Presents, visit www.boweryboston.com.*

Storyville

90 Exeter Street, at Huntington Avenue, Back Bay (1-617 236 1134, www.storyville boston.com). Copley T. **Open** 10pm-2am Wed; 8pm-2am Fri; 7pm-2am Sat. **Admission** free. **Map** p283 G6.

Named after the classic Kenmore Square jazz club that hosted such greats as Billie Holiday, Louis Armstrong, Charlie Parker, Duke Ellington and Ella Fitzgerald, Storyville sure has a lot to live up to. And while the Copley Square space doesn't quite do the historic name justice, it does offer quality, laid-back nightlife and dancing to hip hop and top-40 crowdpleasers. It's more a lounge than a club, but two separate rooms, each with a dancefloor, means that if you don't like the song, you can have a change of scene in seconds.

Comedy

Although small, Boston's comedy scene is thriving. Plenty of big names have tried out their acts here on their way to the top, including Denis Leary, Janeane Garofalo and Conan O'Brien – and the laughs keep coming.

Comedy Studio

3rd floor, Hong Kong Restaurant, 1238 Massachusetts Avenue, at Bow Street, Harvard Square, Cambridge (1-617 661 6507, www. thecomedystudio.com). Harvard T. **Shows** 8pm Tue-Sun. **Admission** $10-$12. **Map** p284 B3.

This spot carries on the Boston-area tradition of top-notch comedy in seedy Chinese restaurants. Perched atop the Hong Kong, the Studio features stand-up Wednesday through Sunday (magicians take the stage on Tuesdays). The shows move quickly, with several comics doing short, punchy sets. Each week-night features numerous gems, but you get the highest calibre of talent at the weekend. Club owner (and frequent host) Rick Jenkins showcases ten of the best local comics, and there's always the potential for a drop-in from national acts such as Mike Birbiglia, Gary Gulman or Joe Wong.

Giggles Comedy Club

517 Broadway, on Route 1, Saugus (1-781 233 9950, www.princepizzeria.com/giggles-comedy). **Shows** varies. **Admission** $20-$27.50.

Though not quite within the city limits, Giggles is an institution of Boston-area comedy. Attached to Prince Pizzeria, the club showcases many of the legends of Boston's rich comedic tradition (Don Gavin, Ken Rogerson, Lenny Clarke) and performers who have been at the top of their game for years. Many of these comics are booked solid with engagements on the road or corporate work and don't get to perform around home much, so Giggles is the spot for classic, no-frills stand-up. No weirdos with PowerPoint presentations here. Just jokes, and lots of them. Look for the replica of the Leaning Tower of 'Pizza' off the side of Route 1.

★ Improv Asylum

216 Hanover Street, at Cross Street, North End (1-617 263 6887, www.improvasylum.com). Haymarket T. **Box office** 2-9pm Mon; noon-9pm Tue-Thur, Sun; noon-midnight Fri, Sat. **Shows** daily; times vary. **Admission** $5-$30. **Map** p281 L3.

Improv Asylum is primarily known for its improv and sketch comedy revues, and is almost always worth checking out. The shows rotate throughout the year, with the main stage cast performing every Thursday through Saturday. Midnight on Saturdays is the 'Raunch' show, which provides a much-needed late-night entertainment option in sometimes-sleepy Boston.

ImprovBoston

40 Prospect Street, at Bishop Allen Drive, Central Square, Cambridge (1-617 576 1253, www. improvboston.com). Central T. **Shows** Tue-Sun; times vary. **Admission** $8-$20. **Map** p284 C3.

ImprovBoston is a clearinghouse for improv, sketch and stand-up comedy. Wednesday night, you can get a sampling of all three at the Comedy Lab, which features experimental shows getting ready for a shot at the prestigious Friday night showcase. Recent offerings include 'Twitterprov', 'The Bigfoot Monologues' and 'Discount Shakespeare: As You Like It in Forty-five Minutes'. The Comedy Lab lets the top local talent breathe life into their weirdest comedy experiments, and you get to watch.

Wilbur Theatre

246 Tremont Street, at Stuart Street, Downtown (1-617 248 9700, http://thewilbur.com). Chinatown or Tufts Medical Center T. **Box office** noon-6pm Mon-Sat. **Admission** varies. **Map** p283 J6.

When the big names in comedy come to Boston, they perform at the Wilbur. Since the closing of the Comedy Connection in 2008, this 1,100-seat venue is your best bet if you want to see nationally renowned comics such as Jim Gaffigan, Lisa Lampanelli, Patton Oswalt and Margaret Cho. The room is classy, and has recently acquired a liquor licence, so you can drink during the show. Spring for the floor-level seats if you're tall (over 5ft 6in), as the balcony does not provide a lot of legroom.

Music

ROCK, POP & ROOTS

The breeding ground of such greats as the Pixies, Aerosmith and the Mighty Mighty Bosstones, Boston has an impressive – and eclectic – musical heritage. Most of the best-known clubs, however, are actually across the river in Cambridge and Somerville. Central Square institutions such as the **Middle East** and **TT the Bear's Place** still attract a hip, music-savvy crowd of all ages, but it's the recent addition of the **Sinclair** that has everyone talking. Located in Harvard Square, the venue opened in 2013 and has since hosted the best and most buzzworthy up-and-coming bands.

In Boston itself, aside from a cluster of rock clubs in the collegiate hipster hub of Allston, you'll mainly find major venues hosting national and international touring acts, such as the **House of Blues** and **TD Garden**. The Remis Auditorium at the **Museum of Fine Arts** offers a great music programme, with an emphasis on cool jazz, pop and indie rock acts, as well as classical offerings. Look out for the MFA's summer series of live music, from indie rock to Latin, in the courtyard.

INFORMATION & TICKETS

For tickets to smaller concerts, your best course of action is to check the venue's website. Tickets for bigger events are sold through **Ticketmaster** (www.ticketmaster.com) or **TicketWeb** (www.ticketweb.com).

Major arenas & stages

Berklee Performance Center

136 Massachusetts Avenue, at Boylston Street, Back Bay (1-617 747 2261, www.berklee.edu/bpc). Hynes Convention Center T. **Box office** *May-Aug* 1-6pm Mon-Sat. *Sept-Apr* 10am-6pm Mon-Sat. **Admission** $10-$50. **Map** p282 F7.

The line-up at Berklee School of Music's concert hall features an impressive roster of big-name artists, as well as student and faculty performances. All kinds of music are showcased here, from hip hop and rock to jazz and folk. The venue is modern, low-key and offers good views of the stage. It is, however, somewhat bland in design, the notable exception being the cool, retro circular moulded plastic seating (think Austin Powers psychedelic '60s pop) that forms the centrepiece of the second-floor lobby area.

Blue Hills Bank Pavilion

290 Northern Avenue, at D Street, Waterfront (1-617 728 1600, www.livenation.com). Silver Line Waterfront to Silver Line Way. **Box office** noon-5pm Mon-Fri (and show days). **Admission** varies.

Boston's major outdoor venue (4,994 capacity) occupies a pleasant, centrally located spot in the South Boston waterfront area. It operates from May to September, featuring mainly mainstream rock, pop and R&B oldies, with a sprinkling of more contemporary acts – Steely Dan, ZZ Top, Jeff Beck, Chicago and REO Speedwagon have recently taken to the stage. The Pavilion is basically a large tent, usually all seated, with an extensive concourse at the rear. Many gig-goers prefer to buy the cheaper concourse tickets so that they can party at the back.

House of Blues

15 Lansdowne Street, at Ipswich Street, Fenway (1-888 693 2583, www.houseofblues.com/boston). Kenmore T. **Box office** 10am-5pm daily. **Admission** $15-$80. **Map** p282 D7.

The world's first House of Blues opened in Harvard Square in 1992 with a capacity of under 200. After closing a decade later despite the franchise itself thriving, the venue found a newer, much larger and more upscale home on Landsdowne Street in 2009. In a city of gritty rock clubs, the House of Blues stands apart as a shimmering outsider. Still, you can't beat the big-name acts that parade through its cavernous expanses, from classic acts such as Dr John and Bob Weir, ageing punks Social Distortion and Dropkick Murphys, to popular newbies like Lana Del Ray and Deadmau5. Just don't get stuck too many rows back in the balcony. The higher levels may look intriguing, but the sights and sounds can be poor and obstructed. Our advice is to stay on the ground floor.

ESSENTIAL BOSTON ALBUMS

The sounds of the city.

THE MODERN LOVERS
THE MODERN LOVERS
(2003 REISSUE)

Recorded mostly in 1972, the proto-punk Modern Lovers' first album didn't actually come out until 1976. The catchy yet brooding LP is packed with local references: cruising the Route 128 belt that encircles Boston in 'Roadrunner' and dropping out of BU in 'Modern World'.

TOYS IN THE ATTIC
AEROSMITH (1975)

It all came together for Steve Tyler and Joe Perry with this third LP. The album soars right away with the screaming title cut, and later leans back for the clenching 'Sweet Emotion'. 'Walk This Way' – both the original and the collaboration with Run-DMC in 1986 – has a place in the classic rock canon.

DOOLITTLE
PIXIES (1989)

The Pixies' second album put them on the map after three years playing Boston clubs like the Rat. Singer-guitarist Black Francis wove vivid, sometimes apocalyptic, stories into his songs that blended melody and noise, with 'Debaser' and 'This Monkey's Gone to Heaven' emerging as alt-rock faves.

FULL HOUSE
J GEILS BAND (1972)

With their mix of originals and covers of blues/R&B gems such as John Lee Hooker's 'Serves You Right to Suffer', the J Geils Band was the first rock band to break out nationally after the largely media-manufactured 'Bosstown Sound' of the late '60s. They were known for their frenzied live shows.

THE CARS
THE CARS (1978)

Songwriter-guitarist Ric Ocasek parlayed his love of Roxy Music and Suicide into the city's biggest new-wave band. The guitar/synth mix was sublime and the eponymous first album was packed with world-weary, ironic-yet-upbeat hits such as 'You're All I've Got Tonight' and 'Good Times Roll'.

LIVE ON LANSDOWNE, BOSTON MA
DROPKICK MURPHYS
(2010)

Ken Casey and his mates picked up on the Pogues' Celtic punk style and Boston-ised it, with songs about the region and its people like 'State of Massachusetts'. Bagpipes and mandolin complement screaming guitars, fast tempos and biting vocals.

ARTS & ENTERTAINMENT

Orpheum Theatre

1 Hamilton Place, at Tremont Street, Downtown (1-617 482 0106, www.crossroadspresents.com/orpheum-theatre). Park Street T. **Box office** noon-5pm Mon-Sat. **Admission** $25-$125. **Map** p280 K4.
Built in 1852, the Orpheum was originally named the Boston Music Hall. Nowadays, it's hard to imagine that this was once a state-of-the-art venue that hosted the New England Conservatory and the Boston Symphony Orchestra. Despite its crumbling appearance, it remains a somewhat regal and ornate space that gives some of the world's greatest bands a chance to play a more intimate theatre show. The Pogues, Allman Brothers, Tom Waits and Arcade Fire have all played sold-out shows here.

★ Sinclair

52 Church Street, at Brattle Street, Harvard Square, Cambridge (1-617 547 5200, www. sinclaircambridge.com). Harvard T. **Open** 5pm-1am Mon-Wed; 11am-2am Thur-Sat; 11am-1am Sun. **Box office** (cash only) noon-7pm Tue-Sat. **Admission** $15-$40. **Map** p284 A2.
Finally, Harvard Square has the music hall it deserves. Classier than any of Cambridge's beloved and historic sonic haunts, the recently minted Sinclair has been attracting indie darlings since its opening, thanks to NYC powerhouse booking crew, Bowery Presents. This is the total package – the venue even has its own restaurant with a highbrow cocktail programme. Order the burger: the kitchen is helmed by restaurateur and Boston burger maestro Michael Schlow.

TD Garden

100 Legends Way, at Causeway Street, West End (1-617 624 1050, www.tdgarden.com). North Station T. **Box office** 11am-7pm Mon-Sat. **Admission** varies. **Map** p280 K2.
Home to sports teams the Celtics (basketball) and the Bruins (ice hockey), the 19,600-capacity Garden also plays host to such mega touring acts as the Rolling Stones and U2, whose multiple-night tenures make the local newspaper headlines and news broadcasts.

Clubs & music bars

The Hub's lively music scene also stretches into its neighbourhood bars and other venues, including indie cinema **Somerville Theatre** (*see p176*), which hosts eclectic acts one or two times a month.

★ Atwood's Tavern

877 Cambridge Street, at Willow Street, Cambridge (1-617 864 2792, www.atwoods tavern.com). Lechmere or Harvard T then 69 bus. **Open** 3.30pm-1am Mon-Wed; 11.30am-2am Thur-Sat; 11.30am-1am Sun. **Admission** $5-$10.
Located just outside Inman Square, this cosy tavern is worth the trek. The low-lit beer bar lights up with live music every night of the week – usually foot-stomping local acts or a curated collection of musicians well known around town. The pub-style food is pretty solid, the beer list commendable and the patio downright pleasant.

Sinclair.

Brighton Music Hall

158 Brighton Avenue, at Harvard Avenue, Allston (1-617 779 0140, www.crossroadspresents.com). Harvard Avenue T. **Box office** at the Paradise Rock Club; *see p192.* **Admission** $15-$25. **Map** off p284 A5.

Known as the smaller sister of the nearby Paradise Rock Club, the BMH holds its own when it comes to quality shows from both touring and local acts. Duelling bars with a decent selection flank the space, ensuring a drink is never far away. Walk past the stage into the mysterious back area for an inexplicable but enjoyable smattering of pool tables and skeeball.

Cantab Lounge

738 Massachusetts Avenue, at Pleasant Street, Cambridge (1-617 345 2685, www.cantab-lounge. com). Central T. **Open** 8pm-1am Mon-Wed; 8pm-2am Thur-Sat; noon-1am Sun. **Admission** varies. **Map** p284 C3.

This delightfully divey Central Square haunt offers everything from bring-your-axe blues jams (Sunday) to singer-songwriter open mics (Monday). There are a couple of undisputed stars: on Tuesday nights, some of the best fiddlers and banjo-pickers this side of the Mississippi trade licks, while host Geoff Bartley sends around a donation hat (more recreational bluegrass players can sharpen their skills together downstairs). On Thursday evenings, a bevy of unbridled grad students dance their cares away to the Chicken Slacks' mix of Motown covers and funky originals. A well-stocked jukebox fills in during quieter moments at the bar, which draws a diverse clientele ranging from twentysomethings to grizzled barflies. The one Cantab constant throughout is high-quality musicianship and an undeniably unpretentious vibe.

Great Scott

1222 Commonwealth Avenue, at Harvard Avenue, Allston (1-617 566 9014, www.greatscottboston. com). Harvard Avenue T. **Open** noon-2am daily. **Admission** free-$15. **No credit cards.** **Map** p284 A5.

A decade ago, Great Scott was a divey bar where you might pay a few dollars to see some college kid playing cover songs. While the interior remains largely unchanged and leaves much to be desired, a great booking policy has transformed the talent draw

and now it consistently competes with any other area club for up-and-coming talent. MGMT, Hot Chip and Of Montreal all gigged at Great Scott long before all the sold-out tours at theatres and arenas. The 240-capacity Allston bar is an unofficial feeder for larger clubs such as the Middle East and the Paradise. The small space has no backstage, which makes this the perfect locale for cornering your favourite singer and cajoling them into grabbing a beer with you. The line-up is mostly various shades of rock, peppered with the occasional influences of folk, electronica and country.

★ Lizard Lounge

1667 Massachusetts Avenue, at Wendell Street, Porter Square, Cambridge (1-617 547 0759, www. lizardloungedb.com). Porter T. **Open** 7.30pm-1am Mon, Sun; 8.30pm-1am Tue, Wed; 8.30pm-2am Thur-Sat. **Admission** $10-$12. **Map** p284 B1.

A short walk from Harvard Square, this diminutive basement bar puts on a jam-packed programme of shows. The beauty of the Lizard Lounge is that there is no stage. It's like watching a band in your living room perform on a well-worn rug – the only delineation between audience and performer. The musical fare runs the gamut from rock and folk to Americana, along with the odd Boston Opera Underground performance. There's great food too, served in the Lounge until midnight, then all night upstairs in the Cambridge Common restaurant.

Middle East

472-480 Massachusetts Avenue, at Brookline Street, Central Square, Cambridge (1-617 864 3278, www.mideastoffers.com). Central T. **Open** 11am-1am Mon-Wed, Sun; 11am-2am Thur-Sat. **Admission** free-$20. **Map** p284 C3.

This sprawling venue is one of America's leading rock clubs, and a major player on the national and local music scenes. A Middle Eastern restaurant as well as a club, it was the nurturing ground for Boston's alternative and indie musicians, beginning in the mid 1980s in the smaller Upstairs room. 'Downstairs' was added later and, like many of Boston's basement clubs, was once a bowling alley. In the restaurant, musicians play the Corner without a cover charge, and, in keeping with the Middle Eastern theme, there are also belly-dancers. ZuZu sits in-between Upstairs and Downstairs, offering food, hip DJ nights and occasionally bands on Monday nights.

O'Brien's Pub

3 Harvard Avenue, at Cambridge Street, Allston (1-617 782 6245, www.obrienspubboston.com). Harvard Avenue T. **Open** 5pm-1am daily. **Admission** $5-$10. **No credit cards.** **Map** off p284 A5.

The music at this tiny, 70-person club leans towards punk and metal outfits with names like Maggot Brain and Rat Corpse. Though it's a fraction of the size of small-scale venues such as Great Scott (see p191), O'Brien's doesn't dial down its sound system, so be sure to pack earplugs. PBR is the drink of choice here – ask for a 'cocktail' and you'll likely get a stiff rum and coke. From the tacky wood panelling to the questionable bathroom upkeep, O'Brien's certainly keeps out folks who require a classy atmosphere – but things are probably better for everybody that way.

★ Paradise Rock Club

967 Commonwealth Avenue, at Pleasant Street, Allston (1-617 562 8800, www.crossroadspresents. com). Pleasant Street T. **Open** *Back room* 7pm-2am Mon-Wed, Sun; 8pm-2am Thur-Sat. *Lounge* 6pm-2am daily. **Box office** noon-6pm Mon-Sat. **Admission** *Back room* $10-$20. *Lounge* free-$10. **No credit cards.** **Map** 276 B5.

One of Boston's must-visit rock haunts, the Dise has hosted everyone from U2 and Elvis Costello to REM and Kings of Leon since it opened in 1977. For years, fans and ego-driven rock stars alike complained about the view-blocking support pillar bang in front of the stage in the two-tiered back room, but during an expansion and renovation in 2010, the simple act of moving the stage just 15 feet or so over dramatically improved the sightlines.

★ Toad

1912 Massachusetts Avenue, at Porter Square, Cambridge (1-617 497 4950, www.toadcambridge. com). Porter T. **Open** 5pm-1am Mon-Wed; 5pm-2am Thur-Sat; 3pm-1am Sun. **Admission** free. **Map** p284 B1.

This Porter Square hole-in-the-wall is one of the few remaining cover-free spots in the city. There's a lot of good roots/Americana, though the joint isn't above booking a solid Beatles tribute band or a well-honed soul singer. Barely the size of a studio apartment, Toad gets packed easily, so expect to rub elbows with complete strangers. Fortunately, this place self-selects for a certain brand of open-minded music fan, so mingling with this amiable bunch is usually a pleasure – and when it's not, the bands should be enough to hold your attention.

TT the Bear's Place

10 Brookline Street, at Massachusetts Avenue, Central Square, Cambridge (1-866 468 7619, www. ttthebears.com). Central T. **Open** 6pm-1am daily. **Admission** $9-$12. **Map** p284 C3.

Named after the owner's pet hamster, TT's is a world-class venue in miniature (275 capacity). To a music geek, the cramped, beer-soaked space is simply Nirvana – who, by the way, played a near-empty show here a mere six months before *Nevermind*'s meteoric rise up the charts. On Saturdays, DJ Chris Ewen (of the Magnetic Fields side project, Future Bible Heroes) spins new wave on a night called 'Heroes', but this is first and foremost a spot for deafening guitars and tight-jeaned frontmen.

JAZZ, BLUES, FOLK & WORLD

In addition to the venues below, the bohemian **Beehive** (see p102), a small restaurant by day and venue by night, hosts diverse acts, from bluegrass to burlesque, while the hippest watering hole in Harvard Square, the **Beat Hotel** (see p132) hosts free, nightly jazz bands.

Thanks to the efforts of the non-profit organisation **CrashArts** (www.worldmusic. org), world music is less of a rarity around Boston these days. **Ryles Jazz Club** runs regular Latin dance party nights, and showcases a global array of artists.

Club Passim

47 Palmer Street, at Church Street, Harvard Square, Cambridge (1-617 492 7679, www.passim. org). Harvard T. **Box office** 9.30am-5pm Mon-Fri. **Admission** $5-$30. **Map** p284 A2.

This small, not-for-profit venue was once at the vanguard of the 1960s folk scene, when it was known as Club 47 and regularly welcomed the likes of Joan Baez and Bob Dylan. The club retains its relaxed, hippie-ish vibe, with plenty of singer-songwriters on the bill.

Johnny D's Uptown Restaurant & Music Club

17 Holland Street, at Davis Square, Somerville (1-617 776 2004, www.johnnyds.com). Davis T. **Open** 4pm-12.30am Mon-Wed; 4pm-1am Fri; 8.30am-1am Sat, Sun. **Admission** $10-$35.

This Davis Square eaterie has been operated by the DeLellis family since the late Johnny DeLellis opened it in 1969. Originally focused on roots music, Johnny D's has expanded to include everything from bluegrass and funk to Afrobeat and zydeco. Wilco, Gillian Welch, Neil Young, Townes Van Zandt and the Dixie Chicks have all graced the stage, and Susan Tedeschi used to head up the Blues Jam, which still happen on most Sundays. Expect no shortage of blues-infused rockabilly acts, as well as some dancey bands.

IN THE KNOW
SOMETHING IN THE AIR TONIGHT

One of the best places to rock out outdoors in Boston is the **Blue Hills Bank Pavilion** (see p188). Interesting architecturally, it's absolutely stunning when the sun sets over Boston Harbor and your favourite band is playing your favourite song. Another alfresco treat is the **Hatch Shell** (www.hatchshell. com). Free classical and classic rock concerts are held throughout the summer at this iconic spot along the Charles River. Pack a picnic and settle on the lawn; it's the perfect way to spend an evening without spending much money.

Club Passim.

The menu is also worth a look, featuring the likes of Southern fried catfish. The old-timer decor is a quirky mish-mash of vintage beer posters and vinyl albums.

★ Lilypad
1353 Cambridge Street, at Springfield Street, Inman Square, Cambridge (1-617 955 7729, www.lilypadinman.com). Central T then bus 83, 91 or 15min walk. **Open & admission** varies. **No credit cards.** **Map** p284 C2.

Just a small performance space with metal folding chairs, and adorned with works by local artists, Lilypad offers an eclectic, experimental line-up, ranging from jazz to psych, singer-songwriter to jam sessions. Local rocker Jesse Gallagher, of Apollo Sunshine fame, has taken over bookings and is getting more off-the-wall acts than ever before. You might find a Brazilian rocker, a punk outfit with a string quintet, or the next Beirut (who played here in 2006). Soak in the tuneage and give thanks that the place finally has a licence to sell beer.

Regattabar
Charles Hotel, 1 Bennett Street, at Eliot Street, Harvard Square, Cambridge (1-617 661 5000, www.regattabarjazz.com). Harvard Square T. **Open** 7.30pm-2am Tue-Sat. **Admission** $15-$30. **Map** p284 A2.

Situated in the lovely Charles Hotel, this sleek modern club serves up jazz, blues, gospel and R&B. It seats around 220 and is smarter than many of the city's other jazz venues, which tend to be quite casual.

Ryles Jazz Club
212 Hampshire Street, at Inman Street, Inman Square, Cambridge (1-617 876 9330, www.ryles jazz.com). Central T then bus 83, 91. **Open** 5pm-1am Tue-Sat; 10am-3pm Sun. **Admission** $6-$15. **Map** p284 C2.

This hopping haunt has become a local institution. Split into two levels, it has live music daily except Mondays, with shows usually at 8pm or 9pm. The ground floor features national and local jazz artists, interspersed with world music, blues and comedy. Upstairs is the dance hall, where spicy salsa and merengue are often the order of the night. Mitch's BBQ dishes add more Southern heat to a night out.

Scullers Jazz Club
Double Tree Suites by Hilton Hotel Boston-Cambridge, 400 Soldiers Field Road, at River Street, Allston (1-617 562 4111, www.scullersjazz.com). **Open** 11am-2am daily. **Admission** $25-$90. **Map** p284 B4.

Housed in the DoubleTree Suites, overlooking the Charles River, Scullers hosts big-name artists (the likes of Jamie Cullum, Michael Bublé and Tony Bennett), as well as rising stars on the jazz, R&B and Latin music scenes. The dimly lit, mahogany-panelled lounge has a sophisticated but relaxed atmosphere.

▶ *Scullers offers special three-course dinner packages, as well as 'Jazz Overnighter' deals for stays at the DoubleTree Suites – a good idea given the out-of-the-way location.*

★ Wally's Café
427 Massachusetts Avenue, at Columbus Avenue, South End (1-617 424 1408, www.wallyscafe.com). Mass Ave T. **Open** 11am-2am Mon-Sat; noon-2am Sun. **Admission** free. **No credit cards.** **Map** p283 G8.

For sheer history and ambience, there's no beating Wally's. Since 1947, this unassuming spot has been the premier showcase for Boston jazz talent, including plenty of students from Berklee, the Boston Conservatory and the New England Conservatory of Music. The crowd is a diverse mix of post-grads, South End yuppies and be-bop-diggin' septuagenarians. The drinks are strong and reasonably priced. Musical highlights include blues on Mondays, funk/fusion on Tuesdays, Wednesdays and Sundays, and jazz on Thursdays. No matter the day of the week, it's invariably jazzy, often inventive and always free. Shows start at 9.30pm.

Performing Arts

Once the home of the fabled 'pre-Broadway try out', Boston is now treasured as a hotspot for touring shows, a home for classic and contemporary theatre, and the birthplace of edgy new work by playwrights from around the globe. And, yes, some of the area's home-grown theatrical magic, especially new works cultivated at American Repertory Theater (ART), goes on to impressive runs on the Great White Way.

The centrepiece of the classical landscape is the internationally renowned Boston Symphony Orchestra, but you can take in everything from contemporary compositions to early music – Boston's Handel and Haydn Society celebrated its bicentennial in 2015. On the dance scene, artistic director Mikko Nissinen has transformed and raised the profile of the Boston Ballet, while small companies that cultivate new choreography are flourishing in Cambridge.

Classical Music & Opera

Boston's classical music scene embraces both the grandeur of the full symphony orchestra and the intimacy of the solo recital, and the stylistic spectrum is equally diverse, from historically informed Renaissance operas to complex, cutting-edge contemporary fare. Performances, workshops and lectures enliven historic concert halls as well as a variety of spaces at some of the area's many top-notch educational institutions, including the **New England Conservatory** (http://necmusic. edu) and the **Boston Conservatory** (www.bostonconservatory.edu). The non-profit organisation **Celebrity Series of Boston** (www.celebrityseries.org) is the area's top presenter of visiting artists from around the world.

Founded in 1881 and considered one of the world's finest musical ensembles, the **Boston Symphony Orchestra** (www.bso.org) is the focus of renewed excitement under its new music director, Andris Nelsons. The BSO's affiliate, the **Boston Pops**, is America's most recorded orchestra, offering wide-ranging performances geared to mainstream audiences, with guest appearances that include pop and jazz favourites, Broadway superstars, and Laureate Conductor John Williams. Other esteemed area orchestras include the **Boston Philharmonic Orchestra** (www.bostonphil.org) and the chamber-sized **Boston Classical Orchestra** (www.boston classicalorchestra.org), which performs in historic Faneuil Hall. Chamber music abounds in Boston, and a number of organisations, such as the **Boston Chamber Music Society** (www.bostonchambermusic.org), have a wide-ranging repertoire. Others, such as **Boston Modern Orchestra Project** (www.bmop.org) and **Boston Musica Viva** (www.bmv.org), dedicate their artistry to the full range of today's music.

The long tradition of vocal music in Boston is fuelled by a profusion of ensembles offering music ranging from chamber pieces to massive choral works and opera, including the **Cantata

In the summer, the **Boston Symphony Orchestra** moves to **Tanglewood** (1-413 637 1600, www.bso.org), in the Berkshire Hills of western Massachusetts. The orchestra's seasonal home since 1937, it's an idyllic, pastoral setting with three primary venues – the Koussevitzky Music Shed and lawn, Seiji Ozawa Hall and the Theatre, which hosts opera and student performances as well as some of the annual Festival of Contemporary Music. Picnickers welcome!

Singers (www.cantatasingers.org), **Boston Cecilia** (www.bostoncecilia.org) and **Emmanuel Music** (www.emmanuelmusic.org), best known for its landmark presentations of Bach cantatas. **Boston Lyric Opera** (www.blo.org) is the largest dedicated opera company in New England and presents works from Mozart to 20th-century classics at the **Shubert Theatre** (*see p199*). Fledgling companies in the area, such as **Guerilla Opera** (http://guerillaopera.com) and **Odyssey Opera** (www.odysseyopera.org), tend to focus on more offbeat, often contemporary fare.

For purists, Boston is a hotbed of early music. The **Handel and Haydn Society** (http://handelandhaydn.org; *see p196* **200 Years of Handel & Hayden**), **Boston Baroque** (www.bostonbaroque.org), **Boston Camerata** (www.bostoncamerata.com) and the **Boston Early Music**

Festival (www.bemf.org) lead the way with a wide variety of instrumental, vocal and operatic concerts performed with lively stylistic authenticity.

INFORMATION & TICKETS
Weekly music listings can be found in the city's broadsheet newspaper, the *Boston Globe* and online at www.boston.com. In addition, the *Boston Musical Intelligencer* (www.classical-scene.com) lists upcoming events, and *ArtsBoston* (www.artsboston.org) offers a comprehensive online cultural calendar and a range of discount ticket options through its **BosTix** programme (www.bostix.org). Dealing directly with venues and organisations is often the best choice, as many offer their own discounts, including special student and young professional tickets as well as rush seats (discounted tickets sold at the box office on the day of performance).

VENUES
Cutler Majestic Theatre at Emerson College
219 Tremont Street, at Lagrange Street, Theatre District (1-617 824 8000, http://cutlermajestic.org). Boylston or Chinatown T. **Box office** 10am-6pm Mon-Sat; noon-4pm Sun. **Tickets** $25-$110. **Map** p283 J5.
Dating from 1903, this jewel-box Beaux Arts opera house was the first venue in Boston designed without pillars or other obstructions to visibility and sound. After a $10 million renovation, the 1,200-seat theatre reopened in 2003 and is now one of the city's busiest arts venues. It hosts a wide range of cultural activities, from performances from touring international opera companies to world music, dance and theatre.

Cutler Majestic Theatre at Emerson College.

ARTS & ENTERTAINMENT

Edward M Pickman Concert Hall

27 Garden Street, at Concord Avenue, Harvard Square, Cambridge (1-617 876 0956, www.longy. edu). Harvard T. **Box office** 1hr before concerts. **Tickets** vary. **Map** p284 A2.

Since 1970, this intimate 300-seat theatre at the Longy School of Music of Bard College has been a choice spot for chamber presentations, not just by Longy students and the school's distinguished faculty, but also by visiting ensembles. Recently it has become one of the prime spots for concerts by Emmanuel Music and recitals presented by the Celebrity Series of Boston.

★ Jordan Hall

30 Gainsborough Street, at Huntington Avenue, Back Bay (1-617 585 1260, http://necmusic.edu/ jordan-hall). Massachusetts Avenue or Symphony T. **Box office** 10am-6pm Mon-Fri; noon-6pm Sat. **Tickets** vary. **Map** p282 F8.

The New England Conservatory's 1,029-capacity auditorium, which opened in 1903, is one of the most prized musical venues in Boston. Known for its excellent acoustics and intimacy, it offers programming that not only features Conservatory faculty and students, but also by local ensembles and world-renowned classical artists.

200 YEARS OF HANDEL AND HAYDN

Boston's oldest orchestra celebrates a major milestone.

During its 200-year history, the **Handel and Haydn Society** has commissioned an oratorio from Ludwig van Beethoven and performed the American premières of Handel's *Messiah*, Haydn's *The Creation*, and Bach's monumental *St Matthew Passion*, to name just a few landmark firsts. The longest-running arts organisation in America, it has emerged with a clear profile as one of the country's pre-eminent period orchestras despite shifting tides and numerous upheavals over the decades. H&H is dedicated to performing the world's most beloved classics with stylistic authenticity on historical instruments, presenting music as it would have been heard in the composer's day. This gives performances an electric freshness that often brings new life to old choral and instrumental pieces.

The Society credits Thomas Dunn with setting the orchestra on its current path of historically informed performance practices when he became music director in 1967. After Christopher Hogwood took over in 1986, the orchestra began its commitment to performing on period instruments and with fewer players, allowing for new interpretations and unique textures to be highlighted. Each new music director over the past two decades – Grant Llewellyn, Roger Norrington and, currently, Harry Christophers – has brought something new and vital to the organisation.

H&H has presented a number of interdisciplinary programmes featuring dance, jazz and theatre with collaborators such as Dave Brubeck, Marian McPartland, Chick Corea, Keith Jarrett, Mark Morris and Claire Bloom. And there are more changes afoot as H&H looks to the future. As part of a bold $12 million capital campaign, there are plans to extend its performance range beyond Greater Boston and forge collaborations with other Boston arts organisations.

★ Sanders Theatre

Memorial Hall, 45 Quincy Street, at Cambridge Street, Harvard Square, Cambridge (1-617 496 2222, www.boxoffice.harvard.edu). Harvard T. **Box office** (1350 Massachusetts Avenue, at Holyoke Street) noon-6pm Tue-Sun. **Tickets** vary. **Map** p284 B2.

Its unusual semi-circular design, church-like wooden interior and wonderful acoustics distinguish Harvard's main concert hall. In addition to the university's major lectures (Winston Churchill and Martin Luther King Jr have graced its stage), the theatre regularly hosts concerts by the Boston Philharmonic and Boston Chamber Music Society, plus the occasional folk, world or rock artist.

★ Symphony Hall

301 Massachusetts Avenue, at Huntington Avenue, Back Bay (1-617 266 1492, www.bso.org). Massachusetts Avenue or Symphony T. **Box office** 10am-6pm Mon-Fri; noon-6pm Sat. **Tickets** $30-$137. **Map** p282 F8.

Symphony Hall, home of the Boston Symphony Orchestra and the Boston Pops Orchestra, opened its doors in 1900 and is considered one of the finest concert halls in the world, renowned for its superb acoustics and state-of-the-art audio technology. In addition to musicians of every stripe, the stately hall hosts world-class lecturers, comedians and political figures.

Dance

The big show in town is the **Boston Ballet** (www.bostonballet.org), founded in 1963 and stronger than ever under the visionary leadership of artistic director Mikko Nissinen. Equally acclaimed for its diverse repertoire of contemporary works and solid productions of classical masterpieces, the company has a full season at home in the **Boston Opera House** (*see p198*) and has begun touring internationally. Across the river in Cambridge, **José Mateo Ballet Theatre** (www.ballettheatre.org) offers an intimate alternative, performing Mateo's well-crafted neo-classic choreography in the company's lovely **Sanctuary Theatre** in the historic Old Cambridge Baptist Church in Harvard Square.

The primary presenters of touring dance companies are the **Celebrity Series of Boston** (*see p194*), which tends to feature more mainstream troupes like Pilobolus and Alvin Ailey at the **Citi Performing Arts Center** (*see p199*), and **World Music/CRASHarts** (www.worldmusic.org), which presents edgier fare, usually at the **Cutler Majestic** (*see p195*) or the **Institute of Contemporary Art**. But what makes Boston's dance scene so distinctive is the wealth of small, independent troupes and

choreographers, who enrich the cultural scene with choreography ranging from ballet to Butoh, hip hop to jazz and modern.

VENUES

Boston University Dance Theater

915 Commonwealth Avenue, at Buick Street, Boston (1-617 358 2500, www.bu.edu/fitrec). St Paul Street T. **Box office** 2-6pm Wed-Sat. **Tickets** from $5. **Map** p284 B5.

This 225-seat state-of-the-art theatre has become a popular performance space for both local and visiting performers, from jazz and modern dance troupes to ethnic-dance companies. It also hosts a variety of popular concerts featuring BU dance faculty and guest artists.

Dance Complex & Green Street Studios

Dance Complex *536 Massachusetts Avenue, at Pearl Street, Central Square, Cambridge (1-617 547 9363, www.dancecomplex.org). Central T.* **Box office** varies. **Tickets** $10-$30. **No credit cards**. **Map** p284 C3.
Green Street Studios *185 Green Street, at Brookline Street, Central Square, Cambridge (1-617 864 3191, www.greenstreetstudios.org). Central T.* **Box office** 1hr before showtime. **Tickets** $10-$20. **No credit cards**. **Map** p284 C3.

These two non-profit grassroots organisations have created a veritable hub of dance in Cambridge's Central Square over the past two decades. Each has new leaders, who have professed goals for the two organisations to work hand in hand. Between the two, classes are offered in virtually any dance form that you can think of, and they host a variety of programmes and residencies geared towards nurturing the development of choreography. Concerts and programmes take place at one or both of the venues almost every weekend. These are the spots to see home-grown Boston choreography.

Institute of Contemporary Art (ICA)

For listing, *see p124*.
The ICA has begun presenting its own provocative series of mostly avant-garde dance performances, and this dynamite little theatre has become a favourite spot for World Music/CRASHarts presentations

ARTS & ENTERTAINMENT

IN THE KNOW JACOB'S PILLOW

Just two hours west of Boston in the lush Berkshire Hills, world-acclaimed dance centre **Jacob's Pillow** (www.jacobspillow.org) presents America's longest-running dance festival each summer. The event offers more than two months of top-notch programming from around the world from both established and emerging talents.

Boston Ballet. *See p197.*

too. With its steep rake, here isn't a bad seat in the house, and when the curtains are fully open, the windowed back and side walls provide a stunning panoramic view of Boston Harbor. The wide array of contemporary art you get to see when the museum is fully open is the icing on the cake.

Theatre

While major troupes, like the **American Repertory Theater** and the **Huntington Theatre Company** at the **Boston University Theatre** have their own venues and often bring in established stars, some of the smaller fringe ensembles, like feisty, ground-breaking **Company One** (www.companyone.org) and **Actors' Shakespeare Project** (www.actors shakespeareproject.org), help discover the stars of tomorrow in ambitious, often provocative productions created on shoe-string budgets and performed in a variety of venues throughout the area. For the big touring blockbuster shows, **Broadway in Boston** (http://boston.broadway. com) is the primary presenter.

Boston's downtown Theatre District includes more than a dozen venues, from grandly opulent theatres for touring shows and big productions to tiny spots offering more intimate fare. Truth be told, however, the area's theatrical magic unfolds all over Greater Boston, from the Fenway and the South End to Cambridge and Watertown. Further afield, **North Shore Music Theatre** (www. nsmt.org) lights up Beverly and the surrounding area with a remarkable array of shows performed in the round. **Merrimack Repertory Theatre** (www.mrt.org) presents provocative stagings in former mill town Lowell.

INFORMATION & TICKETS

The easiest way to get tickets to most theatrical performances in Boston is to go to the company website, where you might just find a deal. If the organisation doesn't have its own dedicated ticket management, you'll be bounced to one of a number of sites to facilitate purchase, from the big agencies like **Ticketmaster** (www. ticketmaster.com) or **TheaterMania** (1-866 811 4111, www.theatermania.com/boston-theatre) to more localised sites, like **Boston Theatre Scene** (1-617 933 8600, www.bostontheatre scene.com) and **BosTix** (www.bostix.org), which often offers appreciable discounts.

MAJOR VENUES

Boston Opera House

539 Washington Street, at Avenue de Lafayette, Downtown (1-617 259 3400, www.bostonopera house.com). Chinatown or Downtown Crossing T. **Box office** 10am-5pm Mon-Fri. **Tickets** vary. **Map** p280 K5.

The great curiosity about the Boston Opera House is that it plays host to just about everything but opera – musicals, touring shows, concerts, ballet (it's the performance venue for Boston Ballet's subscription series). Once a vaudeville theatre, it was revamped in 2004 and is one of the most elegant venues in town.

Charles Playhouse

74 Warrenton Street, at Stuart Street, Downtown (1-617 426 6912, www.charlesplayhouse.com). Boylston or Tufts Medical Center T. **Box office** noon-6pm Mon, Tue, Sun; noon-8pm Wed-Fri; 10am-8.30pm Sat. **Tickets** $60-$100. **Map** p283 J6.

If it ain't broke, don't fix it. That's the rule at the Charles Playhouse, which has kept its two crowd-pleasing acts running for years – *Shear Madness* since 1980, and Blue Man Group since 1995. Blue Man Group offers a wild, noisy, paint-splattered evening of laugh-out-loud fun, while *Shear Madness* provides audiences with a ribald, comic whodunit.

★ Citi Performing Arts Center (Colonial Theatre, Shubert Theatre, Wang Theatre)

270 Tremont Street, at Stuart Street, Downtown (1-617 482 9393, www.citicenter.org). Boylston, Chinatown or Tufts Medical Center T. **Box office** noon-6pm Tue-Sat. **Tickets** $15-$100. **Map** p283 J6.

The big daddy of Boston's theatre scene, Citi Performing Arts Center owns three venues – the 3,600-seat Wang Theatre, the smaller Shubert opposite, and the Colonial, just up the road at 106 Boylston Street. Originally known as the Metropolitan Theatre, the Wang opened in 1925. The theatre's gilt-trimmed interior was restored to its former glory a few years ago; today it hosts everything from Broadway hits to Shakespeare, plus the occasional pop concert. With more than 1,500 seats, the Shubert Theatre opened in 1910, but the Theatre District's 'Little Princess' was given a multi-million

dollar facelift in the mid 1990s. These days, the bill is divided between theatre, music, dance and opera (it's home to the Boston Lyric Opera). Built in 1900, the Colonial is the oldest continuously operating theatre in Boston, with a fan-shaped auditorium that guarantees a decent view from almost anywhere in the house. Once a regular spot for pre-Broadway try-outs, the theatre has a fascinating, illustrious history, but it's now used mostly for smaller touring productions.

Cutler Majestic Theatre at Emerson College

For listing, *see p195*.

Paramount Center

559 Washington Street, at Avenue de Lafayette, Downtown (1-617 824 8400, http://paramount boston.org). Chinatown T. **Tickets** $25-$100. Box office 10am-6pm Mon-Sat; noon-4pm Sun.

Originally a 1930s art deco movie palace, the Paramount Theatre was in serious disrepair when Emerson College bought the building in 2005 and transformed it into a three-theatre complex: the 596-seat Mainstage, the Jackie Liebergott Black Box, and the Bright Family Screening Room. ArtsEmerson (http://artsemerson.org) presents a wide range of intriguing, often international theatrical and musical offerings at the Center, and the college uses it for its major drama productions.

OTHER THEATRES & COMPANIES

★ American Repertory Theater (ART)

Loeb Drama Center, Harvard University, 64 Brattle Street, at Hilliard Street, Cambridge (1-617 547 8300, www.americanrepertorytheater.org). Harvard T. **Box office** noon-5pm Tue-Sun. **Tickets** $30-$60. **Map** p284 A2.

One of the country's top regional theatres, ART has been making waves on the international scene since its inception in 1980. Luminaries such as Philip Glass, Anne Bogart and David Mamet have all worked with the company to produce decidedly edgy world premières. In 2005, ART opened a second stage at the intersection of Arrow Street and Massachusetts Avenue, called the Oberon. This intimate space plays host to even more experimental ventures, many of which transform the theatre into a cabaret-like setting. Tickets are available through the main ART box office.

Boston Center for the Arts (BCA)

539 Tremont Street, at Clarendon Street, South End (1-617 426 5000, www.bcaonline.org). Back Bay or Copley T. **Box office** varies. **Tickets** $10-$35. **Map** p283 J7.

Dominating the South End arts scene, BCA offers theatre, visual arts and dance. The complex has become a hub for small and mid-size theatrical

Paramount Center.

ARTS & ENTERTAINMENT

HARVARD'S CLASS ACT

Under the direction of Tony-winner Diane Paulus, the ART is a smash hit.

Over the past few years, theatregoers have packed prestigious Broadway houses to see the Tony Award-winning musicals *Once*, *Pippin* and the Gershwins' *Porgy and Bess*, all of which went on to tour the US. And families will undoubtedly flock to the musical adaptation of *Finding Neverland*, at time of writing poised to première on the Great White Way. What they may not know, however, is that these hit productions began life at Harvard's **American Repertory Theater** (*see p199*). And a large part of their success is thanks to the ART's innovative artistic director Diane Paulus.

'We never take on a show with the end goal of going to Broadway,' says Paulus, who was named one of *Time*'s 100 Most Influential People of 2014. 'We programme for our ART audiences and we are thrilled when a show is able to have a future life.'

Founded in 1980 by Robert Brustein, the theatre, which also provides training for the university's drama students, had a reputation for staging complex, serious-minded plays; since taking the reins in 2008, Paulus hasn't dumbed down this tradition but she also relishes comedies, musicals, acrobatics and interactivity.

Eve Ensler, best known for *The Vagina Monologues*, has committed to ART projects for three years. The ART staged *OPC*, starring Oscar winner Melissa Leo, in late 2014 and is slated for two more plays, one an adaptation of her memoir, *In the Body of the World*, and another, a musical on which she's collaborating with Paulus.

'It's been my best experience in theatre today, in many ways,' says Ensler. 'Diane is so brilliant and supportive. Diane is not only a visionary director, she's a visionary leader. She has real politics and she has a real sense of what theatre can do, how it can impact communities, change lives and bring people to thought.'

The ART has two venues – the 550-seat Loeb Drama Center in the heart of Harvard Square and Oberon, a 360-capacity performance space/nightclub on the Square's fringe, which stages more left-field theatre, dance and musical acts. Oberon's immersive disco-ised take on *A Midsummer Night's Dream – The Donkey Show –* has been running since 2009, and is set to continue indefinitely every Saturday.

'I'm a great believer of freedom in the theatre,' says Paulus. 'As a creator, you have to be utterly specific and rigorous and personal. And then the beauty of the theatre is that space where the audience completes the equation. They bring their viewpoint and they complete the event.'

Pippin.

ventures, with its Emerging Theatre Company Program and three notable companies in residence – Company One, SpeakEasy Stage Company and the Theater Offensive. In 2004, the BCA entered into a partnership with the Huntington Theatre Company to jointly build and manage the Stanford Calderwood Pavilion (527 Tremont Street), which houses two theatres (the Virginia Wimberly Theatre and the Nancy and Edward Roberts Studio Theatre). These provide secondary stages for the Huntington as well as being venues for smaller arts organisations.

Boston Playwrights' Theatre

949 Commonwealth Avenue, at Harry Agganis Way, Allston (1-866 811 4111, www.bu.edu/bpt). Pleasant Street T. **Box office** 1hr before showtime. **Tickets** $10-$30. **Map** p284 B5.

Founded in 1981 by Nobel Laureate Derek Walcott, this small professional company is dedicated to the creation and performance of new plays. It's a modest venue, tucked away in an alley, but over the years it has nurtured a wealth of theatrical invention. With the closing of the Factory Theatre in the South End, one of the area's most fertile incubators for emerging talents, BPT is beginning to host performances by some of the area's fringe theatres, such as Fresh Ink Theatre Company (www.freshinktheatre.com).

Boston University Theatre

264 Huntington Avenue (Avenue of the Arts), at Massachusetts Avenue, Back Bay (1-617 266 0800, www.huntingtontheatre.org). Symphony T. **Box office** varies; usually noon-7pm Tue-Sun. **Tickets** $65-$99. **Map** p282 F8.

Designed as America's first civic playhouse, the building first opened in 1925 as the Repertory Theatre of Boston. When the resident troupe disbanded, the venue spent decades as a movie house until Boston University bought the building, later founding the Huntington Theatre Company as the resident organisation. Consistently top-notch, Huntington productions often star big names and go on to Broadway glory, winning a clutch of prestigious awards along the way.

Central Square Theater

450 Massachusetts Avenue, at Brookline Street, Central Square, Cambridge (1-617 576 9278, www.centralsquaretheater.org). Central T. **Box office** 11.30am-5pm Tue-Fri. **Tickets** $15-$60. **Map** p284 C4.

Finally two of the area's most admirable little companies, the Nora Theatre Company and Underground Railway Theater, have their own permanent home in this state-of-the-art facility. The mission of the new theatre is to create a vibrant hub of theatrical, educational and social activity where artists and audiences connect 'to create theatre vital to the community'. As befits its name, the Underground Railway focuses on theatrical projects with strong social content. While

the Nora Theatre Company looks whenever possible to represent the feminine voice, productions over the years have been wide-ranging, from modern classics like *Our Town* to local premieres of works that reflect contemporary human concerns.

Charlestown Working Theater

442 Bunker Hill Street, at Main Street, Charlestown (1-617 242 3285, www.charlestownworkingtheater. org). Sullivan Square T. **Box office** 2hrs before showtime. **Tickets** $10-$20.

Housed in a converted Victorian fire station, the Charlestown Working Theater radiates a deeper sense of history than any of its big brothers in the Theatre District. Its versatile staging area means the theatre never looks the same twice, while oodles of community support means tickets are dirt cheap. The organisation sponsors a variety of resident artists and children's programmes.

Lyric Stage Company of Boston

YWCA Building, 140 Clarendon Street, at Stuart Street, Back Bay (1-617 585 5678, www.lyricstage. com). Back Bay or Copley T. **Box office** noon-5pm Tue, Sun; noon-8pm Wed-Sat. **Tickets** $35-$50. **Map** p283 H6.

Boston's oldest professional theatre, Lyric Stage has flourished under the leadership of artistic director Spiro Veloudos, who's been nurturing and inspiring the work of some of the area's most talented playwrights, actors, designers and directors. With repertoire that has ranged from familiar classics to hits such as *Avenue Q*, the company is known for high-quality yet moderately priced performances.

Modern Theatre

525 Washington Street, at Avenue de Lafayette, Downtown (OvationTix 1-866 811 4111, www2. suffolk.edu/moderntheatre). Boylston or Chinatown T. **Box office** 1hr before showtime. **Tickets** vary. **Map** p280 K5.

With 185 seats, Suffolk University's theatre may be small in scale, but it has big ambitions. The theatre's programming is designed to engage both students and the community with a range of thoughtful offerings, from intimate chamber operas to classical drama and theatrical premieres.

New Repertory Theatre at Arsenal Center for the Arts

321 Arsenal Street, at School Street, Watertown (1-617 923 8487, www.newrep.org). Central T then bus 70, 70A. **Box office** noon-6pm Tue-Fri. **Tickets** $30-$60.

One of Boston's most respected repertory companies, the award-winning New Rep prides itself on presenting challenging productions based on thought-provoking ideas, from classics such as *Waiting for Godot* to New England premières by such notable playwrights as Athol Fugard and Suzan-Lori Parks.

ARTS & ENTERTAINMENT

Escapes & Excursions

Escapes & Excursions

Along the rocky coastline of Massachusetts, you'll find seagulls, sand dunes and salty sea air. You'll also discover lonely lighthouses, rattletrap clam shacks and gruff seafaring charm. Many seaside communities still rely on the Atlantic for their livelihood. This is what people are talking about when they refer to the 'real' New England.

It was this coast that drew the early settlers to Plymouth, and then inland to the countryside, where you'll still find a host of charming, sleepy towns. These peaceful backwaters were the settings of dramatic, far-reaching events – the Salem Witch Trials, the first battles of the American Revolution and, later, a gathering of writers and thinkers that helped to shape the country's literary legacy.

One if by Land…

LEXINGTON, CONCORD & LINCOLN

Concord and Lexington, neighbouring towns about half an hour's drive west of Boston, are known as the battleground of American independence. The villages enjoy a friendly rivalry over who hosted the first rumblings of the American Revolution; Lexington can claim the first shot, but Concord entertained the first fight. In fact, the first true battle of the American Revolution started in Lexington

> **IN THE KNOW THREE IN ONE**
>
> A three-house package tour covering the **Buckman Tavern**, **Hancock-Clarke House** and **Munroe Tavern** (for all, see p205) is available from any of them for $12 ($8 reductions).

and ended in Concord, thus forever combining the two in the minds of many.

It all began in 1774, when the Provincial Congress delegated a division of elite militia soldiers known as the Minutemen. They were authorised to form 'for defence only'. But the Minutemen, in anticipation of future battles, had begun stockpiling weapons in the village of Concord. British generals caught word of the arsenal and sent 700 troops to make the 25-mile journey from Boston to Concord. Alerted by a trio of rebels (Paul Revere among them) sent on horseback, 70 Minutemen met the troops at Lexington Green. When the British soldiers arrived, they ordered the Americans to drop their weapons. The colonists refused – and a battle began. During that first struggle, 18 Minutemen were killed or wounded, while not a single British soldier was injured. Emboldened by their victory, the British didn't stop to rest, but marched on to Concord where, unknown to them, more militia were marshalling. As the American troops awaited the Redcoats' arrival outside Concord, they spotted smoke rising from the town. Convinced that the British were burning their homes, they attacked a British patrol sent out to hold the **Old North Bridge**. It is said that the colonial troops were so enraged that Captain John Parker told the militia: 'Stand your ground. Don't fire unless fired upon, but if they mean to have a war, let it begin here!' And so it did. Two Americans and 11 British soldiers were killed there. With that, the war had begun in earnest (*see p226*).

Lexington

All the major sights of **Lexington** centre on **Lexington Green**, the triangular plot upon which the battle occurred. Today, it is anchored by the **Minuteman Statue** and dotted with other markers and memorials. The statue is of Captain Parker, his famous quote engraved below his feet. Turning right as you come out of the green, you'll see the yellow colonial house known as **Buckman Tavern**. Here, the Minutemen assembled to await the arrival of British troops; they later used it as a field hospital. The tavern, one of the oldest buildings in the area, was already 85 years old at the time of the battle. These days, it is staffed by guides in period costume. The high bar counter is said to have been set at this level to prevent under-age drinking: if a boy's chin wasn't above the bar, he couldn't buy a beer. Just behind the tavern is the small but perfectly informed **Lexington Visitors Center**, which has a diorama illustrating the particulars of the battle. It also offers maps of the town's historically significant houses for a self-guided tour.

North of the green, on Hancock Street, sits the **Hancock-Clarke House**. On the night of the battle, largely by coincidence, rebels Samuel Adams and John Hancock were spending the night here, as guests of the owner, Rev Jonas Clarke. In the end, Revere awoke them in time,

and they were hustled out of town to safety. He did not, however, warn the soldiers at Concord, as he was captured by the British. The Hancock-Clarke House now contains a permanent collection of the furnishings and paintings owned by the two families, as well as relics of that night in April 1775.

About a mile east of the green is the **Munroe Tavern**. It was here that the British troops retreating from Concord stopped to rest and treat their injured, shooting the bartender who tried to flee after serving them. George Washington tried to redeem the bar's reputation by visiting it after the war, and several artefacts relating to his stay are kept here today. Further along, at the intersection of Massachusetts Avenue and Marrett Road, is the modern brick building that houses the **National Heritage Museum**. Colonial farm tools and Freemason propaganda mingle with rock concert posters and baseball memorabilia, making the museum a breezy respite from the rest of the area's emphatically colonial history.

Concord

Four miles from Lexington down Route 62 is the village of **Concord**. As well as playing a major role in the War of Independence, Concord is distinguished by its place in American letters. Ralph Waldo Emerson, Henry David Thoreau, Louisa May Alcott and Nathaniel Hawthorne all lived here at various times, and within a few short blocks you'll find a group of houses that once contained an unparalleled flowering of American literary genius. But the first sites most visitors feel obliged to see are tied into the country's earliest days. The most significant is the **Minute Man National Historical Park**, which marks the spot where the Battle of Concord took place after the British marched on victorious from Lexington. Every April, on Patriots' Day

Old North Bridge.

Orchard House

Weekend (*see p29*), thousands of people in traditional Minuteman and Redcoat garb hold a historical re-enactment of the opening events of the Revolutionary War.

Once inside the park, it's best to start at the **North Bridge Visitors' Center**, set on a hill overlooking the bridge and the Concord River. Inside is a diorama, alongside a collection of Revolutionary War memorabilia, including uniforms and weapons from both sides. The helpful park rangers at the centre provide guided tours of the site. From there, it's just a short walk to the reconstruction of the North Bridge, where the 'shot heard around the world' was fired. The **Battle Road Trail** is a five-mile stretch that connects many of the park's points of interest.

Essayist and philosopher Ralph Waldo Emerson lived in two houses in town, but his primary residence was at what is now known as the **Ralph Waldo Emerson House**. He lived here with his family from 1835 until his death in 1882; while he was on tour in Europe, his friend and fellow Transcendentalist Henry David Thoreau kept house. It contains some of the original furnishings and many of Emerson's personal belongings.

Another Emerson residence is the **Old Manse**, built by his grandfather in 1770. Both Emerson and Nathaniel Hawthorne lived here at different times. Emerson stayed here with his wife from 1842 to 1847, and many of their personal effects are on display. Hawthorne's stories inspired by his time here brought him his earliest fame. Not far away is **Orchard House**, once home to the educator Bronson Alcott, another prominent Transcendentalist. However, its best-known resident was his daughter, Louisa May Alcott. Her *Little Women* was written and set at Orchard House. The house, filled with the family's belongings, attracts thousands of fans of the book every year. A ticket includes a highly detailed tour. Alcott also lived at **The Wayside**, a neighbouring residence where, coincidentally, Hawthorne later came to spend his final years. The **Concord Museum**, built on the site of Emerson's orchard, contains a tidy collection of local relics, including a number of Thoreau's effects. But the museum's most famous item is one of the lanterns that was hung in the Old North Church on the night of Paul Revere's famous ride, to signal the approach of British troops.

From the nearby town square, you can catch a glimpse of the steep embankment of **Sleepy Hollow Cemetery** (*see p52* **Six Feet Under**) on Bedford Street, the eternal home of Concord's most celebrated writers-in-residence. At the top of a hill, under the shade of enormous maple trees, lie the graves of Emerson, Thoreau, Alcott and Hawthorne. It's an especially apt tableau for naturalists Thoreau and Emerson, who drew inspiration for their work from the serenity of Concord's landscape.

Thoreau's best-known muse, though, lies just south of town. At **Walden Pond** (*photo p208*) in a one-room cabin off Route 126, he lived in rustic meditation for a year or so from 1846. He wrote the ground-breaking essay *Walden* about the experience, but fame only came with *Civil Disobedience* three years later. The house in which Thoreau sought his simple life is long since gone – a pile of stones marks the spot – but the well-preserved **Walden Pond State Reservation** affords the kind of swimming and hiking the native seer advocated. A full-size replica of the original cabin, with painstakingly reproduced furnishings, is open to visitors. In summer, the pond's wooded banks can become quite crowded with Bostonians hoping to cool off.

Lincoln

Lincoln was originally part of Concord, but became a separate town in 1754, nipping off a few bits of other surrounding towns in the process. (Its piecemeal geography earned it the nickname 'Niptown'.) Like its neighbours, Lincoln boasts Revolutionary history aplenty. Just off Route 2A, in the Minute Man National Historical Park, is the site where Paul Revere was captured by British soldiers on his way to Concord.

Nearby, just off Route 128, is the stunning **DeCordova Sculpture Park & Museum**. The castle-like premises (the former estate of Boston entrepreneur Julian de Cordova, 1850-1945) are home to the largest contemporary art museum in the region, and New England's only permanent sculpture park. Devoted to living New England talent, the DeCordova holds annual shows of accomplished regional artists. A varied and ever-changing array of enormous sculptures bespeckle the 35-acre park, where visitors can wander or picnic.

Tucked into the farmlands and forests along Baker Bridge Road is the spare, minimalist **Gropius House** (see p209 **A Bauhaus in the Country**), the family home of acclaimed mid 20th-century German architect Walter Gropius.

DeCordova Sculpture Park

A half-hour's walk through the woods will bring you to the much more Colonial-looking **Codman Estate**. The grand, Federal-style estate of the Codman family, it dates back to 1735. The grounds are home to extensive gardens, as well as the **Codman Community Farms**, a working, educational vegetable and livestock farm that's open to visitors.

Buckman Tavern
1 Bedford Street, Lexington (1-781 862 1703, www.lexingtonhistory.org). **Open** 10am-4pm daily. Closed late Nov-early Apr. **Admission** $7; $5 reductions; free under-6s.

Codman Community Farms
58 Codman Road, Lincoln (1-781 259 0456, www.codmancommunityfarms.org). **Open** 9am-6pm daily. **Admission** $3; $2 reductions. **No credit cards**.

Codman Estate
34 Codman Road, Lincoln (1-617 994 6690, www.historicnewengland.org). **Open** 11am-4pm 2nd & 4th Sat of mth. Closed mid Oct-May. **Admission** $5; $2.50-$4 reductions.

Concord Museum
200 Lexington Road, Concord (1-978 369 9763, www.concordmuseum.org). **Open** *Jan-Mar* 11am-4pm Mon-Sat; 1-4pm Sun. *Apr, May, Sept, Oct* 9am-5pm Mon-Sat; noon-5pm Sun. *June-Aug* 9am-5pm daily. Closed Nov, Dec. **Admission** $10; $5-$8 reductions; free under-5s.

DeCordova Sculpture Park & Museum
51 Sandy Pond Road, off Route 2 or 128, Lincoln (1-781 259 8355, www.decordova.org). **Open** *Mid Oct-mid May* 10am-4pm Wed-Fri; 10am-5pm Sat, Sun. *Mid May-mid Oct* 10am-5pm daily. **Admission** $14; $10-$12 reductions; free under-12s.

Gropius House
68 Baker Bridge Road, Lincoln (1-781 259 8098, www.historicnewengland.org). **Open** *Tours* (hourly) June-mid *Oct* 11am-5pm Wed-Sun. Mid Oct-May 11am-5pm Sat, Sun. **Admission** $15; $8-$12 reductions.

Hancock-Clarke House
36 Hancock Street, Lexington (1-781 862 1703, www.lexingtonhistory.org). **Open** *Early Apr-late May* 10am-4pm Sat, Sun. *Late May-Oct* 10am-4pm daily. Closed Nov-early Apr. **Admission** $7; $5 reductions; free under-6s.

Louisa May Alcott's Orchard House
399 Lexington Road, Concord (1-978 369 4118, www.louisamayalcott.org). **Open** *Apr-Oct* 10am-4.30pm Mon-Sat; 1-4.30pm Sun.

Walden Pond. See p206.

Nov-Mar 11am-3pm Mon-Fri; 10am-4.30pm Sat; 1-4.30pm Sun. **Admission** $10; $5-$8 reductions; free under-6s.

☐FREE☐ Minute Man National Historical Park

North Bridge Visitor Center: 174 Liberty Street, Concord (1-978 369 6993, www.nps.gov/mima). **Open** dusk-dawn daily. *Visitor centre* Apr-Oct 9am-5pm daily. Nov 9am-4pm Tue-Sat. Dec, Mar 11am-3pm Tue-Sat. **Admission** free.

Munroe Tavern

1332 Massachusetts Avenue, Lexington (1-781 862 1703, www.lexingtonhistory.org). **Open** *Early Apr-late May* noon-4pm Sat, Sun. *Late May-Oct* noon-4pm daily. Closed Nov-early Apr. **Admission** $7; $5 reductions; free under-6s.

Old Manse

269 Monument Street, Concord (1-978 369 3909). **Open** *Mid Mar-late May, Nov-late Dec* noon-5pm Sat, Sun. *Late May-Oct* noon-5pm Tue-Sun. Closed late Dec-mid Mar. **Admission** $8; $5-$7 reductions.

Ralph Waldo Emerson House

28 Cambridge Turnpike, Concord (1-978 369 2236, www.nps.gov). **Open** *late Apr-late Oct* 10am-4.30pm Thur-Sat; 1-4.30pm Sun. **Admission** $9; $7 reductions; free under-6s.

☐FREE☐ Walden Pond State Reservation

915 Walden Street, Concord (1-978 369 3254, www.mass.gov/eea). **Open** varies. **Admission** free.

Wayside

455 Lexington Road, Concord (1-978 318 7863, www.nps.gov). **Open** reopening summer 2015; call for information. **Admission** call for information.

Where to eat & drink

Concord's dining scene recently received a boost with the arrival of high-profile chef Jason Bond's contemporary American restaurant **Bondir Concord** (24 Walden Street, 1-978 610 6554, www.bondirconcord.com). Helmed by former Rialto (*see p132*) chef de cuisine Carolyn Johnson, upscale farm-to-table **80 Thoreau** (80 Thoreau Street, 1-978-318-0008, www.80thoreau.com) is also recommended.

Where to stay

Concord has two historic inns: the 19th-century **Hawthorne Inn** (462 Lexington Road, 1-978 369 5610, www.concordmass.com) and the 18th-century **Concord's Colonial Inn** (48 Monument Square, 1-978 369 9200, www.concordscolonialinn.com), which occupies a prime spot on the square and is home to a highly regarded restaurant. For something a little more intimate, the **North Bridge Inn** (21 Monument Street, 1-978 371 0014, www.northbridgeinn.com) has six suites of various sizes.

Getting there

By car Lexington is 14 miles north-west of Boston on Route 128 (I-95). Concord is 19 miles north-west of Boston and seven miles west of Lexington. Take Route 2A from Lexington, or Route 2 from Boston. Lincoln is 17 miles north-west of Boston and just a few miles south-east of Concord. Take Route 2 from Boston or Concord.

By bus or rail The MBTA Commuter Rail (*see p258*) has services to Concord and Lincoln from North Station. Buses 62 and 76 go to Lexington from Alewife T station in Cambridge. Awkwardly, there's no direct public transport connection between Lexington and Concord or Lincoln.

Tourist information

For the **Minute Man National Historical Park Visitors' Center**, *see left*.

Lexington Visitors' Center

Lexington Green, 1875 Massachusetts Avenue, Lexington (1-781 862 1450). **Open** *Apr-Nov* 9am-5pm daily. *Dec-Mar* 10am-4pm daily.

SALEM

There are few American towns with reputations as dark as **Salem**'s. While there's more to its history than the notorious witch trials of 1692, the mass hysteria that consumed the town during those seven months still casts a pall on its name. According to local lore, Tituba, an Arawak maid who practised voodoo, turned the interest of a

A BAUHAUS IN THE COUNTRY

Discover an unexpected modern architectural gem in colonial Lincoln.

Walter Gropius arrived in Cambridge in 1937 to teach at Harvard's Graduate School of Design after the Nazis closed the Bauhaus, the innovative German design school he'd founded 18 years earlier. Offered a hillside site in rural Lincoln by a wealthy patron to build a home for himself and his family, he turned it into a laboratory of sorts where he and his colleagues could explore new forms and materials, and a new way of life.

Completed in 1939, **Gropius House** (see p207) is a sculptural tour de force, inventively engaging its hilltop site. Its boxy white form may have grown out of 1920s European modernism, but its fieldstone foundation, screened porch and colonnade tie it to the traditions of the region.

A white wooden box dominates the composition, a familiar New England icon stripped of the pitched roof, vertical windows and traditional ornamental features. Instead, there are horizontal ribbons of windows and a series of projecting elements and sculptural cutouts that open it up to the pastoral setting.

An angular, steel-and-glass block entrance entices visitors inside; next to it, a staircase spirals upwards to a sheltered terrace (which gave Gropius and his wife Ise a surreptitious view from inside of their precocious teenage daughter's late-night comings and goings). To the rear, a wafer-thin roof hovers on slender columns above a terrace wrapped in a taut skin of screening. The interior comprises interconnected spaces that are cool and serene. A floating glass dividing wall, steel framed windows and sleek black counters echo the aesthetic of the exterior. The sensuously curving central stairway is a lovingly designed piece of sculpture with its cascade of metal, wood and unpainted plaster.

The house is furnished with pieces collected or designed by Gropius. The dining room chairs by collaborator Marcel Breuer are icons of modern design, and the Miró hanging in the entrance was a gift from the artist. Hour-long tours take visitors around the entire property and site, putting the aspirations and innovations of its designer into the context of their time and place.

group of repressed young Puritan girls towards magic, with devastating results; other stories attribute their behaviour to adolescent hysteria, or even ergot poisoning. The tragic conclusion of it all – the executions of more than 20 people, mostly elderly women – means the town will be forever linked with madness.

Black magic associations aside, Salem is a lovely place. It has a slightly split personality. One side of it is darkly colonial, with red-brick buildings and cemeteries dating back to its earliest days. But it's also a beach town, with a brisk fishing trade and colourful summerhouses by the coast. The colonial section makes a good starting point in terms of chronology, because you move towards the more modern buildings as you get closer to the water.

Though Salem is small, it's sprawling enough to make getting from one end to the other a bit of a hike – but walking really is the best way to get around. Not surprisingly, the town is overrun with witchcraft-related attractions, many of them closer to Halloween spectacles than actual historical points of interest. The few sites worth investigating are mostly scattered around **Salem Common**, a scenic park in the middle of the oldest section of town. The **Witch House**, also known as the Jonathan Corwin House after the former inhabitant and witch trial judge, was where the 200 or more unfortunates suspected of witchcraft were questioned. The house is truly spooky, though probably more for its dearth of windows than for its ominous pedigree. The **Salem Wax Museum** displays re-creations of the characters involved in the trials. Nearby, and the best of the lot, the **Salem Witch Museum** features a very thorough (and somewhat scary) mixed-media re-enactment of the Puritan hysteria. There's also a refreshingly enlightened exhibit on modern-day 'witches', including pagans and Wiccans.

Old downtown Salem is a National Historic District and site of architectural interest. Along Chestnut Street, Samuel McIntyre, a native of Salem and a pioneer of the American Federal style, designed a number of houses. In the heart of the area is the **Peabody Essex Museum**, an exceptional resource for international art and culture. Founded by the East India Maritime Company in the late 18th century, when Salem was prominent in the shipping trade to China, the Peabody collection documents the history of whaling and merchant shipping, and features an extensive collection of exhibits from sailors' travels. Renovations have brought several new galleries and exhibits, including Yin Yu Tang, a spectacular Qing dynasty merchant's house that was shipped over and reassembled in partnership with the Chinese government.

Salem's seafaring past is on display aboard the **Friendship**, a full-scale replica of a

House of the Seven Gables.

three-masted 1797 East India merchant ship. It's docked at the end of Derby Street, amid the nine-acre **Salem Maritime National Historic Site**, which offers tours of reconstructions of wharves, warehouses and stores, as well as the old Customs House where Nathaniel Hawthorne worked before he wrote *The Scarlet Letter*. Salem's most famous son, Hawthorne took the inspiration for his other great novel from his cousin's home, the **House of the Seven Gables**. It's an extraordinary building, large and gloomy, with a peaked roof and turrets. Built in 1668, it's filled with period furniture, much of which is described in Hawthorne's novel. Tours also take in the modest house where Hawthorne was born, which was moved to the grounds from its original site on nearby Union Street in 1958.

House of the Seven Gables
115 Derby Street, at Turner Street (1-978 744 0991, www.7gables.org). **Open** *Mid Jan-June, Nov, Dec* 10am-5pm daily. *July-Oct* 10am-7pm. **Admission** $12.50; $7.50-$11.50 reductions.

Peabody Essex Museum
116 Essex Street, at East India Square (1-978 745 9500, 1-866 745 1876, www.pem.org). **Open** 10am-5pm Tue-Sun; 10am-9pm 3rd Sun of mth. **Admission** $18; $10-$15 reductions; free under-16s.

Salem Maritime National Historic Site
Visitor centre: 2 New Liberty Street, between Brown & Essex Streets (1-978 740 1650, www.nps.gov/sama). **Open** *Park* 24hrs daily; *Visitor centre* 10am-5pm Wed-Sun. **Admission** free.

Salem Wax Museum
288 Derby Street, at Central Street (1-978 740 2929, www.salemwaxmuseum.com). **Open** *Jan-Mar* 11am-4pm daily. *Apr-June, Sept* 10am-6pm daily. *July, Aug* 10am-9pm daily. *Oct* 10am-midnight daily. *Nov, Dec* 10am-5pm daily. **Admission** $8; $6 reductions.

Salem Witch Museum
19 1/2 Washington Square North, at Route 1A (1-978 744 1692, www.salemwitchmuseum.com). **Open** *Jan-June, Sept, Nov, Dec* 10am-5pm daily. *July, Aug* 10am-7pm daily; *Oct* 10am-5pm Mon-Thur; 10am-10pm Fri, Sat; 10am-7pm Sun. **Admission** $9.50; $6.50-$8 reductions.

Witch House
310 1/2 Essex Street, at North Street (1-978 744 8815, www.witchhouse.info). **Open** *Mid Mar-mid Nov* 10am-5pm daily. *Mid Nov-mid Mar* 1-3pm Wed-Fri; noon-5pm Sat, Sun. **Admission** $8.25; $4.25-$6.25 reductions; free under-6s.

Where to eat & drink

Salem offers fairly extensive dining options. The best bet is **Grapevine** (26 Congress Street, 1-978 745 9335, www.grapevinesalem.com), a funky, well-priced New American bistro facing Pickering Wharf. Contemporary seafood spot **Finz** (76 Wharf Street, 1-978 744 8485, www.hipfinz.com) has a raw bar and seasonal outdoor seating on its harbourside deck.

Where to stay

Aside from the usual chains, there are several more colourful options in town. One is the **Salem Inn** (7 Summer Street, 1-800 446 2995, www.saleminnma.com), a complex of three 19th-century houses, all on the National Register of Historic Places. Another is the **Hawthorne Hotel** (18 Washington Square West, 1-978 744 4080, www.hawthornehotel.com), which is nicely furnished, close to the sights and reasonably priced – although it's not as old as its name would suggest. More reasonable still, though a little further off the common, the **Amelia Payson House Bed & Breakfast** (16 Winter Street, 1-520 744 2365, www.ameliapaysonhouse.com) is an 1845 Greek Revival house with a piano in the parlour. The **Coach House Inn** (284 Lafayette Street, 1-800 688 8689, www.coachhousesalem.com), a 19th-century captain's mansion, is another elegant yet inexpensive choice.

Getting there

By car Salem is 16 miles north of Boston. Take Route I-95 north to Route 128, then Route 114 north into Salem. The drive should take around 50mins.

By rail The journey by rail takes 30mins by MBTA Commuter Rail (*see p258*) out of Boston's North Station.

Tourist information

Salem Visitor Center
2 New Liberty Street (1-978 741 3282). **Open** 9am-5pm daily.

PLYMOUTH

As you head south along the scenic coast between Quincy and Cape Cod, aka the **South Shore**, you come into the heart of colonial New England. Near Plymouth, the roadside retailers adopt faux 'Olde English' signage to emphasise the local heritage, and there are lots of 'towne shoppes'. In addition to the glut of historical attractions clustered near the old Pilgrim settlement, the lovely South Shore is home to old colonial trails and parks that remain, for the most part, uncorrupted by the tourist trade.

Famously, this is the spot where the Pilgrims landed in 1620 after their harrowing voyage from England. The landmark in these parts is **Plymouth Rock**, where, according to lore, they first stepped ashore. A replica of the ship in which the Pilgrims made their epic journey is docked close by. The **Mayflower II** is a full-scale version of the original, staffed by

Plymouth Rock

performers in 17th-century garb who recount the tale of the Pilgrims' struggles. The boat seems tiny, and it's hard to imagine how the settlers spent months aboard it, much of that time amid violent storms.

Plymouth itself is charming, its narrow streets lined with 17th- and 18th-century houses, many of which are open to the public. But the main attraction is the **Plimoth Plantation**, a huge, surreal re-creation of the 1627 settlement, developed by historians and archaeologists. The village is populated by actors who speak, work, play, and breathe 17th-century life. The project pays painstaking – some might say obsessive – attention to detail, and visitors can watch the 'settlers' stocking firewood, stuffing sausages and plucking geese. The effect is like entering a time warp and it's extremely entertaining. Also worth seeing are the **Pilgrim Hall Museum**, with its *Mayflower*-era artefacts and exhibits on the native Wampanoag tribe, and the epitaphs on **Burial Hill**, on Carver Street, one of the oldest cemeteries in America and resting place of many of the first settlers.

Just south of the town centre is **Plymouth Long Beach**, a pretty, three-mile stretch of coastline. **Morton Park**, near Summer Street, is another peaceful retreat, with its swimming holes and woodland hiking trails.

Other towns around Plymouth Bay include Hull, Cohasset and Hingham. **Hull** was evacuated during the Revolution after a military fort was constructed on one of its hills. Today, its beaches do a brisk tourist trade, while the **Hull Lifesaving Museum** tells the tales of local superhuman shipwreck rescues.

Close by, **Cohasset** is a picture-perfect colonial village with none of the tourist trade of Plymouth or Hull. The century-old **Minot's Ledge Lighthouse** in Cohasset is a classic piece of New England scenery. At 4 Elm Street, the small, seasonally open **Maritime Museum** commemorates local early American heritage; its neighbour, the **Captain John Wilson House** at no.2, is also worth a look (1-781 383 1434, www.cohassethistoricalsociety.org for both).

Peaceful and bucolic **Hingham**, the next hamlet over, is a good place to while away a few peaceful hours. **Cove Park** is great for a stroll, and the clapboard-clad **Old Ordinary** (21 Lincoln Street, 1-781 749 0013, www.hingham historical.org) is a 17-room museum with period furniture and a tap room.

Hull Lifesaving Museum
1117 Nantasket Avenue, Hull (1-781 925 5433, www.lifesavingmuseum.org). **Open** *May-Dec* 10am-4pm Mon-Thur, Sat; 10am-4pm Sun (July, Aug only). *Jan-Apr* 10am-4pm Mon-Thur. **Admission** $5; $3 reductions; free under-18s.

Mayflower II
State Pier, Water Street, Plymouth (1-508 746 1622, www.plimoth.org). **Open** *mid Mar-Nov* 9am-5pm daily. Closed mid-Dec-mid Mar. **Admission** $10; $7-$9 reductions; free under-5s.

Pilgrim Hall Museum
75 Court Street, Plymouth (1-508 746 1620, www.pilgrimhallmuseum.org). **Open** *Feb-Dec* 9.30am-4.30pm daily. Closed Jan. **Admission** $8; $5-$7 reductions.

Plimoth Plantation
137 Warren Avenue, off Route 3A South at Exit 4, outside Plymouth (1-508 746 1622, www.plimoth. org). **Open** 9am-5pm daily. Closed Dec-mid Mar. **Admission** $26; $13-$24 reductions; free under-5s. *Combined ticket with Mayflower II* $30; $19-$275 reductions; free under-4s.

Where to eat & drink

Dining around Plymouth is a briny business. Top-notch fish and shellfish at the self-service **Lobster Hut** (25 Town Wharf, 1-508 746 2270) are inexpensive and come with a view. The more upmarket **Isaac's** (114 Water Street, 1-508 830 0001) offers another great ocean vista and more elaborate seafood.

In nearby Hull, locals swear by the lobster at **Jake's** (50 George Washington Boulevard, 1-781 925 1024, www.jakesseafoods.com), an award-winning eaterie that overlooks the bay. Hingham has a number of good restaurants, including the Italian-inspired **Tosca** (14 North Street, 1-781 740 0080, www.toscahingham.com) and **Stars on Hingham Harbor** (2 Otis Street, 1-781 749 3200, www.starshingham.com).

Where to stay

Plymouth has a number of serviceable, if undistinguished, motels within convenient reach of downtown. A more pleasant choice, and one with its own private beach, is the moderately priced **Pilgrim Sands Hotel** (150 Warren Avenue, 1-508 747 0900, www.pilgrimsandshotel.com), a few miles out of town. The **Auberge Gladstone** guesthouse (8 Vernon Street, 1-508 830 1890, 1-866 722 1890, www.aubergegladstone.com), a colonial mansion with modern furnishings, is another good option.

If you're looking for water views, check out the **Cohasset Harbor Inn** (124 Elm Street, 1-781 383 6650, www.cohassetharborresort.com), a low-key hotel with two on-site restaurants.

Getting there

By car Plymouth is 40 miles south-east of Boston on the I-93 (Southeast Expressway) to Route 3. Take Exit 6A. It's roughly an hour's drive from Boston.

Rockport.

By bus or rail Plymouth & Brockton Street Railway Co and MBTA Commuter Rail run services from Boston's South Station (*see p258*). The journey takes about an hour.

Tourist information

Plymouth Area Chamber of Commerce
134 Court Street, Plymouth (1-508 830 1620, www.plymouthchamber.com). **Open** 8am-4pm Mon-Fri.

Waterfront Visitor Information Center
130 Water Street, Plymouth (1-508 747 7533, 1-800 872 1620, www.seeplymouth.com). **Open** *Apr, May, Sept-Nov* 9am-5pm daily. *June-Aug* 8am-8pm daily. Closed Dec-Mar.

...Two if by Sea

Cape Ann is the less frequently visited of the Bay State's two capes, and has managed to survive the past 200 years with minimal commercial interruption. Its pride, personality and picturesque panoramas are fully intact, unlike the holiday hotspot and significantly more tourist-clogged **Cape Cod**. This wedge of New England is an area of extremes, and asserts a rough loveliness all of its own: regal schooners are moored next to rickety old rowing boats, while grand, multi-tiered homes are flanked by ramshackle cottages and shacks with the stability of card castles.

CAPE ANN

Cape Ann includes Gloucester, Essex, Rockport and Manchester-by-the-Sea. These towns all started off with post-Pilgrim seafaring histories: shipbuilding, shipwrecks, intrepid sailors crossing the Atlantic, tragedy and heroism, captured by poets and artists such as Winslow Homer and Henry Wadsworth Longfellow.

Gloucester, the largest of the towns, has been a centre of the fishing industry since 1623, and some 10,000 locals are said to have perished at sea over the years (Sebastian Junger's book *The Perfect Storm*, and the subsequent film of the same name, documented a 1991 tragedy). The town's tribute to these men, a bronze statue known as 'The Man at the Wheel', stands sentinel on the harbour promenade, just off Western Avenue.

Further down the street is the more recent – and equally poignant – Fishermen's Wives Memorial, dedicated to the families of the men who risk their lives at sea. **Rocky Neck**, in East Gloucester, is the country's oldest working artists' colony. Here, **Hammond Castle** is a full-scale stone replica of a medieval castle, built between 1926 and 1929 by John Jays Hammond Jr. You'll also find ample opportunity for whale-watching excursions and day-long fishing trips around these parts.

Essex relies on clamming as one of its principal industries, and the sweet, tender Essex clam is about as famous as a clam can get. In 1914, a clam-digging local named Lawrence 'Chubby' Woodman opened a clam shack here, **Woodman's** (*see p215*). Whether Chubby actually 'invented' the fried clam is not important. What really matters is that the ones at Woodman's, where the motto is 'Eat in the rough', are some of the best on the coast.

The main strip in Essex, known as the Causeway, is lined with antiques shops – the most famous of which is the White Elephant. Some look like cluttered, chaotic junk shops, while others resemble mini museums, and are priced accordingly.

Shipbuilding began in Essex in the mid 1600s, and by the 1850s the town was renowned as the North American centre for schooner building. Craftsmen still build ships by hand here today, and you can learn about the history of the industry at the **Essex Shipbuilding Museum**.

In **Rockport**, visitors poke around its narrow streets, lined with little gift shops and galleries. Bear Skin Neck, a small peninsula that juts into the harbour, has a profusion of tiny storefronts and cafés.

ESCAPES & EXCURSIONS

Manchester-by-the-Sea is the most sleepy and residential of the four towns. Nonetheless, its **Singing Beach**, named in honour of the rare 'singing' sand that chirps when you step on it, is lovely. Other notable Cape Ann beaches include **Long Beach** in Rockport, and **Wingaersheek** and **Good Harbor**, both in Gloucester. South of Gloucester, at **Rafe's Chasm Reservation**, the granite ledges open on to a 200-foot-long and 60-foot-deep chasm, where the tides often produce some striking sights and sounds. East of town, **Pebble Beach** has an unusual shoreline of timeworn stones stretching into the horizon.

Although not in Cape Ann proper, **Ipswich** (www.ipswichma.com), to the north of Essex, boasts **Castle Hill**, the **Crane Wildlife Refuge** and **Crane Beach** (Argilla Road, 1-978 356 4354), all once part of the expansive estate of Chicago plumbing magnate Richard T Crane Jr. Crane Beach is a four-mile stretch of sand that's home to the threatened piping plover. The funding for wildlife preservation in this conservation area is raised by hiring out the regal Great House on Castle Hill. It's set in 165 acres, with the Grand Alleé path running from its porches down to the bluffs overlooking Crane Beach.

ESCAPES & EXCURSIONS

JAZZ TUNES AND TYCOONS

Enjoy a summer weekend of music and mansions in Newport, RI.

Newport Folk Festival.

Newport, across the state border in Rhode Island, is a favourite summer seaside trip for Bostonians. A relatively short drive from Boston, the town has two main lures: its magnificent architecture and its Jazz Festival.

Newport was once the summer playground of America's wealthiest industrialists. The Rockefellers and the Vanderbilts came here and built what they called 'cottages'. The size of English stately homes, the sweeping mansions along Bellevue Avenue – each in a different style – are opulent testimony to the wealth of their owners. Some, most notably the **Breakers** – a 70-room Italian Renaissance-style pile built in 1895 for Cornelius Vanderbilt – are open to the public. Roam room after room of imported marble, gold leaf, precious antiques and art. Other tourable mansions in the vicinity include the **Elms**, **Rosecliff** and **Marble House**. Individual or combination tickets are available; for more information, phone 1-401 847 1000 or visit www.newportmansions.org.

The history of the **Newport Jazz Festival** is equally lofty, boasting such musical royalty as Ella Fitzgerald, Dizzy Gillespie and Billie Holiday – and that was just its inaugural year. Miles Davis also performed in Newport, as did Nina Simone and BB King. But it's not all scatting and saxophones: in 1959, the granddaddy of jazz festivals spawned the **Newport Folk Festival**. Bob Dylan, Joan Baez, Joni Mitchell and, more recently, Billy Bragg, Emmylou Harris and Lyle Lovett have all taken to the Newport stage, as well as such fringe indie rockers as Jim James from My Morning Jacket, Calexico and Andrew Bird. Both events are held in late July and August. Call 1-401 848 5055 or visit www.newportjazzfest.org for details.

Newport is about 90 minutes by car from Boston. Take the I-93 South to Route 24 South, then on to Route 114 South. Peter Pan Bus Lines (*see p258*) runs daily services from Boston's South Station.

Essex Shipbuilding Museum

*66 Main Street, Essex (1-978 768 7541, www.
essexshipbuildingmuseum.org)*. **Open** *June-Oct*
10am-5pm Wed-Sun. *Nov-May* 10am-5pm Sat, Sun.
Admission $7-$10; $5-$8 reductions; free under-6s.

Hammond Castle

*80 Hesperus Avenue, Gloucester (1-978 283 2080,
www.hammondcastle.org)*. **Open** *Mid June-early
Sept* 10am-4pm Tue-Sun. *May, Oct* 10am-4pm Sat,
Sun. **Admission** $10; $8-$9 reductions.

Where to eat & stay

For dining, of course there's the famous
Woodman's (121 Main Street, Essex, 1-800 649
1773, www.woodmans.com). In Gloucester, the
Rudder (73 Rocky Neck Avenue, 1-978 283 7967,
www.rudderrestaurant.com, closed winter), in the
heart of the Rocky Neck Art Colony, has a well-
priced, eclectic menu, quirky decor and a festive
atmosphere. The **Franklin Café** (118 Main
Street, 1-978 283 7888, www.franklincafe.com),
sibling to the venue in Boston's South End (*see
p101*), serves contemporary comfort food.

The most interesting choices for a bed for the
night include the **Addison Choate Inn** in
Rockport (49 Broadway, 1-800 245 7543, www.
addisonchoateinn.com), a Greek Revival house
from the 1850s, and the **Inn on Cove Hill** (37
Mount Pleasant Street, 1-978 546 2701, www.
innoncovehill.com), which was reputedly built
with funds from a cache of pirate loot.

Getting there

By car Gloucester is 30 miles north-east of Boston
on I-93 to Route 128 North; Rockport is 40 miles from
Boston, and seven miles north of Gloucester on
Routes 127 or 127A. Ipswich is 25 miles north-east
of Boston. Take Route I-95 North to Route 1 North.
By bus or rail MBTA Commuter Rail (*see p258*)
runs trains to Gloucester and Ipswich from Boston's
North Station. The bus service on the Cape Ann
peninsula is run by the Cape Ann Transportation
Authority (1-978 283 7278, www.canntran.com).

Tourist information

Cape Ann Chamber of Commerce

*33 Commercial Street, Gloucester (1-978 283
1601, www.capeannchamber.com)*. **Open** *June-
Sept* 9am-5pm Mon-Sat; 10am-5pm Sun. *Oct-May*
9am-5pm Mon-Fri.

CAPE COD

Order a Cape Codder at the bar, and you'll get a
vodka and cranberry juice with a wedge of lime –
a cosmopolitan without the Cointreau. And that's
the Cape right there: sharp, strong and a splash

away from being something fancy. It's a mix of
hardy fisher-folk year-rounders and the summer
crowd in their khaki shorts and Polo button-
downs; of sweeping Cape estates and quaint
old clapboard cottages.

Cape Cod was named after the fish found there
in 1605 by English explorer Bartholomew Gosnold.
These days, cranberry-growing and tourism
provide the region's economic support, rather
than the traditional industries of fishing, whaling,
shipping and salt-making. This area is the nation's
largest producer of the red berries (hence the name
of the cocktail), and the burgundy bogs add
swathes of colour to the often austere landscape.
As for tourism, you can expect the summer
weekend traffic over Sagamore Bridge – the
gateway to the Cape – to be backed up for miles.

The Cape is organised into three chunks,
containing the following towns, as well as multiple
villages: Upper (Bourne, Sandwich, Falmouth and
Mashpee); Mid (Barnstable, Dennis, Yarmouth);
and Lower, or Outer (Brewster, Chatham, Harwich,
Eastham, Orleans, Provincetown, Truro and
Wellfleet). Within these larger towns are
settlements such as Hyannis in Barnstable. The
Cape Cod National Seashore boasts 43,685
acres of beaches, sand dunes, heathland, marshes
and freshwater ponds, along with a number of
historic sites.

Sandwich was the first of the Pilgrims' Cape
towns. In the 19th century, the town became a
centre of American glass-making, its plentiful
scrub brush fuelling the artisans' ovens. Today,
its **Glass Museum** contains a wealth of
examples of the work produced here. Meanwhile,
at the restored 17th-century **Dexter Grist Mill**
on the corner of Main and Water Streets, you can

Provincetown. *See p216.*

still buy a bag of freshly ground cornmeal. The nearby 76-acre **Heritage Plantation** is home to a hotchpotch of objects, ranging from vintage cars to Currier & Ives prints. It includes several museums and a Shaker barn, and offers children rides on a 19th-century carousel.

Provincetown (*photo p215*) was the place where Miles Standish and his *Mayflower* boatload of Pilgrims first landed on American soil on 11 November 1620 – they quickly decided against the site, and moved on to that famous rock in Plymouth (*see p211*). Today, Provincetown supports a booming tourist trade and a notorious nightlife, based around its three-and-a-half miles of beach. In summer, it becomes the LGBT community's Disneyland destination, and an anything-goes attitude pervades the scene. Tea dancing at the **Boatslip** (161 Commercial Street, 1-508 487 1669, www.boatslipresort.com), a midnight boogie at **A-House** (4-6 Masonic Place, 1-508 487 3169, www.ahouse.com) and a late-night dinner at **Spiritus Pizza** (190 Commercial Street, 1-508 487 2808, www.spirituspizza.com) are all part of the seasonal routine.

A year-round local artists' community has long been established here. The **Provincetown Art Association & Museum** has been offering exhibitions, lectures and classes since 1914, and you'll find numerous galleries on Commercial Street.

Woods Hole, on the Cape's south-west tip, is one of the world's great centres of maritime research. The **Woods Hole Oceanographic Institute**, which assembled the team that located the remains of the *Titanic* in 1985, has exhibitions on undersea exploration. The more visitor-friendly **Marine Biological Laboratory** gives guided tours on weekends.

Hyannis, halfway out on the Upper Cape, is the transport hub of the area, with rail and airport services and ferries to **Nantucket** and **Martha's Vineyard** (*see p218*). Famously the location for the Kennedys' summer home, it remains inseparably linked to visions of a suntanned JFK at the helm of a skiff. The family's compound is walled off south of town in Hyannisport, but there's an extensive photographic display to admire at the **JFK Hyannis Museum**.

Chatham is a chic little town that has been continuously settled since the mid 17th century. In its earliest days, Chatham's perch on the shipping lanes made it a favourite location for 'moon-cussers' – bands of pirate wreckers who roamed the beaches with false lights that led boats aground to be pillaged. But the most prominent landmark today is one that guides sailors safely to shore: the **Chatham Light** lighthouse. Fishing is still a major industry here, along with the tourist trade – which the town accommodates in genteel style with its downtown crafts and antiques shops.

For a glimpse of a more primal New England, head south of town and past the Chatham Light

Chatham Light.

to **Morris Island**, and take the ferry out to the **Monomoy Island National Wildlife Refuge** (www.fws.gov/northeast/monomoy). This barrier island serves as a stopover point for bird migration in the Atlantic Flyway, and became a designated wildlife sanctuary in 1944. You might spot a grey seal or two here as well.

Along the sandy Cape Cod National Seashore you'll find some of Massachusetts' loveliest beaches. **Nauset Beach**, at the southern tip outside East Orleans, has the best surf and draws the youngest, liveliest crowd. This last, narrow stretch of the Cape has managed to escape most of the horrors of commercialisation. **Wellfleet Harbor**, on the bay side, encloses the 1,000 acres of the **Wellfleet Bay Wildlife Sanctuary**. Here, the Massachusetts Audubon Society (www.massaudubon.org) sponsors tours and lectures and allows camping (for a fee, and for Audubon members only).

Wellfleet and nearby **Truro** have long been known as artists' and writers' retreats. Edna St Vincent Millay and Edmund Wilson lived in Wellfleet in the 1920s, while Edward Hopper admired the bleak light and beauty of the high dunes outside Truro.

Heritage Museums & Garden

67 Grove Street, Sandwich (1-508 888 3300, www.heritagemuseumsandgardens.org). **Open** *Apr-Oct* 10am-5pm daily. *Nov-Dec* 4.30-8.30pm Fri-Sun. Closed Jan-Mar. **Admission** $18; $7 reductions; free under-2s.

John F Kennedy Hyannis Museum

397 Main Street, Hyannis (1-508 790 3077, www. jfkhyannismuseum.org). **Open** *June-Oct* 9am-5pm Mon-Sat; noon-5pm Sun. *Nov* 9am-4pm Mon-Sat;

noon-4pm Sun. Closed Dec-May. **Admission** $9; $5-$6 reductions; free under-8s.

FREE **Marine Biological Laboratory**
100 MBL Street, Woods Hole (1-508 548 3705, www.mbl.edu). **Open** *tours* late June-late Aug 1pm & 2pm, Mon-Fri. **Admission** free.

Provincetown Art Association & Museum
460 Commercial Street, Provincetown (1-508 487 1750, www.paam.org). **Open** *Tours* Late June-Sept 1pm, 2pm Mon-Fri (tours can also be scheduled Oct-May Mon-Fri). **Admission** $10.

Sandwich Glass Museum
129 Main Street, Sandwich (1-508 888 0251, www.sandwichglassmuseum.org). **Open** *Feb, Mar* 9.30am-4pm Wed-Sun. *Apr-Dec* 9.30am-5pm daily. Closed Jan. **Admission** $8; $2 reductions; free under-5s.

Wellfleet Bay Wildlife Sanctuary
291 State Highway, Route 6A, Wellfleet Harbor (1-508 349 2615, www.massaudubon.org). **Open** *Late May-mid Oct* 8.30am-5pm daily. *Mid Oct-late May* 8.30am-5pm Tue-Sun. **Admission** $5; $3 reductions.

Woods Hole Oceanographic Institution
15 School Street, Woods Hole (1-508 289 2663, www.whoi.edu). **Open** *Mid Apr-Oct* 11am-4pm Mon-Fri. *Nov, Dec* 11am-4pm Tue-Fri. **Admission** *Suggested donation* $2; free under-10s.

Where to eat & drink

Dining in Provincetown runs the gamut – but phone ahead wherever you go, as off-season hours are unpredictable and sometimes non-existent. Upmarket interpretations of New American cuisine are the order of the day at **Front Street** (230 Commercial Street, 1-508 487 9715, www.frontstreetrestaurant.com); decent contemporary Italian food can be had at reasonable prices at the venerable **Ciro & Sal's** (4 Kiley Court, 1-508 487 6444, www.ciroandsals.com); and stylish light fare is served at **Café Heaven** (199 Commercial Street, 1-508 487 9639).

It's worth driving to Wellfleet for dinner at **Winslow's Tavern** (316 Main Street, 1-508 349 6450, www.winslowstavern.com, closed in winter), a classy bistro with a focus on fresh, light dishes. Provincetown also has a significant Portuguese community, émigrés from the Azores who came to work on the fishing boats. For an afternoon sandwich, *linguiça* concoction or cod fritters – or a sweet treat after dinner – try the **Provincetown Portuguese Bakery** (299 Commercial Street, 1-508 487 1803), famous for its *malasadas* – a fried dough pastry sometimes filled with cream.

Where to stay

Lodging is extremely varied the whole length of Cape Cod; as a rule, towns on the Cape Cod Bay side of the peninsula are more interesting and relaxing. Rates tend to drop the further down the Cape you are from Provincetown, though there are bargains there, too, if you book well in advance. Off-season rates drop steeply – and the Cape has a wonderful austerity once the tourists have gone.

In Sandwich, the **Belfry Inn & Bistro** (6 Jarves Street, 1-508 888 8550, www.belfryinn.com) occupies three charming 19th-century buildings, including a converted church with stained-glass windows. In Barnstable, the **Beechwood Inn** (2839 Main Street, 1-800 609 6618, www.beechwoodinn.com) nestles among the trees from which it takes its name. The historic district of Chatham has a number of carefully restored 19th-century inns, such as the **Chatham Bars Inn** (297 Shore Road, 1-800 527 4884, www.chathambarsinn.com), but they can be pricey.

To be in the thick of the action, head to the town's most luxurious lodging, the **Brass Key Guesthouse** (67 Bradford Street, 1-800 842 9858, www.brasskey.com). For a free directory of gay- and lesbian-owned hotels, restaurants, bars and services, contact the **Provincetown Business Guild** (1-508 487 2313, www.ptown.org).

Getting there

By car The Sagamore Bridge, linking Cape Cod to the mainland, is 30 miles south-east of Boston on Route 3, and is the most direct route. The trip from Boston to Cape Cod is 77 miles, and takes about 90mins – or considerably longer if traffic is bad. **By bus** The Plymouth & Brockton bus (1-508 746 0378, www.p-b.com) runs several times a day from Boston's South Station to Hyannis and then on to Provincetown. The Cape Cod Regional Transit Authority (1-800 352 7155, www.capecodtransit. org) and Peter Pan Bus Lines (*see p258*) cover the mid-Cape region. Provincetown runs local shuttle bus services in the area in the summer months (see the CCRTA's website for details). **By boat** Bay State Cruise Company (1-877 783 3779, www.boston-ptown.com) runs a high-speed ferry from Boston to Provincetown daily throughout the summer season and for the first few weekends in October. The journey from Commonwealth Pier takes 90mins.

Tourist information

Cape Cod Chamber of Commerce Convention & Visitors Bureau
5 Patti Page Way, Centerville (1-508 362 3225, www.capecodchamber.org). **Open** *Late May-early Sept* 9am-4pm Mon-Sat; 10am-2pm Sun. *Early Sept-late May* varies; call or see website.

ESCAPES & EXCURSIONS

MARTHA'S VINEYARD & NANTUCKET

If well-heeled locals aren't heading to the Cape for long summer weekends, chances are they're off to the islands. Beautiful New England seascapes bring in money by the bucketload, and every summer the beaches, bars, restaurants and air of exclusivity of Martha's Vineyard and Nantucket draw thousands of tourists.

The first recreational use of **Martha's Vineyard** was for Methodist camp meetings in the summer of 1835. Today, summer residents include Spike Lee and the Obamas. **Edgartown** is the largest and oldest of the main towns. A walk along the harbourside, past the stately captains' mansions on Water Street, reveals the prosperity they brought back from the sea. The **Vineyard Historical Museum** is replete with scrimshaw, model ships and other local artefacts. Nearby **South Beach**, also known as Katama, is the island's largest and most popular strand.

In **Oak Bluffs**, the Martha's Vineyard Camp Meeting Association's candy-coloured Victorian cottages and tabernacle (www.mvcma.org), built as a Methodist retreat in the mid to late 19th century, are a National Historic Landmark. Some of the antique dwellings are also available to rent (see website for details). The wonderful 1876 **Flying Horses Carousel** (corner of Lake & Kennebec Avenues, 1-508 693 9481) is reputedly the country's oldest. A prime example of American folk art, it runs every day in summer until 10pm for $2.50 a ride.

Vineyard Haven (also known as Tisbury), on the north coast, was long the island's chief port and it's where the old colonial atmosphere is best preserved. One of the prettiest spots to visit on the island is the town of **Aquinnah** on the western tip. The public beach there is famous for its dramatic mile-long cliffs of multicoloured clay and the panoramic views from the trails above them.

While Martha's Vineyard is only a 45-minute ferry ride away, it takes over two hours on the open seas to get to **Nantucket**, making the 'Faraway Island' an apt nickname. In *Moby-Dick*, Herman Melville calls Nantucket 'a mere hillock, an elbow of sand; all beach without a background'. You can bet there's background now, in the form of eye-poppingly expensive properties – though Nantucket is doing everything it can to control the development of its precious land.

For 150 years, the island was one of the key centres of the whaling industry, and its streets and historic houses are soaked in that history. The Nantucket Historical Association's **Whaling Museum** (13 Broad Street, 1-508 228 1894, www.nha.org) tells the story – complete with a 46-foot sperm whale skeleton. But in the 19th century, with the rise of the petroleum industry, a devastating fire in 1846 and the onset of the Civil War, the

island's economy began to tumble. Between 1840 and 1870, the population decreased from 10,000 to 4,000. Nantucket was revived by tourism.

A sense of history still pervades the island, and in spring and summer the Nantucket Historical Society runs guided walking tours of the downtown hub. Highlights include the last of the town's 18th-century mills, as well as the **Old Gaol**, a lock-up in which the prisoners were allowed to go home for the night. Also offering guided walking tours is the **Museum of African American History**, headquartered in Boston (*see p66*), which maintains the **African Meeting House** and **Florence Higginbotham House** on Nantucket.

These days, the streets are packed with Range Rovers and lined with smart boutiques and antiques shops. But conspicuous consumption aside, in its beaches, foggy moors and ubiquitous grey clapboard houses, Nantucket has a grace that's missing in mainland Massachusetts.

Bring a bicycle – or rent one at **Young's Bicycle Shop** (6 Broad Street, Steamboat Wharf, 1-508 228 1151, www.youngsbicycleshop.com). Bike paths thread around the island, and having two-wheeled transport means you won't have to pay the prohibitively expensive car-ferry reservation, imposed to discourage drivers. A ride out to **Madaket** will be rewarded with a long and lovely stretch of beach on the west side of the island. **Cisco Brewers & Triple Eight Distillery** (5 & 7 Bartlett Farm Road, 1-508 325 5929, www.ciscobrewers.com) is the island's very own oasis of beer, wine and spirits. Tucked away out of town, the brewery is open to the public and offers several bars, lots of outdoor seating, food and, often, live music.

African Meeting House

29 York Street, Nantucket (1-508 228 9833, www.afroammuseum.org). **Open** *Mid Apr-mid Sept* noon-3pm Mon-Sat. *Mid Sept-Nov* noon-3pm Thur-Sat. *Dec-mid Apr* noon-3pm Fri, Sat. **Admission** $5; $3 reductions; free under-12s.

Martha's Vineyard Museum

59 School Street, Martha's Vineyard (1-508 627 4441, www.marthasvineyardhistory.org). **Open** *mid Oct-late May* 10am-4pm Mon-Sat. *Late May-mid Oct* 10am-5pm Mon-Sat; noon-5pm Sun. **Admission** $6-$7; $4-$6 reductions; free under-6s.

IN THE KNOW JOIN THE CLUB

Nantucket's seasonal bar/eaterie the **Club Car** (1 Main Street, 1-508 228 1101, www.theclubcar.com), in an antique pullman coach salvaged from the island's defunct railway, is an atmospheric spot for excellent, overstuffed lobster rolls and cocktails between late May and early October.

Martha's Vineyard

Nantucket Historical Association
15 Broad Street, Nantucket (1-508 228 1894, www.nha.org).
Walking tours (every 30mins) *late May-mid Oct* 11am-4pm daily. **Tickets** $10; $4-$8 reductions; free under 6s.
Whaling Museum hours vary by season; call or see website for details. **Admission** $20; $5-$18 reductions; free under 6s.

Where to eat & drink

As a result of all the super-rich folk on Martha's Vineyard, and the need to import most produce, dining out on the islands is expensive. If you want to splash out on the Vineyard, **L'Etoile** (22 North Water Street, 1-508 627 5187, www.letoile.net) is renowned for its contemporary French fare. The always-packed **Black Dog Tavern** (20 Beach Street, Vineyard Haven, 1-508 693 9223, www.theblackdog.com) is where everyone flocks to load up on a huge breakfast or watch the sunset – and invariably buy the T-shirt.

On Nantucket, pack a picnic with gourmet sandwiches, salads and chocolate brownies from **Something Natural** (50 Cliff Road, 1-508 228 0504, www.somethingnatural.com), or breakfast on a lobster omelette or eggs benedict at Main Street mainstay **Arno's** (no.41, 1-508 228 7001, www.arnosnantucket.com). A decent dinner can be had at the **Brotherhood of Thieves** (23 Broad Street, 1-508 228 2551, www.brotherhood ofthieves.com), followed by live music and more drinks at the **Chicken Box** bar (16 Dave Street, 1-508 228 9717, www.thechickenbox.com).

Where to stay

Good, cheap accommodation can be found on both islands, even in high season, thanks to the youth hostels: **Hostelling International – Nantucket** is at 31 Western Avenue (1-508 228 0433, www.hiusa.org); while **Hostelling International – Martha's Vineyard** is in Edgartown (525 Edgartown–West Tisbury Road, 1-508 693 2665, www.hiusa.org). Beyond that, the cost per night is

going to be pretty high – if you can even secure a room. In Edgartown, comfort and convenience at relatively modest prices can be found at the pretty, white-painted **Victorian Inn** (24 South Water Street, 1-508 627 4784, www.thevic.com), the former home of a whaling captain. In the island's south-west section, the **Beach Plum Inn** (50 Beach Plum Lane, 1-508 645 9454, www.beachpluminn.com) in the picturesque fishing village of Menemsha offers exquisitely simple rooms and cottages and a superb farm-to-table restaurant, none of which comes cheap.

Prices run even higher among the swells of Nantucket, but the local landmark **Jared Coffin House** (29 Broad Street, 1-508 228 2400, www.jaredcoffinhouse.com) isn't too exorbitant, and is packed with history. Nantucket also has a wealth of B&Bs, which are listed through services such as **Nantucket Accommodations** (1-508 228 9559, www.nantucketaccommodations.com).

Getting there

By air Cape Air (1-508 771 6944, www.capeair.com) has flights to Hyannis, Provincetown, Martha's Vineyard and Nantucket from Boston.
By car Check with the ferry services about taking cars to the islands, as there are restrictions. However, car rental firms abound and both islands have extensive shuttle-bus services for most of the year, run by the Martha's Vineyard Regional Transit Authority (1-508 693 9440, www.vineyardtransit.com) and the Nantucket Regional Transit Authority (1-508 228 7025, www.nrtawave.com).
By boat Martha's Vineyard and Nantucket are served by several ferry companies. The Steamship Authority (1-508 477 8600, www.steamship authority.com) has a year-round service from two Cape Cod locations: the trip from Woods Hole to Martha's Vineyard takes 45 minutes. The ferry from Hyannis to Nantucket is two hours and 15 minutes, or an hour on the high-speed ferry. In summer, Island Queen (1-508 548 4800, www.islandqueen.com) and Falmouth Ferry (1-508 548 9400, www.falmouthedgartownferry.com) boats run from Falmouth to Martha's Vineyard; Hy-Line Cruises (1-508 778 2600, www.hylinecruises.com) operates a seasonal service to Nantucket.

Tourist information

Martha's Vineyard Chamber of Commerce
Vineyard Haven, Martha's Vineyard (1-508 693 0085, www.mvy.com). **Open** 9am-5pm Mon-Fri.

Nantucket Island Chamber of Commerce
Zero Main Street, Nantucket (1-508 228 1700, www.nantucketchamber.org). **Open** 9am-5pm Mon-Fri.

History

*How the Cradle of
Liberty became a modern
political and intellectual
powerhouse.*

Visitors from across the USA and beyond come
to Boston to see the sites that begot America:
Faneuil Hall, the 'Cradle of Liberty' turned gift
shop; the hallowed Revolutionary battleground
of Charlestown; and the Old State House, where
the Declaration of Independence was first read
to the public in 1776.

A city with a strong political thrust, Boston
has fostered influential leaders since America's
inception, including John Adams and John F
Kennedy. It has been central in scientific
development and technological innovation,
from Alexander Graham Bell's telephone to the
world's first computer, which was built at the
Massachusetts Institute of Technology (MIT).
And as a dominant force in academia – Harvard
was the first seat of higher education in the
country – the area is known for cultivating
future visionaries, rulers and thinkers.

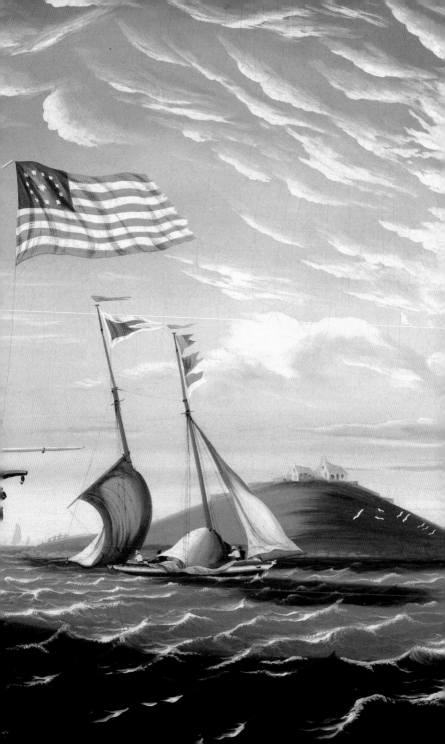

A Salem witchcraft trial

PILGRIMS' PROGRESS

Boston was heavily populated with Native Americans in 1497, when John Cabot's explorations in search of the North-west Passage to the Orient led him to claim Massachusetts for King Henry VII of England. Just over a quarter of a century later, in 1524, Giovanni Verrazano claimed the same land for Francis I of France, thus setting up more than 200 years of squabbling over what had become known as the New World. Word of this 'paradise' reached John Brewster, leader of a strict religious sect known as the Puritans. Facing persecution in England, he began an effort to establish a Puritan colony in America. And so it was that the *Mayflower*, filled with 102 passengers, set sail in September 1620 bound for 'some place about the Hudson River'. It landed nowhere near the Hudson, actually, anchoring instead, after 65 days at sea, at the tip of Cape Cod, near what is now Provincetown. Finding the area too wild for their new town, the Puritans moved on, crossing the bay and ultimately establishing their colony on a protected stretch of sandy beach close to several cornfields maintained by local tribes. They called it Plymouth.

Utopia it surely wasn't. Winters were brutal, and the Pilgrims had little understanding of the land, the kinds of crops that would grow and what native vegetation was edible. They also brought diseases with them that wrought devastation on their population and on the Native American tribes. Nearly half of the Pilgrims died of pneumonia and smallpox that first winter. But, come the spring, local tribes taught them how to plant corn, dig clams and fish for cod. By harvest time, the settlers were sufficiently established to host a three-day feast – celebrated today as Thanksgiving.

Within the next decade, 1,000 more settlers had arrived. They established Salem, on the north shore of Massachusetts Bay. These new settlers would ultimately form the foundation for what is now Boston. Choosing as their leader John Winthrop, many of them migrated south from Salem to the area now known as Charlestown. But the lack of fresh water forced them to relocate to a neighbouring peninsula, known to the natives as Shawmut. Winthrop's settlers bought the narrow 440-acre peninsula from a hermit bachelor and renamed it Tremontaine after its three surrounding hills. They soon changed their minds and renamed it again. This time, they called it Boston, after the Lincolnshire town from which many of them had originally come. As the capital of the Massachusetts Bay Colony, it quickly became the centre of activity.

STRUGGLING SETTLERS

By 1636, there were some 12,000 colonists, primarily Puritans, spread between the townships of Plymouth, Salem and Boston, with new settlements springing up almost monthly. By 1640, the population of Boston alone was 1,200. The lack of ministers to keep up with the growing population led Puritan elders to establish America's first training college, which they later named after a young minister, John Harvard, who died and left the college his library. Colonists found Massachusetts curiously easy to settle and rather empty of the anticipated hostile Indians. The fact was, epidemics of smallpox, pneumonia and influenza brought over by early settlers had decimated the once-robust native population.

Relations with the remaining tribes rapidly deteriorated. The fundamental Puritan notion of a righteous life leading to the accumulation of wealth clashed with native beliefs that it was impossible to own the land. They attempted to rid Christianity of the heathen devil by burning out the Indians' settlements and appropriating their land. The Algonquin nation, under the leadership of Chief Metacomet (known to colonists as King Philip), retaliated in 1675 by raiding several outlying English settlements. But it was all in vain. Metacomet was betrayed by one of his own warriors the following year and gruesomely executed.

The Indians were not the sole targets of Puritan intolerance. Quakers and Baptists arriving in the colonies were sometimes prevented from leaving their ships; those who practised their faith publicly were hanged for heresy. Such religious paranoia ultimately led to the witch trials of Charlestown (1648), Boston (1665) and – most infamously – Salem (1692), where 100 colonists were imprisoned and 19 were hanged in a mass hysteria that became known as the Salem Witch Trials.

'THE SACRED COD'
By 1700, Boston had grown into the third-largest port of the burgeoning British Empire. Some of the Puritans grew extremely wealthy, thanks primarily to the export of dried cod to the Caribbean and the Mediterranean. (To this day, a carved pine cod – known as 'the Sacred Cod' – hangs above the entrance to the House of Representatives in the State House, pointing towards the party in power.) Some got very rich in a notorious triangular shipping trade where sugar cane was harvested by slaves in the West Indies and then shipped to Boston to be distilled into rum. The Puritans shipped most of the rum to West Africa, where it was traded for more slaves, who were, in turn, delivered to the Caribbean sugar plantations.

One of the by-products of the city's rum production was molasses (Boston was the largest American producer of the stuff until the early 20th century). Another, more important, consequence was the introduction of slavery to American soil. By 1705, there were more than 400 black slaves – and a small number of free blacks – living in Boston.

At about the same time, England was mired in a serious financial crisis. The Crown had incurred enormous expenses during its lengthy (and inconclusive) wars with France. As some of the battles were fought in New England, and as the colonists were virtually voiceless in Parliament, it established the Revenue Act of 1764, which placed heavy duties on silk, sugar and wine from the West Indies. The colonists were irate and began the first of a series of boycotts of the imports involved.

DEATH AND TAXES
Ignoring their protest, Parliament enacted another set of taxes a year later. The Stamp Act required a heavy duty to be paid on all commercial and legal documents printed in the colonies, including newspapers. This was viewed by the colonists as an attempt to remove what little voice they had through the freedom of the press. Again they fumed. Again they felt no sympathy from England. Again they boycotted, but this time, with more force. They branded their protest with the tagline 'No taxation without representation'. They were heard, and the Stamp Act was hastily repealed a year later, but the British still attempted to keep their rebellious cousins in line. They next imposed the Townshend Acts of 1767 – a litany of levies on imported lead, glass, paint, paper and tea.

Britain's attempts to pull political rank enraged the colonists, especially those in Boston. Governmental meeting houses such as Faneuil Hall, the Old South Meeting House and the Old State House became hotbeds for revolutionary plotting. Rebels such as Samuel Adams, Daniel Webster, Paul Revere and James Otis gathered secretly to discuss the benefits of splintering off from the British Empire. Prodded by growing public outcry, civil unrest grew so clamorous it carried across the Atlantic and back to the monarch. To quiet the rumblings, George III reluctantly sent troops overseas in 1768, but military occupation in the colonies created more problems than it solved.

IN CONTEXT

Lieutenant General Thomas Gage, commander-in-chief of British forces in the colonies, was faced with a near-impossible situation. 'I wish this cursed place was burned,' he wrote in 1770. 'America is a mere bully, from one end to the other, and the Bostonians by far the greatest bullies.'

But it was the British who looked like bullies when, on 5 March 1770, a group of unarmed anti-royalists sparred with English soldiers in front of the Old State House. The redcoats were antagonised – the gathered assemblage was heckling and throwing things at them. No matter, the Brits came out looking like the bad guys, because during the fray the British troops opened fire. Five colonists were fatally shot, including Crispus Attucks, an African-American slave-turned-martyr who is considered the first casualty of the American Revolution. The colonists were outraged, and impassioned insurgent Sam Adams dubbed the incident the 'Boston Massacre'. The shooting became a rallying cry for those who supported plans for a revolution.

TEA PARTY POLITICS

Word of the incident quickly spread throughout the colonies, causing King George III to fear that this bloodshed might be the match that would light the powder keg. To avert such an outcome, the king quickly abolished the Townshend Acts – all except for its provisions on tea, which would continue to be taxed under the Tea Act of 1773. This was a little jab from the king to his subjects as George III knew it was the most popular beverage in America. Instead of easing the mood of revolt, the move added fuel to the flames and the colonists continued to plot and to boycott.

With the situation growing heated – and with the East India Company (Britain's chief exporter of tea) teetering on the brink of bankruptcy, Parliament attempted to rescue the Asian tea-sellers by exempting them from paying taxes. So while the colonists had to shell out import taxes on tea, the East India Company didn't have to pay tariffs, so it could undercut the prices of local tea merchants and flood the colonial markets. No such luck: every American port slammed shut to English tea ships – except Boston. The state's British governor, Thomas Hutchinson, stuck to the party line, ignoring the incensed citizens and

insisting that all ships could dock in Boston Harbour until the other ports accepted the tea.

The rebels hit back. On the night of 16 December 1773, a group of 60 men, calling themselves the 'Sons of Liberty' and disguised as Mohawk Indians (then seen as a symbol of freedom in the New World), stormed the blockaded ships and dumped 342 chests of tea into the harbour. This defiant act, known as the Boston Tea Party, electrified the colonies.

In September the following year, the first Continental Congress for Independence convened in Philadelphia. Massachusetts sent prominent delegates such as John Adams, John Hancock and Sam Adams to represent it and to help in the writing of the country's manifestos. At the same time, throughout the colonies, local militia began training for a fight.

THE BATTLE FOR INDEPENDENCE

The first shots of the revolution were fired in Lexington, Massachusetts, on 19 April 1775. British garrisons lodged in Boston heard about an arms store located in the nearby township of Concord. When the Redcoats left Boston to seize the Concord stockpiles on the night of 18 April, rebels Paul Revere and William Dawes set out on horseback to warn the local militia that the British troops were on their way. Paul Revere's ride (see p228 **The Ride of His Life**)

Boston Tea Party.

became one of the most famous acts of the War of Independence, and was immortalised in Henry Wadsworth Longfellow's 1861 poem. The message was sent, the British marched forth and early the next morning the world's David and Goliath came to blows. The first shot of the battle, called by the rebels the 'shot heard round the world', rang out on Lexington Green where around 70 Minutemen – an elite force of local militia members – crouched waiting to ambush 700 redcoats. The king's men quickly smothered the skirmish, killing eight rebels, and the war was under way. By then, King George was no longer reluctant to go to war. He is said to have told his counsellors: 'I am glad that blows will decide it.'

It was to be a lengthy, bitter fight, marked by heroism on the part of the outgunned, outmanned rebels, and rugged determination on the part of the British. The Americans were led by military leaders who knew only too well that their troops were fighting more with heart than skill. The colonists were plagued by a shortage of ammunition and weaponry. In the first full-scale battle of the revolution, two months after the shots at Lexington, General Israel Putnam is said to have ordered his American troops: 'Don't one of you fire until you see the whites of their eyes.' Part of the reason Putnam gave the order was to prevent the troops from wasting scarce ammunition.

That famous command came during the gory battle of Charlestown, which started on 17 June 1775, when the British attacked a group of colonists who had fortified themselves at the top of Breed's Hill. (This battle was later mistakenly identified as the Battle of Bunker Hill, which was, in fact, the next mound over.) Having learned from their mistakes earlier in the war, the unflinching colonists waged a tactically masterful fight: British casualties were more than double that of the Minutemen – more than 1,000 redcoats were killed compared to 440 rebels. Unfortunately for the Americans, the fight was so heated that they exhausted their ammunition supplies. The redcoats won that battle, but reports of the bravery of the American troops helped to inspire the spirit of insurrection throughout the colonies.

A NEW NATION

Meanwhile, in Philadelphia, the Second Continental Congress was establishing a new government. Using as an excuse the fact that King George III had not replied to a petition for redress of grievances sent by the First Continental Congress, the Second Congress gradually took on the responsibilities of a national government. In June 1775, the group established a continental army and currency. By the end of July, it had also created a post office for the 'United Colonies'. In August, England issued another proclamation, this one declaring (a bit belatedly) that the colonies were 'engaged in open and avowed rebellion'. Later that year, Parliament passed the American Prohibitory Act, which declared that all American vessels and cargoes were the property of the Crown.

It all reached a crescendo in Philadelphia on 7 June 1776. On that date, the Congress heard Richard Henry Lee of Virginia read a resolution that began: 'Resolved: that these United Colonies are, and of right ought to be, free and independent states, that they are absolved from all allegiance to the British Crown, and that all political connection between them and the state of Great Britain is, and ought to be, totally dissolved.'

The valour of the rebels in Boston ultimately resulted in the penning of the Declaration of Independence. The document, still considered one of the world's great governmental manifestos, has been taught in political science classes ever since. Its introductory paragraph is blunt and unapologetic and tells the story of how America viewed its strength in comparison to England's: 'When in the course of human events, it becomes necessary for one people to dissolve the political bands which have connected them with another… a decent respect to the opinions of mankind requires that they should declare the causes which impel them to the separation. We hold these Truths to be self-evident, that all men are created equal; that they are endowed by their Creator with certain unalienable rights, that among these are Life, Liberty and the pursuit of Happiness.'

On 4 July 1776, in Philadelphia, John Hancock of Boston signed his name to the document with a flourish. His is the largest signature by far – he is said to have written large enough that George III could read it without spectacles. Even today in the US, a 'John Hancock' is an expression for someone's signature.

IN CONTEXT

THE RIDE OF HIS LIFE

How silversmith Paul Revere became an American folk hero.

*Listen, my children, and you shall hear
Of the midnight ride of Paul Revere…*

On 18 April 1775, Boston silversmith **Paul Revere** rode to Lexington, Massachusetts, to warn patriot leaders Samuel Adams and John Hancock, and households en route, of an imminent British attack. The likely targets: the arrest of Adams and Hancock or the seizure of munitions in nearby Concord. Nearly a century later, distressed by the slavery crisis and impending civil war, America's pre-eminent poet, Henry Wadsworth Longfellow, published 'Paul Revere's Ride' in the *Atlantic Monthly* in 1861. Revere became the personification of the Revolutionary ideals of liberty and unity that Americans had seemingly forgotten. He also became a national folk hero.

Born in Boston's North End in 1735, Revere learned the silversmith's trade from his father, a French Huguenot immigrant who anglicised his name from Apollos Rivoire to Paul Revere. The silversmith was both a labourer who made shoe buckles for artisans and an artist who designed elegant rococo tea sets for merchants. Paul Revere moved between the worlds of artisans and gentlemen. In 1760, he became a member of St Andrew's Lodge of Freemasons. Freemasonry, originating in the medieval stoneworkers' guilds, reinforced his ties to the artisans who dominated his lodge.

During the Stamp Act Crisis of 1765, Revere became a 'Son of Liberty'. He and his fellow rebels believed the Stamp Act was unconstitutional because colonists weren't represented in Parliament. Revere and brother artisans and Freemasons such as Gibbons Bouve, a housewright, Adam Colson, a leather-dresser, and Thomas Crafts Jr, a painter and japanner, would be critical actors in Boston's Revolutionary resistance.

Revere's position and skills allowed him to play many roles: trusted courier, engraver of inflammatory political cartoons, and protester. As an engraver, he often adapted ideas from British publications. Using vivid

images and dramatic language, he depicted colonial resistance to the Stamp Act, the Townshend Acts, and the presence of British troops in Boston that resulted in the Boston Massacre. In *A View of the Year 1765*, his review of the Stamp Act crisis, he depicts Boston and the united colonies protecting Lady Liberty from a dragon wearing the Scottish bonnet of Lord Bute, often considered the instigator of Britain's unpopular revenue measures.

On 16 December 1773, Boston patriots took direct action against the Tea Act by destroying 342 chests of tea. Revere and several members of St Andrew's Lodge were participants in the Boston Tea Party. The next day, he began his career as messenger of the Revolution by carrying the news to New York.

IN CONTEXT

His legendary April 1775 ride to Lexington was the culmination of months of spying on British troops by Revere and other rebels. On 15 April, they observed preparations for an expedition. The following day, patriot leader Dr Joseph Warren ordered Revere to Lexington to alert Samuel Adams and John Hancock. Word was forwarded to Concord to hide the munitions.

Concerned that the British Army would arrest messengers leaving Boston for Lexington, Revere arranged the hanging of lantern signals from the Old North Church Steeple ('One, if by land, and two, if by sea'). The signals were not to Revere, as Longfellow wrote, but to patriots across the Charles River in Charlestown who sent a back-up messenger.

On 18 April, when the British marched, Dr Warren ordered Revere and William Dawes to Lexington by different routes. After delivering their news to Adams and Hancock, they decided to continue to Concord. Halfway there, they and Dr Samuel Prescott, a third rider encountered on the road, were intercepted by British soldiers. Dawes and Prescott escaped. Held at gunpoint, Revere brazenly lied that he had alarmed the countryside and there would be 500 colonials at Lexington (in reality, around 70). They released him in Lexington, where he witnessed the first shots of the Revolutionary War.

When he died in Boston on 10 May 1818, aged 83, his contemporaries celebrated Revere's Revolutionary service, as well as his accomplishments after the war: Grand Master of the Massachusetts Grand Lodge of Freemasons and founder of America's first successful copper-rolling mill. As an obituary writer observed: 'His country found him one of her most zealous and active of her sons.'

Jayne E Triber, author of A True Republican: The Life of Paul Revere *(University of Massachusetts Press).*

INDUSTRY AND IMMIGRATION

At that point, of course, the war was still far from over: the fight would last for another five years. But while much of it was fought in New England, there were no more battles in Boston. When America finally did achieve its independence in 1781, Massachusetts was one of the original 13 states constituting the fledgling United States of America.

As might be expected, British trade was cut off following the war. The loss of the English market caused Boston's status as a major port to suffer. The US economy continued to sputter until Boston embraced whaling and Far East trade; eventually, when the demand for fishing clippers grew, Boston's shipyards grew into some of the largest in the world. Other Boston creations that helped the economy were Eli Whitney's cotton gin, Charles Goodyear's vulcanised rubber, Elias Howe's sewing machine and Alexander Graham Bell's telephone.

As the city's wealth and power grew, so did its immigrant population. In the 19th century, shiploads of immigrants were turning up on its shores looking for a better life. The Irish arrived in 1845, escaping the potato famine; they were followed by tens of thousands of European immigrants seeking financial opportunity and religious freedom. By 1860, it was estimated that more than 60 per cent of Boston's population had been born elsewhere in the world.

Boston's skinny peninsula could hardly accommodate such an enormous influx of new citizens, so resourceful denizens looked to the fetid swamps of Back Bay. To make the bogs liveable, two of Boston's three hills were levelled and several feet were shaved off the top of Beacon Hill for fill. But the real work of filling in the marshy Back Bay didn't begin until the mid 1850s, when 3,500 loads of gravel a day were railed in and dumped into the muck. It took 40 years to complete the project – the largest engineering feat of its day. The result was 450 more acres of land, which doubled the city's size.

THE ATHENS OF AMERICA

'Their hotels are bad. Their pumpkin pies are delicious. Their poetry is not so good,' Edgar Allan Poe once wrote about Bostonians. And Poe was indeed correct. For a while, Boston's poetry wasn't so good. But it wasn't just the

IN CONTEXT

city's stanzas that lacked finesse; it was the entire notion of crafted aesthetics that escaped the community's inhabitants. Why had the arts been so neglected? The Puritans didn't consider the arts to be a godly practice. As for the other early colonists, many were preoccupied with gaining independence. 'I must study politics and war so that my sons may have liberty to study mathematics and philosophy in order to give their children a right to study painting, poetry, music, architecture,' wrote future US President John Adams to his wife Abigail in 1780.

Luckily, economic prosperity in the 19th century was to beget a cultural awakening. When the well-heeled 'First Families of Boston', dubbed 'Brahmins' by writer Oliver Wendell Holmes, began to travel abroad, they realised just how unenlightened their city was. It didn't take the wealthy population long to rectify the situation. In the short span between the 1840s and 1880s, Boston gained a music hall, a magnificent public library, a museum of natural history, a museum of fine arts and a symphony orchestra. These new arts showcases, coupled with the talent they attracted, earned the city the sobriquet 'the Athens of America'.

Athens was also the birthplace of the Olympics, and Boston was one of the first American cities to take sports seriously. In 1897, the first Boston Marathon ran from the nearby town of Hopkinton to Back Bay. Soon afterwards, the newly invented game of baseball swung into the city. Boston's first professional team was called the Somersets, but the name only lasted one season. In 1903, Boston's new team, the Pilgrims, hosted the Pittsburgh Pirates at the World Series; by the time Fenway Park opened in 1912, the Pilgrims were renamed the Red Sox. Six years later, the Red Sox won Boston's fifth World Series in 17 years – it would be the last time Boston would win a championship until 2004.

BREAKING THE CHAINS

Talk about being misunderstood: when Bostonian Wendell Phillips joined the Massachusetts Anti-Slavery Society, his Yankee family wanted to send him to a sanitarium. Fortunately, he withstood their persecution and eventually became one of abolitionism's most revered voices. Phillips was swayed to anti-slavery when, at the age of 24, he witnessed a lynch mob drag reputed abolitionist William Lloyd Garrison half-naked through the streets. But such savage bigotry was less common in Massachusetts than anywhere else in the country.

'The reported life expectancy of an Irish immigrant living in Boston was 14 years.'

In 1800, Boston was home to the oldest and largest population of free black people in America (a full five per cent of its then total population of 25,000), and the black community already had its heroes: Crispus Attucks was a martyr of the Boston Massacre, Peter Salem a hero of Bunker Hill. Although the black population hadn't yet been granted suffrage, they were allowed to earn wages as servants, street cleaners, shipbuilders, blacksmiths and barbers. They could also meet freely, worship as they pleased and educate themselves. The first African Meeting House in America was built on Beacon Hill in 1806, and the first black school, Abiel Smith, in 1834.

Hence, it wasn't surprising that, as tensions over slavery mounted between the North and South, Boston became the centre of the abolition movement. The New England Anti-Slavery Society was founded in 1832, and prominent blacks such as Frederick Douglass, William Nell and Maria Miller Stuart began condemning slavery publicly with the support of wealthy whites. Lewis and Harriet Hayden's house at 66 Phillips Street became a station on the Underground Railroad (a network of abolitionists whose members smuggled slaves from the South to freedom in the North). When the Civil War broke out, the first free black regiment of the Union Army – the 54th Regiment of Massachusetts – was organised on Beacon Hill, trained in Jamaica Plain and sent to battle in the Carolinas. All of those soldiers died in the war. Their story was largely forgotten for the better part of a century. Today, it is commemorated by a sculpture in the Boston Common.

NAME THAT TOWN
Boston by any other name.

Visitors may be puzzled by Boston's many monikers, but they all have logical origins. The Native Americans called it **Shawmut**, or 'unclaimed land'. When John Winthrop and his fellow Puritans defied the Indians by claiming it after all, they promptly renamed it **Tremontaine** ('three mountains') after the three local hills that dominated the place. In no time, though, the homesick settlers had redubbed their village **Boston** after the Lincolnshire village from which most of them had come. A torrent of other names soon followed, all of which have stuck around for centuries.

Take, for instance, **Beantown**. In the 18th century, Boston was fairly awash with molasses, a by-product of rum production. Because of its cheap cost and plenitude, the syrup was frequently used by colonial housewives to sweeten ordinary foods. A favourite food at the time consisted of beans that had been stewed in the sugary stuff for hours. Travellers dubbed the place Beantown after this ubiquitous dish.

In the early 1800s, Boston became America's undisputed capital of culture. It's little wonder, then, that the city became known as the **Athens of America**. Later in the 19th century, the writer Oliver Wendell Holmes gave the city the title that Bostonians love the most. In his popular 1858 essay, *The Autocrat of the Breakfast Table*, he described Boston's State House as the 'hub of the Solar System'. In no time, Bostonians had extended the concept, calling their city the hub of the universe – and **the Hub** remains Boston's most widely used nickname today.

IRISH INFLUENCE

It might be hard to believe these days, but Boston didn't always ooze unconditional love for the Irish. When the potato famine of the mid 19th century first sent over 100,000 people from Ireland to Boston, the reported life expectancy of an Irish immigrant living in Boston was 14 years. In this traditionally Brahmin city, blatant discrimination was common. Job postings often bore the clause 'No Irish Need Apply'.

After generations of political struggle, though, prejudices began to subside as the city's Irish political machine fought its way into power. The election in 1885 of the first Irish-Catholic mayor of Boston, Hugh O'Brien, started to chip away at racial biases – so much so, that eventually Irish leaders couldn't lose a race.

'Boss' James Michael Curley was perhaps the finest example of this relative invincibility. Curley was nicknamed the Purple Shamrock – and the moniker suggests, he was a colourful character. Curley served as congressman, governor and mayor, and over a chequered 40-year career in the first half of the 20th century he bought votes, got re-elected to the position of alderman while in the clink and allegedly acquired the mayoral office after threatening to expose the incumbent, John 'Honey Fitz' Fitzgerald (JFK's maternal grandfather; see p232 **Curse of the Clan**), for having a mistress. And holding true to his crooked ways, Curley spent much of his fourth and last term as mayor in a federal penitentiary, charged with mail fraud.

20TH-CENTURY BLUES

By the late 1940s, Boston had lost its major port status to the West Coast and its manufacturing to the South. What's more, it became the only major US city in the post-World War II baby boom to see a decline in population (plummeting from 800,000 to 560,000). Both the city's middle and upper classes migrated to the suburbs, and its infrastructure went with them. With downtown crime on the rise and student demonstrations blocking the streets, tourism suffered, and the city entered an economic crisis. By the mid 1960s, Boston had officially become one of the worst places to live in America.

Panicked by Boston's decline, city officials attempted to hit the brakes. Under Mayor John Hynes and the newly established Boston Redevelopment Authority (BRA), they began a 'clean up' of the city's problem areas. The 1960s saw the completion of three massive building projects, with controversial results. The Prudential Tower rose out of Back Bay's abandoned Boston & Maine railyards. Most of the West End, Boston's only ethnically mixed neighbourhood, was razed to make way for a modern apartment complex, Charles River Park. Seedy Scollay Square, home to Boston's then few gay bars and jazz joints, was levelled to make way for the new Government Center. They called it urban renewal. But, basically, much of the city's character was systematically erased in the name of progress.

However inept, though, these first efforts at regeneration did have their positive side. Organisations such as the Beacon Hill Historical Society were established to protect other neighbourhoods from suffering the fate of the West End. Public outcry caused subsequent developers to be attentive to architectural and historical significance. Today, the city retains many of its most important historical buildings despite the ravages of the planners and developers of the 1960s and '70s.

CURSE OF THE CLAN

The tumultuous history of the Kennedys.

The closest thing America has had to a 'royal family', the Kennedys came from humble beginnings. Patrick J Kennedy was an immigrant from southern Ireland who set up Boston's only Irish-owned bank. His son Joseph (born 1888) attended Harvard, married Rose, daughter of popular Boston mayor John 'Honey Fitz' Fitzgerald, and made millions in boat-building, the stock market, the movie industry and Prohibition-era bootlegging, later serving as ambassador to Great Britain. But after resigning from the position and losing his first-born in World War II, Joseph devoted himself to the political futures of his sons John, Robert and Edward.

John had all the makings of a president. A Harvard graduate, he became a decorated war hero, a Pulitzer Prize winner and a three-term US Senator. In 1960, he beat Richard Nixon to become the 35th US president. He was a popular leader whose beautiful young wife and picture-perfect children led the media to nickname his government 'Camelot'. But everyone knows what happened next.

The Kennedy clan's reversal of fortune began in 1963, when John was shot dead during a Dallas parade. Five years later, younger brother Robert, attorney general during JFK's presidency, fell to an assassin in his own bid for America's highest office. Youngest son Edward 'Ted' Kennedy also had White House aspirations, but a car accident in 1969, in which he drove off a bridge, leading to the death of his young female passenger, but failed to report the incident

until the next day, damaged his reputation and haunted his presidential bid in 1980.

In 1991, Ted's nephew William was indicted for rape, but later acquitted. Then, in 1984, Robert's third son, David, died from a cocaine overdose at the age of 28. In 1997, his fourth son, Michael, slammed into a tree while playing football on skis and died. And in 1999, dashing media darling John F Kennedy Jr was in a plane crash and died alongside his wife, Carolyn Bessette Kennedy.

After close to a century, the family's influence appears to be dwindling. Ted, who was the second most senior member of the Senate and the only one of his brothers to reach old age, died of brain cancer in 2009 after a long career. His son Patrick, former US Representative from Rhode Island, didn't run for re-election. In 2011, Ted's daughter Kara died of a heart attack after a gym workout at the age of 51, once again fuelling media chatter about the 'Kennedy Curse'.

RACE RIOTS

In the midst of financial chaos, Boston entered an emotional and moral morass. The city's 1970s race riots are notorious to this day. Possibly the most striking image from those times was shot on City Hall Plaza, when a white student tried to spear a black passer-by with a flagpole bearing an American flag. Presages of such bigotry began in 1974, when federal judge Arthur Garrity Jr ordered the city to desegregate its public school system. Before the ruling, proximity had dictated school assignment, so poor children (often racial minorities) went to school with other poor children – and received a poor education. The court saw this as a violation of civil rights and forced an end to the practice. It ordered a racial integration policy designed to give each school a ratio of black to white children that reflected Boston's overall population.

That September, under heavy police security, the Board of Education began bussing white students into black neighbourhoods and black students into white neighbourhoods. Huge riots flared up. Crowds of angry white parents and children filled the streets. Rocks were thrown at the black students. Bedlam ensued – most particularly in Irish South Boston and largely black Roxbury. While the violence exposed Boston's ugly underbelly to the nation, critics of bussing – future mayor of Boston Ray Flynn, President Gerald Ford, state politician William Bulger – argued fervently that this fight concerned other issues than racism. Many believed Boston's ethnic ghettos had evolved into close-knit neighbourhoods – both blacks and whites feared losing their hard-earned sense of community. The court disagreed.

Finally, in 1999, precisely 25 years after the racial integration programme began, the Boston School Committee voted to stop using racial quotas for school placement, saying it would never achieve its goal of making the schools truly equal. The ending was anticlimactic, nobody emerged a winner. And in the eyes of many, Boston will always be associated with those scenes of racial intolerance and hatred.

CHANGING SCENES

In the 1970s, city officials courted the emerging high-tech industry aggressively and, by the mid 1980s, Boston had reinvented itself once again. 'The Massachusetts Miracle' – as the media touted Boston's resuscitated economy – was due largely to the leadership of mayors such as Kevin White and Ray Flynn. Within the last couple of decades, Boston has become a popular location for the headquarters of national corporations. Around the turn of the century, Boston also underwent a major facelift. The city's Central Artery, a six-lane elevated freeway jutting through downtown, was one of the most congested highways in the country, as well as a blight on the cityscape. And so in the early '80s, local planners outlined the Big Dig, one of the largest, most technically complicated engineering projects ever undertaken in the United States. Construction began in 1991, giving birth to the Ted Williams Tunnel, a long underground stretch dedicated to one of Boston's most revered athletes; a new Boston landmark, the Leonard P Zakim Bunker Hill Bridge, the widest cable-stayed suspension bridge in the world; and a linear park, the Rose Kennedy Greenway. Neighbourhoods that were cut off by the expressway have become reintegrated and waterfront development continues – the jewel in the crown is the Institute of Contemporary Arts, which, when it opened in 2006, was the city's first new art museum in almost a century.

Boston continues to make national history and produce influential political figures, though none has been elected president since Kennedy. Governor Michael Dukakis ran for higher office in 1988, but was defeated by George Bush Sr; in 2004, Beacon Hill resident and Massachusetts senator John Kerry lost by a famously narrow margin to his son; eight years later, he became secretary of state in the Obama administation. Yet another Massachusetts man, former governor Mitt Romney, a devout Mormon, battled Obama in the 2008 primaries.

The Boston area has also been at the centre of the fight for gay and lesbian rights. In 2004, after a ruling by the Massachusetts Supreme Judicial Court, America's first legally recognised same-sex wedding took place in Cambridge. A proposed constitutional amendment to overturn the court's ruling was defeated by the state legislature in 2007, preserving the sanctity of same-sex marriage in Massachusetts.

IN CONTEXT

Architecture

The city of brick is in the midst of a 21st-century building boom.

IN CONTEXT

Although Boston's cityscape is commonly associated with red-brick rowhouses and the glistening State House dome, its collection of provocative contemporary buildings – as well as bland skyscrapers – is growing. New highrises downtown, in the Back Bay and South End, and a mix of cultural, commercial and residential structures on the South Boston waterfront are challenging the city's image of itself. Whether these projects are expressions of Boston's continuing vitality or eroding its historic character is an issue that is hotly debated. But along with new development has come restoration of many period buildings, and it's hard to argue with the transformation of neglected areas into attractive urban environments. In many ways, the city is looking better than it has in decades.

ARCHITECTURAL FOUNDATIONS

As with so many other urban centres, contemporary Boston grew out of successive waves of destruction and reconstruction. It was a string of massive conflagrations that transformed Boston from a colonial city of wooden structures to one of brick and stone. Fires had plagued Boston since its initial settlement – the city suffered devastating blazes in 1653, 1676, 1679, 1711 and 1761. The Great Fire of November 1872, however, was by far the most catastrophic. It started in a hoop-skirt warehouse on the corner of Kingston and Summer Streets and rapidly spread, consuming most of the city centre. Consequently, very little of Boston's early architecture still exists, and virtually all of Boston's core was rebuilt in masonry.

In fact, the only 17th-century wooden construction that remains within the city limits is the **Paul Revere House** (see p110), built in 1680. After periods as a flophouse, souvenir shop, cigar factory and grocery store, it was saved from destruction by one of Revere's descendants and restored to its original two-storey frame. Today, the house is a National Historic Landmark and museum. Next to Revere's house is the **Pierce/Hichborn House** (see p111), a three-storey brick structure built in 1711 for glazier Moses Pierce and later owned by Revere's cousin, shipbuilder Nathaniel Hichborn. Although the Pierce/Hichborn House was constructed only 30 years after its neighbour, there is a stark contrast between the two: picturesque Tudor gives way to orderly Georgian; clapboard to brick; diamond to gridded panes; a cramped winding staircase to one that is perfectly straight. The Pierce/Hichborn House was restored in the 1950s, and four of its rooms are open for tours.

The **Old State House** (see p56) is another remnant of Boston's Georgian past. Designed and constructed in 1713, this small building served as the colonial governor's offices, hence the lion and unicorn ornamentation on the façade. It was then used as a public meeting place until the Revolution, when it became the headquarters of the British Army. Topped with a richly ornamented steeple, the three-storey brick building, dwarfed by the surrounding downtown skyscrapers, now houses the Bostonian Society's museum – and, oddly, the entrance to the State Street T station.

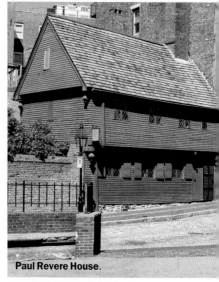

Paul Revere House.

BULFINCH'S BLUEPRINT

Though he was never formally trained, Charles Bulfinch (1763-1844) was America's first notable architect. Born into a wealthy Boston family, Bulfinch travelled extensively in England and Europe, and developed an affinity for the Greek Revival style of architecture that was fashionable at the time. Inspired, he returned to America and began designing his friends' houses for free. This led to public commissions such as the new **State House** (see p65) and the remodelling of **Faneuil Hall** (see p56).

Bulfinch is best known for the development of the Federal style – an Americanisation of the Georgian Greek Revival style – and his crowning glory outside Massachusetts is the US Capitol building in Washington, DC. Typical of this genre is the austere, three-storey brick **Harrison Gray Otis House** (see p66), one of three houses Bulfinch designed for a close friend. Completed in 1796, the flat-faced building, now the Otis House Museum, is a masterpiece of symmetry and proportion. Rooms contain false doors to maintain balance, intricately carved fireplaces and garish colour schemes – all typical of the period. Though the brick building nearly crumbled in the early 1900s, it was rescued in 1916 by the Society for the Preservation of New England Antiquities and painstakingly

IN CONTEXT

restored to its original state. Most of the rooms are now open to the public.

When the Otis family had settled into their home, there was little in the way of neighbours to block the view from its windows to the new **State House**, also designed by Bulfinch. Considered one of his best works, the State House occupies a commanding spot on top of Beacon Hill, and its gleaming gold dome can be seen for miles. Completed in 1798, it has a red-brick façade supporting white Corinthian columns flanked by tall arched windows. In 1895, the yellow-brick Brigham Annex was added to the rear, while white marble wings were added in 1917. The dome was originally clad in white wood shingles, but in 1802 Paul Revere recovered the curvature with copper sheeting and painted it grey. In 1872, as the nation's wealth grew, a coating of 23-carat gold leaf was applied. Except when it was painted grey during World War II for fear of Axis bombers, the dome has retained its glistening place on the Boston skyline.

Today, Beacon Hill is considerably more populated. Its tightly packed rowhouses reveal the extent of Bulfinch's impact, which stretched beyond his own designs.

His influence can be spotted in the brick and granite detailing, green wooden doors topped with fanlights, wrought-iron grillwork and gracious bay windows that form undulating walls along the neighbourhood's narrow, sloping streets. The preponderance of black shutters you see today are a 19th-century afterthought.

'First to spring up was the bourgeois South End, with its red brick and bay windows.'

GAINING GROUND

As the city expanded, the surrounding tidal marsh was filled in, the soft ground shored up, and new neighbourhoods were built. First to spring up was the bourgeois South End, with its red brick and bay windows. Its architecture reflects Beacon Hill's Federal traditions, and many of the side streets are modelled after Bulfinch's beloved English squares. (Two wonderfully preserved examples that are worth a visit are **Union Park** and **Rutland Square**.) The South End townhouses, however, are noticeably larger than those on Beacon Hill – their high ceilings, soaring windows and mansard roofs speak of a 19th-century preoccupation with slenderness and verticality.

Back Bay, on the other hand, takes most of its architectural cues from France's Second Empire. A fetid swamp along the Charles River in the 1850s, the Back Bay was painstakingly filled with stone and soil in the 1860s to create new land for an expanding population. This is where much of Boston's upper class moved when Beacon Hill became crowded with immigrant families. The area favours Parisian avenues over English squares, and the house façades tend towards marble and sandstone rather than red brick.

Both public and private buildings are studded with embellishments. The **Ames-Webster House** (306 Dartmouth Street), for example, sports an elaborate porte cochère that kept the ladies dry as they descended from their carriages. The **Burrage Mansion** (314 Commonwealth Avenue) is a neo-Gothic

IN CONTEXT

State House.

Burrage Mansion. *See p237.*

confection modelled on the Vanderbilt mansion in Newport, Rhode Island, itself based on the Château de Chenonceau in France's Loire Valley.

Throughout the Victorian era, the city embraced ostentation. The favoured styles of the time were Italian Renaissance, neo-Gothic and neo-Romanesque. An area then known as Art Square was one of the first parcels of land set aside in Back Bay purely to showcase the city's fledgling cultural institutions. Later renamed Copley Square, it housed imposing examples of institutional architecture, such as the Museum of Fine Arts (later relocated to make way for the Fairmont Copley Plaza), the Museum of Natural History (now occupied by upscale interiors store Restoration Hardware) and the magnificent **Boston Public Library** (*see p77*).

The library design by Charles McKim (1847-1909) is usually attributed to the Italian Renaissance style, though he claimed its ornate stone façade was equally inspired by a library in Paris, a temple in Rimini and the Marshall Fields department store in Chicago. The library was not an easy project, only completed after ten years of construction in 1895. The lobby doors were designed by Daniel Chester French, the artist who also created the statue of Abraham Lincoln in the Washington, DC memorial to the assassinated president, as well as the statue of John Harvard on the university campus in Cambridge. McKim didn't spare any expense when it came to the library's interior, commissioning murals by John Singer Sargent and Pierre Puvis de Chavannes, and sculptures by Augustus Saint-Gaudens.

While the new wing of the library (designed in 1972 by Philip Johnson) is seen as an uninspired attempt to strip down and reinterpret historic forms, McKim's original is worth a visit. Its grand staircase, vaulted reading room and enchanting cloistered garden have all been meticulously restored.

GRAND DESIGNS

Henry Hobson Richardson (1838-86) is considered one of the great American architects, his libraries, train stations and courthouses giving form to new institutions in a country on the threshold of modernity. A dozen Boston suburbs are graced by his buildings, but his masterpiece, **Trinity Church** (*see p80*), as well as the lovely **First Baptist Church** (*see p84*), are in Back Bay. A student of the Ecole des Beaux-Arts in Paris, Richardson was influenced by the heavy masonry, deep arches and elemental composition of 11th-century Romanesque architecture. The First Baptist Church, completed in 1871, is a characteristically asymmetrical composition, with a tall bell tower encircled at the top with a bas-relief by Frédéric Auguste Bartholdi, best known as the sculptor of the Statue of Liberty.

Commissioned in 1872, Richardson's Trinity Church opened in 1877 and cost almost four times the original budget. It seems it was worth the expense, as it is often cited as one of the most influential works of architecture in America. Like most of Richardson's buildings, Trinity is built with multicoloured stone walls, round arches and heavy ornamental flourishes that are rooted in history but show his inventive spirit and keen eye for composition. Stained-glass windows and other decorative elements in the interior are the work of some of the most talented artists of the day. Although the church is so solid it appears to grow out of bedrock, it actually rests on 4,502 wooden pilings driven deep into the Back Bay landfill.

Richardson's influence can be seen in a number of buildings around town, including

Trinity Church.

the **New Old South Church** (645 Boylston Street, at Copley Square) and the flamboyant **Flour & Grain Exchange Building** (177 Milk Street, near Quincy Market). His academic buildings at **Harvard** (Sever and Austen Halls; *see p135*) and suburban libraries (the **Crane Memorial Library** in Quincy is among the best) are architectural gems that all merit a visit.

URBAN OASES

The desire to develop Boston's green spaces was spurred by the development of New York's Central Park in the 1850s. Its renowned landscape architect, Frederick Law Olmsted (1822-1903), was hired by Boston's Metropolitan Parks Commission to design a five-mile corridor of continuous parkland, called the 'Emerald Necklace'. **Franklin Park**, **Arnold Arboretum**, **Jamaica Park**, **Olmsted Park**, **Riverway** and the **Back Bay Fens** are connected to each other and – through the grassy median mall of Commonwealth Avenue – to the Public Garden and the Common. The **Charles River Esplanade**, although conceived by Olmsted, wasn't developed until the 1930s. After the MBTA extended the Orange Line to the South End, the **Southwest Corridor Park** was designed as a 'new strand' of the Necklace in the 1980s.

A bleak irony shrouds the epilogue to Olmsted's career: he also refurbished the grounds of McLean Hospital in

Belmont – the sanatorium where he was to spend his final days.

HIGHS AND LOWS

Boston's first skyscraper came in 1915, with a 30-storey tower inexplicably stuck on top of the neoclassical **Custom House** (*see p57*). Shortly thereafter came the Depression, and aside from a number of art deco buildings from the late 1920s and '30s (such as the **Batterymarch** at 60 Batterymarch Street and the **John W McCormack Post Office and Courthouse** at 5 Post Office Square), few new buildings were built until the 1960s, when a new round of demolition and construction began in the name of urban renewal.

The **Prudential Center** (*see p77*), a bland, cheese grater of a tower, is widely considered to be among Boston's ugliest structures. Built in 1965, it grew out of the former site of the Boston & Albany railyards, with other towers rising around it. Its raised plazas, isolated from pedestrians, have been knit back into the streetscape with new retail and residential developments – although the glitzy 111 Huntington Avenue, with its theme-park spaceship top, makes the subtlety of the original tower look almost appealing.

Not long afterwards, most of the old West End's red-brick rowhouses, by then in disrepair, were replaced by a forest of

WALK HARVARD ARCHITECTURE

Take a stroll through the hallowed grounds of academia.

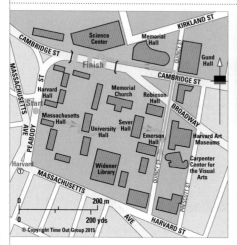

Johnston Gate.

Widener Library.

The challenging academics may take place inside Harvard's eclectic collection of buildings, but its outdoor spaces are the institution's heart and soul, offering a tree-lined vision of serenity amid the cut-throat Ivy League competition. **Harvard Yard** is the oldest; enclosed by buildings and a wrought-iron fence, it feels a world away from its surrounding neighbourhood, Harvard Square.

The most prominent entry to the yard is through **Johnston Gate** where, until the 1970s, the governor of Massachusetts arrived for students' graduation ceremonies in a carriage with scarlet-clad mounted lancers. Johnston Gate is flanked by **Massachusetts Hall** on the right and **Harvard Hall** on the left, two of the few remaining 18th-century Georgian buildings on the site.

Aligned with the gate is **University Hall**, a grey Chelmsford granite structure that has housed offices for a series of administrative functions since 1813. Its architect, Charles Bulfinch, also designed the State House in Boston and is credited with proposing the system of interconnected yards that would guide Harvard's growth for the next century.

On the other side of University Hall is **New Yard**, dominated by **Widener Library** and

Memorial Church, both built in the early 20th century. Between them stands one of Harvard's finest buildings, **Sever Hall**, designed by seminal American architect HH Richardson in 1878. Its monumental red-brick mass is penetrated by a deep archway, and a fluid system of ornamentation gives an elemental strength to the building's many bays and towers.

A short walk through or around Sever leads to a court that opens on to Quincy Street. **Robinson Hall**, to the north, was designed by New York architects McKim, Mead and White and sits opposite the even grander **Emerson Hall**. Both halls are rendered in a refined classical style that speaks of early 20th-century America: wealthy, powerful and increasingly led by the very people who wandered these walkways.

Across Quincy Street you'll see a remarkable series of buildings that challenge Harvard's stodginess. The most prominent is the **Carpenter Center for the Visual Arts** (*see p136*). A masterful sculptural composition of

Memorial Hall.

rectangular and curvilinear concrete forms built in 1960, it is the only building in the US by Le Corbusier. The towering concrete columns and ramp allow views down into studios, reinterpreting the traditional tree-lined diagonal pathways of Harvard Yard for a community of artists and filmmakers.

Next door, and now connected via a new walkway, is the rechristened **Harvard Art Museums** (see p137). Newly expanded by Renzo Piano, the structure knits together the 1927 Georgian Revival Fogg Museum façade and its travertine replica of a 16th-century Italian courtyard with a cedar-clad extension and a new glass roof.

Anchoring the other side of Cambridge Street is John Andrew's **Gund Hall**, home to Harvard's Graduate School of Design since 1972. Four gargantuan concrete 'trays' holding open studios step upwards under a vast, sloping (and sometimes leaking) roof, giving dramatic expression to the work taking place inside.

Dominating the corner, and the skyline, is **Memorial Hall**. Although it looks like a cathedral, it actually houses the dining hall and **Sanders Theatre** (see p197). Its multicoloured Victorian gothic masonry and steep slate roofs have gone in and out of fashion since 1878, when its doors opened to commemorate Harvard's contribution to the Civil War. Its neighbour is almost a century younger: the **Science Center** was the creation of Spanish architect and Design School dean Josep Lluís Sert in 1970. Its interior courtyards and walkways are a celebration of technology and community, from which future leaders will emerge.

apartment towers in a suburban-style park. Scollay Square – which in its respectable past was where Alexander Graham Bell invented the telephone, and, later, where debauchees flocked to drink, dance and visit brothels – was razed to make space for the vast expanse of **Government Center** and **City Hall Plaza**.

The respected architect IM Pei designed the master plan for Government Center, which paved red brick over acres of now prime urban real estate and reduced 22 city streets to six. Architects Kallmann, McKinnell and Knowles designed City Hall itself, and Walter Gropius's Architects Collaborative created the adjacent **JFK Buildings**. City Hall was among America's most acclaimed works of architecture when it was completed in 1968, but its intimidating scale and isolation from its context have left it an object of scorn for most Bostonians. Plans to reinvent the plaza, renovate the building, or tear it down and sell the land to developers pop up from time to time. Despite all the complaints, the transformation of neighbouring **Quincy Market** (see p55) from decaying warehouse district to successful urban marketplace – and of Boston itself into a thriving metropolis – was sparked, at least in part, by this reinvestment in the city's downtown.

DRAMATIC DEVELOPMENT

The 1970s and '80s saw a new generation of skyscrapers sprout up against the historic backdrop of brick and stone. One of the best is still IM Pei and Partners' 62-storey **John Hancock Tower** in Copley Square. Its slender profile, mirrored glass reflecting Trinity Church and angular shape, recognising the shifting street grid at the edge of Back Bay, connect it to its surroundings, using a contemporary architectural language. Although instantly more popular than the Prudential Center with most Bostonians, the Hancock did not escape controversy. While it was still under construction in 1973, a flaw in the glazing caused the windows to pop out and crash on to the streets below. Every one of its 10,344 panes had to be replaced – first with plywood, and finally with newly engineered glass.

The 1980s saw the emergence of so-called 'post-modernism', which reinterpreted historic forms in new, often exaggerated structures. Philip Johnson's grotesquely ornamented **500 Boylston Street** and his

IN CONTEXT

Boston Convention and Exhibition Center.

International Place (on Atlantic Avenue), plastered top to bottom with what appears to be Palladian-window wallpaper, typify the genre. Newer high-rises, such as Gary Handel's **Ritz-Carlton Towers** on Tremont Street by the Common, use modern forms and materials and thoughtful detailing to reflect the scale and pedestrian orientation of traditional Boston buildings.

Today, the cycle of renewal continues. The elevated highway that ripped through the city in the 1950s has finally been buried by the Big Dig, leaving a broad swathe of land for parks and public buildings, along with a renewed connection between downtown and the waterfront. The tall masts and slender cables of the 2002 **Leonard P Zakim Bridge** to Charlestown anchor one end of the Rose Kennedy Greenway.

On the harbour, Boston is slowly converting what was a post-industrial wasteland into a thriving waterfront district. Rafael Viñoly's huge but elegant **Boston Convention and Exhibition Center**, Diller Scofidio + Renfro's 2006 **Institute of Contemporary Art** (see p124) and a number of mediocre office buildings have already gone up. Elsewhere, the city is gaining several cloudbusting condos, including downtown's **Millennium Tower** (625 feet) and **1 Dalton Street**, a luxe Four Seasons hotel/apartment building designed by the John Hancock Tower's original

architect, Henry Cobb, which at 60 storeys will be Boston's tallest residential building.

Three of the city's top museums have gained high-profile extensions. In 2010, after five years and $345 million, the Museum of Fine Arts (see p90) opened its **Art of the Americas wing**, designed by London-based firm Foster + Partners. The addition comprises a central glass unit and two glass and granite pavilions decorating the north and south faces – the stone comes from the same Deer Island quarry in Maine used by the museum's original architect, Guy Lowell (1870-1927), to create the 1909 Beaux-Arts building. Museum designer du jour Renzo Piano is behind a 2012 building connected to the **Isabella Stewart Gardner Museum** (see p89), which combines glass walls with pre-patinated copper and red brick. In November 2014, the Pritzker Prize-winning architect unveiled his renovation and expansion of the **Harvard Art Museums** (see p137), which includes a contemporary cedar-clad addition to the 1927 neo-Georgian **Fogg Museum** building.

PURELY ACADEMIC

The conurbation's colleges contain a wealth of impressive modern architecture, especially across the Charles river in Cambridge. The **Massachusetts Institute of Technology (MIT)** has spent decades commissioning

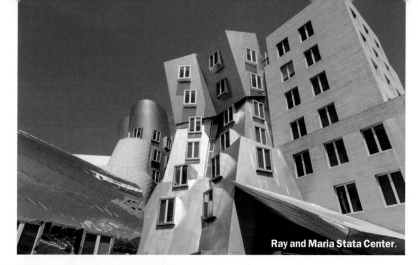

Ray and Maria Stata Center.

Kresge Auditorium.

The MIT campus also features several works by alumnus IM Pei, including the 1984 **Wiesner Building** (20 Ames Street) and the 1959 **Green Tower** (near the centre of the campus) which, at 295 feet, is the tallest building in Cambridge.

At the end of the last century, innovative New York architect Steven Holl built the ten-storey dormitory **Simmons Hall** (243 Vassar Street). The exterior is wrapped in gridded aluminum with a dozen tiny square windows for each bedroom and large amoeba-shaped openings at lounges that snake up through the building. A cross between a cave dwelling and a spaceship, it's called home by the kids who are busy inventing the future.

MIT enlisted the services of Frank Gehry, best known for his Guggenheim Museum in Bilbao, to create the **Ray and Maria Stata Center** (32 Vassar Street), a colliding series of sculptural towers and canopies held together by webs of glass, completed in 2004. The complex features a 'Toon Town' colour scheme in the interior and canted brick walls that come crashing down through the skylights.

The area's other colleges offer further exemplary works of modern architecture, suggesting that tradition and innovation can go hand in hand. Josep Lluís Sert's buildings lining the river at **Boston University**, Le Corbusier's **Carpenter Center** at Harvard and Rafael Moneo's 1993 **Davis Museum** at Wellesley provide the kind of challenging forms and spaces that keep greater Boston on the cutting edge – despite occasional protests from some of its citizens.

ground-breaking works from the world's great architects. Its campus, beside the Charles River near Kendall Square, is studded with some of the most innovative designs in the country.

In 1949, **Baker House** (362 Memorial Drive) opened its doors; one of only two works in the country by iconic Finnish architect Alvar Aalto. The six-storey student dorm is distinguished by its curvilinear plan, which gives 80 per cent of its rooms views of the Charles, and the cascading stairs at the back.

In 1955, the **Kresge Auditorium** (48 Massachusetts Avenue), brainchild of another Finnish master, Eero Saarinen, was unveiled. Kresge has an outer shell that is exactly one eighth of a sphere, balanced on delicately intersecting arches, filled in with glass, below. Saarinen's small chapel next door is a revelation, lit by rippling sunlight reflected off its own moat.

Essential Information

Hotels

American history is a big lure for many visitors to Boston, but not everyone wants to stay in historic digs. Travellers who prefer contemporary style and conveniences will be glad to hear there is now a good choice of up-to-date boutique hotels alongside the old-school luxury establishments and quaint inns. Budget options remain lean, but moderately priced hotels continue to sprout up around Boston, many of them converted from existing properties. The trendy Revere Hotel Boston Common recently reinvigorated a haggard Radisson, and the Verb, a new incarnation of a classic motel, is a retro-cool addition to the Fenway neighbourhood. New openings need to keep up with growing demand – 2014 marked the fifth straight year of increased citywide occupancy rates.

WHERE TO STAY

At the heart of the action, **Back Bay** – with its lively dining, shopping and arts scene – is the most popular area for visitors, and has a good choice of high-end and more moderately priced hotels. There's a modest sprinkling of small-scale accommodation in the hip **South End**, a prime spot for dining, drinking and taking in some culture, and **Beacon Hill**, which offers a glimpse of historic Boston. Luxury names are lining up on the waterfront to take advantage of the harbour views and lure both business travellers to the convention centre, World Trade Center and the burgeoning tech district and touristsdrawn by the increasing number of attractions and restaurants in the area.

Reflecting the needs of its most frequent visitors – academics and parents of students – **Cambridge** accommodation tends to be of the guesthouse or chain variety, with some notable exceptions.

INFORMATION & PRICES

Boston can be a pricey place to lay your head – the average hotel room rate topped $200 a night in high season, according to the latest figures from industry research specialist STR. It's wise to book ahead, particularly in the traditionally busy autumn season, and during May and June, when more than 60 college graduation ceremonies take place in the Boston area. Prices may fluctuate wildly according to season, but as a guide you can expect to pay $500 or more per night in the Deluxe category, $300-$500 for Expensive hotels, $150-$300 for Moderate accommodation and under $150 for properties listed as Budget. Rates do not include room occupancy taxes, which reach nearly 15 per cent in Boston and Cambridge.

DOWNTOWN

Deluxe

Ritz-Carlton, Boston Common
10 Avery Street, at Washington Street, Boston, MA 02111 (1-617 574 7100, www.ritzcarlton.com). Boylston T. **Rooms** 193. **Map** p280 K5.
Thanks to revitalised theatres, an influx of interesting restaurants and rapidly rising new residential towers, Downtown Boston feels more vital and vibrant than it has in years. Early to the wave of developments was this typically luxurious Ritz property, which eschews old-fashioned opulence for contemporary styling. A creamy, neutral palette creates a warm, relaxing atmosphere, and the suites are fabulous, with sweeping floor-to-ceiling

windows and imposing fireplaces. In the lobby you'll find rustic-chic American cuisine at the hotel's Artisan Bistro and a swanky cocktail scene in its Avery Bar. Guests can access the adjacent Equinox Sports Club and the Spa for a $15 fee per room, per day.

Expensive

Ames Boston Hotel

1 Court Street, at Washington Street, Boston, MA 02108 (1-617 979 8100, www.ameshotel.com). State T. **Rooms** 114. **Map** p281 L4.

Built in 1893, the 13-storey Ames Building was Boston's first 'skyscraper'. Now home to a contemporary upscale hotel, it offers expansive views of the neighbouring Financial District. Romanesque masonry meets modern design courtesy of the style wizards at Rockwell Group, which dialled down its splashier instincts for simpler drama: a massive lobby chandelier of glittering reflective discs, clear 'curiosity boxes' displaying decorative antiques and oddities, and guest rooms swathed in sophisticated mauve, tan and silver tones. In many rooms, glass partitions separate the bathroom from the bed – light the in-room fireplace and leave the curtains open, and it makes for quite a shower show. But aside from chic, the spot lacks a strong identity. There's a tiny, functional fitness centre, and the expensive downstairs restaurant, King St Tavern, has a limited menu. Still, the City Hall-side location is an excellent selling point, and Ames is well suited for business travellers who need a convenient, high-end base.

★ Langham Hotel Boston

250 Franklin Street, at Post Office Square, Boston, MA 02110 (1-617 451 1900, www.langhamhotels. com). State T. **Rooms** 318. **Map** p281 L4.

The Boston outpost of this small, international luxury chain is housed in the 1920s former Federal Reserve Bank on pretty Post Office Square. Unsurprisingly, its style leans toward Gilded Age opulence: Renaissance Revival-style public rooms with lots of polished bronze and ornate woodwork. Bottles pop and cups clink at the Reserve, a champagne lounge that also hosts a traditional afternoon tea service. Guests and locals party at BOND, a moneyed nightspot where DJs spin and a dressed-up crowd dances under glittery chandeliers. Nurse your hangover at the popular weekend Chocolate Bar in the hotel's Café Fleuri, a gloriously rich chocolate-based buffet of sweet and savoury selections, then make amends in the health club, which has a gym, saunas and a 40ft pool.

Millennium Bostonian Hotel

26 North Street, at Clinton Street, Boston, MA 02109 (1-617 523 3600, www.millenniumhotels. com). Haymarket or State Street T. **Map** p281 L3.

Part of the British hotel chain, the Millennium was revamped less than a decade ago, exchanging the demeanour of an English country inn for a more modern, if somewhat nondescript, design. Guests can gather over board games by a fireplace in the Eastern-inflected lobby, and the guest rooms – though beige and a bit ho-hum – are large and comfortable, and many have balconies. The hotel's location is the main selling point. Housed in two adjoining converted warehouses and arranged around a central brick courtyard, it sits next to historic Faneuil Hall Marketplace; Boston Harbor, the Financial District, and the North End are within easy walking distance. The hotel's contemporary American restaurant, North 26, is a retreat from Faneuil Hall's tourist bustle, but also offers patio dining for superb people-watching opportunities.

ESSENTIAL INFORMATION

Ames Boston Hotel.

Revere Hotel Boston Common.

Nine Zero

90 Tremont Street, at Bosworth Street, Boston,
MA 02108 (1-617 772 5800, www.ninezero.com).
Downtown Crossing or Park Street T. **Rooms** 190.
Map p280 K4.

When it opened in 2002, Nine Zero was one of
a select sprinkling of boutique-style hotels in
Boston. Now part of the Kimpton group, it retains
its aura of chilled-out chic – 'relax' is etched in
brass lettering on the sidewalk outside the entrance
as a welcome mantra – and exclusivity. The white-
painted rooms are sleekly modern, with plush
bed linens and oversized black vinyl headboards
(Christian Grey would approve). Extras here
include Kimpton's signature leopard-print robes,
free Wi-Fi and a complimentary 'wine hour' in the
evening. It's home to one of the city's newly celebrated cocktail joints, Highball Lounge (*see p51*),
a chic hipster-skewing den stocked with board
games, vinyl records and whimsical flourishes,
such as rubber ducks as drink garnishes.

Omni Parker House

60 School Street, at Tremont Street, Boston, MA
02108 (1-617 227 8600, www.omnihotels.com).
Downtown Crossing or Park Street T. **Rooms** 551.
Map p280 K4.

IN THE KNOW
DINNER AT CAMELOT

For a classically romantic evening,
dine at Parker's in the **Omni Parker**
House (*see above*), the country's oldest
continuously operating hotel. Reserve
table number 40, where JFK proposed
to Jackie, and split a Boston cream pie
(invented here) for dessert.

Established in 1855 as the Parker House, this is the
oldest continuously operating hotel in the country. No
opportunity is missed to remind guests that Charles
Dickens once stayed here, holding court in the Last
Hurrah bar – which became a famous literary hangout
for the likes of Longfellow, Hawthorne and Emerson.
And that's not all: Ho Chi Minh and Malcolm X were
both among the staff, and the place has put up a string
of presidents since Ulysses S Grant.

★ Revere Hotel Boston Common

200 Stuart Street, at Charles Street, Boston, MA
02116 (1-617 482 1800, www.reverehotel.com).
Tufts Medical Center T. **Rooms** 356. **Map** p283 J6.

A one-time Radisson has been transformed into a
24-floor independent property with an eye towards
hip luxury and a prime location steps from Boston
Common. A slick marble lobby and a glass of champagne greet guests at check-in. Each of the urbane
guest rooms has its own balcony offering one of several city views, from the Common to charming Bay
Village brownstones. In fine weather, pretty people
sun and swim at Rooftop at Revere, with its 50-foot,
glass-enclosed pool and open-air terrace for tippling
tropical cocktails while sunning on a chaise or kick-
ing back in one of a half-dozen cabanas. The hotel
also houses Emerald Lounge, an iridescent nightclub with a loose Land of Oz motif, a single-screen
cinema, which regularly hosts screenings and special events, and Space 57, a warehouse-sized venue
for cool city events. There's no on-site spa, but guests
receive a $25 voucher towards the nearby Exhale.

W Boston Hotel

100 Stuart Street, at Tremont Street, Boston,
MA 02116 (1-617 261 8700, www.wboston.com).
Boylston or Chinatown T. **Rooms** 235. **Map** p283 J6.

This young professional-skewed urban hotel chain
continues to expand around the country, but it hasn't
yet reached the point where ubiquity cancels out

fashionability. For that, full credit goes to the design, which eschews grand flourishes in favour of a simple, unobtrusive stylishness in public spaces and rooms, with their predictably plush beds and classy brown and blue palette. Immediately on entering the hotel, you'll find yourself in a buzzing lobby bar, crowded with visitors and after-work locals. (The restaurant space, though, still awaits a tenant after the departure of Jean-Georges Vongerichten's short-lived Boston eaterie.) The brand's Bliss Spa Boston has six treatment rooms for massages and more. At night, descend to Tunnel – a long and narrow subterranean nightclub lined with LED lights and booths where international crowds booze it up.

Moderate

Harborside Inn

185 State Street, at John F Fitzgerald Surface Road, Boston, MA 02109 (1-617 723 7500, http:// harborsideinnboston.com). Aquarium T. **Rooms** 116. **Map** p281 L4.

Occupying a converted warehouse at a prime downtown address, the sister hotel to the Charlesmark in Back Bay is one of the city's best bargains. Guest rooms feature atmospheric exposed-brick walls and simple, classic furnishings, such as mahogany sleigh beds and hand-woven Middle Eastern rugs, plus the usual modern amenities. The lobby – a bright, eight-storey atrium – is gorgeous. Although the building once bordered the harbour, due to the changing coastline there are no water views, just the bustle of business-oriented State Street and the lively bar scene around Faneuil Hall.

BEACON HILL
Deluxe

★ XV Beacon

15 Beacon Street, at Somerset Street, Boston, MA 02108 (1-617 670 1500, www.xvbeacon.com). Park Street T. **Rooms** 63. **Map** p280 K4.

Housed in a former office building just steps from the State House, XV Beacon conveys an appropriate air of discretion and exclusivity that carries considerable cachet. The sleek, spacious guest rooms are decorated in browns and beiges, enlivened by contemporary patterns, marble bathrooms and a lounge area with a grand gas fireplace (which, in our experience, seems to emit heat whether you want it or not, battling with the air-conditioning). The modern four-poster beds are a bit twee, but provide a comfy spot from which to watch the flatscreen TV. (Take note: a roof deck offers guests a rare, perfect view of the city's famed Fourth of July fireworks.) Swanky restaurant Mooo offers some of Boston's best steakhouse dining with a tongue-in-cheek twist. The hotel's free chauffeured car service is a boon, especially in winter, and the prime Beacon Hill location means you're close to most corners of the city.

Expensive

Beacon Hill Hotel & Bistro

25 Charles Street, at Chestnut Street, Boston, MA 02114 (1-617 723 7575, www.beaconhillhotel. com). Arlington or Charles/MGH T. **Rooms** 13. **Map** p280 J4.

The location for this charming hotel couldn't be lovelier: on Beacon Hill's pretty main drag, steps away from Boston Common and Public Garden, and a short stroll to Back Bay. Rooms are airy, decorated in an unfussy, updated New England style to maximise space, and equipped with flatscreen TVs and free Wi-Fi. The busy ground-floor bistro, open to the public, has a reputation for fostering fledgling talent on the local culinary scene. Only guests have access to the simple but comfy second-floor lounge and private roof deck.

► *For the bistro, see p67.*

★ Liberty Hotel

215 Charles Street, at Cambridge Avenue, Boston, MA 02114 (1-617 224 4000, www.libertyhotel. com). Charles/MGH T. **Rooms** 298. **Map** p280 H3. *See p250* **Do Some Time**.

Moderate

John Jeffries House

14 David G Mugar Way, at Charles Street, Boston, MA 02114 (1-617 367 1866, www.johnjeffries house.com). Charles/MGH T. **Rooms** 46. **Map** p280 H3.

Named after the co-founder of a free eye clinic for Boston's poor (now the renowned Massachusetts Eye and Ear Infirmary), this building was originally a nurses' residence. These days it's a comfortable guesthouse, modestly done up with reproduction Victorian decor, but kept quite simple. Rooms range from small studios to full suites; most include a kitchenette, complete with refrigerator, stove and microwave. Complimentary continental breakfast is served each morning in the common room on the ground floor, and there's also free Wi-Fi. The shops and restaurants of Beacon Hill's Charles Street are on your doorstep, and Back Bay is within strolling distance.

WEST END
Moderate

Boxer Hotel

107 Merrimac Street, at Staniford Street, Boston, MA 02114 (1-617 624 0202, http:// theboxerboston.com). North Station T. **Rooms** 80. **Map** p280 K3.

The 110-year-old Flatiron building, a minor West End landmark, recently swapped tenants. Out went the Bulfinch Hotel, and in is the Boxer, a smartly updated incarnation with era-jumping nods to history. The lobby ceiling is emblazoned with an 1860 map of Boston, while the 1960s are referenced with the *Mad Men*-evoking Finch restaurant, which serves New England comfort food and cocktails in a parlour-like space with exposed brick and comfy club chairs. The rooms received an industrial-chic makeover that incorporates blue slate, riveted-steel wardrobes, tech-friendly amenities and some retro-inflected design elements. There's even a collection of bunk rooms, which stack a full-size and twin bed – less expensive than a two-double-bed option, they're great for families or room-sharing friends. Crisp and comfortable, the Boxer is a solid new entry to an area that is woefully underserved for accommodation.

Onyx Hotel

155 Portland Street, at Valenti Way, Boston, MA 02114 (1-617 557 9955, www.onyxhotel.com). Haymarket T. **Rooms** 112. **Map** p280 K3.

This Kimpton property is a tasteful, pet-friendly bolthole amid a surprising dearth of accommodation by TD Garden, the city's largest sports and concert venue. The small rooms are decorated with clean, elegant lines and a bold red, black and taupe colour scheme. It may be short on space, but the Onyx doesn't skimp on style or service. Top-of-the-line amenities are in abundant supply, from feather-down pillows to in-room spa services (at an extra charge), and forgotten toiletries and other

DO SOME TIME

Spend the night in prison – in style.

Fancy spending the night in a cell? It's a lot more appealing than it sounds at the luxurious **Liberty Hotel** (*see p249*), set inside the former Charles Street Jail, which once housed a number of famous – and infamous – inmates: Malcolm X; Sacco and Venzetti, whose controversial trial and subsequent execution are often cited as an argument against the death penalty; and early-20th-century politician James Michael Curley.

Built in 1851 by the Charles River near Beacon Hill, it was a model prison for the times – but by the 1970s, the facility was outmoded and in disrepair, known for its dire conditions. A district court ruled that the jail violated prisoners' constitutional rights, and it finally closed in 1990.

Needless to say, there's no trace of its former squalour. For its conversion into a luxury hotel, some $120 million was pumped into renovations and the construction of an adjacent 16-storey wing, which contains most of the 298 guest rooms. As the jail is a National Historic Landmark, the refurbishment has preserved the cruciform-shaped building's original features. The airy 90-foot central rotunda, which houses the main lobby, is topped by a cupola that was formerly covered over; magnificent, original floor-to-ceiling windows overlook the landscaped patio. The catwalks that link the jail's public spaces were also kept, along with the cells in the cocktail lounge, Alibi.

Inside the restored landmark are two restaurants, Clink and Scampo, which also milk the vestiges of prison architecture for all they're worth. The food at Clink, the fine-dining option, treats local ingredients with modern American flair, but has received

mixed reviews. Scampo is a more reliable option, offering casual elegance and Italian cuisine from Lydia Shire, a flame-haired chef who is noted as one of the city's best.

Rooms are more comfortable than cutting edge, with pale, neutral decor, mahogany furniture and handmade patchwork throws. Luxuries abound, from plush bedlinen and Molton Brown toiletries to flatscreen HD-LCD TVs, wireless internet and VoIP telephones.

essentials are free on request. Be sure to stop by the lobby for the complimentary early evening wine hour. There, you'll also find the crimson-swathed cocktail bar, Ruby Room, which is serviceably swanky in an early 2000s way.

BACK BAY & FENWAY
Deluxe

Four Seasons
200 Boylston Street, at the Public Garden, Boston, MA 02116 (1-617 338 4400, www.fourseasons. com). Arlington T. **Rooms** 273. **Map** p280 J5.
The five-star Four Seasons is known for its famous guests. When the Stones roll into town, this is where they set up camp. Problem: there's only one Presidential Suite, an apartment complete with baby grand piano and dedicated maid or butler service. So who gets it, Mick or Keith? Or do they bunk up together? Apparently, Keith defers to his Glimmer Twin and takes the less lavish – but still deluxe – Ambassador Suite. Built on the site of a former Playboy Club, the hotel boasts an ideal location in the Back Bay, with swooning views of the Public Garden and impeccable service and amenities, such as a 44ft swimming pool and spa, neither of which is open to the public.

★ Mandarin Oriental
776 Boylston Street, at Fairfield Street, Boston, MA 02199 (1-617 535 8888, www.mandarinoriental. com/boston). Copley or Hynes Convention Center T. **Rooms** 136. **Map** p282 G6.
Blending global luxury, Back Bay style and New England charm, the Mandarin Oriental is a posh, relaxing retreat from the crowds outside: some of the city's most sought-after shopping and dining is just steps away. But inside the Mandarin, elegant and modern guest rooms wow with stately, east-meets-west decor, marble-covered bathrooms, and small luxury-minded details, like sumptuous Frette linens, that satisfy upper-crust tastes. Adjacent to the lobby is an outpost of star chef Daniel Boulud's accessibly upscale bistro and wine bar, Bar Boulud, which serves seasonal French fare in a warm, inviting dining room that subtly suggests the interior of a wine barrel with curved oak ceiling panels overhead. The five-star spa pampers guests with hydrotherapy, steam rooms, vitality pools and more.

Taj Boston
15 Arlington Street, at Newbury Street, Boston, MA 02116 (1-617 536 5700, www.tajhotels.com). Arlington T. **Rooms** 273. **Map** p283 H5.
After 80 years, the venerable Ritz-Carlton on Arlington Street was taken over by the Indian hotel group Taj in 2007. While tea at the Taj may not have quite the same ring to it as tea at the Ritz, very little has changed about the old girl, really. As the Ritz, it had already undergone refurbishment that kept to

its old-world European style. Decor is unremarkable but pleasantly pastel, with plenty of ruffled window adornments and dark woods, creating a classic, elegant feel. Rooms vary from standard deluxe and garden view (the only difference being they overlook the Public Garden) to the 1,540sq ft Presidential Suite, with its own jacuzzi, parlour, kitchen and a dining area that seats six. Taj Boston Club guests have members-only services and privileges, and a dedicated, catered lounge. As the Ritz, the place had a mystique engendered by decades of famous guests, from Frank Sinatra to Winston Churchill. It may look basically the same, but there's no doubt that an era ended when the new nameplate went up.

Expensive

Colonnade Boston Hotel
120 Huntington Avenue, at West Newton Street, Boston, MA 02116 (1-617 424 7000, www. colonnadehotel.com). Prudential T. **Rooms** 285. **Map** p283 G7.
Out went fuddy-duddy floral decor and in came sleek, modern elegance: the genteel Colonnade Hotel's renovations create a boutique hip, but with a smart, individual edge to the design. Rooms are a blend of geometric patterns, blond woods, chrome and a soothing neutral colour palette. A small, shimmering guests-only rooftop pool, 11 storeys above street level, is another enticement to check in. The art deco-inspired bar offers great cocktails and the ground-floor restaurant, Brasserie Jo, serves classic French cuisine.

Eliot Hotel
370 Commonwealth Avenue, at Massachusetts Avenue, Boston, MA 02215 (1-617 267 1607, www.eliothotel.com). Hynes Convention Center T. **Rooms** 95. **Map** p282 F6.
This tried, true, traditional hotel will satisfy visitors who want a Brahmin-style stay in the Back Bay. With just under 100 rooms, the stately brick building conveys Old World class. At once relaxed and refined, the Eliot has the air of a mini grand hotel – from its marble reception area to the snug but elegant guest rooms, which are accessed by an old-fashioned turnkey. Downstairs, celebrated chef Ken Oringer presides over Clio, serving expensive, slightly esoteric French cuisine, and Uni Sashimi Bar, both among Boston's best restaurants. Free access to a nearby Boston Sports Club is a perk for gym-goers. *Photo p252.*

★ Fairmont Copley Plaza
138 St James Avenue, at Copley Square, Boston, MA 02116 (1-617 267 5300, www.fairmont.com/ copleyplaza). Copley T. **Rooms** 383. **Map** p283 H6.
The little sister to New York's Plaza occupies a prime spot overlooking Copley Square. Built in 1912, its mirrored and gilded lobby and function rooms are quite spectacular, with beautiful murals and ornate ceilings.

ESSENTIAL INFORMATION

Eliot Hotel. See p251.

The place has long hosted presidents, diplomats and dignitaries, but it doesn't coast on its dignified past. The Copley Plaza has introduced modern comforts while preserving its old-fashioned charm; rooms have high-speed internet access as well as stately armchairs, wooden headboards, and abundant marble in the bathrooms. On the fourth floor, the discreet Fairmont Gold hotel-within-a-hotel has its own dedicated check-in and concierge, business centre and lounge. Draped in tones of gold and burgundy with tufted leather seats, the reimagined Oak Long Bar + Kitchen breathes handsome new life into the former Oak Room, a Boston institution and one of the best spots for a (correspondingly high-priced) martini.

Hotel Commonwealth

500 Commonwealth Avenue, at Kenmore Square, Boston, MA 02215 (1-617 933 5000, www.hotel commonwealth.com). Kenmore T. **Rooms** 149. **Map** p282 D6.

While Boston old-timers can tell you about the punk shows and rave days on club-filled Lansdowne Street, these days the area around Fenway Park is a much more family-friendly place. Loads of new restaurants and residential buildings have sprung up, and this sprawling Kenmore Square property was early to the transformation. Inside, spacious suites and rooms have a rustic, boutique elegance, good soundproofing and superbly comfortable, Italian-linen-clad beds. (Themed accommodations include the new Rathskeller Suite, a rock memorabilia-stocked, graffiti-brushed nod to the famously grungy punk club that once stood on the site.) Attached to the hotel are Eastern Standard, a hip American brasserie, lauded seafood restaurant Island Creek Oyster Bar, and the Hawthorne, a subterranean cocktail lounge that is among the city's best.

★ Inn @ St Botolph

99 St Botolph Street, at West Newton Street, Boston, MA 02116 (1-617 236 8099, www. innatstbotolph.com). Prudential T. **Rooms** 16. **Map** p283 G7.

Named for the patron saint of travellers, this gem of a guesthouse flies as much under the radar as its sister property XV Beacon (*see p249*) hogs the spotlight. The Back Bay brownstone is outfitted as a series of suites, each with kitchenettes, and entrances accessed by passcodes provided prior to arrival. The property lends itself well to extended stays in a vibrant corner of town, with in-room amenities that run deep: from 42inTVs to gas fireplaces and video intercoms. And the team threw its weight behind impressive interior design: guest room decor is stylish and handsome, modern and metro with oaky woods, thick striped upholstery, and houndstooth fabrics. All rooms have big bay windows, while certain suites enjoy the cool, curved alcove formed by the building's charming turret. There's basic maid service, and a laundry facility where long-stay guests can wash their own clothes. It's a pretty hands-off property – which may be just what the independently minded tourist ordered.

Lenox

61 Exeter Street, at Boylston Street, Boston, MA 02116 (1-617 536 5300, www.lenoxhotel.com). Copley T. **Rooms** 214. **Map** p283 G6.

The privately owned Lenox, which first opened in 1900, boasts a prime location next to the Boston Public Library (*see p77*). The hotel's old-style gold and blue decor oozes quiet elegance, while its rooms are outfitted with brass chandeliers, dark wood furniture and marble bathrooms; several also feature

ESSENTIAL INFORMATION

working fireplaces, as does the charmingly restored lobby. The Lenox also houses the chic American eaterie City Table, its sibling City Bar, typically a young-professional cocktail klatch, and the homey, casual Irish pub Sólás.

Loews Boston Hotel

154 Berkeley Street, at Stuart Street, Boston, MA 02116 (1-617 266 7200, www.loewshotels. com). Arlington or Back Bay T. **Rooms** 224. **Map** p283 H6.

Formerly known as the Back Bay Hotel, and before that Jury's, this modern lodging is housed in the former headquarters of the Boston Police Department. The classic 1920s exterior is in sharp contrast to the contemporary, playful interior design, which features a cool glass staircase, waterfall, lobby fireplace and quirky elevators with night-clubby neon lighting. Guest rooms are superb and spacious, eschewing minibars in favour of fridges that guests can fill with their own supplies. You might find laptop warriors working in the library-like lounge, Apothecary, or tossing back cocktails in Precinct Kitchen + Bar, a seafood- and charcuterie-focused restaurant that spills from a subway tiled interior onto a sidewalk patio warmed by fire pits.

Moderate

Copley Square Hotel

47 Huntington Avenue, at Exeter Street, Boston, MA 02116 (1-617 536 9000, www.copleysquare hotel.com). Back Bay or Copley T. **Rooms** 143. **Map** p283 G6.

Back Bay's first hotel, the Copley Square opened for business in 1891; in recent years, millions of dollars in renovations have given it a trendier sheen. Rooms are small, but the location is excellent, and the hotel has a solid reputation, with friendly and efficient staff. Come weekends, there's even a small social scene. Restaurant XHALE rarely attracts locals, but the same can't be said of Minibar, a cloistered contemporary cocktail lounge. And though the subterranean nightspot Storyville named for the now-defunct Boston jazz bar that hosted legends like Ella Fitzgerald and Billie Holiday, today you'll find DJs spinning house music in a flock wallpaper-lined bordello filled with international party people.

enVision

81 South Huntington Avenue, at Craftson Way Boston, MA 02130 (1-617 383 5229, http:// envision-hotel-boston.com). Back of the Hill T. **Rooms** 39.

This affordable option is located in a residential area just a few stops on the T's above-ground Green Line from the Museum of Fine Arts and the Isabella Stewart Gardner Museum. Guests trade an in-the-thick-of-it location for competitive rates in clean, contemporary guest rooms of green and

yellow that won't surprise but will satisfy: you'll find iPod docks and Keurig coffee makers, robes and slippers, and microwaves for reheating restaurant leftovers. There's a small but useful fitness area, a serviceable café for coffee and grab-and-go snacks, and the hotel hosts near-nightly 'soirées' for guests, such as a Wednesday ice-cream social. Depending on your priorities, enVision can do the trick at a nice price.

Gryphon House

9 Bay State Road, at Beacon Street, Boston, MA 02215 (1-877 375 9003, www.inboston.com). Kenmore T. **Rooms** 8. **Map** p282 E6.

Occupying an old townhouse tucked between Back Bay and Kenmore Square, this comfy, upscale bed and breakfast couldn't be accused of minimalism. If you're not averse to a bit of Victorian-style clutter, it's a charming, warm retreat, pleasantly situated off the main drag. Each of the eight suites is individually decorated; some have gas fireplaces and all are equipped with refrigerators and your own cocktail or 'wet' bar.

Hotel 140

140 Clarendon Street, at Stuart Street, Boston, MA 02116 (1-617 585 5600, http://hotel140.com). Back Bay or Copley T. **Rooms** 65. **Map** p283 H6.

Sharing a landmark 1920s building with original tenant the YWCA, private apartments and the Lyric Stage Company, Hotel 140 is great value. While it may not be the pinnacle of luxury – the modern decor is plain but unassuming, with blond wood and neutral colours – the rooms come with all modern conveniences (including high-speed internet and nice bathroom products), the staff are very friendly and the Back Bay location is hard to beat.

Newbury Guest House

261 Newbury Street, between Gloucester & Fairfield Streets, Boston, MA 02116 (1-800 437 7668, www.newburyguesthouse.com). Hynes Convention Center T. **Rooms** 32. **Map** p282 F6.

Perfect for shopaholics or anyone who wants to stay on Boston's chicest strip, this pleasant townhouse B&B is set amid retail heaven. Rooms are fitted out with reproduction Victorian furnishings, in keeping with the building's hardwood floors and high ceilings. There's a homey atmosphere, though the noise from the street does filter into the guest quarters. A breakfast buffet is served in a bright parlour that opens on to a small terrace. It's good value for the location – and what you save on hotel rates you can spend in the shops.

Verb Hotel

1271 Boylston Street, at Yawkey Way, Boston MA 02215 (1-855 695 6678, www.theverbhotel.com). Fenway or Kenmore T. **Rooms** 93. **Map** p282 D7. *See p255* **Playing Away**.

Budget

Florence Frances Guest House

*458 Park Drive, at Medfield Street, Boston, MA
02215 (1-617 267 2458). Fenway or St Mary
Street T.* **Rooms** 3. **No credit cards.**
Former actress Florence Frances offers three
guest rooms in her 19th-century townhouse. Each
is lovingly decorated around a theme – take the
flamenco-fabulous 'Spanish' room, which features
a bold red and black colour scheme and decorative
fans. Depending on your taste, you'll either find
it delightfully kitsch or bordering on tacky – the
communal bathroom (there are no private ensuites)
features a toilet seat inlaid with silver coins. There's
also a comfortable lounge, a roof terrace and free
parking at the back.

Oasis Guest House

*22 Edgerly Road, at Stoneholm Street, Boston,
MA 02115 (1-617 267 2262, www.oasisgh.com).
Hynes Convention Center or Symphony T.* **Rooms**
8. **Map** p282 F7.
With its peaceful yet central location and reasonable
prices, the Oasis is a welcome find. Its clean, comfortable rooms have up-to-date amenities, including
Wi-Fi, attracting non-expense-account business
travellers as well as tourists. Complimentary continental breakfast is served in the cosy lounge – which,
like the outdoor deck areas, is a pleasant place to
relax. There's also a kitchen for guests.

SOUTH END
Moderate

Chandler Inn

*26 Chandler Street, at Berkeley Street, Boston, MA
02116 (1-617 482 3450, www.chandlerinn.com).
Back Bay T.* **Rooms** 56. **Map** p283 H7.
If you fancy staying in one of Boston's chicest
residential neighbourhoods, book a room at this
gay-friendly South End guesthouse. Rooms have
ensuite bathrooms and are equipped with all mod
cons: satellite TV, voicemail and free Wi-Fi. Several
have been revamped as 'deluxe' quarters with
boutique-style design and amenities, including
plasma TVs, iPod docks and marble bathrooms
with walk-in showers. Complimentary coffee and
tea are offered throughout the day in the lobby.
Trophy Room, located on the ground floor, is a sleek
but affordable American bistro with a popular
brunch and bar scene. It can be noisy at weekends;
non-party people are advised to request a room on
the upper floors. Across the street, the affiliated
Chandler Studios offers tricked-out accommodations for longer stays.

Clarendon Square Inn

*198 West Brookline Street, at Warren Avenue,
Boston, MA 02118 (1-617 536 2229,
www.clarendonsquare.com). Back Bay or
Prudential T.* **Rooms** 4. **Map** p283 H8.
Housed in a beautifully renovated 1860s merchant's
townhouse, this luxury bed and breakfast is a far
cry from Boston's staid image – take the rooftop hot
tub, for instance, with its views over Back Bay. Guest
rooms are individually designed and furnished with
impeccable attention to detail, mixing carefully chosen antiques with sleek contemporary pieces. Some
rooms have original (non-functioning) fireplaces.
Marble and limestone bathrooms and high-thread-
count linens add to the appeal, but there are no
king-sized beds, only queens. The Clarendon suite,
with its splendid freestanding Victorian bath, is popular with romantics. Wi-Fi is complimentary, and
two guest parking spaces (which they recommend
reserving in advance, $30) are a boon in the area.

Budget

40 Berkeley

*40 Berkeley Street, at Appleton Street, Boston,
MA 02116 (1-617 375 2524, www.40berkeley.
com). Arlington or Back Bay T.* **Rooms** 200.
Map p283 H7.
Formerly a YWCA, this centrally located property
offers private and dorm-style rooms for those with
leaner pockets. Though comfortably furnished,
it's a no-frills operation. The rooms have free
Wi-Fi but no telephones or televisions; you will
find them in the public spaces, which include a
living room with fireplace and game room with
billiards table. If you're travelling on a tight budget, you could do a lot worse.

WATERFRONT
Deluxe

Boston Harbor Hotel

*70 Rowes Wharf, at Atlantic Avenue, Boston,
MA 02110 (1-617 439 7000, www.bhh.com).
Aquarium T.* **Rooms** 230. **Map** p281 M4.
The Big Dig blighted the Harbor Hotel's west side
for years, but now – overlooking the Rose Kennedy
Greenway (*see p118*), as well as the harbour – the
hotel is having the last laugh. It's in a superbly
central location, close to the Financial District and
the restaurant-rich Fort Point neighbourhood.
Although the decor is old-fashioned by most hotel
standards – New England country-house-style flo-
rals and heavy woods – it's understated, not fussy,
and the lobby's high ceilings and cool marble add
an air of classic elegance. Rowes Wharf Bar has
the atmosphere of a gentlemen's club, while the
stunning restaurant Meritage (*see p118*) offers
first-class dining; the Alley Bar is less formal. The
hotel's spa and fitness rooms are among the best in
the city, with a welcomingly warm 60ft pool as the
centrepiece. Outdoor movies and music keep its
waterfront plaza lively in the summer.

PLAYING AWAY

An amped-up classic motel welcomes baseball and music fans alike.

Best known as the stomping ground of the Boston Red Sox at Fenway Park, Kenmore Square is now in the midst of a condo and restaurant boom. But for decades it was the grungy nexus of the greater Boston rock scene. Although Lansdowne Street is still the location of one of the city's biggest music venues, House of Blues (*see p188*), the area was once rocking with numerous nightspots, including the Rat, Jumpin' Jack Flash and megaclub complex Metro and Spit. These days, you're more likely to find an artisanal cocktail than an underground gig, but you can get a taste of the area's gritty glory days at the **Verb Hotel** (*see p253*), a remodelling of the 1959 Fenway Motor Hotel ('Verb' references reverb). In addition to hosting baseball players, the two-storey, horseshoe-shaped lodging put up an impressive line-up of pop stars over the years, from Tony Bennett and Connie Francis in the '60s to Joe Strummer and the Ramones in the '80s.

In its new incarnation, the hotel is decorated with rock and pop culture ephemera and memorabilia, curated by David Bieber, veteran special projects manager at former rock stations WBCN and WFNX, and the late alternative weekly, the *Boston Phoenix*. Bieber selected around 300 items from his massive collection, which will rotate at the Verb. 'It's Boston-oriented as much as possible,' he says. There's an

autographed cover of the first Boston album signed by all members; matching Velvet Underground 'banana' albums signed by Lou Reed, and a stairwell admonition to 'Walk this way' after the Aerosmith song.

The small lobby is adorned with original framed posters of Boston rock shows (The Who, Led Zeppelin and the Velvet Underground at Lansdowne's old Tea Party club in May, 1969, for example), dozens of neatly stacked old *Rolling Stone* magazines, and 300 era-spanning LPs and 45s, many by Boston-based artists, which you can play on a vintage Realistic turntable.

Framed *Phoenix* covers adorn the walls of each of the 93 guest rooms. In keeping with the property's midcentury roots, the contemporary furnishings have a retro edge, with lighting and fabrics that evoke the Kennedy era. In each room, a Modernica saucer ceiling light pendant, originally designed by George Nelson in 1947, hangs over a sleek, minimalist sofa. And while there's free Wi-Fi, you can also type an old-school letter home on the in-room manual or electric typewriter. The TV, however, is an up-to-date 47-inch flatscreen.

Further perks include a 15-foot by 30-foot courtyard pool and a Japanese restaurant/bar, Hojoko, helmed by Tim and Nancy Cushman, the James Beard Award-winning duo behind O Ya (*see p58*), due to open around the time of publication of this guide.

ESSENTIAL INFORMATION

THE CHAIN GANG

Stay with someone you know.

In addition to the hotels listed in this chapter, many moderately priced chains have outposts in Boston and Cambridge. **Marriott** (1-888 236 2427, www.marriott. com) has several branches downtown and beyond, including the remarkable Custom House in the landmark tower (see p57) and the Courtyard Boston Tremont, housed in a splendid 1920s building.

Westin and **Sheraton** (1-888 625 5144, www.starwoodhotels.com) offer comfortable options in convenient locations downtown, and the **Hyatt** chain (1-888 591 1234, www.hyatt.com) has a downtown address as well as its unusual pyramid-style property overlooking the Charles River in Cambridge. More budget-conscious options include **Best Western** (1-800 780 7234, www.bestwestern. com), which has several locations in the Boston area.

Expensive

InterContinental Boston

510 Atlantic Avenue, at Pearl Street, Boston, MA 02210 (1-617 747 1000, www.intercontinental boston.com). South Station T. **Rooms** 424. **Map** p281 L5.

What the InterContinental lacks in front entrance grandeur – its shallow forecourt is parked on a busy street – it makes up for with a snazzy, Vegas-style glamour. Locals and guests enjoy sleek Sushi-Teq, an unusual hybrid of a sushi bar that also specialises in premium aged tequilas, and RumBa, a waterfront place to party. The sunny restaurant Miel (*see p118*), meanwhile, serves excellent Provence-inspired food 24/7; its name references the honey that's harvested from the hotel's rooftop beehives. The inviting rooms are chic and contemporary, but warm woods and rich accent colours save them from clinical minimalism. Some have splendid canopied four-poster beds, others stunning harbour views; all are kitted out with large HD TVs and soaking tubs. Club InterContinental offers high flyers a dedicated floor of extra pampering and exclusive business services, but even non-guests are baited by the body treatments at its tranquil, sprawling spa, which also boasts a heated indoor lap pool.

Seaport Hotel

1 Seaport Lane, between Seaport Boulevard & Congress Street, Boston, MA 02210 (1-617 385 4000, www.seaportboston.com). Silver Line Waterfront to World Trade Center. **Rooms** 428. **Map** off p281 N5.

Before the harbour area development, the Seaport was a lone beacon, accommodating business types attending the adjacent Seaport World Trade Center. Now that the nearby Institute of Contemporary Art (*see p124*) has broadened its attractions and Fort Point is blossoming, putting up here offers a different perspective on the city. Facilities are faultless: the spa is highly recommended, while the third-floor fitness centre has a wonderful 50ft pool with sky views and underwater music. There's also plentiful parking in the adjacent garage, and an in-house restaurant, Aura, along with TAMO Bistro & Bar, offering quirky noshes. Innovations include the touchscreen in-room 'Seaportal' service, which provides guests with VoIP telephone calls, information on local dining spots, cultural attractions and events, and the latest flight information from Logan International's website – all at the tap of the monitor screen.

CAMBRIDGE

Expensive

Charles Hotel

1 Bennett Street, between University Road & Eliot Street, Harvard Square, Cambridge, MA 02138 (1-617 864 1200, www.charleshotel.com). Harvard T. **Rooms** 295. **Map** p284 A2.

Sophisticated, modern, but with still a hint of quaintness, the Charles Hotel has an air of relaxed refinement that befits its smart Harvard Square location. Rooms are kept simple, with a New England aesthetic that includes Shaker furniture and handmade quilted comforters on the beds. DVD players, flatscreen TVs and sleek Seura 'in mirror' bathroom televisions add to the air of unobtrusive luxury. The Charles is home to an impressive line-up of bars and restaurants: the renowned Rialto (*see p132*); Henrietta's Table, whose menu highlights organic and local produce; the seductive bar Noir; and the Regattabar (*see p193*), a nationally recognised jazz hotspot. In winter, a skating 'pond' is set up in the hotel's courtyard. All in all, a unique place to stay.

Hotel Marlowe

25 Edwin H Land Boulevard, at Cambridgeside Place, Cambridge, MA 02142 (1-617 868 8000, www.hotelmarlowe.com). Lechmere T then 10min walk. **Rooms** 236. **Map** p280 H2.

The nondescript exterior of this modern block near the Cambridgeside Galleria mall doesn't prepare you for the flamboyant melange of fake animal prints and rich colours within. The decor may be loud, but the atmosphere is laid-back, unpretentious and fun. The early evening complimentary wine hour – a Kimpton chain-wide perk – offers the opportunity to unwind and meet other guests in the lobby guests in the lobby lounge, with its huge fireplace. Although the hotel feels removed from the main cultural and commercial areas of the city (the mall notwithstanding), it's within walking distance of the bars and restaurants of Kendall Square (and a short subway ride to Central and Harvard Squares). If you don't feel like a trek, Bambara Kitchen & Bar is a casual-chic American restaurant and cocktail haven that is also frequented by non-guests. Some of the rooms offer wonderful views over the river.

Hotel Veritas

1 Remington Street, at Massachusetts Avenue, Harvard Square, Cambridge, MA 02138 (1-617 520 5000, www.thehotelveritas.com). Harvard T. **Rooms** 31. **Map** p284 B3.

Smack in the middle of Harvard Square, this delightfully lush boutique hotel turns heads. The 31-room property is old Cambridge meets Italian minimalism – hints of both can be found everywhere, from the crown moulding in every room to the luxurious Anichini bed linens. Guest rooms are definitely small, but the art deco-inflected decor is refined. Unapologetically indie, Veritas will appeal to travellers who like local flavour without cringeworthy tourist pandering: works by local artists line the walls, and the intimate lobby lounge offers charcuterie from revered Cambridge cheese shop Formaggio Kitchen, and beers and spirits from local microbreweries and distilleries. A business centre is a nice bonus, especially since many guests are staying for its proximity to the university.

Moderate

A Bed & Breakfast in Cambridge

1657 Cambridge Street, at Trowbridge Street, Harvard Square, Cambridge, MA 02138 (1-617 868 7082, http://cambridgebnb.com). Harvard T. **Rooms** 3. **Map** p284 B2.

A few minutes' walk from Harvard University, this family-run B&B offers three rooms (with shared bathroom), each furnished in keeping with the Colonial Revival-era house, built in 1897. The complimentary breakfast features crêpes, Belgian waffles and home-made jams, and, in a deliciously quaint gesture, guests are offered complimentary afternoon tea. But old customs meet New Age here – the proprietor is also an Alexander Technique teacher, handy should you wish to book a session or two during your stay.

A Cambridge House Inn

2218 Massachusetts Avenue, at Haskell Street, Davis Square, Cambridge, MA 02140 (1-617 491 6300, www.acambridgehouse.com). Davis or Porter T. **Rooms** 20.

On busy Massachusetts Avenue, a few miles north of Harvard Square, this lovely Greek Revival house was constructed in 1882. Rooms are furnished in a somewhat fussy – but lovely for its type – Victorian style. The hotel may be off the beaten track, but free parking is available. If you plan to explore further than Cambridge and Boston, it offers easy access to all points west and north. Continental breakfast is included in the rate.

Budget

Monastery of the Society of Saint John the Evangelist

980 Memorial Drive, Harvard Square, Cambridge, MA 02138 (1-617 876 3037, www.ssje.org). Harvard T. **Rooms** 13. **Map** p284 A3.

Run by an order of monks affiliated with the Anglican and American Episcopal churches, this Italianate monastery is a short walk from Harvard Square. It's a place for peaceful reflection and spiritual renewal, so silence is maintained in the common spaces. The tiny guest rooms served as monk's cells for eight years before the main monastery and its beautiful church were built in 1936. The white-painted quarters are sparsely furnished, and there is only one double room with a queen-sized bed for couples. Breakfast is served in the guest house, but visitors can take other meals with the community in the refectory (as long as they refrain from chitchat). There are no TVs or phones, and mobile phone use is kept to a minimum, permitted only in designated rooms or out in the garden.

BED & BREAKFAST AGENCIES

Whether you're after a more 'authentic' taste of local life or all the comforts of home in your own apartment, B&B agencies can hook you up with accommodation in Boston and beyond. Rates start from as little as $80 per night off-season for a single room with a shared bath.

Bed & Breakfast Agency of Boston

47 Commercial Wharf No.3, Boston, MA 02110 (1-617 720 0522, www.boston-bnbagency.com). Aquarium T.

This agency offers high-quality, child-friendly accommodation in central Boston, ranging from waterfront lofts to rooms in historic Victorian Back Bay homes. It's especially good at finding short-term studios and apartments.

Bed and Breakfast Associates Bay Colony

453 Beacon Street, at Hereford Street, Boston, MA 02115 (1-800 347 5088, www.bnbboston. **Open** *Office* 8.30am-6pm Mon-Fri; 10am-4pm Sat, Sun.

With a far-reaching list of accommodation in B&Bs, inns, suites and furnished apartments throughout the city and western suburbs (Newton, Wellesley and Needham), this agency also covers the coast, Nantucket and Martha's Vineyard.

ESSENTIAL INFORMATION

Getting Around

ARRIVING & LEAVING

By air

Boston Logan International Airport
1-800 235 6426, www.massport.com.
Located on a spit of reclaimed land east of Boston, the airport is three miles from downtown. Its four terminals – A, B, C and E – are connected by walkways and shuttle buses. The subway (known as the T; *see p259*) is the cheapest route to and from the airport. The **Airport** station is on the Blue Line, which runs downtown to the State and Government Center stations, a trip that takes about 15mins. Massport's airport **shuttle buses** (22, 33, 55 and 66) take passengers from the airline terminals to the Airport T station. Alternatively, the **Silver Line Waterfront** route SL1 (*see p259*) stops at each terminal and goes to South Station. T maps are available from information booths in terminals A, C and E.

The **taxi** rank is outside the airport's baggage reclaim area. The fare to downtown Boston or Cambridge will set you back anything between $25 and $45, with an extra $5.25 toll for travelling through Sumner Tunnel and Ted Williams Tunnel from Logan to Boston, plus a $2.25 Massport tunnel fee. On your return, heading into Logan from Boston, you'll have to pay a $2.75 toll for travelling through Callahan Tunnel or Ted Williams Tunnel. For a list of reputable taxi firms, *see p259*.

If you want to travel in style, make a booking with **Boston Limo** (1-617 933 9077) or **Commonwealth Worldwide Chauffeured Transportation** (1-617 787 5575).

One of the most pleasant ways of getting to and from the airport is by boat. **Rowes Wharf Water Transport** (1-617 406 8584, www.roweswharfwatertransport.com) runs services between Rowes Wharf and Logan's dock (accessible via the free 66 airport shuttle bus). In winter (Nov-Mar), boats run 7am-7pm daily. For the rest of the year, services run 7am-10pm Mon-Sat, 7am-8pm Sun; tickets are $10 one way. The MBTA **Harbor Express** (1-617 222 6999, www.mbta.com) runs a similar service between the airport, Hull and Long Wharf in downtown Boston. Finally, **Boston Water Taxi** (1-617 227 4320, www.bostonharborcruises.com) operates year-round (6.30am-10pm Mon-Sat, 6.30am-8pm Sun), running from the airport to the World Trade Center, Congress Street (near South Station) and other stops. A one-way ticket costs $10.

Major airlines

Aer Lingus *1-800 474 7424.*
Air Canada *1-888 247 2262.*
Air France *1-800 237 2747.*
AirTran *1-800 247 8726.*
Alaska Airlines *1-800 252 7522.*
Alitalia *1-800 223 5730.*
American Airlines *1-800 433 7300.*
British Airways *1-800 247 9297.*
Cape Air *1-800 352 0714.*
Cathay Pacific *1-800 223 2742.*
Copa Airlines *1-800 359 2672.*
Delta Air Lines *1-800 221 1212.*
Emirates *1-800 777 3999.*
Hainan Airlines *1-888 688 8813.*
Iberia *1-800 772 4642.*
Icelandair *1-800 223 5500.*
Japan Airlines *1-800 525 3663.*
JetBlue Airways *1-800 538 2583.*
Lufthansa *1-800 645 3880.*
Midwest *1-800 452 2022.*
PenAir *1-800 448 4226.*
Porter Airlines *1-888 619 8622.*
SATA *1-800 762 9995.*
Southwest Airlines *1-800 435 9792.*
Spirit Airlines *1-800 772 7117.*
Sun Country *1-800 359 6786.*
Swiss *1-877 359 7947.*
TACV *1-866 359 8228.*
Turkish Airlines *1-800 874 8875.*
United Airlines *1-800 241 6522.*
US Airways *1-800 428 4322.*
Virgin America *1-877 359 8474.*
Virgin Atlantic *1-800 862 8621.*

By bus

The following bus services arrive at and depart from the **South Station Transportation Center** (700 Atlantic Avenue, at Summer Street).

BoltBus
1-877 265 8287, www.boltbus.com.
Owned by Greyhound and booked online, this Wi-Fi equipped fleet connects Boston with New York City, Newark, NJ, and Philadelphia.

Concord Coach Lines
1-800 639 3317, www.concord coachlines.com.
For New Hampshire and Maine.

Greyhound
1-800 231 2222, www.greyhound.com.
For national services.

Peter Pan
1-800 343 9999, www.peterpan bus.com.
For New England (including Cape Cod and Providence), plus New York.

Plymouth & Brockton
1-508 746 0378, www.p-b.com.
For Plymouth (and other towns along the South Shore) and Cape Cod.

By car

The three main highways that lead into town are the **I-95**; the **I-93**, which runs all the way to Vermont; and the **I-90** (the Massachusetts Turnpike, or 'Mass Pike'), which runs into New York state.

By rail

National rail service **Amtrak** (1-800 872 7245, www.amtrak.com) runs from **South Station**, **North Station** and **Back Bay Station** (*see p259*).

PUBLIC TRANSPORT

Local public transport is run by the **Massachusetts Bay Transportation Authority (MBTA)** and consists of the subway system (known as the T), commuter rail, buses and ferries. For a map of the T and commuter rail lines, *see p288*.

Fares & tickets

Although you can still pay for buses with exact change, Boston's public transport system is accessed through rechargeable plastic **CharlieCards** and paper **CharlieTickets**. (The name derives from a character from a 1948 Kingston Trio protest song, in which Charlie was doomed to ride the T forever because he couldn't pay the full fare.) The cards work via an embedded micro-chip and simple touch-in system. Fares are slightly cheaper

ESSENTIAL INFORMATION

with a CharlieCard: rides cost $2.65 with a CharlieTicket, or $2.10 using a CharlieCard. Ask for a card at the ticket windows at Back Bay, Harvard Square, Kenmore, North Station or South Station, or order one on MBTA's website, and add credit using machines in T stations. Transfers between subway lines are free, but a transfer from subway to bus is only free with a CharlieCard.

LinkPasses for one day (at $12, not a great deal), one week ($19) or one month ($75) can be used on the T, local buses, ferries across Boston Harbor and local commuter rail. Passes can be bought from ticket vending machines at airport terminals and T stations.

Up to two children aged 11 or under can ride for free when accompanied by a paying adult. For information about additional reduced fare availability, see the MBTA website.

MBTA
1-617 222 3200, 1-800 392 6100, www.mbta.com.

Subway

Boston's **T** was America's first subway, and it's easy to use and cheap, though delays often cause grumbles (for fares, *see p258*). Trains run from 4.56am to 1.05am Mon-Thur, from 4.56am to 2.45am Fri, from 4.45am to 2.45am Sat, and from 5.20am to 1.05am Sun (first and last trains vary by line). Free T maps are available from the larger stations.

'Outbound' and 'Inbound' services sometimes have different subway entrances. Inbound trains will always be heading towards downtown stations Park Street, State, Downtown Crossing and Government Center; Outbound trains head away from them.

Although the two **Silver Line** routes appear on subway maps, they actually use buses. Silver Line Waterfront (SL1) serves the airport, South Station and the South Boston waterfront. Silver Line Washington Street (SL5) serves Downtown Crossing, Washington Street and Dudley Square in Roxbury, and charges a local bus fare. SL4 operates on a slightly different route from the latter, while SL2 branches off the former to the Design Center.

Not many people know that each subway-line colour was chosen to reflect a characteristic of the area it covers. The Green Line, for example, was named in honour of

the Emerald Necklace, the chain of parks that links Boston and the western suburbs. The Red Line, serving Harvard, pays homage to Harvard Crimson, the university's official colour. The Blue Line is supposed to mirror the colour of the waterfront, and the Orange Line runs along Washington Street, once known as Orange Street. The newer Silver Line was so named in an effort to convey a sense of speed.

Buses

The MBTA runs around 175 bus routes in Boston and the suburbs. The flat fare is $2.10 if you use a CharlieTicket or pay cash on board, or $1.60 if you use a CharlieCard. Express buses are $3.65-$5.25. Transfers to the subway are discounted if you use a CharlieCard, and bus-to-bus transfers are free with a CharlieTicket or CharlieCard. If you overpay in cash, you'll get a CharlieTicket with the change on it.

Bus routes and timetables are available from major T stations or the MBTA central office (10 Park Plaza, between Boylston, Stuart & Charles Streets, Downtown); they're also on the MBTA's website. The busiest bus routes run from 5.30am to 1am daily.

Rail

Boston has three main train stations: **South Station** (700 Atlantic Avenue, at Summer Street), **North Station** (135 Causeway Street, at Canal Street) and **Back Bay Station** (145 Dartmouth Street, at Stuart Street).

The MBTA Commuter Rail runs from Back Bay, North Station and South Station, serving the Greater Boston area and Massachusetts, as far away as Providence, Rhode Island; fares range from $2.10 to $11.50 a trip. Tickets can be bought on the train, but it's cheaper to buy them at the station.

TAXIS

Taxis can be hailed at any time of day or night, although it becomes difficult after 1am. Taxi ranks can be found near major hotels, big train stations and in Harvard Square in Cambridge. Call ahead for wheelchair-accessible vehicles or vans (for the latter, there may be a surcharge). Normal meter fares cost $2.60 for the first seventh of a mile, then 40¢ for each seventh of a mile.

If you have a complaint about a taxi, or to report lost property, phone the police department's **Hackney Carriage Unit** at 1-617 343 4475.

The following taxi companies offer a 24-hour service. Most accept major credit cards, but it's always best to phone to check first.

Boston Cab *1-617 536 5010.*
Independent Taxi Operators Association *1-617 426 8700.*
Metrocab *1-617 782 5500.*
Top Cab/City Cab *1-617 266 4800/ 1-617 536 5100.*

DRIVING

Thanks to the Big Dig project, driving in Boston isn't the purgatory it used to be. But traffic can still be painfully slow and motorists' tempers often fray.

The speed limit on many major highways is 55mph, going up to 65mph on sections of the Mass Pike. Elsewhere in Boston, speed limits range from 20mph to 50mph. State law requires seatbelts to be worn.

The **American Automobile Association** (AAA) provides maps and other information, free if you're a member or belong to an affiliated organisation such as the British AA. It also offers a 24-hour breakdown service (except on the privately run Mass Pike, which has its own patrol cars to help with breakdowns). The Boston office (125 High Street, Downtown, 1-617 443 9300, www.aaa.com) is open 9am-5pm Mon-Fri.

Car hire

To rent a car, you'll need a credit card and a driver's licence (UK licences are valid, but those from non-English-speaking countries may need to be accompanied by an International Driving Permit). Some firms refuse to rent to under-25s or charge an additional fee. Rental rarely includes insurance.

Car rental companies

Alamo *1-888 233 8749, www.alamo.com.*
Avis *1-800 331 1084, www.avis.com.*
Budget *1-800 218 7992, www.budget.com.*
Dollar *1-800 800 4000, www.dollar.com.*
Hertz *1-800 654 3001, www.hertz.com.*
National *1-888 826 6890, www.nationalcar.com.*

Parking

Despite the city's ample public transport, Bostonians still love their cars; traffic congestion is dreadful and parking spaces are rare – many are metered and only available to non-residents for up to two hours between 8am and 6pm.

A parking fine costs from $25, and retrieving a towed car can be as much as $90. If you do get a ticket, call the **Boston Office of the Parking Clerk** (1-617 635 4410) or pay online at www.cityofboston.gov/parking.

Boston's two main car parks are under Boston Common (entrance on Charles Street, directly opposite the Public Garden, 1-617 954 2098) and under the Prudential Center (800 Boylston Street, Back Bay, 1-617 236 3060). Other garages can be found at Government Center (50 New Sudbury Street, Downtown, 1-617 227 0385), near the New England Aquarium (70 East India Row, Waterfront, 1-617 720 5135) and Post Office Square (Zero Post Office Square, Downtown, 1-617 423 1430).

CYCLING

Boston was once consistently rated one of the worst cities in America for bikers by cycling magazines, but recently designated bike lanes have improved the terrain; still, given the bad reputation of local motorists, it's advisable to exercise caution. Inexperienced cyclists might want to stick to special trails such as the **Paul Dudley White Charles River Bike Path** – a 17-mile stretch running between the Science Museum and Watertown – and the **Minuteman Bikeway** (www.minutemanbikeway.org), a ten-mile ride from Alewife T to Lexington and Bedford along a former rail line. For bike rentals, try either **Community Bike Supply** in the South End (496 Tremont Street, 1-617 542 8623, www.communitybicycle.com), or **Back Bay Bicycles** (362 Commonwealth Avenue, 1-617 247 2336, www.papa-wheelies.com). Across the river, there's **Cambridge Bicycle** (259 Massachusetts Avenue, Cambridge, 1-617 876 6555, www.cambridgebicycle.com).

In 2011, the city introduced a bike-sharing scheme, **Hubway** (www.thehubway.com). Visitors can purchase 24- or 72-hour passes ($6 or $12 for unlimited rides of no more than 30 minutes each within the designated period) at self-serve kiosks at any of the system's 140 stations in Boston, Cambridge, Somerville and Brookline.

WALKING

Boston is not called 'America's Walking City' for nothing. You can easily cover the city centre on foot, and walking through the different neighbourhoods is a pleasurable way to explore.

TOURS

For self-guided walking trails, see p47 **Trail Blazers**. For child-oriented tours, see p173.

Boston By Foot

1-617 367 2345, www.bostonbyfoot.org. Tours leave from a variety of locations (phone for details). **Tours** May-Oct times vary. Nov-Apr occasional tours, call for details. **Rates** $12-$15; $8 reductions.

A broad array of 90-minute historical and architectural tours, led by volunteer guides who encourage questions. Tours focus on neighbourhoods or themes, such as Victorian Back Bay or Literary Landmarks.

Boston Duck Tours

1-617 267 3825, www.bostonducktours.com. Tours leave from the Prudential Center, at Huntington Avenue (Copley, Hynes, Convention Center or Prudential T); or from the Museum of Science, Science Park (Science Park T). **Tours** (every 30-60mins) Apr-mid June 9am-5pm. Mid June-early Aug 9am-7pm. Early Aug-mid Sept 9am-6pm. Mid Sept-3rd wk in Oct 9am-5pm. 3rd wk in Oct-late Nov 9am-3pm. **Rates** $21-$31; $5-$24 reductions. **Map** p283 G7/p280 H2.

You can travel by land and sea – in a restyled World War II amphibious landing craft. Manned by so-called conDUCKtors, tours are informative and especially fun for kids. Shortened tours are also available, which depart from the New England Aquarium (Aquarium or Haymarket T); check the website for details.

Boston Harbor Cruises

1-617 227 4321, 1-877 733 9425, www.bostonharborcruises.com. Tours leave from Long Wharf, Waterfront. Aquarium T. **Tours** USS Constitution Cruise March-Nov 10.30am-4.30pm daily (every hr). Historic Sightseeing Cruise May-Aug 11am, 1pm, 3pm daily. Sept 11am, 1pm, 3pm Sat, Sun. Sunset Cruise May-Aug 7pm daily. Sept 6pm Thur-Sun. **Rates** $22-$26. **Map** p281 M4.

BHC offers a variety of themed sightseeing, entertainment and meal cruises, as well as whale-watching excursions (call or visit website for seasonal schedules).

Boston Old Town Trolley Tours

1-617 269 7150, www.trolleytours.com. **Tours** Apr-Oct every 15-20mins 9am-5pm daily. Nov-Mar every 25-30mins 9am-4pm daily. **Rates** $41; $18-$39 reductions; free under-4s. **Map** p281 M4.

One of these faux trolley cars (they ride on wheels, not rails) always seems to be passing, no matter where you are. You can leave and rejoin the tour at will, which is useful if you want to get a better look at a particular neighbourhood. Seasonal tour themes range from Chocolate to Ghosts & Gravestones.

Charles Riverboat Company

1-617 621 3001, www.charlesriverboat.com. Tours leave from Lechmere Canal Park, at CambridgeSide Galleria, 100 CambridgeSide Place, Cambridge. Lechmere T. **Tours** Charles River Sightseeing Tour May-Oct 10am, 11.15am, 12.30pm, 1.45pm, 3pm, 4.15pm daily. Architectural Boat Tour May-Oct 10am Fri; 10am, 2.30pm Sat, Sun. Boston Harbor Sunset Cruise June-Aug 6pm, 8pm daily. **Rates** $15-$25; $8-$20 reductions.

The Charles River tour departs from the Lechmere Canal then cruises the river basin, taking in the sights along the way.

Urban AdvenTours

1-617 379 3590, www.urbanadventours.com. Tours leave from 103 Atlantic Avenue, North End. Aquarium or Haymarket T. **Tours** (weather permitting) 10am, 2pm, 6pm daily. **Rates** $35-$50. **Map** p281 M4.

A variety of cycling tours around Boston are on offer, with themes such as a tour along the Emerald Necklace (see p84 **In the Know**), a waterfront tour that highlights the Rose F Kennedy Greenway and a monthly re-creation of Paul Revere's Midnight Ride. Tours last 90mins to three hours and rates include a bicycle, helmet and water. Urban AdvenTours also rents hybrid bikes for $35/24hrs.

ESSENTIAL INFORMATION

Resources A-Z

AGE RESTRICTIONS

Buying/drinking alcohol 21.
Driving 16.
Sex 16.
Smoking 18.

BUSINESS

Conventions & conferences

Boston Convention & Exhibition Center *415 Summer Street, at D Street, Waterfront (1-617 954 2000, www.massconvention.com). Silver Line Waterfront to World Trade Center.*
John B Hynes Veterans Memorial Convention Center *900 Boylston Street, at Gloucester Street, Back Bay (1-617 954 2000, www.massconvention.com). Hynes Convention Center T.* Map p282 F6.
Seaport World Trade Center *200 Seaport Boulevard, at Seaport Lane, Waterfront (1-617 385 5000, www.seaportboston.com). Silver Line Waterfront to World Trade Center.*

Couriers & shippers

DHL Express *1-800 225 5345, www.dhl.com.*
FedEx *1-800 463 3339, www.fedex.com.*
Metro Cab *1-617 782 5500, www.metro-cab.com.* **Open** 24hrs daily.
New England Courier *1-866 286 4500, www.newenglandcourier.com.* **Open** 24hrs daily.
Usground *1-617 457 7800, www.usground.com.* **Open** 7am-6pm Mon-Fri; 7am-5pm Sat; by appt Sun.
US Postal Service *1-800 275 8777, www.usps.com.*

Office services

Boston Translation Company *Suite 805, 31 St James Avenue, at Arlington Street, Back Bay (1-617 778 0594, www.bostontranslation company.com). Arlington T.* **Open** 8.30am-6pm Mon-Fri. Map p283 H6. Translation and interpreting services for all major languages.
FedEx Office *10 Post Office Square, at Congress Street, Downtown (1-617 482 4400, www.fedex.com). State T.* **Open** 7am-midnight Mon-Fri; 8am-9pm Sat; 9am-9pm Sun. Map p281 L4.
On-site computer rental, printing, Wi-Fi, copying, faxing and mailing. **Other locations** 2 Center Plaza, Downtown (1-617 973 9000); 187 Dartmouth Street, Back Bay (1-617 262 6188); 1 Mifflin Place, Cambridge (1-617 497 0125).
Regus *Suite 1900, 101 Federal Street, between Franklin & Matthews Streets, Downtown (1-617 342 7000, www.regus.com). South Station T.* **Open** 8.30am-5pm Mon-Fri. Map p281 L5.
Meeting rooms and office space for rent.
Sir Speedy *827 Boylston Street, between Fairfield & Gloucester Streets, Back Bay (1-617 267 9711, www.sir-speedy.net). Copley T.* **Open** 8.30am-6pm Mon-Fri; 10am-5pm Sat. Map p282 G6. Copying, printing, binding and graphic design.
Other location 1 Milk Street, at Washington Street, Downtown (1-617 227 2237).
TransPerfect *Suite 502, 100 High Street, at Berkeley Street, Back Bay (1-617 523 6936, www.transperfect. com). Arlington T.* **Open** 8.30am-6pm Mon-Fri. Map p281 L4. Translation and interpreting, plus a multilingual secretarial service.

CONSUMER

Better Business Bureau *1-508 652 4800, www.bbb.org.* Contact the bureau if you wish to file a complaint about a business in the north-eastern US.

Office of Consumer Affairs & Business Regulation *1-617 973 8787, www.mass.gov/ ocabr.*
If you have a complaint to make regarding your consumer rights, contact the OCABR. It also provides arbitration services for disputes involving home improvement contractors and car sales, and can refer you to mediation or legal services.

CUSTOMS

During your inbound flight, you will be given a customs declaration form to fill in and hand in when you land at the airport.

US Customs allows visitors to bring in $100 worth of gifts duty-free (generally $800 for returning Americans), 200 cigarettes or 100 cigars, and one litre of spirits. Any amount of currency can be brought into the US, but you must fill in a form (available from the airport) for amounts over $10,000. Prescription drugs must be clearly marked; be prepared to produce a written prescription on request. No meat or meat products can be taken through customs, while seeds, plants and fruit are heavily restricted.

For more information, call Logan Airport's **Customs & Border Protection Office** (1-617 568 1810) or visit the US Customs website (www.cbp.gov).

The UK's **HM Revenue & Customs** allows returning

travellers to bring in £390 worth of 'gifts, souvenirs and other goods' into the country duty-free, along with the usual duty-free goods.

DISABLED TRAVELLERS

Boston is generally well equipped for disabled travellers. Hotels must provide accessible rooms; museums and street kerbs have ramps; and MBTA buses and certain subways are wheelchair-accessible. That said, it's always best to phone a venue first to double-check facilities and accessibility.

Free **Transportation Access Passes** (TAP), entitling disabled passengers to reduced fares on public transport, are available from the **MBTA Office for Transportation Access** (1-617 222 5123, www.mbta.com) in Back Bay. Applications for passes must be completed by a licensed healthcare professional. The office also supplies a map that shows disabled access points to the T.

For information on access to more than 200 local arts and entertainment facilities, contact **VSA Massachusetts** (1-617 350 7713).

Massachusetts Office on Disability

1-617 727 7440, 1-800 322 2020, www.mass.gov/mod.
Information on rights enforcement and building access.

ELECTRICITY

The US uses 110-120V, 60-cycle AC voltage. Laptops and most travel appliances are dual voltage and will work in the US and Europe, but it's a good idea to check with the manufacturer before you plug them in – older computers have been known to blow. Adaptors can be bought at the airport or at pharmacies.

EMBASSIES & CONSULATES

Australia *1601 Massachusetts Avenue NW, Washington, DC (1-202 797 3000, www.usa.embassy.gov.au).*
Canada *Suite 400, 3 Copley Place, at Huntington Avenue, Back Bay (1-617 247 5100, www.can-am.gc.ca/boston). Copley T.* Map p283 G6.
Ireland *3rd Floor, 535 Boylston Street, at Clarendon Street, Back Bay (1-617 267 9330, www.dfa.ie/irish-consulate/boston). Copley T.* Map p283 H6.
New Zealand *37 Observatory Circle NW, Washington, DC (1-202 328*

4800, www.nzembassy.com/usa-washington).
South Africa *9th Floor, 333 E 38th Street, New York (1-212 213 4880, www.southafrica-newyork.net).*
UK *7th Floor, One Broadway, Cambridge (1-617 245 4500, www.gov.uk/government/world/organisations/british-consulate-general-boston). Kendall/MIT T.*

EMERGENCIES

For all emergency services, dial **911**. The call is toll-free from any payphone. For more information, *see below* **Accident & emergency**, *p263* **Helplines** and *p264* **Police**.

GAY & LESBIAN

For gay and lesbian resources, as well as shops, restaurants and bars catering to the lesbian and gay community, *see pp178-184*. For HIV/AIDS information, *see p263*.

HEALTH

Foreign visitors should ensure they have full travel insurance, as treatment can be costly. Contact the emergency number on your insurance policy before seeking treatment, and you'll be directed to a hospital that deals directly with your insurance company.

Accident & emergency

The following hospitals have 24hr emergency rooms:

Boston Children's Hospital *300 Longwood Avenue, at Binney Street, Brookline (1-617 355 6000, 1-800 355 7944, www.childrens hospital.org). Brigham Circle or Longwood Medical Area T.*
Brigham & Women's Hospital *75 Francis Street, at Binney Street, Brookline (1-617 732 5500, 1-617 732 6438, 1-800 294 9999, www.brighamandwomens.org). Brigham Circle or Longwood Medical Area T.*
Floating Hospital for Children *755 Washington Street, Downtown (1-617 636 8100, www.floating hospital.org). Tufts Medical Center T.* Map p283 J6.
Massachusetts General Hospital (MGH) *55 Fruit Street, at Charles Street, West End (1-617 726 2000, www.massgeneral.org). Charles/MGH T.* Map p272 J3.
Mount Auburn Hospital *330 Mount Auburn Street, at Memorial Drive, Cambridge (1-617 492 3500, 1-800 322 6728, www.mountauburnhospital.org).*

Harvard Square T then bus 71, 73. Map p284 A2.
Tufts Medical Center *800 Washington Street, Downtown (1-617 636 5000, www.tuftsmedical center.org). Tufts Medical Center T.* Map p283 J6.

Complementary medicine

Market Street Health *214 Market Street, at North Beacon Street, Brighton (1-617 787 3511, www.marketstreethealth.com). Cleveland Circle T then bus 86.* **Open** varies.
Market Street Health offers a wide variety of complementary medicine and holistic therapies, including acupuncture, chiropractic therapy, homeopathy, Chinese medicine, massage and psychotherapy.

New England School of Acupuncture *3rd Floor, 150 California Street, Newton (1-617 558 1788, www.nesa.edu). Kenmore T then bus 57.* **Open** 8.30am-8pm Mon; 8am-6.30pm Tue; 8am-7.30pm Wed, Thur; 9am-7pm Fri; 8.30am-2pm Sat.
The oldest college of acupuncture and Oriental medicine in the country, this well-known school offers a wide array of treatments.

Contraception & abortion

Planned Parenthood Greater Boston Health Center *1055 Commonwealth Avenue, at Alcorn Street, Brookline (1-617 616 1617, www.plannedparenthoodppbm.org). Babcock Street T.* **Open** 8.30am-7.15pm Mon; 7.30am-7.15pm Tue, Thur, Fri; 7.30am-4.15pm Wed; 7.30am-3.45pm Sat.

Dentists

Dental Referral Service *1-800 511 8663.* **Open** 24hrs daily.
Massachusetts Dental Society *1-800 342 8747, www.massdental.org.* **Open** 9am-5pm Mon-Fri.
Tufts School of Dental Medicine *1 Kneeland Street, at Washington Street, Downtown (1-617 636 6828). Chinatown or Tufts Medical Center T.* **Open** *Emergency walk-in clinic* 9am-4pm Mon-Fri. Map p283 J6.

Opticians

Eye Q Optical *12 Eliot Street, at Bennett Street, Harvard Square, Cambridge (1-617 354 3303, www.eye-q-optical.com). Harvard Square T.* **Open** 10am-6pm Mon, Wed; 10am-5.30pm Tue, Fri;

ESSENTIAL INFORMATION

10am-7pm Thur; 10am-5pm Sat; noon-4pm Sun. **Map** p284 A2.
This mini chain has its own range of cool specs that runs from minimalist styles to striking retro looks. High-tech eye exams, same-day service and contact lenses are offered.
Other location 615 Centre Street, Jamaica Plain (1-617 983 3937).

Pharmacies

Several branches of chain **CVS** (www.cvs.com) are open 24 hours.

STDs, HIV & AIDS

Fenway Health
1340 Boylston Street (1-617 267 0900, 1-888 242 0900, www. fenwayhealth.org). Fenway or Kenmore T. **Open** 8am-8pm Mon-Thur. **Map** p282 D7.
The clinic offers HIV, hepatitis and STD testing and services.

HELPLINES

Alcoholics Anonymous
1-617 426 9444, www.aaboston.org.
Open 9am-9pm Mon-Fri; noon-9pm Sat, Sun.
Child-At-Risk Hotline
1-800 792 5200. **Open** 24hrs daily.
Drug & Alcohol Helpline
1-800 327 5050. **Open** 24hrs daily.
Rape Crisis
1-617 492 8306, 1-800 841 8371.
Open 24hrs daily.
Samaritans
1-617 536 2460, 1-877 870 4673, www.samaritanshope.org. **Open** 24hrs daily.

ID

The legal drinking age of 21 is rigorously upheld, and photo ID checks are taken very seriously. Not all forms of out-of-state ID are accepted, so it's always best to carry your passport with you.

INSURANCE

You should take out comprehensive insurance cover before travelling to the US: it's almost impossible to arrange once you have arrived. Make sure that you have adequate health cover, since medical expenses can be sky-high. (For a list of hospitals and clinics, *see p262* **Health**.)

INTERNET

Wi-Fi access is generally available for free at chain cafés, such as Starbucks and Au Bon Pain, and at many boutique coffeehouses in the Boston area. The main **Boston Public Library** (*see p77*) offers free 'express' internet access (30-minute sessions for non-members). You'll need to drop by the computer desk and make a reservation in advance.

Alternatively, you can pay to use a computer at a copy/office centre (*see p261* **Office services**) – some branches of **FedEx Office** offer high-speed access. Another option is to swing by the free internet terminals in the **Shops at Prudential Center** (*see p77*), located near the entrance to the Sheraton hotel. But be warned: there are no seats, and there's often a queue.

For a list of useful websites, with information on the city and the local area, *see p270* **Websites**.

LEFT LUGGAGE

At the time this guide went to press, no luggage storage facilities were available at Logan Airport due to FAA restrictions. South Station bus terminal (adjacent to the train terminal, at 700 Atlantic Avenue, 5th Floor) has left luggage facilities ($10 per item). Look for the sign for Package Express.

LEGAL HELP

If you run into legal trouble, contact your insurers or your embassy or consulate (*see p262*).

LIBRARIES

Boston Public Library
700 Boylston Street, at Copley Square, Back Bay (1-617 536 5400, www.bpl.org). Copley T. **Open** 9am-9pm Mon-Thur; 9am-5pm Fri, Sat; 1-5pm Sun. *Print department, rare books & manuscripts* 9am-5pm Mon-Fri. *Young adults' room* 10am-6pm Mon-Thur; 9am-5pm Fri, Sat; 1-5pm Sun. **Map** p283 G6.
The city's enormous main library.
Other locations 25 Parmenter Street, North End (1-617 227 8135); 685 Tremont Street, South End (1-617 536 8241); 151 Cambridge Street, West End (1-617 523 3957).

LOST PROPERTY

For lost credit cards, *see p264*.

Airport

Logan Airport *1-617 568 7514.*
The Massachusetts State Police also run an airport lost-and-found office at 2 Service Road (1-617 561 2047), across from the Airport T station.

Public transport

If you lose something on a bus or the subway, phone 1-617 222 5000 (9am-4pm Mon-Fri). For property lost on the Commuter Rail from North Station, phone 1-617 222 3600 (7am-7pm Mon-Fri); for South Station, call 1-617 222 8120 (7am-7pm Mon-Fri).

Taxis

If you leave something in a taxi, call the police department's **Hackney Hotline** (1-617 536 8294), open 8.30am-4pm Mon-Fri.

MEDIA

Newspapers & magazines

Boston magazine
www.bostonmagazine.com.
A general-interest glossy monthly magazine with a mix of lifestyle features and pieces on city issues, catering mostly to an upmarket audience. The annual 'Best of Boston' issue and the restaurant reviews are highly regarded.
Boston Globe
www.bostonglobe.com.
The city's oldest and most popular daily newspaper generally takes a cautiously liberal line, covering local politics quite well and regaining its national stride with a growing stable of Pulitzer-winning journalists. 'G', a daily events insert, functions as a fluffy arts and entertainment guide.
Boston Herald
www.bostonherald.com.
A raucous, conservative-leaning tabloid newspaper in the style of the *New York Post*, the *Herald* has a strong following among working-class Bostonians. It has been very successful in unearthing local political scandals, and the sports coverage is extensive.
Dig Boston
www.digboston.com.
Boston's popular free weekly covers local listings and news from an indie standpoint. Its columnists take strong political stances and take great pleasure in lashing out at anyone and anything in the Boston scene – from local politicos to other newspapers and their editors. Grab a copy from dispensers around town.
GateHouse Media
www.wickedlocal.com.
This chain of newspapers caters to particular cities or neighbourhoods; publications include the *Cambridge Chronicle* and *Brookline TAB*. Mostly focused on community issues and local arts coverage.

ESSENTIAL INFORMATION

Improper Bostonian
www.improper.com.
Glossy bi-weekly magazine covering lifestyle, dining and entertainment, plus the local social scene.

Radio

WBOS *92.9 FM, www.myradio929. com.*
Expect alternative bands – anything from the Offspring to the Crash Kings.
WBUR *90.9 FM, www.wbur.org.*
A public radio station, dedicated almost completely to news and talk – including the flagship NPR (National Public Radio, the US equivalent of the BBC) programmes. The nationally syndicated *Car Talk* is produced here.
WBZ-FM *98.5 FM, www.cbslocal.com.*
The Sports Hub, an upstart WEEI competitor with CBS backing, is the official flagship radio station of the Boston Bruins and the New England Patriots.
WEEI *850 AM, www.weei.com.*
A station for die-hard Red Sox and Celtics fans – just about everyone in Boston, then.
WERS *88.9 FM, www.wers.org.*
A high-quality semi-professional college radio station, run by students at Emerson College. Daily slots are dedicated to folk, rock, jazz, world music, reggae and hip hop, with lots of interviews and live performances thrown into the mix.
WGBH *89.7 FM, www.wgbh.org.*
This public radio station airs the main NPR news shows, including *Morning Edition* and *All Things Considered*, along with classical music, folk, blues and jazz.
WHRB *95.3 FM, www.whrb.org.*
Harvard University's station plays a combination of classical and jazz during the day. Punk, indie, rock and hip hop take over in the small hours.
WJMN *94.5 FM, www.jamn945.com.*
Mainstream hip hop and R&B.
WRKO *680 AM, www.wrko.com.*
Talk radio and news programmes with a mainly conservative bent.

Television

Boston's local PBS (Public Broadcasting Service, www.pbs.org) station, **WGBH**, on channels 2 and 44, is one of the best in the country, producing acclaimed shows such as *Nova* and *Frontline*. The local affiliates of national commercial networks are:
WBZ Channel 4 (CBS)
WCVB Channel 5 (ABC)
WHDH Channel 7 (NBC)
WFXT Channel 25 (Fox).

MONEY

The US dollar ($) equals 100 cents (¢). Coins range from copper pennies (1¢) to silver-coloured nickels (5¢), dimes (10¢), quarters (25¢) and rarely seen silver dollars ($1). Paper money 'bills' come in denominations of $1, $2 (rare), $5, $10, $20, $50 and $100 – and all, confusingly, are the same size and colour.

Since counterfeiting of $50 and $100 bills is a booming business, many small shops will not accept them. On the whole, it's better to restrict your paper money to smaller denominations.

Tax is applied to hotels (12.45%), meals (5%) and retail purchases (5%), excluding food bought from supermarkets and clothing under $175; and for a brief period in summer, when the state has a 'tax holiday'.

ATMs

Automated teller machines (ATMs) are easy to find. Most will accept American Express, MasterCard, Visa and selected international debit and cash cards. Most charge a fee. You can get directions to your nearest ATM location by calling the Visa Plus System (1-800 843 7587) or MasterCard (1-800 424 7787). If you have forgotten your PIN or have de-magnetised your card, most banks will dispense cash to cardholders with valid ID. You can also get cash back at supermarkets with a card with the Cirrus or Plus logo.

Banks & bureaux de change

If you arrive in Boston after 5pm, exchange money at the airport. If you want to cash travellers' cheques at a shop, ask first if a minimum purchase is required. You can obtain cash on a credit card account from certain banks; check with your credit card company before you leave, and be prepared to pay interest rates that vary daily. You will need some kind of photo ID, such as a passport, to cash travellers' cheques or obtain cash from a credit card.

Bank of America *100 Federal Street, at Franklin Street, Downtown (1-617 434 3412, www.bankof america.com). Downtown Crossing or South Station T.* **Open** 8am-5.30pm Mon; 8.30am-5pm Tue-Fri. **Map** p281 L5.
Other locations throughout the city.
Citizens Bank *28 State Street, at Congress Street, Downtown (1-617*

725 5900, www.citizensbank.com). State T. **Open** 8.30am-5pm Mon-Thur; 8.30am-6pm Fri. **Map** p281 L4.
Other locations throughout the city.
OneUnited Bank
133 Federal Street, between Milton Place & Matthews Street, Downtown (1-617 457 4400, www.oneunited. com). South Station T. **Open** 9am-5pm Mon-Fri. **Map** p281 L5.
Travelex *745 Boylston Street, Back Bay (1-617 266 7560). Copley T.* **Open** 9am-7pm Mon-Fri; 10am-6pm Sat; noon-5pm Sun. **Map** p281 L5.
Western Union *1-800 325 6000, www.westernunion.com.*

Credit cards

Less disastrous if you're robbed, and accepted almost everywhere, credit (and not debit) cards are required by almost all hotels, car-rental agencies and airlines. The cards most widely accepted in the US are American Express, Discover, MasterCard and Visa. If you lose your credit card (or travellers' cheques) call the appropriate number:

American Express *1-800 221 7282, travellers' cheques 1-800 221 7282.*
Discover *1-800 347 2683.*
MasterCard *1-800 307 7309.*
Visa *1-800 336 8472, travellers' cheques 1-800 227 6811.*

OPENING HOURS

Shops tend to open around 10am and close around 7pm, though many stay open later, especially during the tourist season. **Banks** are usually open 9am to 4pm or 5pm Monday to Friday, and some open from 10am to noon or 1pm on Saturdays. **Post offices** are usually open from 8am to 5pm Monday to Friday, and 8am to noon on Saturdays.

POLICE

For emergencies, dial **911**. Otherwise, call the **Boston Police** on 1-617 343 4200. Police HQ is at 1 Schroeder Plaza, Mission Hill, with another outpost at 650 Harrison Avenue, at East Dedham Street, South End (1-617 343 4250). Also, visit www.bpdnews.com.

POSTAL SERVICES

Contact the **US Postal Service** (1-800 275 8777, www.usps.com) for details of your nearest post office and mailing facilities (be ready with a post code or zip code).

Stamps can be bought at any post office, as well as at many hotels, grocery stores and convenience stores. It costs 49¢ to send a 1oz letter within the US. Each additional ounce costs 21¢. Postcards mailed within the US cost 34¢. Airmailed letters or postcards to Canada and Mexico cost 85¢ for the first ounce. The Global Forever Stamp ($1.15) can be used to send a postcard or 1oz letter anywhere in the world. Express mail costs extra and guarantees 24-hour delivery within the US, and two- to three-day delivery to international destinations with no guarantee. Call 1-800 275-8777 for more information.

Main Post Office *25 Dorchester Avenue, behind South Station, Downtown (1-617 654 5302). South Station T.* **Open** *6am-midnight daily.*
Beacon Hill *136 Charles Street, between Cambridge & Revere Streets. Charles/MGH T.* **Open** *8am-5.30pm Mon-Fri; 8am-noon Sat.*
Cambridge *Suite 1, 125 Mount Auburn Street, at Harvard Square. Harvard Square T.* **Open** *7.30am-6.30pm Mon-Fri; 7.30am-3pm Sat.*
North End *217 Hanover Street, near Mechanic Street. Haymarket T.* **Open** *8am-6pm Mon-Fri; 8am-2pm Sat.*

RELIGION

Baptist

First Baptist Church of Boston
110 Commonwealth Avenue, at Clarendon Street, Back Bay (1-617 267 3148, www.firstbaptistchurch ofboston.org). Copley T. **Services** 11am Sun. **Map** p283 H5.

Buddhist

Cambridge Zen Center
199 Auburn Street, Cambridge (1-617 576 3229, www.cambridge zen.com). Central T. **Daily practice** 5.45am, 6.10am, 6.30am, 6.30pm, 7pm, 7.30pm. **Map** p284 C3.

Catholic

Sacred Heart of Jesus Parish
49 Sixth Street, at Otis Street, Cambridge (1-617 547 0399). Harvard Square T then bus 69. **Services** 9am Mon, Wed-Fri; 9am, 6pm Tue; 5pm Sat; 7.30am, 9am, 11am Sun.
St Anthony Shrine
100 Arch Street, at Summer Street, Downtown (1-617 542 6440, www. stanthonyshrine.org). Downtown Crossing T. **Services** 6am, 7am, 10am, 11.45am, 12.30pm, 1.15pm,

5.15pm Mon-Fri; 8am, 10am, noon, 4pm, 4.15pm, 5.30pm Sat; 6am, 7.30am, 9am, 10am, 11.15am, 11.45am, 12.30pm, 4pm, 5.30pm Sun.

Christian Science

First Church of Christ, Scientist
250 Massachusetts Avenue, at Huntington Avenue, Back Bay (1-617 450 2000, www.christian science.com). Symphony T. **Open** 9am-4.15pm Mon-Fri. **Services** noon, 7.30pm Wed; 10am, 5pm Sun. **Map** p282 F8.

Episcopal

Church of the Advent
30 Brimmer Street, West End (1-617 523 2377, www.theadventboston. org). Charles/MGH T. **Services** 9am, 12.15pm, 5.30pm Mon, Tue, Thur, Fri; 9am, 5.30pm, 6pm Wed; 8.30am, 9am Sat; 7.30am, 8am, 9am, 11.15am Sun. **Map** p272 H4.
Old North Church (Christ Church)
193 Salem Street, at Hull Street, North End (1-617 523 6676, www.oldnorth.com). Haymarket T. **Services** 9am, 11am Sun. **Map** p281 L2.
For information about the church's history, *see p114.*

Jewish

Temple Israel of Boston
477 Longwood Avenue, at Riverway, Brookline (1-617 566 3960, www. tisrael.org). Longwood T. **Services** 6pm Fri; 9am, 10.15am Sat.

Methodist

Old West Church
131 Cambridge Street, at Staniford Street, Downtown (1-617 227 5088, www.oldwestchurch.org). Bowdoin or Charles/MGH T. **Services** noon Wed; 11am Sun. **Map** p272 K3.

Muslim

Islamic Society of Boston Cultural Center
100 Malcolm X Boulevard, at Elmwood Street, Cambridge (1-617 427 2636, http://isbcc.org). Roxbury Crossing T. **Services** Check online for daily prayer times. **Map** p284 C3.

Presbyterian

Church of the Covenant
67 Newbury Street, at Berkeley Street, Back Bay (1-617 266 7480, www.cotcbos.org). Arlington or Copley T. **Services** 10.30am Sun. **Map** p283 H5.

Quaker

Beacon Hill Friends House
6 Chestnut Street, at Walnut Street, Beacon Hill (1-617 227 9118, www. bhfh.org). Park Street T. **Meetings** 10.30am Sun. **Map** p272 J4.
The Friends House on Beacon Hill also has rooms for rent (in the Quaker style) for $90-$115 per night.

SAFETY & SECURITY

Boston is one of the safest cities in the US. However, as in any big city, it's wise to take basic precautions. Don't fumble with your map or wallet in public, and always plan where you're going and walk with brisk confidence. Avoid walking alone at night, and don't park in questionable areas of town (if in doubt, use valet parking when you can). Always keep your car doors locked when parked and while driving.

Central Boston is generally well lit, but pedestrians should probably avoid Boston Common, the Public Garden and the walkways along the Charles River after dark. Although the old red-light district, the Combat Zone, is all but gone bar a couple of clubs, the section of Washington Street between Avery and Stuart Streets still has a slightly rough edge late at night. As on all urban mass-transit systems, don't flash your mobile phones or other valuables on the MBTA.

SMOKING

Smoking is banned in all indoor public places statewide, including bars, clubs and restaurants. Smokers now have to congregate out on the pavement to get their nicotine fix, although some bars have set up beer gardens equipped with heaters to help them get through Boston's brutally cold winter months.

STUDY

As Boston has the world's largest number of colleges and universities per square mile, the choices for study are plentiful. The city is a great place to be a student, with a huge variety of courses and summer schools, and a jumping social scene.

Harvard University (1-617 495 1000, www.harvard.edu) is the oldest and most prestigious university in America – not to mention one of the most difficult colleges in the world to get into.

Other prominent institutions include **Boston College** (1-617 552 8800, www.bc.edu); the massive

Boston University (1-617 353 2000, www.bu.edu); and the renowned **Massachusetts Institute of Technology** (MIT; 1-617 253 1000, www.mit.edu), one of the world's top science and technology universities.

Devoted to the arts and communication, **Emerson College** (1-617 824 8500, www.emerson.edu) has a famously artistic student body and an award-winning radio station, WERS (*see p264*).

In Back Bay, there is **Northeastern University** (1-617 373 2000, www.northeastern.edu), while **Suffolk University** (1-617 573 8000, www.suffolk.edu) sits plum in the heart of Boston, perched on Beacon Hill.

North-west of the city, in nearby Medford, is **Tufts University** (1-617 628 5000, www.tufts.edu), founded in 1852. The **University of Massachusetts Boston** (1-617 287 5000, www.umb.edu) is a branch of the state-wide university system (commonly known as UMass). Situated on the Columbia Point peninsula in Dorchester, it's blessed with one of the most dramatic campus locations in the city.

TELEPHONES

Dialing & codes

The area codes for metropolitan Boston (including Cambridge, Somerville and Brookline) are **617** and **857**. The first ring of suburbs are in the 781 and 339 area codes, considered a local call from metropolitan Boston. The northern suburbs and north coast are served by 978 and 351, while the western and southern suburbs (including Cape Cod and the islands) use 508 and 774. Western Massachusetts uses area code 413. These are all long-distance calls from Boston.

Toll-free calls generally start with 1-800, 1-888 or 1-877, while costly pay-per-minute calls usually start with 1-900 or 1-976. Many hotels add a surcharge on all calls.

Collect calls To make a collect (reverse charge) call, dial 0 for the operator followed by the area code and phone number. For help, dial 0 for an operator.

Direct dial calls Calls made from any of the nine area codes should be dialed using all ten digits: area code + seven-digit phone number – even when calling within the area the code covers. If you are trying to reach a Boston number from elsewhere within the US, dial 1 + area code + seven-digit number.

International calls When you're calling Boston from abroad, dial the international access code of the country from which you are calling (00 from the UK), followed by the US country code (1), the area code and the number.

To phone abroad from Boston, dial 011 followed by the country code, area code and phone number. For countries not listed below, check the White Pages of the telephone book for a full list of country codes.

Australia 61
New Zealand 64
Republic of Ireland 353
South Africa 27
UK 44

Mobile phones

Whereas in Europe mobile phones work on the GSM network at either 900 or 1800 megahertz, the US does not have a standard mobile phone network that covers the whole country. This means that many European handsets will not work, and travellers may need to rent a handset once they arrive. Check with your service provider before you travel. **AT&T Wireless** (1-888 333 6651) and **T-Mobile** (1-800 937 8997) both offer pre-paid services at outlets across the city.

Operator services

Operator assistance 0
Emergency (police, ambulance, fire) 911
Directory enquiries 1-617 555 1212

Public phones

A local call costs 50¢; operator, directory and emergency calls are free. Public payphones only accept nickels, dimes and quarters – not ideal for long-distance calls. Pick up the receiver and check for a dial tone before parting with your money; many payphones are broken and battered, and once you put your money in, it's gone. Some phones require you to dial the number first and wait for an operator or recorded message to tell you how much change to deposit.

Phone cards are widely available, ranging in price from $5 to $50, with call costs as low as 3¢ per minute. Read the card information carefully before buying; some have a 'connection charge'. Alternatively, you can charge calls to your MasterCard with AT&T (1-800 225 5288).

TIME & DATES

Massachusetts operates on **Eastern Standard Time**, which is five hours behind Greenwich Mean Time, one hour ahead of Central Time (Manitoba to Texas), two hours ahead of Mountain Time (Alberta to Arizona and New Mexico) and three hours ahead of Pacific Time (California). Daylight Saving Time, when the clocks are put forward one hour, is observed from the second Sunday in March to the first Sunday in November, .

In the US, dates are written in month, day and year order; so 12/5/04 is 5 December, not 12 May.

TIPPING

Tipping is a way of life in the US, as the service industry is based largely on cheap labour. Waiters and bartenders, in particular, often make little more than $2 per hour outside of tips. That's why Americans tip much more than people in other countries, spawning the myth that US residents throw their money around trying to impress people by tipping heavily.

If service isn't included in your bill, tip waiters 15 to 20 per cent and bartenders around 15 per cent. Leave a 15-20 per cent tip for cabbies, hairdressers and food delivery people. In hotels, it's the norm to give bellhops and baggage handlers $1-$2 per bag and to tip housekeepers around $2 a night.

TOILETS

Shopping malls are your best bet for public toilets. Central locations include the Copley Place and Prudential Center malls, and Faneuil Hall Marketplace.

TOURIST INFORMATION

Boston Common Visitor Center *147 Tremont Street, Downtown (1-617 536 4100, advance information 1-888 733 2678). Park Street T.* **Open** 8.30am-5pm Mon-Fri; 9am-5pm Sat, Sun. **Map** p272 J5.
Boston National Historical Park Visitor Center *Faneuil Hall, at Congress & North Streets, Downtown (1-617 242 5642, www.nps.gov/bost). State T.* **Open** 9am-6pm daily. **Map** p281 L4.
A useful source of information on Boston and New England; there's also a bookshop.
Cambridge Office of Tourism *4 Brattle Street, at John F Kennedy Street, Cambridge (1-617 441 2884,*

1-800 862 5678, www.cambridge
usa.org). Harvard Square T.
Open 9am-5pm Mon-Fri. **Map**
p284 A2.

Drop in for general enquiries
on Cambridge. The office also
publishes the *Cambridge Visitor
Guide*, which has information on
accommodation, sights and
attractions as well as maps, a
seasonal calendar of events and
a walking-tour map. The office
runs the **Visitor Information
Booth** in Harvard Square (open
9am-5pm Mon-Fri; 9am-1pm Sat,
Sun), which has a touch-screen
service to help you find your way
around Cambridge.

**Greater Boston Convention
& Visitors Bureau**
*Suite 105, 2 Copley Place, Back
Bay (1-617 536 4100, 1-888
733 2678, www.bostonusa.com).
Copley T.* **Open** *Phone enquiries*
8.30am-5pm Mon-Fri.

The GBCVB provides information
on attractions, restaurants,
performing arts and nightlife,
shopping, and travel services.
The main office operates as a
telephone information service,
but the bureau also runs the
visitor centres at Boston Common
and the Prudential Center.

**Massachusetts Office
of Travel & Tourism**
*1-617 973 8500, 1-800 227 6277,
www.massvacation.com.* **Open**
9am-5pm Mon-Fri.

**Prudential Center Visitor
Information Center**
*Center Court, Prudential Center,
800 Boylston Street, Back Bay
(1-617 236 3100, www.
prudentialcenter.com). Hynes
Convention Center or Prudential T.*
Open 10am-9pm Mon-Sat;
11am-6pm Sun. **Map** p283 G6.

VISAS & IMMIGRATION

Visas

Currently, 37 countries participate
in the Visa Waiver Program (VWP;
www.cbp.gov/esta), including
Australia, Ireland, New Zealand
and the UK. Citizens of these
countries do not need a visa for
stays in the US shorter than 90
days (business or pleasure) as
long as they have a machine-
readable passport (e-passport)
valid for the full 90-day period,
a return ticket and authorisation
to travel through the ESTA (Electronic
System for Travel Authorization)
scheme. Visitors must fill in the
ESTA form at least 24 hours before
travelling (72 hours is recommended)

and pay a $14 fee; the form can be
found at www.cbp.gov/xp/cgov/
travel/id_visa/esta/).

If you do not qualify for entry
under the VWP, you will need a
visa; leave plenty of time to check
before travelling.

Your airline will give all visitors
an immigration form to be presented
to an official when you land. Fill it
in clearly and be prepared to give
an address at which you are staying
(a hotel is fine). Upon arrival in the
US, you may have to wait an hour
or, if you're unlucky, considerably
longer, in Immigration, where, owing
to tightened security, you can expect
slow-moving queues. You may be
expected to explain your visit; be
polite and prepared. Note that all
visitors to the US are now
photographed and electronically
fingerprinted on arrival on every trip.

WEIGHTS & MEASURES

The US uses the imperial system.
Here are a few basic metric
equivalents.
1 foot = 0.305 metres.
1 mile = 1.61 kilometres.
1 square foot = 0.093 square metres.
1 pound = 0.454 kilograms.
1 pint (16fl oz) = 0.473 litres.

WHEN TO GO

Weather-wise, the best time of
year in Boston is the autumn.
Temperatures are generally in
the low 70s°F (20s°C) and the
skies are clear for days. Of course,
this also means that the city is
packed to bursting point, prices
soar, and booking a hotel room
becomes difficult. It's also the
time when students from more
than 60 colleges return to town;
many professional conventions
take place, and autumn foliage

sightseers arrive by the busload.
In other words, it is the best of
times and the worst of times to
find yourself in Boston.

Summer is much quieter,
Bostonians are more relaxed and
it's easier to get around town. But
temperatures can soar, with almost
100 per cent humidity. This can
make sightseeing arduous and
sleeping difficult (make sure
your hotel has air-conditioning).

Spring is also quieter, when
blossoms appear and the city is
quite beautiful. But the weather can
be very unpredictable, and tends to
be rainy; bring an umbrella.

Winter is often grey, cold and
dreary, which is why hotel rates
drop. The city is lovely after a light
dusting of snow, but there can be
debilitating blizzards in January
and February, bringing the city
to a standstill.

Whichever season you visit,
pack plenty of layers of clothing.
The old saying – 'If you don't
like the Boston weather, wait ten
minutes' – holds true. Hat, gloves
and scarf are essential in winter,
and an umbrella or waterproof
gear is a good idea at any time of
year. Call 1-617 936 1234 for free
daily weather information, or
check the forecast online.

For information on public
holidays, *see p29*.

WORK

Non-nationals seeking work in
the US must be sponsored by a
US company and get an H-1B
visa, which permits the holder
to work in the US for up to six
years. For the visa to be approved,
your prospective employer must
convince the Immigration
Department that no American
could do the job.

LOCAL CLIMATE

Average temperatures and monthly rainfall

	High (°C/°F)	Low (°C/°F)	Rainfall (mm/in)
Jan	2 / 36	-5 / 23	92 / 3.6
Feb	3 / 38	-4 / 24	86 / 3.4
Mar	7 / 45	0 / 32	98 / 3.9
Apr	14 / 57	5 / 41	92 / 3.6
May	20 / 67	10 / 50	82 / 3.2
June	25 / 77	15 / 59	80 / 3.1
July	28 / 82	18 / 65	80 / 3.1
Aug	27 / 80	18 / 64	91 / 3.6
Sept	22 / 72	14 / 57	81 / 3.2
Oct	17 / 63	8 / 47	84 / 3.3
Nov	11 / 52	4 / 39	99 / 3.9
Dec	4 / 40	-3 / 27	93 / 3.7

ESSENTIAL INFORMATION

Further Reference

BOOKS

Fiction

Nathan Aldyne
Canary; Cobalt; Slate; Vermilion
Four tongue-in-cheek mystery novels set in the gay communities of Boston and Provincetown, c1980.

Margaret Atwood
The Handmaid's Tale
Dystopian, post-nuclear fallout set in Cambridge.

Edward Bellamy
Looking Backward: 2000-1887
A socialist Rip Van Winkle tale that inspired a number of utopian communities – one of the most popular books of its day.

Nathaniel Hawthorne
The Scarlet Letter; The House of the Seven Gables
Two classics by the Salem native.

Henry James *The Bostonians*
James's tale of a Boston feminist.

Stephen King *Cell*
Old-school, Boston-set zombie romp.

Dennis Lehane *Shutter Island*
A psychological thriller set on a fictitious Boston Harbor island.

Henry Wadsworth Longfellow
The Works of Henry Wadsworth Longfellow
Includes the famous poem 'Paul Revere's Ride'.

Robert Lowell *Life Studies; For the Union Dead*
The poet's account of growing up privileged in Boston – and hating it.

Norman Mailer
Tough Guys Don't Dance
Boston's ultimate cynic tells another hard-edged tale.

Robert McCloskey
Make Way for Ducklings
The classic children's tale about ducks in the Boston Public Garden.

Michael Patrick McDonald
All Souls
A bittersweet story of growing up in South Boston's Irish ghetto.

Herman Melville *Moby-Dick*
The great American novel. Melville's 19th-century search for the great white whale.

Henry David Thoreau *Walden*
Thoreau's most famous work, written while living in isolation in a cabin for two years, two months and two days.

John Updike *Roger's Version*
The writer's updated take on *The Scarlet Letter*.

Non-fiction

Jack Beatty *The Rascal King: The Life and Times of James Michael Curley, 1874-1958*
Thoroughly researched biography of the charismatic Boston mayor.

David Hackett Fischer
Paul Revere's Ride
Fine account of the legendary ride, related as a historical narrative.

Noel Riley Fitch *Appetite for Life: The Biography of Julia Child*
All about America's favourite TV chef and Boston icon.

Barney Frank *Improper Bostonians: Lesbian and Gay History from the Puritans to Playland*
Comprehensive history of homosexuality in Boston.

Doris Kearns Goodwin
The Fitzgeralds and the Kennedys: An American Saga
America's answer to royalty.

Sebastian Junger
A Death in Belmont
The author of *The Perfect Storm* turns his attention closer to home to explore whether a murder in the 1960s was by the Boston Strangler.

J Anthony Lukas *Common Ground: A Turbulent Decade in the Lives of Three American Families*
The 1970s busing crisis, seen through the eyes of an Irish-American, a black and a white middle-class family.

Dan McNichol & Andy Ryan
The Big Dig
The turbulent story of the biggest highway project in US history.

Robert S Morse *25 Mountain Bike Tours in Massachusetts: From the Connecticut River to the Atlantic Coast*
Guidelines and trips.

Douglass Shand-Tucci
The Art of Scandal: The Life and Times of Isabella Stewart Gardner
Biography of Boston's famous patron of the arts.

Dan Shaughnessy
The Curse of the Bambino
Entertaining look at the Red Sox 'curse' by local sports journo.

FILM

The Boondock Saints (1999)
A silly crime thriller with a cult following about two brothers from Southie who become vigilantes after killing members of the Russian mob.

The Brink's Job (1978)
William Friedkin's film about the infamous bank heist of 1950 (*see p111* **The Brink's Job**).

A Civil Action (1998)
John Travolta stars in the real-life tale of a town that was poisoned by a chemical company, sued and lost.

The Crucible (1996)
Film version of the Pulitzer Prize-winning play about the Salem witch trials, with Winona Ryder.

The Departed (2006)
Adapted from the Hong Kong thriller *Internal Affairs* (Triad mole vs undercover cop), Scorsese's Oscar-winner moves the action to South Boston with Jack Nicholson, Leonardo DiCaprio and Matt Damon.

Edge of Darkness (2010)
Mel Gibson is a cop investigating the murder of his daughter in this adaptation of a BBC TV series.

The Friends of Eddie Coyle (1973)
A Robert Mitchum vehicle about snitching and organised crime, often touted by locals as the best Boston movie ever.

Gone Baby Gone (2007)
Ben Affleck's foray into directing, based on a Dennis Lehane story.

Good Will Hunting (1997)
Academy Award-winning film by and about Boston residents. Filmed on location all over town, particularly in Southie and in Cambridge, around MIT.

Legally Blonde (2001)
Bubbly West Coast blonde sets out to win her blue-blooded fraternity crush by attending Harvard Law School – though the film wasn't actually shot in Cambridge.

Love Story (1970)
Ali MacGraw and Ryan O'Neal star in the classic weepie set at Harvard.

Mona Lisa Smile (2003)
Chick flick based on Wellesley College's campus in the 1950s, starring Julia Roberts.

Mystic River (2003)
Clint Eastwood directs this serious drama starring Sean Penn – check out his take on the Boston accent.

Next Stop Wonderland (1997)
Wonderful, low-budget romantic comedy with nods towards Boston's immigrant communities.

No Cure for Cancer (1992)
Concert film with local comedian Denis Leary, who both typifies and spoofs Boston's angry young Irish.

ESSENTIAL INFORMATION

Prozac Nation (2008)
Christina Ricci acts out Elizabeth Wurtzel's famous novel about being stressed and depressed at Harvard.
The Social Network (2010)
David Fincher's fast-paced Facebook origin story chronicles the rise of Harvard undergrad Mark Zuckerberg and subsequent legal disputes.
The Thomas Crown Affair (1968)
Steve McQueen and Faye Dunaway star in the Boston-set original, about pulling off the perfect crime.
The Town (2010)
This Ben Affleck crime thriller focuses on Charlestown, alleged to be the US bank robbery capital.

MUSIC

Aerosmith *Toys in the Attic* (1975)
Essential album by the '70s rock band before they quit doing drugs.
Boston *Boston* (1976)
The city's namesake band had one of the best-selling albums of all time.
Buffalo Tom *Let Me Come Over* (1992)
A seminal alternative rock band, one of the best of the era.
The Cars *Greatest Hits* (1978)
Popular 1970s new wave band.
The Dresden Dolls
The Dresden Dolls (2004)
Boston-based duo combining punk beats with Weimar-era cabaret style.
Dropkick Murphys
Do or Die (1998)
Irish-American working-class punk anthems to shout along to.

Galaxie 500 *On Fire* (1989)
Second album from Dean Wareham's early band of Harvard peers, considered their defining moment.
J Geils Band *Full House* (1972)
Known for its live shows, this local rock group was requently compared to the Rolling Stones.
Tom Lehrer *The Remains of Tom Lehrer* (2000)
Box set of snarky satire from Harvard University.
The Lemonheads *Car, Button, Cloth* (1996)
Funny, sad, wonderful songs by this quirky rock band, led by Boston-born singer Evan Dando.
Mighty Mighty Bosstones *More Noise & Other Disturbances* (1992)
Just watch the video for 'Where'd You Go?' and you'll know all you need to know about Boston.
Mission of Burma *Signals, Calls and Marches* (1981)
The album that made a name for Boston's indie godfathers.
Morphine *Cure for Pain* (1993)
The quirky Boston rock band with no guitar that was fronted by the late Mark Sandman.
Pernice Brothers *Overcome by Happiness* (1998)
Joe Pernice's first album with his brother Bob, featuring 'exquisitely sad' song 'Chicken Wire'.
Pixies *Doolittle* (1989)
Boston's own: these guys (and one girl) had it all: the rock, the quirks and the hooks.

Jonathan Richman & the Modern Lovers
Modern Lovers (1988)
Influential Boston-based proto-punk garage-rock band.

WEBSITES

See also p263 **Media** *and p266* **Tourist Information**.

www.timeout.com/boston
Our inspiring online guide to Boston includes things to do, restaurants and bars, shops and movies – all rated and reviewed by *Time Out* critics.
www.boston.com
The free companion website of the *Boston Globe*, the city's daily broadsheet.
www.bostonusa.com
The tourist office's site is packed with information about the city.
www.cityofboston.gov
The city's official website, with a section for visitors.
www.mass.gov
Includes extensive information about outdoor activities, culture and events in Massachusetts.
www.mbta.com
Transport maps, bus schedules, ticket information and interactive route planners.
www.universalhub.com
Local website regurgitating blog comments and chiming in on mainstream media's inadequacies.

BOSTON ACCENT & GLOSSARY

When a Boston native tells you to 'pahk the cah ovah by Hahvahd Yahd,' you may wonder where all the r's have got to. They're not gone, they've just relocated – ask someone if they grew up in Southie, and they may well answer: 'Yeahr, I did.'

The Boston accent, so often mangled by Hollywood, sports a pedigree that goes back four centuries. Boston's first settlers, mostly Puritans from East Anglia, brought with them the slighted 'r' of 'yahd' and the broad 'a' of 'bahthroom.' Later waves of immigrants, particularly the Irish in the 19th century, infused the dialect with their own linguistic quirks. Today, the accent may be fading downtown, but thrives in Boston's older neighbourhoods and the inner suburbs.

'Bawstin' English is renowned as one of the most difficult American accents for outsiders to understand. Add in some unique regional slang, a whacking number of place names with inscrutable pronunciation, and a tendency among locals to do the neat trick of mumbling while talking at top speed, and you may feel you've stumbled across a foreign language. Have no fear – a little practice and you'll be well on your way to comprehension. Just knowing how to pronounce 'Woburn' will set you apart from the garden-variety tourist.

Here's a brief guide to some of the odd place names, pronunciations and colloquialisms you'll hear about town:

Bang a U-y Make a U-turn
Big Dig The most expensive highway project in US history
Comm Av e Commonwealth Avenue
Frappe A milkshake – pronounced 'frap'
Hang a louey Take a left
Jimmies Chocolate sprinkles on top of ice-cream
JP Jamaica Plain
Khakhis What you use to unlock the 'cah' (car)
Mass Ave Massachusetts Avenue
Mem Drive Memorial Drive
Packie A liquor store (short for package store)
Quincy Pronounced 'Quinzy'
Shattered Very, very drunk
Southie South Boston
Spa Convenience store that sells food
The Pats The New England Patriots
The Pike The Massachusetts Turnpike
The Pit The centre of Harvard Square
The Pru The Prudential Tower
The Sox Boston's beloved baseball team, the Red Sox
Tonic Old Boston word for soft drink
Woburn Pronounced 'Woobuhn'

ESSENTIAL INFORMATION

Index

Bags packed, milk cancelled, house raised on stilts.

You've packed the suntan lotion, the snorkel set, the stay-pressed shirts. Just one more thing left to do – your bit for climate change. In some of the world's poorest countries, changing weather patterns are destroying lives.

You can help people to deal with the extreme effects of climate change. Raising houses in flood-prone regions is just one life-saving solution.

**Climate change costs lives.
Give £5 and let's sort it *Here & Now***

www.oxfam.org.uk/climate-change

Be Humankind 🧍 Oxfam

INDEX

THE WORLD CAN BE AN UNJUST AND TREACHEROUS PLACE, BUT THERE ARE THOSE WHO STRIVE TO MAKE IT SAFE FOR EVERYONE.

© 2003 Human Rights Watch; © 2009 Andrew Pars

Operating in some of the world's most dangerous and oppressed countries, **Human Rights Watch** conducts rigorous investigations to bring those who have been targets of abuse to the world's attention. We use strategic advocacy to push people in power to end their repressive practices. And we work for as long as it takes to see that oppressors are held accountable for their crimes.

© 2009 Susan Meiselas/Magnum; © 2008 Human Rights W

KNOWLEDGE IS POWER.
LEARN ABOUT LIFE-CHANGING EVENTS IN YOUR WORLD THAT DON'T ALWAYS MAKE THE HEADLINES AND HOW YOU CAN HELP EFFECT POSITIVE CHANGE.

Stay informed, visit HRW.org

HUMAN
RIGHTS
WATCH

INDEX

Maps

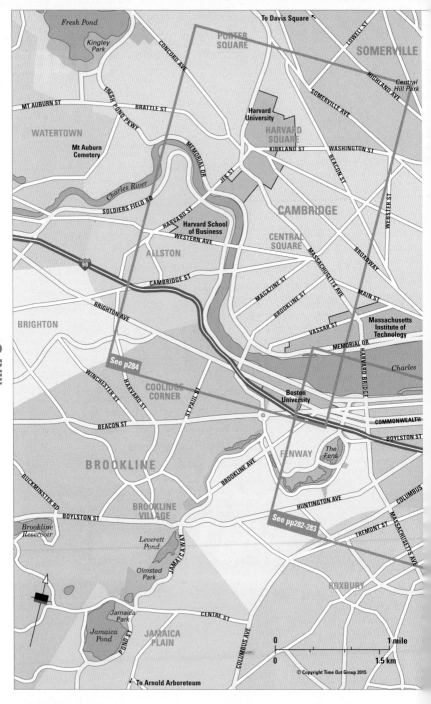

Fresh Pond

Kingley Park

To Davis Square

POTTER SQUARE

SOMERVILLE

CONCORD AVE

LOWELL ST

HIGHLAND AVE

Central Hill Park

MT AUBURN ST

FRESH POND PKWY

BRATTLE ST

WATERTOWN

Mt Auburn Cemetery

Harvard University

HARVARD SQUARE

SOMERVILLE AVE

WASHINGTON ST

KIRKLAND ST

BEACON ST

MEMORIAL DR

JFK ST

Charles River

SOLDIERS FIELD RD

CAMBRIDGE

HARVARD ST

Harvard School of Business

WESTERN AVE

CENTRAL SQUARE

WEBSTER ST

BROADWAY

ALLSTON

90

CAMBRIDGE ST

MAGAZINE ST

MASSACHUSETTS AVE

BROOKLINE ST

MAIN ST

BRIGHTON

BRIGHTON AVE

VASSAR ST

Massachusetts Institute of Technology

MEMORIAL DR

HARVARD BRIDGE

Charles

See p284

WINCHESTER ST

HARVARD ST

COOLIDGE CORNER

ST PAUL ST

Boston University

COMMONWEALTH

BEACON ST

BOYLSTON ST

BROOKLINE

BROOKLINE AVE

FENWAY

The Fens

BUCKMINSTER RD

BOYLSTON ST

BROOKLINE VILLAGE

Leverett Pond

JAMAICAWAY

HUNTINGTON AVE

COLUMBUS

See pp282-283

TREMONT ST

MASSACHUSETTS AVE

Brookline Reservoir

Olmsted Park

ROXBURY

Jamaica Park

CENTRE ST

COLUMBUS AVE

Jamaica Pond

POND ST

JAMAICA PLAIN

0   1 mile

0   1.5 km

© Copyright Time Out Group 2015

To Arnold Arboreteum

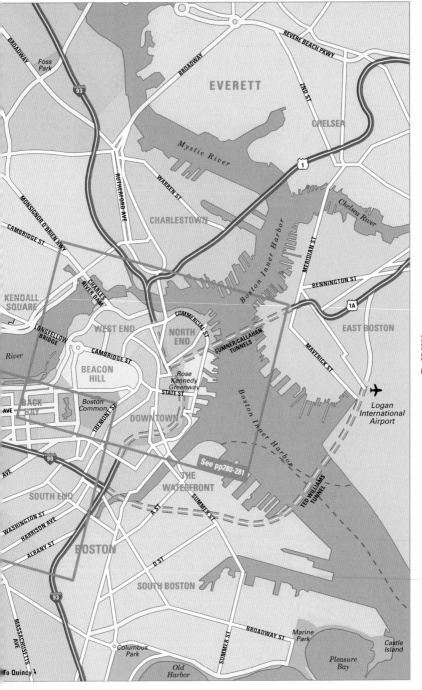

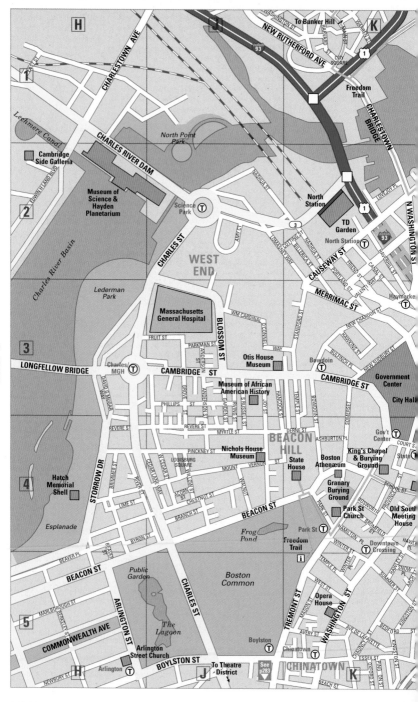

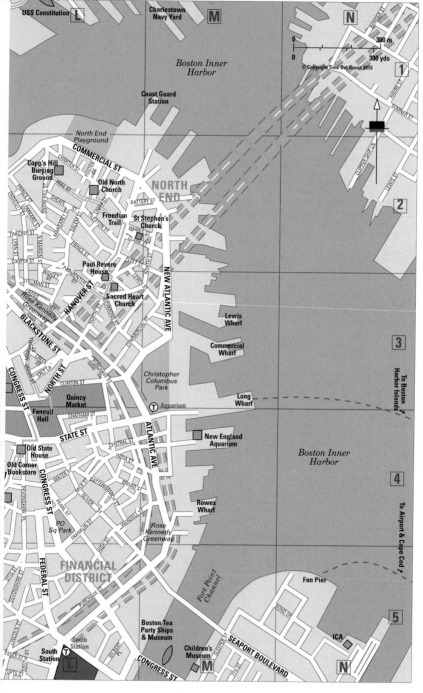

USS Constitution

Charlestown Navy Yard

Boston Inner Harbor

Coast Guard Station

North End Playground

COMMERCIAL ST

Copp's Hill Burying Ground

Old North Church

NORTH END

BATTERY ST

Freedom Trail

St Stephen's Church

Paul Revere House

HANOVER ST

Sacred Heart Church

NEW ATLANTIC AVE

BLACKSTONE ST

Rose Kennedy Greenway

NORTH ST

Lewis Wharf

Commercial Wharf

Christopher Columbus Park

Quincy Market

Faneuil Hall

Aquarium

Long Wharf

CONGRESS ST

STATE ST

ATLANTIC AVE

Old State House

Old Corner Bookstore

New England Aquarium

Boston Inner Harbor

To Boston Harbor Islands

PO Sq Park

Rowes Wharf

Rose Kennedy Greenway

To Airport & Cape Cod

FINANCIAL DISTRICT

FEDERAL ST

Fan Pier

Boston Tea Party Ships & Museum

Children's Museum

SEAPORT BOULEVARD

ICA

South Station

CONGRESS ST

0 300 m
0 300 yds
© Copyright Time Out Group 2015

MAPS

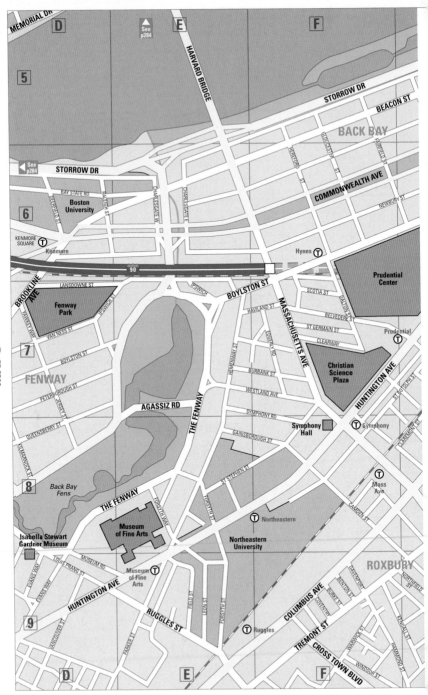

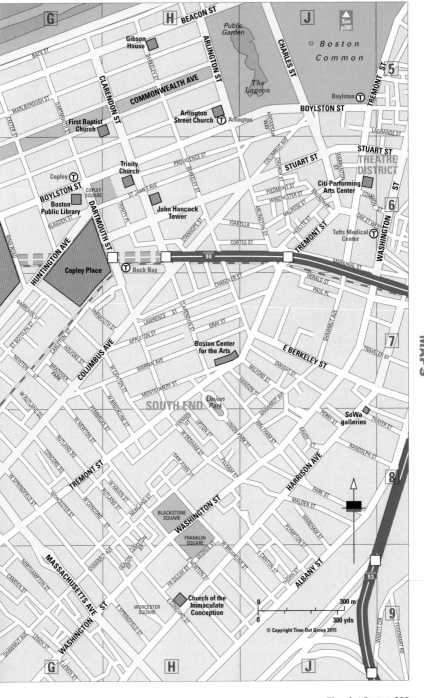

MAPS

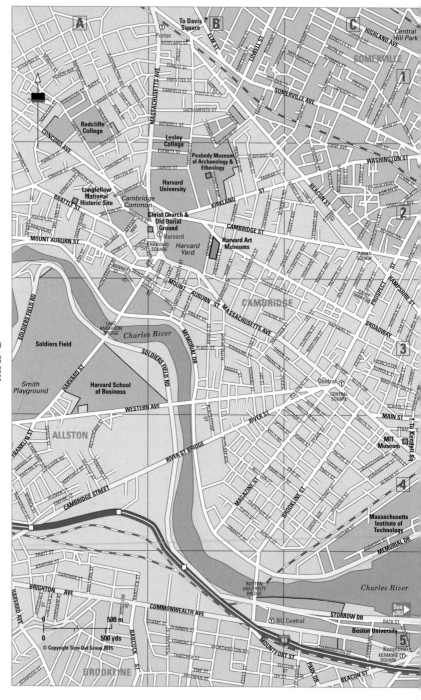

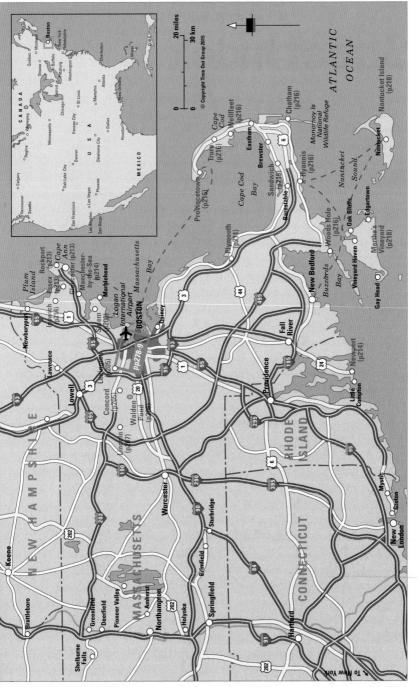

MAPS

Street Index

STREET INDEX

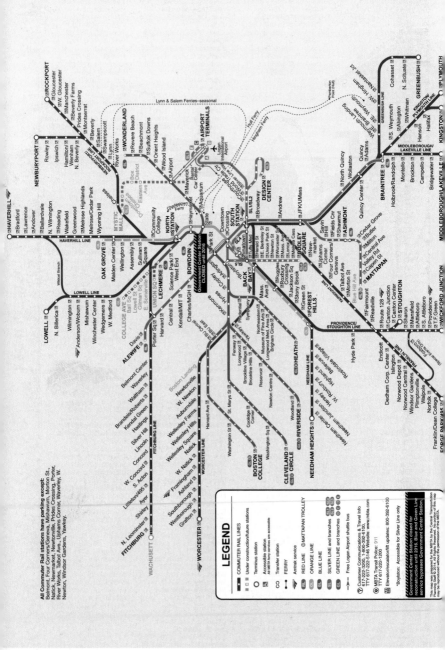